GERMAN AND EUROPEAN
CULTURAL HISTORIES, 1760–1830
BETWEEN NETWORK AND NARRATIVE

T0407893

German and European cultural histories, 1760–1830
Between Network and Narrative

Edited by

CRYSTAL HALL

and

BIRGIT TAUTZ

Published by Liverpool University Press on behalf of
© 2024 Voltaire Foundation, University of Oxford
ISBN 978 1 83764 472 8
Oxford University Studies in the Enlightenment 2024:01
ISSN 2634-8047 (Print)
ISSN 2634-8055 (Online)

Voltaire Foundation
99 Banbury Road
Oxford OX2 6JX, UK
www.voltaire.ox.ac.uk

The correct style for citing this book is
Crystal Hall and Birgit Tautz, eds, *German and European
cultural histories, 1760–1830: between network and narrative*
Oxford University Studies in the Enlightenment
(Liverpool, Liverpool University Press, 2024)

Cover illustration created by Jennifer Edwards from the sections of: *Gravure
en Géographie, Topographie, & en Musique*. PLANCHE II. *Encyclopédie, ou
dictionnaire raisonné des sciences, des arts et des métiers, etc.*, eds. Denis Diderot
and Jean le Rond d'Alembert. 1751-1772. Volume 22. University
of Chicago: ARTFL Encyclopédie Project (Autumn 2022 Edition),
Robert Morrissey and Glenn Roe (eds).

Printed and bound by CPI Group (UK) Ltd, Croydon CR0 4YY

Oxford University Studies in the Enlightenment

GERMAN AND EUROPEAN CULTURAL HISTORIES, 1760–1830
BETWEEN NETWORK AND NARRATIVE

This volume plays on the double meaning of network in German and European studies: configurations of people, objects, and texts as well as network analysis, the dominant digital humanities (DH) method featured in the book. Contributions from art history, history of the book, history, literary studies, and musicology contemplate the strengths and weaknesses of treating the period between 1789 and 1810 as either continuous with or a departure from the centuries before and after by examining different facets of the longer period between 1760 and 1830. While many essays investigate German material, nearly all expand into other European cultures and cover important regions, protagonists, objects, and constellations of bi- and multilingual life. They intersect Italian, French, and English networks and reach across the Atlantic into New England. The period's bookends indicate a threshold or terminus for traditions, institutions, and national identities in Europe: marking the French Revolution (and its effects across the continent culminating in the Napoleonic Wars) and at times reactionary responses with delineation of national, regional, or group identities, and perhaps most pronounced in the aftermath of the Congress of Vienna (1814–1815). Overall, the collection of eleven essays, introduction, and an epilogue explores European cultural histories at the turn of the nineteenth century in a nonlinear manner, that is, by accumulating critical perspectives on people, objects, and texts that test the boundaries of narratives of transmission, organization, and cohesion that often mark scholarly evaluations of this period in European history. This book is accompanied by a digital collaboration hub which can be found at https://liverpooluniversitypress.manifoldapp. org/projects/german-and-european-cultural-histories.

Contents

List of figures

List of tables

Preface and acknowledgments

At first glance, 1760–1830 in the title of this volume comes off as nebulous or at best vague. And yet it perfectly captures the fault line-like terrain of European and German cultural production at the time; even the widely agreed-upon framing of broader continental reverberations due to the French Revolution (1789–1810) remains arbitrary to us: after all, the networked effects we seek to chronicle defy any neat periodization. We therefore invite readers—and this is the first of many such invitations we propose in this book—to construct their own frames for periodization, including embedded challenges and alternatives, by perusing an interactive graph of the people, places, and ideas that are connected in the articles of this volume. This network graph, like the illustrations, dynamic visualizations, abstracts, as well as an introduction can be found on the website that accompanies the volume, published on the Manifold platform.

Thinking along the lines of "network effects" was also what we had in mind when we first started to conceptualize this project. How do the multifaceted ways in which the digital humanities (DH) think about networks (e.g., via network analysis) intersect with more traditional understandings of eighteenth-century European networks? And how do today's scholarly collaborations, which form networks of people, embrace the various understandings and practices of network theories and analyses, all in an effort to continue to tell the assorted, often competing, stories of eighteenth-century cultural histories? What role do narrative and the quest for seamless, causality-driven understandings play in understanding and upending partially obscure networks? We felt that the best way to explore these questions was to bring scholars together for one of Bowdoin College's academic symposia, which we were able to expand into a Humboldt-Kolleg.

Thus, the idea for Network@1800 was born, and a small conference took place in spring 2017, generously funded by Bowdoin College, the American Friends of the Alexander von Humboldt Foundation, and a Deutsche Akademische Austauschdienst (DAAD) Conference grant. We wholeheartedly thank these institutions for enabling us to initiate a collaboration that ultimately culminated in this book.

First and foremost, we would like to thank the many colleagues and students in the audience, but especially the presenters, moderators, and discussants in what turned out to be a great event: Karin Baumgartner, Dana Byrd, Melanie Conroy, Gregory Crane, Mary Helen Dupree, Matt Erlin, Pamela Fletcher, Sean Franzel, Nacim Ghanbari, Alice Goff, Crystal Hall, Burkhard Henke, Jim Higginbotham, Joachim Homann, Karin Höpker, Peter Höyng, Ann Louise Kibbie, Jens Klenner, Alexander Košenina, Elizabeth Millan, Mary Oleskiewicz, Daniel Purdy, Renata Schellenberg, and Birgit Tautz. Thanks to Marjorie Hassen, college librarian, and the Harold and Iris Chandler Family Lecture Fund for inviting Matt Erlin to be the 2017 Chandler lecturer on the eve of the symposium, bringing community members to campus and setting us up on a path of innovation and rethinking the legacies of European cultural histories in a data-driven age. The contributions of all participants shaped the contents of this volume considerably, even if they did not each amount to a chapter. Our colleagues in the Bowdoin Museum of Art, first and foremost then-curator Joachim Homann and Ann and Frank Goodyear, co-directors, hosted a spectacular tour and open house on "Traveling artists/Circulating images," while Cara Martin-Tetrault and Cindy Stocks invited colleagues and students to explore the entire suite of funding opportunities offered for research in Europe. The George J. Mitchell Special Collections and Archives provided engaging examples and an atmospheric site for the panel on "Reading cultures." Crystal Hall hosted a superb Gephi workshop that turned fearful DH skeptics into enthusiasts. Michelle Morin of Bowdoin's Events Office assured seamless operations and provided far-ranging and expert advice and support; Bowdoin's legendary Dining Services made sure that some of the participants are still raving about their time on campus.

That this volume exists owes a lot to the contributors' patience and dedication to this project. It really took off when we contacted Oxford University Studies in the Enlightenment, following on the heels of their volume on the digital humanities. We could not have wished for a more dedicated and enthusiastic series editor than

Greg Brown. He secured phenomenally helpful readers' reports and input from editorial board members that allowed us to sharpen our arguments and make the final product more compelling. Greg was our biggest supporter; we learned so much from him and took our enthusiasm to working with the entire editorial and production team at Oxford University Studies in the Enlightenment and Liverpool University Press, most notably Rebecca Graham, Leah Morin, Sarah Warren, and Ally Lee. Sarah Davison was instrumental in finalizing the proofs.

But, before we handed over this volume, there were other collaborations: in our joint work, which we thoroughly enjoyed, we have been ably assisted by talented and dedicated students, beginning with Silas Wuerth, along with Quyen Ha, Sabina Hartnett, and Micaela Simeone. Our colleague Stephen Houser in Academic Technology and Consulting made sure that the digital components were stored safely for eternity. Monica Birth has provided invaluable editing services; she stands out among all others in a great pre-final-submission team. The Dean of Academic Affairs Office, especially Dean Jen Scanlon, Ann Ostwald and Saari Greylock, have supported this project beyond its initial symposium stage, and helped us with funding editing services as well as final reproduction and digital maintenance fees.

Finally, a special thanks to the libraries, museums, and digital repositories that have made this research possible.

Editors' notes

All translations into English are by the essay authors unless otherwise noted; whenever they deemed necessary, the original language is quoted in the notes. High-resolution and color images can be found on the accompanying website for the book, https:// liverpooluniversitypress.manifoldapp.org/projects/german-and-european-cultural-histories. Interactive versions of the network graphs and supplemental explanatory materials are also available on the website, supported by Manifold.

Social capital, material cultures, reading: German and European cultural histories between network and narrative around 1800

Crystal Hall

Bowdoin College

Birgit Tautz

Bowdoin College

What is in a name? On what this book is and why it matters

Between February and April of 2017, nearly 3500 Twitter accounts posted content that included #Goethe. This sample of data represents a relatively small subset of social media, but one that is instantly complicated by the content and agency of the participants in this online gesture to the German writer Johann Wolfgang von Goethe (1749–1832). With retweets (posting the content of another user) and mentions (posting the name of a Twitter account), there were only 3900 connections between them. So, while these users were connected by a common medium and content, they connected to an average of less than one other account in conversation. Even that connection might have been driven by automated content creation: #Goethe was used most often in conjunction with #Nietzsche and #Schiller, posted primarily by the account @NietzscheSource. This handle, the term for a Twitter identity, appears to be associated with what is referred to as a bot, an account that posts based on programmed instructions rather than ad hoc or creative human intervention. @NietzscheSource automatically tweets quotations culled from Project Gutenberg texts by Friedrich Nietzsche. The agency of association between Goethe, Nietzsche, and Schiller could exist then in three formulations that feed the automated content generation for the bot: Nietzsche explicitly mentioned the other authors, editors established connections across their works, or automated text analysis identified a stylistic or thematic relationship among the texts of these three authors (in translation). The first two situations are recognizable acts of contextualized, historicized, critical interpretation, but the third (which may or may not be part of the bot's programming) implies the detection of relationships based on counting words and the identification of patterns often invisible to the scholar.

All these observations point to a *network* of agency and resonance, which is the conceptual architecture that seeks to capture the richness of imagining the workings of social capital, material cultures, and reading around 1800. Adding further complexity to networks' reverberations today, nearly 90 percent of the tweets were retweeted, meaning that the tweet did not generate new content, but reproduced a limited amount of material already in circulation. While @NietzscheSource earned hundreds of these, almost forty were a retweet from @crassusmedia, the handle for an independent publishing house that specializes in journals for writers. The @crassusmedia posts adopted Goethe's legacy quite differently: "'A man sees in the world what he carries in his #heart.' #Goethe#inspiration#quotes#writing." Goethe takes on a new local valence for the publishing house, but one that is shared around the world in other local contexts. The famed author, who like no other came to define both German literature and *Weltliteratur* (world literature), appears to have reached the pinnacle of his existence almost 200 years after his death: Goethe's becoming commodity, his persistence as both (inter)national icon and misunderstood cipher, designates an anonymous social media network that is at once popular and still relevant to scholars of German and European cultures. Perhaps since 2004 (the founding of Facebook) but certainly since 2006 (Twitter), social media has become the means through which we often see networks, with their elusive and illusive representations of community, sharing, cultures, and activism. The #Goethe example reveals that a network after 2000 might be one that exists only in a certain medium, reflects multiple local variations of a larger phenomenon, and shifts critical attention across the digitally present individuals and the multiple natures of their connections. It most certainly does not stand for intention or collaboration among the networks' actors.

What, then, is (a) network in or around 1800? First, it is a historical fact: a plurality of constellations thriving on relation and marking literary production, dissemination, and reception that existed as the eighteenth century turned. Some narrative patterns evolved, and their subsequent stories proliferated well beyond their origination, often forming legacies and historiographies that gave the impression of linear processes; other stories receded, were eclipsed, or simply vanished from view and the interest of historiographers. People and places, objects and media aligned and intersected in exchange and collaboration, marking connections or simply reverberations and allowing the circulation of things as well as of people and ideas. Second, the term "network" points to a method or approach that became possible at the turn of the twenty-first century and that catapulted established literary and cultural geography into new contexts (such as the one circumscribed by #Goethe).

German and European cultural histories brings the perspective and architecture of established, geographically situated humanities and digital humanities methods to a well-researched yet foundational period in German and European cultural studies and historiography (*c.*1760–1830). While Goethe's status was a little more circumspect at the time, he quickly emerged as a key figure around whom German cultural history around 1800 revolved—indeed the *Goethezeit* (age of Goethe) remains a lingering term to describe the period within German literary and cultural studies—and reclaimed a lasting modernity that continues to impact the stories, debates, and interactions in which we are absorbed today, not least the aforementioned status of and debates around world literature. But these historiographies revolving around individual protagonists or concepts (such as Goethe or the national author) are now being articulated in a more complex manner, namely as ego networks in which the adaptation of Goethe to the Twitter-sphere forms but one of the components. Many others, unified by the centrality of one element—no matter whether it is a person, object, or concept—can be retrieved and constructed through digital humanities (DH) methods. Goethe thus recalls the not always bygone legacy of ego historiography, while exemplifying the workings of an ego network beyond the actual Goethe, his works, and his times.

The volume represents interventions that engage with the concept of networks, both analog and digital, with their establishment, their successes, and their borders; these interventions offer an opportunity to explore the relationship of DH to traditional areas of scholarship. About half of the contributions rely on close reading practice and explore actually existing networks around 1800—documented personal, material, or social intersections—for their cultural effects (Dupree, Homann, Franzel, Schellenberg, Ghanbari). The digital humanities interventions in other essays serve as a backdrop and inspiration to test and reaffirm these tools and methods (Conroy, Hall, Baumgartner, Höyng, Erlin and Walsh, Tautz). Without entering the ceaseless debate on the definition of digital humanities, the editors and contributors consider three aspects of the field: humanistic inquiry about digital objects (text, image, space, networks), digital or computational methods employed in the service of humanistic inquiry, and humanistic intervention in the development of digital objects or computational analytical methods. Simply put, we collectively pursue this project knowing about the meaningful ways in which digital humanities may alter—even transform—our thinking about the eighteenth century and its impact on human existence and history, without necessarily having to employ DH methods.

In any case, going beyond the protagonists, objects, and relationships of the actual period in cultural history, as well as the hidden histories revealed through DH methods, the year 1800 serves as a metaphor for the massive cultural transitions affecting Europe in the last decades of the eighteenth and first decades of the nineteenth centuries; the turn of the century marks a nodal point in the stories we tell about the objects that signal the advent of modernity. While each essay in this volume adds but one story to the small archive of cultural production assembled here, they can be arranged in sections reflecting the exchanges around 1800: social capital, material cultures, and reading. An additional, final set of contributions addresses the infinite nature of networks as well as the unpredictability of outcomes when applying digital methods. These sections are framed by contributions addressing process-oriented approaches to networks and exploring cultural effects and contexts of reaching beyond "nation" and "1800," two keywords that consistently surface in this volume.

In some ways, this volume complements *Digitizing Enlightenment: digital humanities and the transformation of eighteenth-century studies* (2020), which brought similar intentions to the study of French Enlightenment culture in a European context. Like the editors and contributors of *Digitizing Enlightenment*, we asked ourselves how DH methods revise or at least impact the field of eighteenth-century German and European studies. While *Digitizing Enlightenment* sets out to capture a titular state-of-the-art approach through several DH methods, offering a wide array of case studies in the second part of the book, we situate our project at the intersection of distant and close, conventional readings. We hope to illustrate the productive symbiosis, despite all tension, that novel and conventional approaches bring to exploring the vexing questions of relating the telos of history to the momentary in time, the neat story to more disruptive tales. We readily acknowledge that this volume can only winnow the view and that it must remain, sadly but inevitably, a snapshot in time. Such awareness informs this book, paired with the knowledge that German-language cultural production was far more decentralized and existed outside the nation. Scholarly (and popular) views of the late eighteenth century have been informed by the legacies that this bygone period has had, and, by turning to networked relations, we attempt to refocus some of the more mundane, abridged, eclipsed, or forgotten moments of innovation and creativity—or knowledge production, for short—that humans engaged in, especially in communal settings. Finally, the materials and methods presented here rely on the ability to comprehend the breadth and variety of the network components, which is significantly assisted through visual representations that can be found embedded in the print volume and expanded upon in the online component of this book.

This book and its interactive representation as a graph of connections deliberately play on the double meaning of network: They refer to configurations of people, social constellations, and objects around 1800 as well as to network analysis, the one digital humanities method prevailing in the book.[1] The contributions in this volume provide a glimpse into the expanded modes of scholarly collaboration and dissemination, which, unlike older models, emphasize process over results and invite ongoing dialogue and contestation. This focus on process extends to reconsiderations of seemingly established scholarship on historical networks, redirecting attention to their making on either side of 1800. Examples capture multiple stages in this process: They range from the visualization of documented attendees at Parisian salons (Conroy) or the creators and imitators of travel networks (Baumgartner) to the reconstruction of networks of artistic exchange (Homann and Schellenberg) to the documentation of relationships that were in formation between literary authors (Ghanbari) and between expressive modes and values (Franzel, Hall, Dupree) or that attached concept to author (Tautz). The connections between the essays can also be understood through the sites of the networks: a focus on objects as the connective tissue

---

1. See the online figure currently available in the digital collaboration hub for this volume at https://liverpooluniversitypress.manifoldapp.org/projects/german-and-european-cultural-histories/resource/VolumeIndex and https://learn.bowdoin.edu/network-1800/social-capital-material-cultures/ (last accessed June 21, 2023).

between historical figures (Franzel, Ghanbari, Homann, Höyng), capturing the fleeting elements of local instantiations of larger systems of exchange (Franzel, Hall, Schellenberg), the inverse relationship when the local resists the national (Dupree), and interdisciplines in the eighteenth-century sense of the word (Erlin and Walsh, Hall, and Homann). Likewise, the dialogue between the object of study and the methods available for analysis is reflected in the kinds of arguments posited in the volume: linear (Franzel), conceptual (Höyng, Tautz), and reflective (Erlin and Walsh). Previewing these lines of possible renetworking speaks to our intention with this volume, which is to invite open dialogue and exchange, beyond the necessarily confining time and space of a book with a publication date. The open invitation of *German and European cultural histories* thus captures examples of the permutations of the network as historical fact and methodological approach. It signals that the stories we tell in this book, as well as the archives and remediations these stories draw upon, must remain unfinished, incomplete, and, yes, inconsistent at times, in order to be productive and insightful.

In the process, both the book and its digital apparatus encourage, in reciprocal ways, reading one with and without the other; experiencing the materiality of reading, as well as its virtual impulse, sequel, and accompaniment that suggest alternate modes of perception and gateways into the text; and reflecting on alternate forms of storytelling that emerge as competitors to neatly organized textual convention. Entering the book through an image file or topical tag contained in the digital apparatus, assisted by the network graph of co-occurrences of people, places, and things in the book, organizes a different reading experience from working through an entire section of essays and treating the digital apparatus as an illustration of sorts. This side-by-side arrangement of narratives intersects two trends emerging in this volume, both of which reflect the stage of digital humanities approaches vis-à-vis more conventionally defined work in and across the disciplines devoted to cultural history. While some of the contributors embrace DH in very broad terms, others work primarily with conventional and digital methods of network analysis and, on occasion, reference the tensions between digital and conventional methods of reading. The book form of our work reflects a thematic narrative of eighteenth-century European cultural studies that considers broadly what a network can represent: social capital, artistic influence, material exchange, textual proximities, and national identities. The network representation of the volume through the graph and tags for images in the online digital collaboration hub space allows for the experience of the underlying connections and similarities in methodologies: historiography, network analysis, literary criticism, spatial analysis, and text mining. Moreover, the linked format of digital representations of the books, artworks, people, places, and data visualizations creates an opportunity to see how these objects of study cut across the themes and modes of inquiry. Through this digital, hyperlinked network, the objects can be seen in their multiple contexts, highlighting an affordance of networks as representations and objects of study. Networks intersect, stretch, and encapsulate more conventional modes of narrative storytelling and more linear models of historiography, and thus simultaneously upend and produce tools of cultural analysis. Together, these layers create alternative networks to document processes and outcomes as a way to draw attention to the questions answered and raised by the contributions.

These contributions neither endorse a full-fledged, data-driven, or "enumerated" reading practice, nor dismiss the meaningful intervention enabled by digital humanities. Instead, they seek to recapture a few generative moments of what scholars have described as "reading nations," that is, communities formed through shared interests or engagement in reading materials, along with nascent processes of culture formation abandoned and/or fueled later on. But, rather than confining themselves to the results of imagining community, the contributions direct our attention to the ancillary elements of the process. Embracing one set of methods does not signal a rejection of the validity or value of others: The complementarity of the results of all of the contributions allows us to learn about the connections between approaches as much as we learn about the cultural phenomena under analysis. In the end, we made the decision to represent and disseminate scholarship by anchoring it in a conventional book—in part, because we wanted to show how digital humanities has altered the lines of inquiries pursued by German and European studies and therefore altered the tradition of scholarship.

Evidently, the essays collected here begin with and return to literary texts, visual culture objects, and historical documents. While a focus on the German lands emerges, the essays' authors mostly represent the fields of European literary and cultural studies and thus bring a distinct cross- or transnational focus to the German-language resources. Collectively, our contributors tackle a series of questions intended to illuminate the turn of the nineteenth century.

How did people communicate and collaborate around 1800? Which networks were actually formed? How were these networks enhanced and/or eclipsed by subsequent cultural historiographies that mostly favored national or author-driven narratives over local, group, or otherwise fractured collaborations? How did these networks mitigate and negotiate the internal, always perpetuating forces that interacted in order to sustain the network in a self-organizing manner, no matter how hidden it seemed? How can we describe the complex and dynamic (hence always emergent) system-nature of networks? Or can we? And, perhaps towering above them all, there is the question about the seemingly privileged status of the book—or rather the texts that books contain: How do they outline, proscribe, or subvert the more amorphous relationships we circumscribe in the preceding questions?

To be sure, for long periods of literary historiography, texts and books have been treated, almost exclusively, as inventions and reflections of their individual authors, rather than indicators (and parts) of something at once larger and more circumspect, vague, and all-encompassing—origin and effect. This volume problematizes the privileged status of the book in order to examine its contingency upon and complicity within chains of communication, attempts at collaboration, and the construction of identities and relationships beyond the author. Thus, as several contributions show, the text can be the node, the connective edge between nodes, or the site of the network through its representations. The content, conditions of production, and ownership of the object are connected to other writers, producers, and owners. Yet the text also represents and gives structure to the connected people, places, concepts, and objects within it. In short, it seeks to arrest moments of the eighteenth-century present that today seem lost amidst subsequent historization. But can text as object reveal new questions about the period?

Perhaps evading or eliding these far-reaching philosophical questions, the volume's contributors are interested in unearthing the small, sometimes isolated instances of linguistic and rhetorical constellations that they believe point to or upset larger, often homogenizing, patterns of narrative organization. Other than microhistories that identify those large stories in an individual episode, these subsets of the overall network simultaneously help to build the narrative while necessarily departing from it. Local contributions cannot all exist at the center of the network. Essay authors suggest a surplus or nuance to the material worlds whose stories are told through evidence, empirically gained data, and technologies that have challenged established studies of literary and cultural traditions, canons, and legacies. Several contributions ask to what extent collections assembled around 1800 challenge or define canons in ways that run counter to nineteenth-century (and later) interpretations of the period (Franzel, Schellenberg, Hall). They aim at a larger context of cultural media and mediation, engaging with, yet surpassing, the minutiae of texts. Ghanbari, for instance, uses first letters to expose the power structures of patronage and social hierarchies that are otherwise obscured when mediated via friendships. Dupree shows how popular oral art forms (declamation), though modeled on texts, bridge the social disparity that is thought to have defined engagement with print media and access to salons. By bringing these new materials and perspectives to bear on well-established traditions, the essays propose alternate, forgotten, or eclipsed histories and open paths into new modes of reading, while retaining a critical perspective toward the potentials and shortcomings of data-driven approaches that are increasingly shaping our understanding of digital humanities. Collectively, they show that we should think of innovation and creativity as much more broadly based; thriving no less in relative anonymity and even obscurity, they nevertheless bore dynamic ideas projecting beyond their present moment.

The online material underscores this goal in several ways: The collections section with data visualizations, prints and paintings, texts, and maps puts different media on display, and showcases data-driven methods of exploring networks, including their dynamics of mediation. The design of the online component also adds an important layer. Rather than following a linear way of "illustrating" the essays (cued through abstracts), it invites alternative modes and perspectives of reading and exploration. The index graph represents an example of "expansive networks" that, like the contributions in the fourth section of the book, supplement rather than illustrate the thought processes. Engaging with the index graph and reentering the book invites yet another way of exploring its contents and argument. Above all, we guide the reader to an item that impacts every part of this project, straddling both book and online components: a set of fourteen theses intended to guide and disrupt, reorganize and broaden any conventional reading expectations from the outset (see Figure 1, page 26). The theses conclude this introduction while pivoting to the online component.

Networked people, objects, routes + network analysis = noncausal effects and transformation

In developing the volume's argumentation and architecture, we proceed from the following: The broad cultural transitions around 1800 were visible not only in life and politics (e.g., revolutions) but also in the organization, production, and dissemination of knowledge represented by the aforementioned categories of exchange that organize the contributions to the volume: social capital, material culture, reading, and challenges to well-worn conceptual anchors of literary historiography such as national imagination (and its often-posited conceptual opposite, cosmopolitan claim). The last section also forms an epilogue, projecting toward new, hitherto underpursued methods of researching and writing. By examining the margins of networks, the extreme edges where people, objects, or routes begin to lose their connectivity to the whole, the section begins to suggest alternatives to narrative, seemingly linear presentations of cultural histories, while underscoring the lingering effects that Germany and Europe and their correlate networks around 1800 continue to have today.

We refrain here from an extensive research overview, focusing instead on broad contours that admittedly simplify and thus distort the research landscape by distilling trends. Influential studies on late-eighteenth-century European cultural networks seem unified by one impulse and goal, namely, to account for the cultural impact of loosely defined, often geographically far-reaching arrangements of interaction and exchange that seemed eclipsed but never eradicated by domineering narratives of cultural history. The latter seek to privilege a teleologically oriented process over constellation at any given moment. Often, as scholars tried to resurrect the networks' relevance and restore them to their rightful place in history, images of networks emerged that came to resemble a historical looking glass: magnifying a mediated social constellation, often by discerning one formative vector—gender and/or religion, orality and/or performance, the bourgeois household and/or the urban environment come to mind. Almost always, these histories focus on patterns of power marked by dispersion and imbalance by domesticating them in literary genres, the idea of the nation, or literally in the bourgeois home. Public lives are remediated in and through personal, individual expression, simultaneously co-producing and challenging nascent notions of privacy. In the end, networks often appear as an illustration of a temporary event, though occasionally also as an aberration, in a more or less linear story of culture, one that proceeds from a point of origin, often arranges itself in a binary structure, and always toward a telos or conclusion. In short, networks relate to but are not necessarily an integral, easily subsumed part of a narrative organization of literature, culture, history, and, ultimately, life.

Scholars have observed networks' disruptive patterns in studies on salon culture, travel literature, and trade practices and book exchanges. These studies turn our attention to local events. So-called inter-arts studies, research on "marginal genres" such as letters and autobiographies, and, last but not least, budding interdisciplinary work on epistemological technologies—from performing to publishing to experimenting and exhibiting—have greatly enriched our views of the century that all too long has been defined by concepts of bold narrative histories on either side of the French Revolution and the ensuing Napoleonic Wars.[2] While the latter seek to give a sense of completeness and intention, the focus on networked relations emphasizes incomplete, infinite readings that perpetually open new models for thinking about history while avoiding randomness or particularities. While such studies seeking to capture networked *European* cultures around 1800 remain sparse, an abundance of scholarship testifies to the nation as an emergent and domineering concept shaping textual exchange. However, national thinking is but one network of ideas that emerged in texts and through the exchange of texts.[3]

In this volume, we also think of the involved shifts in intellectual cultures vis-à-vis their products; perplexingly, along with dominant legacies, we have to confront the errant and diffuse when delineating the outcome of these shifts: The emergence of modern academic disciplines stands next to knowledge and information overload;

2. See, for example, recent research on epistolary discourse: *Was ist ein Brief? Aufsätze zu epistolarer Theorie und Kultur / What is a letter? Essays on epistolary theory and culture*, ed. Marie Isabel Matthews-Schlinzig and Caroline Socha (Würzburg, 2018). On knowledge and performance, see *Performing knowledge, 1750–1850*, ed. Mary Helen Dupree and Sean Franzel (Berlin, 2015); on cultural objects, see Anke Te Heesen, *The World in a box: the story of the eighteenth-century picture encyclopedia* (Chicago, IL, 2002), and the work by The Multigraph Collective, discussed in greater detail below.

3. A case in point is the vigorous discussion of trade networks and their nonalignment with nation—for example, in several presentations and sessions at the 2022 convention of the American Society of Eighteenth-Century Studies (ASECS).

complaints about too many writers, translators, and pseudo-experts; and nascent descriptions of what we today call a media explosion. While all of these descriptors are apt in accounting for the complexity of the Enlightenment and the onset of modernity that progressed, albeit dialectically, all the way into the twentieth century, they also draw attention to another aspect, namely the local (i.e., nonnational) and collaborative atmosphere of cultural life that often reverberated globally. Underlying this sense of overload is a vast corpus that is seldom read with close analysis yet through a broader analytical lens reveals the penetrations and permutations of themes, anxieties, and representations. Pockets of similarity appear across delineations that were once treated as fixed boundaries of medium, genre, nation, and identity. They become visible through a mode of *scalable reading* that zeroes in on the quantity (of data), patterns, and distance, and that, through the combination of established philology with digital approaches, delineates interpretive case studies as a result.[4] They gesture to an expansive landscape of knowledge production and reception around 1800, while seemingly glossing over the resistance harbored in the physicality of archival materials, including the dimensions of a book, library, or other artifact.[5] Here, traditional and novel approaches intersect, and, consequently, the volume brings this aspect to the fore in both its physical and online components and the actual and virtual intersection of the storylines they harbor.

Between network and narrative: forms

Because network analysis and related digital humanities methods allow scholars to identify communities that are densely interconnected, highly connected central figures, or eccentric and marginalized members, network is the method and the metaphor underlying the collection and through which we imagine the working of social capital, material cultures, and reading. Although we see this book as a culture-historical project, we are less concerned with causally produced effects

---

4. Jan Horstmann and Rabea Kleymann, "Alte Fragen, neue Methoden: philologische und digitale Verfahren im Dialog—ein Beitrag zum Forschungsdiskurs um Entsagung und Ironie bei Goethe," *Zeitschrift für digitale Geisteswissenschaften* (2019), DOI: 10.17175/2019_007.
5. Matthew G. Kirschenbaum, *Bitstreams: the future of digital literary heritage* (Philadelphia, PA, 2021), p.13. See also Horstmann and Kleymann, "Alte Fragen, neue Methoden."

and their narration than with the conditions of meaning that resonate through and are sometimes eclipsed by time. We trace conditions of meaning, "accounting," in the words of Matthew Kirschenbaum, "for all people and things that make meaning possible, each in their own irreducible individuality."[6] We add genres, concepts, and technologies to this list. And, rather than surveying a number of pathbreaking studies on network analysis and digital humanities,[7] we probe contributions to our discussion that introduce unanticipated angles. One example is Caroline Levine's *Forms: wholes, rhythms, hierarchies, networks* (2015). What seems, at first glance, another attempt at litigating the relative merits of formal versus contextual literary analysis—or a focus on text and social worlds, respectively—yields unexpected insights for our understanding of the intersection between network-driven, DH-mediated approaches and "traditional" close readings. Levine's point of departure, namely that form is the basic constituent of aesthetic and sociopolitical patterns, resonates with our understanding of transformation in German and European cultural history around 1800. Indeed, as we shall see throughout the volume and in the accompanying online materials, the various components and effects of networked constellations constrain, differentiate, overlap, and intersect—even "stretch" and travel amongst each other. Collision replaces causation; affordance or potential replaces intent.

Forms, including the quest for wholesome imageries and repetitions, structure the networks and cultural practices under investigation—or at least our discussion of them, no matter how erratic they appear to be or how much we labor to identify their uniqueness and departure from well-known "linear" histories. Rather than contributing to a narrative told through time, possibly moving from one perspective to the next and thus envisioning change as an orderly or even causal process, these networked practices generate a simultaneity of narratives that at times cross and disrupt each other, often collapsing time and exposing

6. Kirschenbaum, *Bitstreams*, p.14.
7. We are indebted to the work of Scott Weingart for introductory and conceptual research on network analysis across the disciplines in *The Network turn: changing perspectives in the humanities* (Cambridge, 2020) and *Exploring big historical data: the historian's macroscope* (London, 2015). In general, conventional studies embracing network terminology grapple with cultural history and its inherent ordering impulse. See for example Ann Blair, *Too much to know: managing scholarly information before the modern age* (New Haven, CT, 2011), and Chad Wellmon, *Organizing enlightenment: information overload and the invention of the modern research university* (Baltimore, MD, 2015).

cracks and fizzles in a neatly ordered understanding of history and culture.[8] Such linear and nonlinear histories intersect to explore the tension and constant replication between totality and gaps. In this way, for example, the contents of a letter can be problematized against other correspondence, yes, but also among other correspondents with similar network features. Or, for instance, the local, seemingly isolated salon can be contextualized within a larger structure of social exchange to evaluate its commonalities or differences from those other structures. Attaining hierarchies reveals a surprisingly disorderly impact of hierarchical thinking.

Not surprisingly, though, Levine's work with "network" proves most challenging and affirming in our context. Like us, she begins by acknowledging that networks seem to resist form and certainly confound any idea of form as containing. And, while they are defined by connectivity, they nevertheless espouse knowable rules and patterns.[9] The network offers a way to compare the role of qualitative features of these interactions, that is, to explore at a larger scale the (in)consistencies of relationships once the people, texts, and places have been described. Rather than precisely linear, this process can be centripetal or centrifugal. For example, the network might reflect authors' attempts to connect with a powerful central subject, editor, patron, or printer. Conversely, it could provoke the scholar to explore an avant-garde movement away from those centers. The centers close to which or away from which the pieces of the network appear are identified not necessarily by nations, but by themes, images, and experiences. As shown by the directors of the project Nineteenth-Century Publishers' Series in the British Library, Katie McGettigan and Paul Raphael Rooney, network representation can challenge post hoc categorization by nationality and even chronologies limited by the life dates of an author by addressing the pull of readership, editors, and seriality. The individuals, texts, and objects often occupy the same spaces and milieus, but can also cut across social hierarchies. Labor, materials, and physical realities play important roles in the eventual labels of connectivity and eccentricity. In other words, networks endorse distinct forms and reveal hitherto unknowns.

8. For an example drawn from Scottish literature, see Andrea Stewart, "'The limits of the imaginable': women writers' networks during the long nineteenth century," *Victorian review* 45:1 (2019), p.39–57.

9. Caroline Levine, *Forms: wholes, rhythms, hierarchies, networks* (Princeton, NJ, 2015), p.112–13.

At the same time, networks put intense pressure on well-worn, traditional forms. They work against the whole as a unifying, binding expression—or telos—of cultural experience. Among our contributions, Baumgartner's study on travel networks reveals the tension between movement and nation, the ideas of domestic ideals and the foreign, as well as the at once unifying and transcending impulse that comes from repeating, imitating, and translating existing narratives of the Grand Tour. By drawing attention to translations, Baumgartner probes an important force that may destroy and substitute forms; this suggestion is also at play in Hall's discussion of library collections and Tautz's engagement with the conceptual rise of cosmopolitanism. Through a completely different gesture, Höyng's focus on Beethoven's *Konversationshefte* (*Conversation notebooks*)—a chronicle and pattern of the composer's deafness—challenges well-known assumptions and tales of the composer's biography. Conversely, the intersection with established, bounded wholes (e.g., nation, biography) stretches the network, which provokes a useful distortion for understanding our objects of study. As Dupree documents, while national narratives take hold and from the outset reach beyond the nation, they find resistance in local instantiations of an event, text, or grouping; they not only give concomitant rise to ideas of the popular, but also trace a festering oral culture. Conroy, in contrast, highlights how challenging national myths with local network identification allows the historian to gain new perspectives on the temporal unfolding of metaphors or narratives previously thought as closed. Similarly, her insights force a rethinking of transposing scholarship on salon cultures into other national contexts, encouraging us instead to proceed from local conditions and repercussions, including nonurban settings.

Nodes, edges, narratives

The combination of approaches involves several shifts and fractures that expose *our* epistemic threshold moment: Not only have we begun to think of networks in a succinct conceptual manner along the lines of cultural, institutional, and structural parameters—and always against the background of data models and infrastructures—but we have also embraced the toolkit of digital humanities as one that allows us to view and consider tradition in new ways. While contributors engage with this mode of analysis at different depths, certain terms and principles remain consistent across essays. Chief among these is establishing the connections (called edges) between people, objects, cities, texts (called nodes). The nodes exist in all of their complexity: They are a name in a ledger, a woman, a foreigner, a Catholic, and an actress all at once, thus collapsing the single formative vectors of gender, religion, language, and nation into a single abstraction. Edges represent attributes of historical, material, literary, or social conditions of the nodes: that two people attended a salon (Conroy), two words appeared in a title (Erlin and Walsh), two cities formed the leg of a tour (Baumgartner), or two subject headings are used to describe a book (Hall). The strength of the network as an analytical tool derives from being able to compare the connectivity of a pair of nodes (a local or micro instance) with patterns of connectivity in the network overall (Ghanbari, Homann, Tautz). Critical attention is given to the groups of nodes that are highly interconnected with one another and the nodes that bridge those groups or are eccentric to them, such as attendees at one salon and notable figures who were invited to the events of several *salonnières* (Conroy). The scholar must therefore toggle between the local and the general features of the edges, and between the specific and abstract features of the nodes—for example, the exchange of a drawing and the symbolic capacity of its content. Moreover, in this volume, the section on textual spaces emphasizes the edges (the different types of connections that bind ideas and objects), while the social capital essays focus on the nodes (the identities and characteristics of people, places, and things). This allows us to compare how catalogs and inventories can document relationships (edges) and the agency of individuals (nodes) to create those constellations. These contributions take configurations as their object of study.

Established cultural histories are arranged typically as grand narratives engaging with origin, telos, or the binary (or a dialectic) of inclusion and exclusion. Networks, conceived within this model of thinking, illustrate but one possible configuration of participation in that narrative, contingent upon the attributes of participants. For example, as Conroy argues in her contribution to the volume, salon attendees were often literary, political, and artistic, moving through multiple networks and multiple identities in their social lives, even though conventional approaches depict one attribution as more defining than others. Importing the network idea as conceived by digital humanities, even if its methods are not employed, upsets the established logic; it recognizes constitutive force, creates the ability to challenge narrative, exposes gaps, and destabilizes the origin story or purposes that have been inherited from epistemologies with their own histories and priorities.

Though well versed in this language of digital network analysis, several essays marshal alternative methods against this backdrop, using modes of thinking along edges and nodes to challenge more conventional presentations of influence, development, and cultural shifts (Franzel, Dupree, Ghanbari, Tautz). They participate in a trend that emphasizes the archive as a primary cognitive figure, not an actual place, to structure scholarly work. The last decades have seen new archives emerge and generated new practices of engaging with these archives and moving toward generative scholarship. Projects such as the Early Caribbean Digital Archive have demonstrated compellingly that the latter, in turn, not only produced new research questions but challenged us toward new observations about the old and recovered a richly textured, even more ethical knowledge of the past. In the process of constructing this volume, synchronically and diachronically arranged insights emerge regarding cultural moments shaping the decades at either side of 1800 as an epistemic threshold as well as insights into the subsequent 250 years, with select moments/periods coming into sharp relief, all of which have shaped the ways in which we view the late eighteenth century and write tradition. Any book on multifaceted networks is therefore also one of revision, reexamination, and retellings of tradition, leading up to the formulation of nonlinear histories. Somewhat antithetical to what scholarly books are, namely a capsule of knowledge at any given point or period in time, this one attempts to shift focus toward multifaceted processes that capture a plurality of voices, sets of knowledges, and forms that open lines of inquiry. Often these openings occur simply by trying to read through the lens of new interpretive orders.

The power of data, the power of convention, the power of networks

Another observation shapes our engagement with the facets of network analysis. In creating the historical and theoretical framework of exploring and reconstituting networks, the volume provides an exhibition of different ways of engaging with network and network theories that today appear tied to European (especially German) and North American scholarly contexts. But these geographical attributions are deceptive at best and have become ever more porous, even during the development of the present project. Whereas the European tradition has pursued a pragmatic, somewhat intuitive use of sociological approaches to group dynamics, to multidirectional and interpersonal exchanges, and, eventually, to network formation, US-based scholars enlist models appealing to Bruno Latour's writing on networks (at least when it comes to moving beyond the application of computer science methods and technical capabilities). Where European, in particular German, scholars remain indebted to philological traditions—leading to the coinage of the term *Medien-philologie* (digital philology) and associated theory and practice—and have long shied away from crossing into the messier territory of data as the purview of digital humanities,[10] scholars based in North America are deploying new modes of reading, revolving around data generated by network analysis and laying the foundation for—and indeed representing—new, *exploratory material.* This material includes the metadata about our objects of study, that is, the data about the data: the contours of its creation, use, preservation, and place in the archive. Metadata and new interpretations of text corpora, text context, and text archiving support what scholars suggest may arise from reading the *exploratory material*; at this juncture in the scholarly dialogue, both "schools" remain cautious to surrender sole authority to the *explanatory power of data.* While recent studies have moved toward data-driven methods, culminating in the data modeling of and for processes of reading literature—intending to advance, deepen, and revise central tenets of literary study—we prefer to focus on illuminating the tensions at the core of a practice that straddles exploration and explanation.[11] We aim to focus on divergences, approaching what some might consider the earliest debates lingering in the decades before any sustained, academy-driven practice of literary and cultural interpretation. By demonstrating how divergences work together in an observation of nonlinear, noncausal effects of collaboration, exchange, and articulation, we provide a fuller picture of the potential and risks of distant readings.

10. A robust example countering this preference is the *Zeitschrift für digitale Geistes-wissenschaften*, published online at https://zfdg.de/ (and in printed issues that are also available as open access).

11. The example that comes to mind is Andrew Piper, *Enumerations: data and literary studies* (Chicago, IL, 2018). While he does not use terms like "explanatory" and "exploratory data," advancing instead "distributive semantics" in order to emphasize alliances with information science, computer science, and linguistics, we prefer our terms to address more realistically the (opportunities for) work with data across the humanities and in academic institutions of different sizes and options for networking. See also our discussion below.

Despite their differences, both approaches are complementary and united as they seek responses to one predominant, vexing question: In an age like the eighteenth century, where we witness an explosion of exchanges—of people and goods, ideas and information, to name a few—how can we articulate the ensuing networks if the individuals involved and co-creating them cannot? Does it matter whether networks, which always involve relations and, inevitably, degrees of cooperation, posit themselves intentionally and institutionally or simply aggregate? European approaches seem to emphasize the social aspect of historical networks, charting their paths away from a premodern culture of patronage, dependency, and dominance and convergence with modern societies' functional transformation and moves away from social hierarchies, etiquette, and form.[12] Emphasizing immanent dynamics, these approaches nevertheless unfold (or correlate with) linear historiographies that they interpret through synchronic moments. In fact, by cycling through elements of accumulation and disruption, and diving deep into the archive of the communication network and its bibliographic traces, contributors redirect our collective gaze to the conditions of historiographical narrations and their implied continuity, progress, and linearity that have erased nuance, individuality, and singularity. Anglo-American approaches underscore, at least at first glance, the techné dimension of the network; they thus define network primarily in technical terms, namely as an expression of the technologies—and the modes of expression and reception (e.g., seeing and hearing, writing, and reading)—involved in constituting modernity. In their complementarity, these approaches straddle the manifold lines between the lives of individuals and their relationships with people and to things (objects and archives). To return to Levine's approach, they expose the forms of literary and artistic life and of sociohistorical context in all of their messy intersection rather than correlation. Therefore, these approaches also bring into sharp relief the question of designating power: What matters in constituting networks—the intention of actors or the aggregate effects of their actions? That is, to what

---

12. On sociological network theory, see Nacim Ghanbari, "Netzwerktheorie und Aufklärungsforschung," *Internationales Archiv für Sozialgeschichte der deutschen Literatur* 38:2 (2013), p.315–35. Furthermore, for a succinct research overview, see Hannes Fischer and Erika Thomalla, "Forschungsbericht: Literaturwissenschaftliche Netzwerkforschung zum 18. Jahrhundert," *Zeitschrift für Germanistik, Neue Folge* 26:1 (2016), p.110–17.

extent does the scholar reveal a structure that determined those relationships or a structure upon which the individual capitalized on personal achievement? Conceptually, these effects have been linked to archives that, since they have the capacity to store both material and techniques, seem to encompass objects. In relation to the year 1800, to what extent do these objects document the shift between what we now understand broadly as the Enlightenment and modernity?

The individual actor and the network turn out to be the crucial elements in mapping the constellations of modernity by conglomerating the media of communication, action, and the relations they signify and, ultimately, archive. Whoever chooses to save an object, chooses to give agency to the networked nodes it represents; exclusion is continued rejection (obliteration) of agency. Traditionally, that translated into a repository along the lines of actual collections, archives, and libraries, whereas today these relations may create virtual depositories simulating ideas of order, storage, and documentation that we all know to be part of the physical library,[13] or elusive social media networks such as the one described in our opening section. While efforts to gain advantage through networks predate our period of study, this research on 1800 outlines a shift in power structures for mobility, visibility, and accessibility. Particularly with networks that arise from texts (Baumgartner, Ghanbari, Höyng), our attention is drawn to the connective edges, to their existence rather than to the agency of the nodes involved in their creation or perpetuation. Conversely, networks derived from personal interactions privilege the nodes, the individuals, and their subjectivity within those structures. Importantly, this reempowers the audience and parodist, not just the author, in the creation and preservation of culture (Dupree). The scales and contexts for communicating, acting, and interacting expand networks beyond traditional loci of power and invite a reconsideration of the archives that they, in many senses, have determined.

Digital humanities enable and expose this multilayered archiving. They redirect, if not preserve, our access to different, stubborn materials that each on their own encapsulate a moment. Though doomed and "a medium to be out-engineered [...] they become our hedge against oblivion."[14] They provide a way to recreate and evaluate multiple perspectives and multiple possible orderings of the

---

13. See, most recently, Venkat Mani, *Recording world literature* (New York, 2017).
14. Kirschenbaum, *Bitstreams*, p.8.

repository. Network graphs built from different assumptions about the relationships between people, materials, and themes can juxtapose a retrospective scholarly order against a conceptual schema that arises from lesser-studied or less visible attributes of those same objects of study. In this way, standard biographical and bibliographical metadata do more than demarcate the representational value of that content; the metadata are in conversation with the content of primary sources. The network becomes a site for an implosion of both: established modes of writing cultural histories—hermeneutic interpretations of texts and contexts undertaken by individual authors—and the traditional delineation of discreet, academic disciplines. But, rather than supplanting the single author with a collective and allowing concepts, terms, and microhistories to emerge in professed synergy, as has most recently been proposed by The Multigraph Collective's *Interacting with print* (2018), we suggest alternative modes. The network allows for a reassembly of attributes that is generative, as a representation of relationships to analyze, evaluate, and problematize. It also allows for a better understanding of how scholarly work in literary studies may be organized, distributed, and hierarchized, or simply unfold, now and in the future.[15]

Thus, whereas The Multigraph Collective draws our attention to the media ecology of materials of study (and relegates hitherto important constitutive elements of the archive, such as the *Werkedition*—edition of author's works—to the margins), *German and European cultural histories* capitalizes on the media ecology of literary, historical, and cultural scholarship; it uncovers the fault lines, priorities and omissions, values and distortions of linear, mostly national historiographies. As Matt Erlin and Melanie Walsh identify in their reflective contribution, the creation of the network representation of the objects leads to a broader understanding of the features of those objects. Similarly, our book emphasizes the process at the heart of generating concepts, terms, and microhistories in the historical network, while the contributors step back and record this process. In other words, where The Multigraph

---

15. In this sense, we agree with Jo Guldi, "The common landscape of digital history: universal methods, global borderlands, longue-durée history, and critical thinking about approaches and institutions," in *Digital histories*, ed. Mats Fridlund and Mila Oiva (Helsinki, 2020), p.327–49 (337): "Just as critical theory pushed out the set of uncritical liberal targets of research that came before it, so, it might be expected, will the new goals of digital history displace some of the focus of the scholarly record before them."

Collective emphasizes the joint writing among scholars, we document the networks that arise in the essays and between the essays in *German and European cultural histories*, signaling that scholarship is always in the making.[16]

At the same time, the evidence and arguments presented by some of the contributions push back against the impression that digital humanities struggles to produce results. Erlin and Walsh expand upon this idea in their reflections on their large-scale project, and the essays by Baumgartner, Conroy, Hall, and Höyng offer examples of how the representation interacts with our understanding of the objects, the individuals, or the contexts in which they existed. By offering the ability *to see* connections between materials, approaches, and digital representations of scholarly engagement with 1800, the index graph to this volume engages the reader in this generative, nonlinear problematization of connectivity in the organization, production, and dissemination of knowledge today. It showcases new views of the historical networks around 1800. Like *Interacting with print*, the essays collected here also resist the alignment of social and material culture with national cultures.[17] Nevertheless, alignments with different modern languages do emerge. The communities analyzed here are not imagined, but documented, primarily through textual sources; they attest to local thematic affinities that are similar across national borders. But, unlike existing studies of such local networks, *German and European cultural histories* does not fold back onto the local textual source to tell the story and historical legacy of the locale, but uses it to highlight and interrogate the eccentricities of cultural history.

Thus, something else we hope to accomplish comes to the fore: Here, as elsewhere, the outcomes of digital humanities research are often iterative results. They are iterative in the sense that the addition or removal of an element has the potential to significantly alter a digital, quantitative representation of the relationships between materials. Likewise, a newly considered qualitative aspect of the object of study will provoke a different network representation. By extension, our aspiration is that reading or seeing the chapters in their different networked configurations will prompt the same iterative process. Although this shift in interpretation has always occurred, as scholars

16. The "Epilogue" of The Multigraph Collective, *Interacting with print: elements of reading in the era of print saturation* (Chicago, IL, 2018), p.305–10, closely resembles our approach.

17. See The Multigraph Collective, *Interacting with print*, p.5 and 13.

problematize the roles of different works within a given context, the impact on the overall understanding of a period, national literature, or genre has felt more incremental, slowed by publishing schedules and access. With a network graph, the microstructures of smaller communities can immediately be compared to similar structures (see Conroy, Hall, Höyng). Canonical pieces are in constant conversation with secondary and minor texts, but the result is dependent on analytical choices and the priorities of the graph's designer.

Questions of scale and granularity dominate—in particular, intratextual network analysis, which documents the connections across texts via the shared appearance of names, terms, or concepts. The consequences of choices about the number of documents or data points to consider and the size of the text to analyze limit the representational capacity of the resulting graph. Does the network capture all titles, all letters, or all destinations? Are the relationships driven by co-presence, exchange of dialogue, or diegetic attributes? How are items defined as being present together—by being mentioned together in a chapter or by sharing the same diegetic time and space? The representation can only answer the questions encoded into the data collection and organization. If the feature extraction is automated, based on patterns assumed to exist with a certain regularity in the text, then certain nuances of expression are inevitably invisible to the graph. At the same time, redefining centrality mathematically can reveal other kinds of marginalization and eccentricity. In all likelihood, the online representations of data, while fueling the scholarly readings put forth in the contributions, also challenge any dominant narratives emerging in the sections and across the printed book.

Nevertheless, we are wary of taking definitive stock as Andrew Piper does, perhaps unintentionally, in *Enumerations: data and literary study* (2018). In reflecting on and erstwhile concluding his personal process of engaging with digital humanities, he offers an important account of the possibilities and pitfalls, pros and cons of reading digitally and quantitatively. While one could challenge the binary structure embedded in the title—one that is subverted across the book—our intention is, again, different. We agree with Piper's observations, the first of which he makes in an uncanny allusion to Levine—namely, the repetitions that data-driven approaches reveal and that are at work in producing and reproducing literary and cultural life. In a second observation, he compellingly argues that literary studies have been defined by generalizations. In the purview of this collection, it seems that we ought to challenge these general observations, in order to advance both DH methods and literary studies, which, behind the curtain of seemingly impartial data, always draw attention to figuration, singularity, and the nongeneral. Only by unleashing the humanistic, nonautomatic potential of DH in literary studies will either have a future.

Effects: the architecture of this book

We named the four sections of this book for the discursive trends we saw emerging in the knowledge networks, which defined our exchanges.

While, at first glance, a focus on people—the social actors—and the capital they possess seems to unify the three contributions in the "Social capital" section, a more complex understanding of capital comes to the fore, one that entwines actors and their movements, the products they forge and the stories they tell. But we also see the tokens of exchange that these actors leverage for more idealist and immaterial outcomes, such as friendship (Homann), recognition, and elusive power (Conroy)—or, more circumspect already then, caricature (Dupree); in the process, the fragility of those terms becomes visible, in addition to their accumulative effects. By pinpointing and circumscribing these concepts, social capital marks a tension: between continuity and linearity, or even between teleology and progress, which have traditionally been associated with the respective events and the disruptions or movements that become visible through the network. Conroy's debunking of the narrative that the French Revolution was the disrupting event par excellence serves as perhaps the most impressive example.

If social actors form nodes in thus imagined networks, their products resemble nodes in the "Material cultures" section. But paper and books, collections, and libraries also engender the edges, the entailed impact, and the connections that these materials may have had. These edges cannot just be described as transactions, but also make up chains of transmission that become entangled, interlaced, and knot-like. Attempts to organize the proliferation of print material both constrain the possibility of transnational knowledge networks (Hall) and speak to the Weimar appropriation of European cultural trends (Franzel). In contrast to that outward-facing construction of national identity, Schellenberg documents local resistance to that overarching characterization and homogenization. Agency here is diffused beyond centralized figures since the objects (the inventories and itineraries) create both things to mediate and ways to mediate them. Although the contributions to the "Material cultures" section draw heavily on textual sources, we distinguish here between the text as a vehicle of transmission to establish connections between people and places and the text as the (only) site in which a network can be said to exist.

The section entitled "Reading" approaches the latter, drawing attention to edges that are defined by nodes collocated in a document and perhaps nowhere else found together. For example, Höyng outlines individuals who may have never met but appear on the same page of Beethoven's conversation notebooks in networks that reveal a previously lost glimpse of daily life. The section asks what networks of such textual neighbors can reveal about the larger cultural environment in which they were created. Ghanbari and Baumgartner both reveal nascent networks of patronage and tourism. Whereas Ghanbari chronicles how writers, via their "first letters," attempted to forge as well as stifle networks of communication, at times disrupting or leaning on existing correspondents' networks, Baumgartner redirects our attention to the networked, loose intertextuality that travel guides formed with prior, model guidebooks and through translation. Cities may have been connected only by circuitous routes or through local knowledge rather than by direct road access. Networks arise from the contents of the text rather than from the configuration of authors or agents in their production. And by tuning in to texts only, rather than paying attention to the reputation and legendary standing of the person behind the page, we allow different, nonlinear histories of culture to emerge. They are nearly always more complex than established scholarship would have it, and often implode long-held beliefs.

Operating behind all of these sections is the question of nation (and national identity) in a moment of knowledge expansion, bringing with it translation and transmedia expression—even if the national is not articulated as a center around which networks revolve. The concluding pieces, in the "Expansive networks" section, encourage the reader to consider what (if any) boundaries can be attached to the network. Erlin and Walsh consider methodological questions and challenges to networks (and digital humanities, more broadly), while Tautz chronicles the rise of cosmopolitanism as a concept that juxtaposed nation, creating and simultaneously undoing networks in favor of teleological history. The authors of the epilogue problematize the finality of any hermeneutic structure—no matter how much we desire it as scholars and authors—and they challenge the interpretative traditions that rest upon hermeneutics. Their approach invites a reconsideration and reconfiguration of the network metaphor, which the reader should take as a prompt to explore the alternative configurations suggested/invited/enabled by the index graph for the book. Finally, the short theses in Figure 1—with an obvious nod to Emily Apter who introduced the format in similar fashion in *The Translation zone* (2006)—seek to capture and provoke yet another mode of thinking about the underlying architecture of *social capital, material cultures, reading,* and take the titular cue provided by the "Expansive networks" section quite literally.[18]

---

1. Networks are everything, anything, and nothing.
2. The local and the global co-create the concept of networks. They also destroy it.
3. Network is deceptively limitless. It is meaningless without limits.
4. Networks undo the illusion of stability.
5. Networks are tasked with preserving—that is, creating—stability.
6. Networks require attributes.
7. Networks are open, but they strive to be closed. Synonyms for "closed" are "described," "whole," "neat," and "linear."
8. Networks are chaotic, therefore resistant.
9. Where there is network, there are keywords.
10. Networks stand against a binary, but they rely on two vectors. Read: they are often translated into binaries.
11. Networks preserve, and yet they are always already obsolete.
12. Networks affect. They are effects.
13. Networks are deceptive in that they pose as alternative to the linear. Instead they are forever contingent on the linear.
14. Scholars are produced by networks, and they are part of multiple networks.

Figure 1: Fourteen theses on networks. Content and image by Birgit Tautz and Crystal Hall.

---

18. Emily Apter, *The Translation zone: a new comparative literature* (Princeton, NJ, 2006).

I
Social capital

French salons as networks, before and after 1800

MELANIE CONROY

University of Memphis

Introduction

The memory of postrevolutionary French salons is paradoxical. On the one hand, early-nineteenth-century salons like those of Mme de Staël and Mme Récamier are some of the most famous events of the era. On the other hand, postrevolutionary salons have often been presented in the historical literature as inferior copies of Old Regime salons or else not been discussed at all. The French Revolution has frequently served as an end point for histories of the salons. In Habermas's account, the eighteenth century was the great age of public discourse, during which enlightened publics came together to discuss a broad range of topics in informal settings that lent themselves to egalitarian forms of communication; in France, the preeminent institution of such enlightened conversation was the eighteenth-century salon.[1] This Habermasian reading of French salons and their history has been influential in studies of the salons, so much so that even accounts that run counter to Habermas's narrative tend to take the French Revolution as their end date. Such is the case with Dena Goodman and Antoine Lilti, whose accounts of eighteenth-century mondain sociability differ significantly—concerning the nature of salons and salon sociability, as well as their contribution to the Enlightenment,

---

1. Jürgen Habermas, in *The Structural transformation of the public sphere: an inquiry into a category of bourgeois society*, translated by Thomas Burger (Cambridge, MA, 1978), argues that the rise of the salons spans the Revolution as part of the larger rise of the bourgeois public sphere (p.33–39). However, beyond this general revolutionary timeline, Habermas does not offer any specific dates, either for the move from an order led by aristocrats to one led by the bourgeoisie, or for the eventual end of the bourgeois public sphere and of salons.

which Goodman considers to be more significant than does Lilti.[2]
Yet both Goodman and Lilti take 1789 as a convenient end point of
French salons. Literary historians, by contrast—both contemporary
and of the time—have largely taken for granted the existence of salons
after 1789, but they have not made the case for these gatherings as
culturally significant, instead casting salons primarily as background
material for the biographies of famous writers.[3]

Literary salons, especially of the nineteenth century, are often
studied separately from so-called philosophical salons and so-called
mondain salons. This is, in part, because they were thought to bring
together very different publics. Salons of both the late eighteenth
century and the early nineteenth century assembled the literary elites
of their respective eras. But, rather than being separate, the literary
elite and other elites—including the noblesse, academic elites, and
administrative elites—were often the same people. French salons
both before and after 1800 assembled a public of elite bourgeois
and aristocrats, often with an interest in the literary arts, as well as
politics, philosophy, and, to a lesser extent, the sciences. The socioeconomic demographics of French salons did not change radically with
the Revolution, even when these salons were forced to move abroad
for a time and then return, generally for political reasons.

It has been relatively easy to ignore the fact that literary elites
and other elites were often the same people because literary and
political histories of the salons are not forced into dialogue with one
another. In this essay, I attempt to do just that, by examining the
multiple networks in which salon participants were members, both
salon networks and other social and knowledge networks.[4]

2. The Revolution led many salons to close or move abroad. For this reason,
    many histories of the salons use the term only to refer to social gatherings in
    the period before the Revolution. These include Antoine Lilti's *The World of
    the salons: sociability and worldliness in eighteenth-century Paris* (Oxford, 2015) and
    Dena Goodman's *The Republic of Letters: a cultural history of the French Enlight-
    enment* (Ithaca, NY, 1994).
3. Steven D. Kale's *French salons: high society and political sociability from the Old
    Regime to the Revolution of 1848* (Baltimore, MD, 2004) and Anne Martin-Fu-
    gier's *La Vie élégante, ou la Formation de Tout-Paris, 1815–1848* (Paris, 1990)
    make the strongest case for salons existing well into the nineteenth century and
    continuing to play a central role in French culture.
4. For "Procope," the full schema for classifying the networks of early modern
    networks, as well as a discussion of eighteenth-century French social networks,
    see Maria Teodora Comsa *et al.*, "The French Enlightenment network," *The
    Journal of modern history* 88:3 (2016), p.495–534.

I argue that the network is a concept that can profitably be used to understand relations within the salons and the relations of salons to the rest of society. Salons have traditionally been thought of as groups more or less set in their orientation by the hostess—for example, Mme de Staël's salon at Coppet, like her mother Mme Necker's previously, was a bastion of liberalism due to the influence of Mme de Staël herself. Thinking about salons as networks, in which the hostesses play a pivotal role but do not determine the social relations of the group, allows for a more nuanced analysis of the interests and politics of salons. Similarly, seeing salons as networks makes their connections to other institutions more apparent. In the terms of network analysis, salon networks are ego networks, comprising the hostess and her guests, but members of salons are included in other networks in which they may be more central or even the core of the network. Seeing salon guests as nodes in other networks, rather than as subordinate to the salon hostess, encourages us to see the salon networks as integrated into larger society and susceptible to other social pressures.

Methods

I examine French salon networks from the prerevolutionary and postrevolutionary periods using methods developed to study early modern networks within the project Mapping the Republic of Letters.[5] The data are drawn from The Salons Project, a database of salon participants in Europe from 1700 to 1914, which I co-direct with Chloe Edmondson.[6] To the list of participants, I apply the ontological schema "Procope," developed with Maria Teodora Comsa, Dan Edelstein, Chloe Edmondson, and Claude Willan.[7] I use this schema to place individuals into social, knowledge, and professional networks. Social networks are large social groups (e.g., "Nobility," "Elite," "Military," "Court") whose members were more likely to know one another and move in the same social circles. "Nobility" or "Aristocracy" is only applied to titled nobility in France, although the criteria may be different in other countries.

---

5. For more on Mapping the Republic of Letters and The Salons Project, see http://republicofletters.stanford.edu (last accessed June 23, 2023).
6. For more on The Salons Project, see http://www.salonsproject.org (last accessed June 23, 2023).
7. Comsa *et al.*, "The French Enlightenment network."

"Elite" is used for members of elite institutions like the Académie française, high-ranking members of the clergy and nobility, as well as for famous writers and illustrious scientists; it can also be used for powerful members of *le monde*. Knowledge networks, most notably the "Letters" and "Sciences" networks, are based on publications in those fields and election to academies in those fields. Professional networks are smaller groups of people who work in related fields and would be more likely to come into contact with one another—for example, education, banking, medicine, or cultural professions.

The Salons Project aims to understand the role of salons within the early modern Republic of Letters and eighteenth- and nineteenth-century culture more broadly, while this essay will examine the specific aspects of six *salonnières* before and after the Revolution. The overall database contains lists of hosts and guests of notable salons. It also includes basic demographic data about these individuals, such as birth and death years, gender, nationality, profession, social status, military ranks, and titles. The format of this database is indebted to the work of the Electronic Enlightenment project at the University of Oxford, although most of the entries do not come from that database.[8] We use this format because it has become somewhat of a standard in eighteenth-century French studies. To this database, we apply the schema "Procope," which was designed to identify potential networks larger than those suggested by specific data, such as birth years and military ranks. As an example, military officers of different ranks interacted frequently, so one rank by itself would not form a discrete network of people who socialized or served together.

The data for the current study consist of the membership lists of salon networks of six prominent French *salonnières*: Geoffrin, Lespinasse, Necker, Genlis, Stäel, and Récamier (see Table 1).

8.   For more on the Electronic Enlightenment project and their data model, see http://www.e-enlightenment.com/ (last accessed June 23, 2023).

Table 1: Pre- and postrevolutionary French salons, 1750–1830.

Salon network	Gatherings	Location(s)	Estimated dates of activity	Total number of members
Geoffrin	Geoffrin (92) Geoffrin_dinner (3)	Rue Saint-Honoré, Paris	1750-1777	95
Lespinasse	Lespinasse (52)	Rue Saint-Dominique, Paris	1764-1776	52
Necker	Necker (16) Necker_Clery (8) Necker_SaintOuen (5) Necker_Control-General (4) Necker_dinner (3) Necker_Beaulieu (4) Necker_Rolle (4)	Rue Michel Le Comte, Paris Rue de Cléry, Paris Château de Saint-Ouen, Paris Côntrole-général, Paris	1766-1781	36
Genlis	Genlis (1) Genlis_PalaisRoyal (6) Genlis_Arsenal (55)	Palais-Royal, Paris Bibliothèque de l'Arsenal, Paris	1770-1814	62
Stäel	Stael_Paris1 (9) Stael_Paris2 (8) Stael_Coppet (98) Stael_Blois (5) Stael_Fosse (1)	Rue du Bac, Paris Coppet, Switzerland Blois, France Fosse, France	1793-1817	127
Récamier	Recamier_Paris (6) Recamier_Paris1 (29) Recamier_Paris2 (2) Recamier_Paris3 (9) Recamier_Lyon (9) Recamier_Clichy (2) Recamier_Dieppe (3)	Rue du Mont-Blanc, Paris Abbaye-aux-Bois, rue de Sèvres, Paris Lyon, France Clichy, France Dieppe, France	1800-1849	81

All six women held culturally significant salons between 1750 and 1789 or between 1800 and 1830. These two periods correspond, roughly, to the so-called high Enlightenment and the postrevolutionary period. In previous research, we found that the public of French salons did not change a great deal in socioeconomic terms over the eighteenth century, even as philosophy and politics became more prominent topics for the publications of salon guests and as government officials and diplomats became more invested in the salon world. To reiterate, the purpose of the present study is to compare the demographics and networks of these late-eighteenth-century salons with those of the early nineteenth century. I wanted to measure the extent to which these two trends continued: (1) the consistency of demographic *mixité*, such as the presence of multiple classes, professions, genders, and ages; (2) the increase in interest in politics and employment in government. These two factors have been seen as markers of late-eighteenth-century salons.[9] If they continue past 1800, that indicates that the Revolution was not a dramatic break from the late Enlightenment; if they end, that indicates a rupture within the salon world.

Historiography of pre- and postrevolutionary French salons

The history of French salons has been written many times—from Sainte-Beuve's hagiographical account of individual salon hostesses to Benedetta Craveri's more nuanced account in *The Age of conversation*.[10] The French Revolution has marked a turning point in the history of the salons even in the first, less systematic accounts of salons. That history was largely written in the 1830s, when salon participants like Sainte-Beuve and the *salonnière* Sophie Gay set down the first accounts of salons as a continuous institution. For classicists like Sainte-Beuve and Gay, the salon world was tied to the aesthetics of the Old Regime—to wit, regularity, concision, and balance. The early-nineteenth-century horizon of many of the first chroniclers of

9. On the network of foreign ambassadors in late-eighteenth-century Parisian salons, see Charlotta Wolff, "'Un admirateur des philosophes modernes': the networks of Swedish ambassador Gustav Philip Creutz in Paris, 1766–1783," in *Networks of European Enlightenment*, ed. Chloe Edmondson and Dan Edelstein (Liverpool, Liverpool University Press / Voltaire Foundation, 2019), p.173–200.

10. Charles Augustin Sainte-Beuve, *Portraits of celebrated women* (Boston, MA, 1868), and Benedetta Craveri, *The Age of conversation* (New York, 2006).

salon history led them to place the summit of *mondanité* in the recent past. This focus on salons of the late eighteenth century has led our concept of salons to accrue numerous associations: the clash between Enlightenment philosophy and the conservative aristocracy, classical tastes in poetry and music, and an awkward relation to politics, particularly of the liberal sort. Habermas advanced the strongest version of this argument, making salons into a model for the public sphere itself, which seemingly declined even as democratic institutions and mass media rose.[11]

A network approach to salons borrows from the sociological impulse to see groups in ways that examine social relationships before imposing any fixed meanings on those relationships. In other words, instead of seeing salons as emblematic of particular eras and characterizing them by the relationship of their hostess to their era, we can first examine the demographics of salons from a more dispassionate angle and then attribute meaning to those structures. And, indeed, from a sociological perspective, we see that gatherings in women's homes existed throughout the nineteenth century, as did other kinds of informal gatherings that included literary conversations. Salons continued after the multiplication of restaurants and cafés made casual public gatherings, banquets, and weekly or monthly dinners possible.[12] Thus, we cannot say that salons flourished because of a lack of other social options. Rather, salons offered unique characteristics that other social spaces lacked: their openness to new members, but also their separation from the general public. That writers were admitted to the salons in large numbers only added to the general desirability of the salons as these writers gained fame.

The gatherings in elite private homes were normally organized by women and brought together a public that was diverse in age, gender, and, to a lesser degree, social class. *Salonnières* learned the art of "holding a circle" from older women who were sometimes family members: mothers, aunts, or family friends. Before the first institutional histories were written, salons—referred to as *cercles* or *sociétés*—were seen as a core part of the French social calendar, which also included dinners, informal visits, trips to the theater, and other gatherings that overlapped with salons, often drawing together the

11. Habermas, *The Structural transformation*.
12. On the various forms of male-led or male-only literary sociability of the nineteenth century, see Anthony Glinoer and Vincent Laisney, *L'Age des cénacles: confraternités littéraires et artistiques au XIXᵉ siècle* (Paris, 2013).

same people; thus, the first histories of the salon were doing some heavy conceptual interpretation of the patterns of daily life in setting salons apart from other visits.[13] Nevertheless, salons, with conversation as their primary activity, supplemented by literary readings, theatrical performances, and other entertainments, were thought of separately from smaller gatherings like dinners.

But if the salons of the Old Regime were idealized in the early-nineteenth-century works of Sainte-Beuve and Gay, salons of the Restoration were diminished in the works of contemporaneous novelists. For Stendhal, the insularity of Restoration salons ensured that nothing of any real interest could be discussed there, least of all politics or philosophy, as he wrote in *The Red and the black* (1830):

> Provided that there was no joking at the expense of God, the clergy, the king, or the powers that be, artistic and literary figures currently enjoying favor at Court, or indeed any part of the establishment; provided that no good word was spoken of Béranger, the opposition press, Voltaire, Rousseau, or anyone venturing to be in any way outspoken; provided above all that there was never any mention of politics, it was permissible to discourse freely on any subject.[14]

Stendhal's description of salons falls in line with the common claim that salons were not open to political or ideological diversity, which, at the time of Stendhal's writing, was already something of a cliché. The salons of the Restoration, as described by Stendhal, were particularly aristocratic and potentially more ideologically closed than other nineteenth-century salons. Nevertheless, male authors of the nineteenth century often continued to see the salons as cultural battlegrounds, unappealing environs controlled by meddling women seeking to restrict the conversation of freethinking *philosophes*, as they were sometimes cast in the late eighteenth century, despite the fact that *philosophes* attended the salons in large numbers.[15]

Similarly, the idea flourished that salons, particularly conservative salons, were so *démodés* as to be dead, politically and culturally. In *The Cabinet of antiquities* (1838), for example, Balzac depicts a provincial

---

13. See Lilti, *The World*.
14. Stendhal, *The Red and the black: a chronicle of the nineteenth century* (1830), translated by Catherine Slater (Oxford, 2009), p.263.
15. Melanie Conroy and Chloe Summers Edmondson, "The empire of letters: Enlightenment-era French salons," in *Networks of European Enlightenment*, ed. C. Edmondson and D. Edelstein, p.80–91.

salon attended by members of the local aristocracy as a virtual museum piece:

> Beneath that ancient ceiling, the glory of days now dead, sat or moved about ten or a dozen dowagers, some with shaking heads, others as withered and dark as mummies; some stiff and erect, others bent, but all caparisoned in gowns more or less fantastically in opposition to the fashion; powdered heads were there, with heavy curls, caps with bow-knots, and rusty laces.[16]

The women depicted here are dressed at great expense in elaborate gowns that would be more at home in the eighteenth century, complete with powdered hair and bows in the Old Regime fashion. Having missed both the simple fashions of the Empire period and the more structured dresses of the 1820s, these widows have not evolved in forty years. Their dress is emblematic of their ideas and social mores, which have remained in a state of suspended life, since their faction of the old nobility rejected collaboration with the man they saw as a plebeian usurper, Napoleon Bonaparte. Here again, the salons are aligned with the eighteenth-century past; yet here, the eighteenth-century influence is aristocratic and conservative rather than philosophical and liberating.

Despite their ideological differences, Stendhal and Balzac see the salons as stuck in a world that is essentially of the eighteenth century and therefore not natural to the nineteenth. Criticism from within sounded similar to, yet strongly pushed back against, outside voices. *Salonnières* themselves often railed against these discourses of decline that consistently found *le monde* to be lacking in comparison to the recent past. As the *salonnière* Delphine de Girardin wrote in *Parisian letters*:

> For twenty years people have been decrying the salons, the sterility of the salons, the childishness of the salons, without noticing that all of our men of government, all of our men of genius are men of the salons. [...] we have forgotten all of the creators of beautiful speeches to whom the elegant world has given birth; and now again, despite our experience, people speak of the intellectual poverty of the salons.[17]

Girardin's claim is not just that commentators are overly negative about the quality of the salons. It is also that they are wrong *in the same*

16. Honoré de Balzac, *The Gallery of antiquities*, in *The Works of Balzac*, translated by Katharine Prescott Wormeley, vol.15 (Boston, MA, 1896), p.1–184 (15–16).
17. Delphine Girardin, *Œuvres complètes*, vol.4: *Lettres parisiennes* (Paris, 1860), p.99.

way about salons, consistently seeing the salons of the last generation as superior to the current crop. Nonetheless, few took seriously Girardin's argument that postrevolutionary salons were reflective of the best of that generation. The voices of more famous writers and the classical literary historians were more influential in accounts that were to come. Network analysis helps us counter that influence and contextualize Girardin's observations within the structures of cultural and knowledge exchange of the period.

Le monde, or the people of the salons

French salons before 1800 were characterized by *mixité*, or the intermingling of people of different socioeconomic classes, social statuses, vocations, and genders.[18] In previous research, I studied the demographics of eighteenth-century French salons with Chloe Edmondson as an investigation into the characteristics of salons.[19] We found that the *habitués* were more likely to be male, elite, and aristocratic, compared to the broader French population. Looking at the salons of Geoffrin, Lespinasse, and Necker, for example, we see that 75 to 87 percent of the attendees were male, between 63 and 83 percent were members of an elite institution, and between 45 and 65 percent were noble (see Table 2).

This socioeconomic picture validates Lilti's claim that eighteenth-century salons were populated by nobles and characterized by an aristocratic habitus. But we must not forget that late-eighteenth-century salons also brought together members of the political elite (between 33 and 50 percent), especially diplomats and ambassadors. At the same time, all three of these major salons accepted women (between 13 and 25 percent) and had a significant presence of military elites (between 9 and 19 percent) and courtiers (15 to 23 percent). The fact that the military and the court are consistently represented at numbers far lower than the nobility suggests that the "price of admission" to eighteenth-century French salons could be paid by nobility and was not specifically aligned with either the military or the court. Salons provided a space for serious political discussion, especially at the end of the eighteenth century.

18. Antoine Lilti claims, for example, that the mixing of genders is the "touchstone" of Old Regime mondain sociability; Lilti, *The World*, p.22.
19. Data from The Salons Project.

Table 2: Documented members of pre- and postrevolutionary French salons and their networks.

Salon	Geoffrin	Lespinasse	Necker	Genlis	Staël	Récamier
Women %	17	13	25	35	18	28
Nobility %	45	65	61	45	38	56
Elite %	63	81	83	66	62	78
Political elite %	33	50	39	18	31	34
Military %	9	19	14	8	20	22
Court %	23	15	17	11	8	17
Nobility & Letters %	17	35	33	11	14	14
Elite & Letters %	28	56	53	23	30	28
Total number of members	95	52	36	62	127	81

In the years after 1800, salons retained a similar demographic character. Postrevolutionary salons, especially of a literary bent, remained elite affairs. Examining three of the largest and best-documented salons (Genlis, Staël, Récamier), I found that the majority of members were affiliated with elite institutions (between 62 and 78 percent). Large proportions (38 to 56 percent) were nobles, although slightly less than in the late-eighteenth-century salons we studied. Interestingly for our purposes, members of the military and the court continued to be present in similar proportions. The number of salon participants who were in the military stayed roughly similar—between 9 and 19 percent pre-1800 and from 8 to 22 percent post-1800. Thus, despite the intervening Revolutionary and Napoleonic Wars, the participants of salons were not more likely to have served in the military than were salon participants of the late eighteenth century. The proportions of people who were regularly received at court or made a living from the court were slightly lower—8 to 17 percent versus 15 to 23 percent—but not radically so.

The portrait of the salons that emerges from the study of their demographics is of an elite network whose structure is very little changed despite the disappearance of some of its members and the transformation of the society around the salons by successive regime changes. Despite the loss of individual members—such as Genlis's husband, who was guillotined—the network remains remarkably stable. One difference is that there was a greater preponderance of women in salons like those of Mme de Staël, Récamier, and Genlis than in late-eighteenth-century salons, aside from Deffand's salon, which was notable for its large number of female guests.[20] Otherwise, the differences between salons in terms of the socioeconomic status of their members appear to reflect not changes over time, but rather the openness of particular salons to people of various classes and the degree to which historians and others have been able to document the members of the salons.

We see, for example, that Geoffrin's salon has a large number of documented members (95). That salon also has a lower proportion of noble or elite people than either Lespinasse's or Necker's salon, which both have fewer documented members (52 and 36, respectively). The same is true for postrevolutionary salons; Staël's salon has the largest number of documented members (127 versus 62 for Genlis and 81 for

---

20. For more on Deffand's salon in relation to the other salons of the eighteenth century, see The Salons Project.

Récamier). Staël's salon also has a smaller proportion of documented nobles (38 percent versus 45 for Genlis and 56 for Récamier) and elites (62 percent versus 66 for Genlis and 78 for Récamier). The difference between salons with larger numbers of documented attendees may be due to the greater openness of these salons, thus a function of the fact that the salon had more members, including less-elite members. It could also be a function of the better documentation of these salons, with less-elite individuals being recorded as attending alongside their higher-ranking and better-known peers. The fact that smaller salons appear to be more elitist shows that the "eliteness" of the salon was not a function of its popularity; rather, more sought-after salons were less "elitist" if we look only at the number of attendees.

Both pre- and postrevolutionary salons that I examined attracted members from the societal elite, yet this does not mean that salons were primarily noble affairs divorced from the world of letters and philosophy. Indeed, the aristocrats and their upper bourgeois acquaintances were often themselves literary types, or *gens de lettres*. A majority of members in Lespinasse's salon (67 percent) and Necker's salon (61 percent) contributed to the field of *belles-lettres* ("All letters"), meaning both literature and works of a religious, philosophical, historical, or difficult-to-classify nature (see Table 3).

Most of these authors did write some literature, meaning that the literary group ("Literary") is nearly as well represented as the "All letters" group in these salons—58 percent in Lespinasse's salon and 56 percent in Necker's salon.

Both the general "All letters" and the specifically "Literary" knowledge networks were *less* represented in postrevolutionary salons, despite the fact that postrevolutionary salons are *more* associated with literature by total numbers of participants (see Table 3). The "Letters" network constituted between 32 and 40 percent of the postrevolutionary salons that I studied, compared to 39 to 67 percent of prerevolutionary salons. The "Literary" network was 22 to 34 percent of postrevolutionary salons, instead of 35 to 58 percent. While the three postrevolutionary salons that I studied can hardly stand in for all postrevolutionary French salons, it is instructive that the proportion of writers in these salons actually declines after 1800, especially because Genlis and Staël are two of the most prominent writers of the era, yet their salons were not much more "literary" than the salon of Récamier, herself not a writer. Indeed, the salons of Lespinasse and Necker—neither of whom wrote significant works—are the high point in terms of the proportion of both *belles-lettres* and literary writers.

Table 3: Knowledge networks in pre- and postrevolutionary French salons.

Salon	Geoffrin	Lespinasse	Necker	Genlis	Staël	Récamier
All letters %	39	67	61	40	39	32
Literary %	35	58	56	34	31	22
Sciences %	11	8	6	3	6	4
Political economy %	5	27	25	N/A	8	4
Philosophy %	9	15	11	2	6	9
Total number of members	95	52	36	62	127	81

This presents the clearest case in this dataset of the reputation of the *salonnière* overshadowing the characteristics of a salon. It appears that the literary reputations of Staël, perhaps the greatest novelist of her generation, and Genlis, one of the most renowned children's writers and also a writer of bestselling conduct books and historical fiction, have made it appear as though more of the people who attended their salons were writers than was actually the case. In reality, the smaller salons of Lespinasse—a lover and confidante of the *encyclopédiste* D'Alembert but no writer herself—and Necker—Staël's mother—actually welcomed a larger proportion of writers.

Similarly, the proportion of salon attendees who wrote philosophical works is often rather different from what the reputation of the *salonnière* would imply. Geoffrin's salon was a famed meeting place of eighteenth-century *philosophes*, where their works were read and debated. Nevertheless, the openness of Geoffrin's salon and its size meant that the authors of philosophical works constituted only 9 percent of documented attendees (see Table 3). By contrast, Lespinasse's and Necker's salons had a higher proportion of writers of philosophical works (15 and 11 percent, respectively), despite their lesser reputations as sites of philosophical discussion. The authors of philosophical works were even less represented in postrevolutionary salons (between 2 and 9 percent). The low of 2 percent—or one philosophical author—is not surprising, since Genlis was a known rival of the *philosophes* and skeptical of their influence. It is even less surprising that the one philosophical author is Germaine de Staël, who wrote philosophical and literary historical works, as well as novels. It is more unexpected that only 6 percent of the attendees of Staël's salon, which included philosophical luminaries like Wilhelm von Humboldt and August Schlegel, and was renowned for its influence, produced philosophical works. Récamier's salon contained a slightly higher proportion of authors of philosophical works than did Staël's—including the French philosophers Pierre-Simon Ballanche and Félicité Robert de Lamennais. Despite their presence in all salons studied, philosophers were never a majority, and their numbers declined in salons after 1800, even in those with the most philosophical hostesses.

Authors of works on political economy—that is, economics, politics, and what would come to be known as sociology—formed the largest proportion of participants in the salons of Lespinasse (27 percent) and Necker (25 percent). One possible explanation for this higher representation of writers of philosophical, political, and economic works is that the salons of Lespinasse and Necker contained more government officials and diplomats than other salons, at 50 and 39 percent (see Table 2).[21] Postrevolutionary salons contained fewer writers on political economy: none in the case of Genlis's salon, 4 percent in Récamier's, and 8 percent in Staël's (see Table 3). This may be in part because fewer of their members worked in government: 18 percent of Genlis's salon, 34 percent of Récamier's salon, and 31 percent in Staël's (see Table 2). Thus, the rise in interest in politics and employment in government that we saw at the end of the eighteenth century did not continue into the nineteenth.[22]

One consistent aspect of these salons is that the authors of scientific works never formed a very large part of salon attendees, even though they were always present (see Table 3). Authors of scientific works and members of scientific academies accounted for a relatively minor portion of salon attendees, at only 6 to 11 percent before 1800 and 3 to 6 percent after 1800. The reduced presence of scientists in postrevolutionary salons perhaps points to a bifurcation in the social worlds of the *gens de lettres* and *gens de science* that had started in the eighteenth century, but appears more pronounced in these later salons, which had fewer authors of all kinds but especially fewer scientists and authors writing on political topics.

We can see that the traditional picture of the nineteenth-century salon world as primarily literary is not entirely justified, in comparison with late-eighteenth-century salons. Similarly, the view of the eighteenth-century salon world as "mondain" or "amateurish," with a more diverse set of interests, is only true insofar as there were slightly more scientists and political economists who attended prerevolutionary salons. Eighteenth-century salons had a larger proportion of literary writers who attended them, despite also having more nobles and more people associated with the court. This is largely because many of the aristocrats in eighteenth-century salons were also involved in letters. About half of the nobles in the three prerevolutionary salons were also writers (see Table 2). While the association of the nobility with letters became weaker in the postrevolutionary salons, there is still significant overlap.[23] In Genlis's salon 11 percent of the guests

---

21. Salons shifted from more literary to more political over the course of the eighteenth century. See Craveri, *The Age of conversation*, p.374.

22. The Salons Project.

23. My study does not take into account broader societal currents or the deep historical context, nor does it map all the changes in "reading cultures." On the latter, see Dupree's essay in this volume.

were noble and writers; in Staël and Récamier's salons, 14 percent of the guests were documented nobles and writers. In these three salons, high status and being a published author remained intertwined, but at a lesser rate than nobility and literature were intermixed under the Old Regime.

Compared to the general population, salons were elite and exclusive environments, yet they were more open to the young and old, female and male participants, and people of diverse interests than more formal institutions, despite their limits. The salon world was characterized by *mixité*, but it is important to remember that this idea was forged in comparison to closed institutions like academies, schools, and the government, which were more segregated in terms of gender, class, and age. When considered from a socioeconomic perspective, the public of the most elite salons remained remarkably similar before and after 1800. The nobility made up a substantial minority or majority in all salons, but they were always together with people from other social classes, specifically elite segments of the bourgeoisie. Even when interests changed—for example, with the rise and fall of philosophy, politics, and diplomacy—literature remained a dominant interest and salons remained socially consistent. The most elite Parisian salons brought literary and political elites together with a broader population of nobles and members of the *haute bourgeoisie*, both of whom were disproportionately writers.

Salons as networks

Demographic analysis can also be useful in examining large numbers of people, especially when we are not sure whether the sample that we have is representative of some larger whole. Sociological categories of analysis, such as gender, social class, and age, are useful but not sufficient for the humanistic study of such large groups. Thinking about societies as networked interactions means looking at abstract structures that might influence relationships, rather than seeing the person's social network from their subjective position. For example, a woman attending a salon a few times in a short period might not personally know many of its other members; however, from the perspective of the network, she would be linked to the other salon guests as much as the host and any regular guests who had met the vast majority, if not all, of the salon members. Network analysis is useful not only for identifying who is important to a network, but also for how they are important: those who have the highest number of connections (measured by high degree), the parts of the network that are most and least integrated (measured by modularity), and those people and institutions that connect disparate parts of the network to each other (known as bridges or connectors).

The fundamental tool of network analysis is the network diagram, in which edges form connections between nodes. Edges in social network diagrams normally represent social relationships, either a direct relationship person-to-person, or an indirect one: common membership in some organization, co-authorship of a book, joint participation in an activity. It can be difficult to decipher particular details within large network diagrams containing many nodes and edges, but their overall shape does illustrate the broad structure of the network. In my own analysis of salon networks, the nodes are individual salon attendees, and the edges signify common attendance of an elite French salon in the period leading up to 1800.

The network diagram also makes it very easy to identify at a glance individuals with no documented connection to the central figures in the network; these are the nodes around the periphery of the diagram. The ease with which network analysis allows us to quickly ascertain these relationships is in many cases far greater than what was experienced by the people represented in the diagram themselves. The participants, of course, knew of their own direct relationships, but even as common a relationship as the friend of a friend, or further degrees of separation, might remain unknown during a lifetime. Yet even if such indirect relationships were unknown to the people in these extended social networks, they surely exerted a nudge on the course of their lives, influencing what news they heard, what books they read, and what opportunities they encountered. In other words, networks had impacts on their members of which even those members were unaware.

The shape of salon network diagrams reflects not only the actual historical relationships that are their basis, but also the manner in which the data are collected. Importantly, the diagrams tend to overrepresent the *salonnières* since the salon members whose presence is easiest to document tend to be their hosts. Thus, the best model for salon networks is the ego network, which consists of one node and its neighbors, and perhaps the neighbors of these neighbors. In a salon network, this central node is the salon's host. Beyond this, data on salon attendance is fragmentary. Particularly noteworthy guests—the famous, the desirable, the infamous—are more likely to be mentioned in records, and thus are likely to be overrepresented in the same

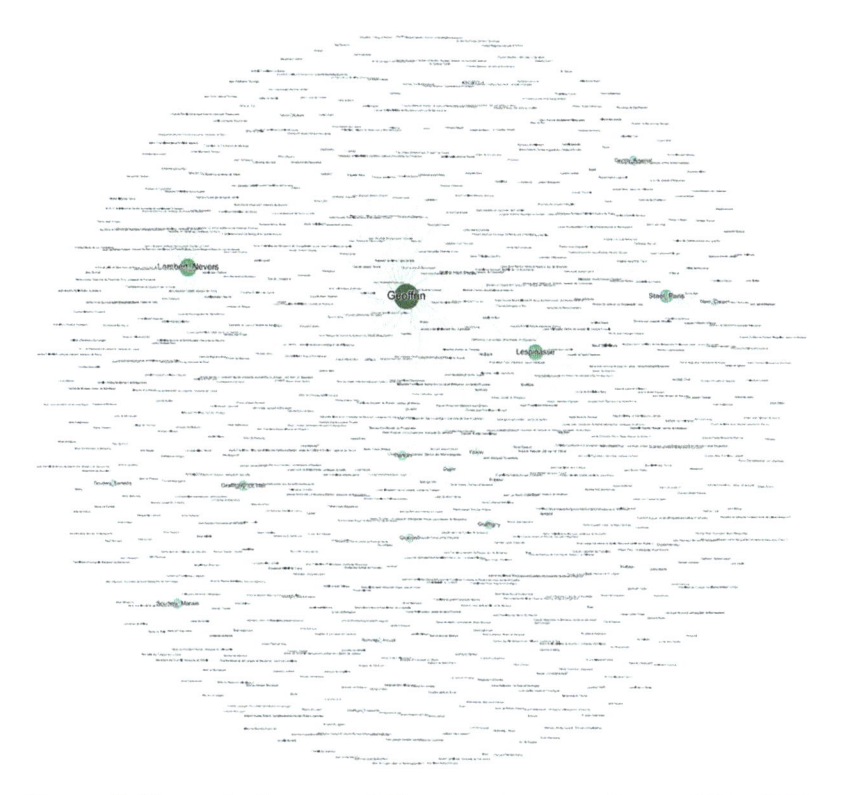

Figure 2: Network diagram of French salon attendance, 1700–1830. Data from Conroy and Edmondson, The Salons Project. Nodes are salon attendees; edges signify that two individuals attended the same salon. Node size and color indicate degree (larger, darker nodes co-attended salons with more individuals). Layout highlights individuals who are connected to one another. Visual created by Melanie Conroy.

manner as the host. For these reasons, we cannot make definitive statements about the structure of the social networks of salons based on network analysis. Still, network analysis can help us identify the most socially significant figures within each salon as well as the figures that connect one salon to another. For instance, considering Geoffrin's salon as an ego network centered on her, we can examine which other salons were most strongly connected to hers—that is, which salons shared the most members with hers (see Figure 2).

Each green-colored dot in this network diagram is a node that represents one person, a salon host or guest. The size of the node represents the number of connections that node has with other nodes. Edges between nodes represent a direct real-life connection between people. The proximity of each node to other nodes illustrates how closely these people were connected through the social network of salons. The names on the periphery of the diagram have little or no documented connection to Mme Geoffrin's salon, the central node.

Geoffrin's Paris salon, which is paradigmatic of Enlightenment-era salons, shares the greatest number of connections with Lespinasse's salon, as well as a significant number with Tencin's salon. Thus, these two *salonnières* are located near Geoffrin on the diagram: Tencin directly below, and Lespinasse below and to the right, with their shared guests clustered about. By contrast, Graffigny's salon shares fewer members with Geoffrin's and more with Quinault's and d'Epinay's, and so Graffigny's node on the diagram is further from Geoffrin's and closer to Quinault's and d'Epinay's. The large node well to the left of Geoffrin's belongs to Lambert, whose salon had many members, but few of whom shared direct connections with Geoffrin and her salon. It is hardly surprising that Geoffrin's salon shared many members with Lespinasse's salon, given that they were contemporaneous and both had connections to the *philosophes*. But time is not a sufficient explanation of their many connections, since d'Epinay's salon was held roughly concurrently.

Examining the diagram more closely, we can identify which individuals connected one salon to another. In the case of the close connection between Geoffrin's and Lespinasse's salons, these shared guests included the abbé de Bon, Etienne Charles Loménie de Brienne, and the baron d'Holbach, a well-known atheist who was himself an important host of dinners. Geoffrin's salon shared with Mme Tencin's such guests as Charles Pinot Duclos and Bernard Le Bovier de Fontenelle. D'Epinay's, Dupin's, Quinault's, and Graffigny's salons shared fewer members with Geoffrin's, though they belong to the same social network through indirect connections, such as shared members with Tencin's salon, which itself shared other members with Geoffrin's.

Most of the connections between paradigmatic Enlightenment-era salons like Geoffrin's and the salons of the early nineteenth century came through the salons of Lespinasse and Mme Necker. Lespinasse's late-eighteenth-century salon shared connections with the later salons of Mme de Staël and Mme de Genlis, the latter of whom was also active in the early nineteenth century. Again, time is an important factor but not decisive. Mme de Staël's Parisian salon has significantly more connections to Lespinasse's salon than does Genlis's more conservative postrevolutionary salon. While most analyses of this type have focused on the presence of more notable attendees, such as the *philosophes*, from this diagram we can see that it is broadly the case that Staël's Paris salon was more closely related to both Geoffrin's and Lespinasse's salons than was Genlis's, even accounting for less notable attendees.

This analysis of salons based on shared members rather than the personal characteristics of the hostess allows us to locate salons that shared large numbers of members more quickly. While it is not too hard to keep the shared members of three or four salons in mind, it can be very difficult to track the memberships of many salons, especially over time. By studying salons as networks, we create pieces of a larger map that can be expanded by future projects to include many more salons, which can be plugged into our "map" of Parisian salons. By creating a framework for studying salons instead of looking at them from a biographical perspective, we can see connections more objectively. In the diagram of Geoffrin's network, we can see that all of the major French salons of the eighteenth and early nineteenth centuries included in our database can be connected to one another by a relatively small number of hops, or moves from one node to another. The French salon world over this 150-year period from 1700 to 1850 remained quite integrated, specifically through the lens of shared guests.

Exile and new European frontiers

Thus far, I have talked a great deal about continuities in French salons before and after 1800. There were, however, discontinuities—most notably the relocation of postrevolutionary salons to other locations in Europe, as a result of the political upheavals in France from 1789 to 1815. A small number of the most mobile women of the postrevolutionary era were responsible for a disproportionate amount of the geographic diversity. Whereas most nineteenth-century literary salons were held in Paris, Mme de Staël, Mme Récamier, and Sophie Gay, all women with a troubled relationship with Napoleon, were responsible for the establishment of salons outside Paris. Most famously Germaine de Staël and her parents Jacques and Suzanne Necker were exiled to Switzerland, where they hosted guests from throughout Europe at a château in Coppet.

Figure 3 shows the 137 major literary gatherings of nineteenth-century France that I have mapped.[24] In this diagram, it is evident

24. Data from Melanie Conroy, 19th-Century Networks.

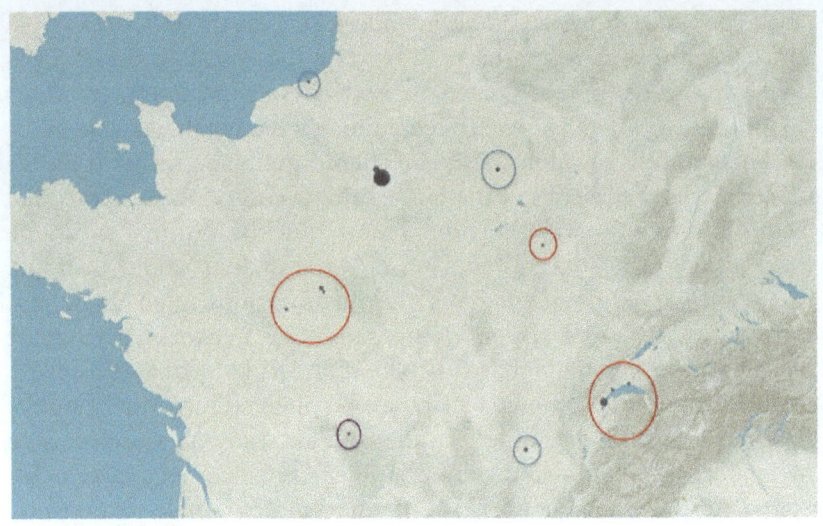

Mme de Staël
Mme Récamier
Sophie Gay

Figure 3: Map of 137 nineteenth-century salons in France. Data
from Melanie Conroy, 19th-Century Networks. Black dots indicate
salons, sized by frequency of occurrence at that location. Salons are
circled according to host: Mme de Staël (red), Mme Récamier (blue),
and Sophie Gay (purple). The largest black dots, not circled, are the
Paris salons. Visual created by Melanie Conroy.

from the dense cluster of dots that the city of Paris was the defining
institution of literary sociability, in which the most notable literary
gatherings, especially the longest-running and most successful ones,
were held. Some of these "salons" were short-term gatherings of
largely Parisian residents. In this map, the dominance of Paris as the
geographical center of literary life is evident.

Staël, Récamier, and Gay, all three Parisian women, presided over
provincial gatherings but held Parisian salons as well. The salon in
Coppet stands out as one of the rare literary gatherings outside of Paris
that brought together a large number of people and had an outsized
cultural significance. Even in that case, the very existence of the salon
in Coppet owed largely to events in Paris—that is, Napoleon's exile of
Mme de Staël and his suppression of free speech within Paris.

Yet, contrary to received opinion, eighteenth- and nineteenth-
century salons did not differ in the overall characteristics of their

publics, even when they took place outside of Paris. Parisians were frequent participants in salons outside of Paris, and elite Parisian salons often hosted foreigners as guests. Even the size of the most successful salons was remarkably similar. For example, Geoffrin's salon is estimated to be about the same size (approximately 500 total guests) as Mme de Staël's.

Aside from a few gatherings outside Paris, most successful *salonnières* and *salonniers* of the nineteenth century held their events in Paris, where literary connections were plentiful and varied. As we shall see, there was an explosion in the number of gatherings but no fundamental change in their structure or purpose after the Revolution. Similarly, female-led salons persisted throughout the nineteenth century, despite some claims that salons ended with the French Revolution.[25] In addition to long-running salons, such as Mme de Genlis's salon at the Arsenal, which was active from 1802 to 1813, women held salons and other gatherings associated with all of the major movements of nineteenth-century literature (Romanticism, realism, naturalism, etc.). Female-led salons found their guests in the same extensive networks of literary sociability as male-led gatherings like dinners and *cénacles* (literary cliques) did. They were held throughout the city of Paris, though limited to private spaces like homes.

But, even when salons did not travel, the world often came to Paris. The Parisian elite included native-born Parisians, as well as provincials and foreigners. Most salons were largely populated by French nationals. Lespinasse's salon was 94 percent French, with small numbers of dual nationals and people of foreign origin, including small numbers of people from many European countries (see Table 4).

Genlis had the same percentage of French nationals as Lespinasse, but less variety in terms of dual nationality or individuals born outside France. However, foreign visitors and people from other parts of France comprised a significant number of guests in some salons; for example, the salon of the duchesse de Praslin welcomed diplomats of all nationalities,[26] and Geoffrin's salon had a relatively large proportion of Polish members (9 percent). While 75 percent of the members of Geoffrin's salon were French, Récamier's salon was 84 percent French with a significant number of English people (7 percent)

25. Most notably by historians of the eighteenth century such as Dena Goodman; see *The Republic of Letters*, p.11.
26. Lilti, *The World*, p.53.

Table 4: Nationalities in pre- and postrevolutionary French salons.*

Salon	Geoffrin	Lespinasse	Necker	Genlis	Staël	Récamier
French %	75	94	64	94	47	84
Swiss %	N/A	2	6	2	19	N/A
Polish %	9	N/A	N/A	N/A	N/A	N/A
English %	3	4	3	N/A	12	7
Italian %	4	6	6	2	4	N/A
German %	1	2	3	3	9	2
Other** %	3	11	N/A	N/A	9	5
Total number of members	95	52	36	62	127	81

*Percentages can add up to more than 100 because some individuals have more than one nationality.
**Includes Irish, Scottish, Russian, Finnish, Danish, and Swedish individuals. We use modern designations for nationalities due to changes over time in distinctions between nationalities and the geographic boundaries of European countries. We also collect birth city and death city to make classifications according to other schemas possible. We distinguish between English, Irish, and Scottish nationalities in line with the Electronic Enlightenment schema.

and others from the British Isles. While most French salons had few foreign guests, larger, more successful gatherings almost all attracted visitors from other countries.

The displacement of salons outside of Paris was the largest source of diversity in national origin, although the form of the French salon remained remarkably similar, despite the geographic moves to places in the south of France and Swiss cities such as Geneva and Coppet. Predictably, given their Swiss origin and their exile to Geneva, the Necker family welcomed many Swiss people into their salons. Necker's salon was only 64 percent French and had a large proportion of Swiss (6 percent) and Italians (6 percent). Staël's salon, including her salon in Coppet, had the smallest proportion of French at 47 percent and included a large proportion of Swiss (19 percent), English (12 percent), and German (9 percent) visitors, as well as guests from other European countries. Geographic analysis of this kind vindicates the view of salons as loci of *mixité* and the worldly traditions that upheld it. Most importantly, it shows that salons persisted in large numbers through the nineteenth century, and did not decline with the French Revolution or with the geographic displacement caused by the Napoleonic Wars. Salons continued to bring together relatively elite groups of writers and nonwriters, regardless of where they were located in Europe or the nationality of the people who populated them.

Conclusions

French salons after 1800 have been unfairly thought of as inferior copies of their eighteenth-century counterparts. Whereas literary writers and historians alike have found postrevolutionary salons to be lacking in prestige and sociability, elite salons of all eras contained the most gifted writers of their time and provided invaluable opportunities for socializing with literary and nonliterary elites. Even as salons expanded geographically and culturally, the socioeconomic status of salon participants remained very exclusive. Although the proportion of aristocrats declined, the elite bourgeoisie that replaced them was similarly integrated into the elite societal networks that the aristocracy had previously dominated, such as academies, government, the military, and literary and cultural institutions. The new elite that emerged after 1800 was only marginally more open to people of different classes than the high society of the *Ancien Régime* had been. This core group of literary writers and aristocrats allowed the salon world to maintain its traditions. It also allowed *le monde* to maintain its social capital, continuing to draw the most accomplished people from other spheres, with the exception of the sciences. Conversely, we must rethink the transformative effect of the French Revolution on social space and capital outside France, giving serious consideration to other forces at work in eighteenth-century German-language salons in the northern German countryside or early-nineteenth-century Berlin.

The narrative of the decline of the salons is part of a Habermasian narrative about the decline of the public sphere with the rise of print culture and mass media. For Habermas, salons before 1800 were places where one could exercise reason and develop ideas; gatherings after 1800 could not have had the same function because the traditions of the salons had died out. The central facet of this narrative is that face-to-face contact within egalitarian social circles declined. This narrative is false for two reasons: (1) Salons did not decline, either in number or in cultural significance, and (2) salon networks remained integrated into other networks, including elite institutions, publishing networks, military networks, and noble families. Even as the variety of face-to-face gatherings increased in the nineteenth century, and as salons competed with male-led literary and nonliterary gatherings in restaurants, cafes, and elsewhere, salons did not lose their social desirability or their appeal to elites. The reputation of the salon leader was crucial in forging this appeal rather than being simply a gender marker.

Thinking about salons as networks, we see that the late-eighteenth-century salons were well integrated with the salons of the first decades of the new century, despite geographic displacements. Salons continued to be well integrated with elite networks outside the salons and formed a core part of French society. While the geographic expansion of 1800 to 1815 was short-lived, it brought the traditions of eighteenth-century Paris to a broader world than the Old Regime salons had by integrating more people of different nationalities, who often brought tales of their experiences in the French salons back to their compatriots. It is fair to say that salons, much like other networked constellations discussed in this volume, were increasingly on the move, traversing Europe and making incursions in imagined but barely existing national discourses, for example in German lands.

Plappermann's *Wanderjahre*: traveling declamators and knowledge circulation around 1800

MARY HELEN DUPREE

Georgetown University

In 1816, the Swiss author David Hess (1770–1843) published a story entitled "Der wandernde Declamator" ("The traveling declamator") in a collection of short stories bearing the programmatic title *Scherz und Ernst (Joking and seriousness)*.[1] As indicated in the volume's title, the story combines silliness and seriousness, lampooning the cultural practice of the declamatory concert or *Deklamatorium*, in which familiar literary works were read aloud by an actor or a self-styled "declamator" or "declamatrice." Literary history has since largely forgotten the story and its author, who distinguished himself during his lifetime as a composer, caricaturist, and author of short prose texts and biographical portraits.[2] Hess's best-known cultural contribution today is probably his *Hollandia Regenerata*, a series of political caricatures satirizing the French Revolution and the Batavian Republic.[3] Nonetheless, "The traveling declamator" appears to have

1. David Hess, *Scherz und Ernst* (Zürich, 1816).
2. Hess sometimes wrote under the pen name "Daniel Hildebrandt." The only work of his currently in print is *Die Badenfahrt*, a humoristic guide to Baden (Baden, 2017). See Verena Bodmer-Gessner, "Heß, David," *Neue Deutsche Biographie* 9 (1972), p.1–2, https://www.deutsche-biographie.de/pnd116764570.html#ndbcontent (last accessed June 23, 2023); and Meyer von Knonau, "Heß, David," *Allgemeine Deutsche Biographie* 12 (1880), p.273–77, https://www.deutsche-biographie.de/pnd116764570.html#adbcontent (last accessed June 23, 2023).
3. Hess composed the series of drawings in 1796, after having been stationed in Holland as an army officer for several years. The series, which includes captions in English, French, and Dutch, is sometimes incorrectly attributed to James Gillray. According to the *Neue Deutsche Biographie*, Hess's antirevolutionary political attitudes were typical of "reactionary Zürich" before and during the

been circulated fairly widely during Hess's lifetime. The full text of the story accompanies Hess's biography in a literary encyclopedia published in 1839, and a Dutch translation even found its way into an anthology of entertaining stories entitled *Tag- und Nachtstukken (Day- and night-pieces)*.[4] The story relates the tale of an ill-fated performance by an out-of-work actor named "Fabianus Plappermann"—the name translates roughly as "Fabian Blabbermouth"—who is forced to go on a declamatory tour as a way to make money after his troupe disbands. When this down-on-his-luck declamator attempts to stage a performance in a remote, provincial small town (*Städtchen*), a series of comic disasters ensue. Here, Hess applies his talents as a caricaturist to the literary realm, populating the small-town tableau with a range of generic types and eccentric characters.

The comic premise of Hess's story is not a particularly original one: "The traveling declamator" draws somewhat on the plot of *Schill, oder das Declamatorium in Krähwinkel (Schill, or the Declama- torium in Krähwinkel)*, a farce written in 1812 by August Klingemann, in which a pair of out-of-work actors terrorize a small town, whose denizens mistakenly believe their "declamatorium" to be a kind of military drill.[5] In both Klingemann's and Hess's texts, the traveling declamator is both an outcast and an antihero, a hack artist who oscillates between genuine love for his chosen art form and willingness to exploit his audience's gullibility. However, while the declamatorium serves more or less as a comic contrivance in Klingemann's farce, Hess's short story offers a more comprehensive satire and critique

Biedermeier era (Bodmer-Gessner, "Heß, David," p.1–2). See David Hess, *Hollandia Regenerata* (London, n.n., 1797).

4.   David Hess, "Der wandernde Declamator," in *Enzyklopädie der deutschen Nation- alliteratur oder biographisches-kritisches Lexikon der deutschen Dichter und Prosaisten seit den frühesten Zeiten; nebst Proben aus ihren Werken*, ed. O. L. B. Wolff, vol.4 (Leipzig, 1839), p.83–88. The quotations in this essay are from this edition. Hess is not credited as the author of the Dutch version, "De reizende Deklamator," which appears in the short story collection *Dag- und Nachtstukken uit de Portefeuille van de gebroeders Spiritus Asper und Spiritus Lenis*, vol.2 (Leeuwarden, 1833), p.1–32.

5.   See August Klingemann, *Schill oder das Declamatorium in Krähwinkel: eine Posse in drei Acten; Fortsetzung der deutschen Kleinstädter und das Carolus Magnus* (Helmstedt, 1812). As the title indicates, the farce was written as a continuation of August von Kotzebue's *Die deutschen Kleinstädter (The German smalltowners)*. The play was apparently widely known and performed; according to the title page, it was performed in Berlin, Hamburg, Frankfurt am Main, Mannheim, Stuttgart, Lübeck, Bremen, Magdeburg, Braunschweig, and Hannover.

of the declamatory concert, which in turn affords some important insights into the mobility and cultural reach of literary declamation around 1800, as it traversed various social, cultural, geographic, and epistemic networks. The local and regional culture depicted in the story ultimately resists inclusion in the urban, national knowledge network brought to them by the farcical Plappermann.

Being parodied is often a sign that a performer, genre, or art form has achieved success. By the time Hess's story was first published in 1816, literary declamation had become an established feature of bourgeois German cultural life and was at least partially professionalized.[6] As a number of recent scholars have shown, the practice of literary declamation around 1800 fed into a larger concern with the spoken dimension of literature and an impulse to explore the boundaries between music and literature.[7] Declamatory concerts were held in theaters, ballrooms, and spa resorts, and were reported on extensively in fashionable journals and memoirs of prominent artists and intellectuals such as Johann Friedrich Reichardt and Helmina von Chézy.[8] They contributed to the popularity of certain poems, particularly ballads by Schiller and Gottfried August Bürger; helped to disseminate the cult of Weimar classicism; and, in some cases, provided a forum for readings of works by less well-known authors, including women. The early-nineteenth-century boom in

6. On literary declamation as an aspect of bourgeois salon culture, see Karin Wurst, *Fabricating pleasure: fashion, entertainment, and cultural consumption in Germany, 1780–1830* (Detroit, MI, 2005), p.295–301.

7. See, for example, Joh-Nikolaus Schneider, *Ins Ohr geschrieben: Lyrik als akustische Kunst zwischen 1750 und 1800* (Göttingen, 2004); Reinhart Meyer-Kalkus, *Stimme und Sprechkünste im 20. Jahrhundert* (Berlin, 2001), p.213–50; and, more recently, R. Meyer-Kalkus, *Geschichte der literarischen Vortragskunst* (Berlin, 2020); Karl-Heinz Göttert, *Geschichte der Stimme* (Munich, 1998); and Irmgard Weithase, *Zur Geschichte der gesprochenen deutschen Sprache*, vol.1 (Tübingen, 1961).

8. See Mary Helen Dupree, "From 'dark singing' to a science of the voice: Gustav Anton von Seckendorff, the declamatory concert and the acoustic turn around 1800," *Deutsche Vierteljahrsschrift für Literaturwissenschaft und Geistesgeschichte* 86:3 (2012), p.365–96. On women declamators, see M. H. Dupree, "Elise in Weimar: 'actress-writers' and the resistance to classicism," in *The Enlightened eye: Goethe and visual culture*, ed. Evelyn Moore and Patricia Anne Simpson (Amsterdam, 2007), p.111–26; and M. H. Dupree, "Sophie Albrechts Deklamationen: Schnittstellen zwischen Musik, Theater, und Literatur," in *Verehrt. Verflucht. Vergessen: Leben und Werk von Sophie Albrecht und Johann Friedrich Ernst Albrecht*, ed. Rüdiger Schütt (Hannover, 2015), p.353–68.

literary declamation generated a wealth of publications: In 1816, the same year that Hess's story was published, the most prominent declamator of the era, Gustav Anton von Seckendorff, published a two-volume collection of his lectures on declamation and gesture, and his colleague Karl Friedrich Solbrig published the first of four volumes of the *Taschenbuch für die Freunde der Declamation* (*Pocketbook for the friends of declamation*), an anthology of poems by various authors marked for emphasis.[9]

As a medial phenomenon, the declamatory concert raises some significant questions about audience, reception, and knowledge networks around 1800. For whom did these latter-day German "rhapsodes" perform, and what expectations did their audiences bring to the table? Were declamatory concerts strictly limited to large metropolitan areas, or did smaller towns such as the *Städtchen* depicted in "The traveling declamator" also make up part of their audience? These questions also feed into larger considerations about the relationship between print, performance, and visual media around 1800. Since the publication of Friedrich Kittler's *Grammophone, film, typewriter* in the 1980s, a concern with processes of textualization (*Verschriftlichung*) has dominated analyses of eighteenth-century media history.[10] One could certainly read "The traveling declamator" as a confirmation of this idea, as it depicts a small town in the process of becoming literate (and text saturated), and ultimately argues for the superiority of print to oral media. Moreover, by incorporating the figure of the declamator into a literary narrative, the text accomplishes what Werner Faulstich has described as the bourgeois literary appropriation of oral media.[11] In fact, the fading into obscurity of this particular text, which enjoyed a certain level of popularity in the early nineteenth century but is unknown today, may represent a further step in the eclipsing of oral or auditory culture by print media. While Hess was well connected to various literary, political, musical, and artistic networks, his specific encounter with networks of literary

9.   See Gustav Anton von Seckendorff, *Vorlesungen über Deklamation und Mimik*, 2 vols. (Braunschweig, 1816); and Karl Friedrich (=Christian Gottfried) Solbrig, *Taschenbuch für die Freunde der Declamation*, 4 vols. (Leipzig, 1816–1818).

10. See for example Friedrich Kittler, *Grammophone, film, typewriter* (Berlin, 1986); Albrecht Koschorke, *Körperströme und Schriftverkehr: Mediologie des 18. Jahrhunderts* (Munich, 1999); and Werner Faulstich, *Die bürgerliche Mediengesellschaft (1700–1830)* (Göttingen, 2002).

11. Faulstich, *Die bürgerliche Mediengesellschaft*, p.62–82.

declamators—which would have presumably inspired him to write this story—is unclear.

However, the wealth of details that the story provides about the practice of declamation around 1800 suggests a more complex and less linear relationship between declamation and print culture during this period. As readers and interpreters of texts, declamators participated in what Robert Darnton has famously described as the "communication circuit" linking various actors involved in the making and circulation of books.[12] Recent scholarship on acoustic histories of knowledge before 1900 may help us to widen the circle further, showing how both oral media and print were implicated in knowledge networks that linked different parts of the German-speaking world during this period.[13] To borrow Bruno Latour's terminology, one might then ask: How did declamatory performers, as "mutable mobiles," collude with print media and other "immutable mobiles" to transmit knowledge about German literature, culture, and identity in an era prior to the advent of train travel and mass communication technologies?[14] This collusion may in fact have been more of a collision, as oral practices associated with a "national" canon and cultural values collided with local and regional practices.

Reading Hess's story against the comic-satirical grain, this essay will explore how "The traveling declamator" illuminates the popular reception of traveling declamators and their participation in social networks and practices of knowledge circulation in the German-speaking world around 1800. Not only does Hess's story offer some examples of how declamatory concerts influenced the reception of the German literary canon during this period, it also acknowledges the place of the declamatory concert within a larger context of the

12. On the "communication circuit," see Robert Darnton, "What is the history of books?," *Daedalus* 111:3 (1982), p.65–83.
13. See for example the collective volume *Wissensgeschichte des Hörens in der Moderne*, ed. Netzwerk Hör-Wissen im Wandel (Berlin, 2017), and the website of the Epistemes of Modern Acoustics research group of the Max-Planck-Institut für Wissenschaftsgeschichte, directed by Viktoria Tkaczyk, https://www. mpiwg-berlin.mpg.de/research/projects/RGTkaczyk (last accessed June 23, 2023). For an introduction to the methodologies of historicist sound studies more generally, see Jonathan Sterne's *The Audible past: cultural origins of sound reproduction* (Durham, NC, 2003).
14. On "mutable" and "immutable" mobiles, see Bruno Latour, "Visualization and cognition: drawing things together," in *Knowledge and society: studies in the sociology of culture past and present*, ed. Henrika Kuklick (New York, 1986), p.7–13.

circulation of ideas and the performance of knowledge around 1800. Through its depiction of Plappermann's misadventures, the story reflects on the ways in which literature and theater were being used to negotiate identities and relationships across rural/urban and class boundaries and thus forge larger social networks in the German-speaking world, which could not yet lay claim to political unity. In its consideration of how the circulation of ideas is impacted by acoustic media in particular, "The traveling declamator" offers some important insights into the shifting status of hearing and listening vis-à-vis print and visual media around 1800.

"The traveling declamator" is set in an unnamed small town somewhere in the German-speaking world. (The small town is never referred to as a village or *Dorf*, but is close to being one as it possesses only one church steeple.) In its depiction of small-town life, the story lacks the attention to cultural and geographical markers of local or regional identity typical of later nineteenth-century novellas by Swiss writers such as Gottfried Keller and Jeremias Gotthelf. Unlike Keller's fictional "Seldwyla," there is nothing particularly Swiss about this town. In its very anonymity, this small town or *Krähwinkel* ("crow's corner"/"screecher's corner"; the term is used at least once) serves as a stand-in for the German "nation"; Hess could be describing any German-speaking small town. The story is divided up into ten short, numbered chapters; the action extends over two days. In the first five chapters, the setting and the main characters are established; the focus remains on Plappermann, the declamator, as he refreshes himself at the local tavern, negotiates with the mayor for permission to perform the next day, and charges the town crier with advertising the upcoming performance. As the second day begins, the focus shifts away from Plappermann. The town crier announces the upcoming declamatorium, leading the townsfolk to speculate as to what that unfamiliar term might mean. Two new characters are introduced in this scene: Freimuth, a "well-traveled" pastor's assistant who acts as the story's voice of reason, and Schableder, a tanner with misplaced literary ambitions, who has written a verse epic in fifty-nine cantos on "The invention of gunpowder." When summoned by the townsfolk to explain the concept, Freimuth offers a resounding critique of the current practice of literary declamation, condemning declamators like Plappermann as opportunists and hacks. Plappermann, who shows up shortly thereafter, inadvertently affirms this critique by giving an impromptu lecture and demonstration of his craft, in which he reads a newspaper dramatically, as if it were an epic poem.

Meanwhile, Schableder, who has been listening all the while, sees a chance to lend his terrible verse epic some legitimacy by having it performed by a real artist. Catching up with Plappermann as he exits the tavern, he explains that he has himself declaimed the poem ad nauseam to his fellow villagers, and that they have long since tired of hearing it. If Plappermann will only read his epic as part of the declamatorium, Schableder promises, he will not only give him free bed and board but will also petition his brother, the mayor, for an extended engagement for the declamator. Plappermann, who cannot refuse such material advantages, reluctantly accepts. In the final chapter, the promised declamatory concert unfolds with predictably disastrous consequences. The stage is set, the whole town appears, and Plappermann is ready to give his performance, for which the mayor has provided a room in the local slaughterhouse, where the livestock auctions usually take place. When Plappermann starts in on the first stanzas of the tanner's gunpowder epic, the audience members respond with fury—"That's just the tanner's same old tune!"[15]—and demand their money back. The scene erupts in fisticuffs, with the disgraced declamator narrowly escaping a severe beating until Freimuth finally drags him to safety.

Through this series of comic episodes, the text asks some important questions about the reach of medial and cultural technologies into the German-speaking provinces and the significance of small towns and villages as public spheres around 1800, as well as the changes taking place in collective life during this period and the power of different media to influence that life. It depicts a provincial bourgeois society in transition, which is mostly literate and engages with print media on a regular basis but is in other ways somewhat backward, particularly in its attitudes toward theater and the performing arts. The town in "The traveling declamator" has a bookbinder and a lending library, and newspapers are read at the local coffeehouse, which functions as a kind of public sphere. When Plappermann first arrives at the tavern, tired and thirsty and clutching his well-worn copies of Bürger and Schiller, he quickly figures out that no professional declamator or

---

15. The original reads: "Das ist wieder die alte ewige Leier des Gerbers! riefen einige, das gilt nicht!" (Hess, "Der wandernde Declamator," p.87). I am grateful to Jared Boddum for providing a translation of the Dutch-language edition published in 1833. For the quotations in this essay, I use a somewhat adapted version of his translation from the Dutch. For the German quotations, I have retained the original spellings.

traveling theater has ever visited there (although it is mentioned later in the story that some of the townsfolk have read about declamatoria in literary journals).[16] There is no printing press in town, which means that the declamator is forced to advertise his performance via the town crier, alongside advertisements for local vendors and announcements of rewards for finding a lost dog.[17] In short, Hess's story depicts a small town that is in the process of becoming part of the German "reading nation."[18] However, this process is still very much incomplete, and the townsfolk are still to some extent dependent on early modern acoustic media such as town criers. This is a dangerous situation for the declamator, for his performances require an audience that has been socialized to know what to expect and how to react, not only to the theater but also to books, printed programs, and reviews in journals. Without the support of print media and a literate audience, his performances are destined to fall flat.[19]

The image of a "standing army of declamators" infiltrating every German-speaking town and village was often evoked in early-nineteenth-century German periodicals and declamation handbooks. But how often did real-life declamators find their way into such provincial *Krähwinkel*?[20] Was the small-town declamatorium really a significant cultural phenomenon around 1800? While most reports of declamatory concerts from around 1800 come from larger cities such as Vienna, Dresden, and Leipzig, there are a few extant reports from smaller towns and court centers, such as Lignitz (Lignica) in Silesia and—not at all surprisingly—Weimar in Thuringia, the home of Goethe's *Musenhof*.[21] In 1811, one of the most influential declamators of the early nineteenth century, Gustav Anton (Freiherr) von Seckendorff, alias "Patrik Peale," performed a series of well-documented declamatoria in the town

---

16. Hess, "Der wandernde Declamator," p.83.
17. Hess, "Der wandernde Declamator," p.84.
18. See *Publishing culture and the "reading nation": German book history and the long nineteenth century*, ed. Lynne Tatlock (Rochester, NY, 2010).
19. On the rise of literacy in eighteenth-century Germany, see Hans Erich Bödeker and Ernst Hinrichs (ed.), *Alphabetisierung und Literalisierung in Deutschland in der frühen Neuzeit* (Tübingen, 1999).
20. See the connection with the discomforts and delays of travel highlighted in Karin Baumgartner's essay in the current volume.
21. A report of a performance in Liegnitz appears in *Schlesische Provinzialblätter* 50 (1809), p.54–60. On declamatory concerts in Weimar, see Dupree, "Elise in Weimar."

of Eutin, in Schleswig-Holstein.[22] Seckendorff was an enthusiastic traveler, having spent two years in Philadelphia (from 1796 to 1798) and reported on it for the German journal *Der neue teutsche Merkur* (*The New German Mercury*).[23] From his travels in the United States, Seckendorff took the stage name "Patrik Peale." The American painter and museum director Charles Willson Peale was apparently one of Seckendorff's personal role models, and he appears to have wanted to style himself as a member of Peale's artist family; "Patrik" may be a reference to Patrick Henry. About ten years following his return to Germany, Seckendorff began performing declamatory concerts and *tableaux vivants* under his stage name; his German-American wife, Elisabeth Lechler, also performed with him, as "Betty Peale."[24] Curiously, none of Seckendorff's performances as "Peale" appear to have involved any texts or cultural images from America or the English-speaking world. The name may have signaled a certain worldliness or "originality" to his German-speaking audiences, but those expecting a transatlantic cultural exchange would have been disappointed; instead, "Peale's" performances, like most declamatoria around 1800, were concentrated on interpretations of works from the "national" German literary canon.

In the spring of 1811, Seckendorff had an extended stay in the small north German city of Eutin at the invitation of the painter Tischbein and gave several performances there, including a declamatory concert performed on March 14, 1811, which was reviewed in a regional magazine, the *Neue Schleswig-Holsteinische Provinzialberichte* (*New provincial reports from Schleswig-Holstein*).[25] For this engagement, Seckendorff had obtained permission to use a large hall in a private household, where he set up a proscenium stage lit by more than fifty

22. On Seckendorff's life, see Johannes Tütken, *Privatdozenten im Schatten der Georgia Augusta: zur älteren Privatdozentur (1734 bis 1831)*, vol.2 (Göttingen, 2005); also Lodewijk Muns, "Gustav Anton Freiherr von Seckendorff, *alias* Patrik Peale: a biographical note," https://hcommons.org/deposits/objects/hc:28472/ datastreams/CONTENT/content (last accessed June 23, 2023).
23. Gustav Anton von Seckendorff, "Filadelfia: Literatur und Vergnügungen der Nordamerikaner," *Der neue teutsche Merkur* 2 (1791), p.168–72.
24. The Seckendorff family tree is written up in the *Gothaisches genealogisches Taschenbuch der freiherrlichen Häuser* 58 (1908), p.717–20. According to the *Gotha*, the marriage produced five sons who survived into adulthood.
25. "Patrik Peale: aus einem Schreiben aus Schleswig," *Neue Schleswig-Holsteinische Provinzialberichte* 20 (1811), p.234–36.

lights. The concert attracted a large audience, including members of
the local aristocracy. The program included ballads and monologues
by Schiller, Goethe, and August Wilhelm Schlegel, as well as comic
pieces by Hagedorn and Voss, followed by a series of *tableaux vivants*.
On the declamatory portion of the evening, the reviewer noted that
the speaker's voice sometimes sounded "monotonous and flat" during
the more serious pieces and that the comic ones were delivered more
successfully. In addition to this report, accounts of Seckendorff's
concerts in Eutin are also preserved in the letters written by members
of the local educated bourgeoisie. For example, a local teacher named
Wilhelm Hellwag wrote to his brother, Ernst, that he was "very
satisfied" with Seckendorff's performance, even if the declamator was,
according to him, "too much of a devotee of Schelling" and tended to
shorten his syllables too much.[26]

Sociologically speaking, Seckendorff's Eutin performances bear
few similarities to the one depicted in "The traveling declamator."
They were witnessed by members of the aristocracy and educated
bourgeoisie, who were familiar with the texts being read and were
able to comment in great detail on the declamator's stylistic choices,
and they were written about in journals and newspapers. Indeed,
Eutin was by no means a backwater, but rather a culturally lively
place that had been home to the *Eutiner Kreis* (Eutin circle) that
included Stolberg, Gerstenberg, Voß, and Jacobi and was now the
residence of the painter Tischbein, whom Seckendorff visited and
profiled in an essay that was published in a fashionable journal.[27]
This visit, and the series of engagements in Schleswig-Holstein,
would probably not have taken place without Seckendorff's extensive
social and literary connections. It seems likely that the appointments
were arranged long in advance, via letter, rather than informally
and on short notice. In short, the accounts of Seckendorff's Eutin
performances depict a small town that was well connected with the
rest of the German "reading nation" via newspapers, artists' circles,
and traveling performers. The denizens of Eutin could fill a hall at
a declamatory concert and could boast of an educated middle class

26. *Eutin–Heidelberg 1811: Briefwechsel des Studenten E. Hellwag mit seiner Familie in
    Eutin*, ed. Henry A. Smith (Eutin, 2009), p.49–50.
27. Gustav Anton von Seckendorff (writing as "Patrik Peale"), "Aus Eutin," *Zeitung
    für die elegante Welt 161* (August 13, 1811), p.1287–88. Around 1800, Eutin was
    part of the so-called Danish Unitary States (1773–1864).

capable of producing finely nuanced critiques of a declamator's performance.[28]

Speaking more broadly, the example of Seckendorff's performances in Eutin reflects, already in 1811, a German-speaking world in which the provinces were remarkably well connected to the cities through knowledge networks. Indeed, Hess himself appears to have been an agent of such connections, interpreting the German and European *Zeitgeist* for a Swiss readership through his literary and artistic works. It is unclear why Hess chose to focus on the figure of the traveling declamator as an agent of cultural connection; to be sure, the trope of the declamator traveling from small town to small town looking for work seems to be a largely fictional or parodic construct rather than an accurate reflection of the state of knowledge and social networks in Germany around 1800. It may be that the ignorant small-town audience depicted in the story works as a kind of tabula rasa that shows up the puffery and pretense of literary declamation around 1800. This contrastive technique is highlighted in the scene in which Plappermann approaches the town mayor with a petition to perform. The mayor, a model of provincial Biedermeier-era cosiness, or *Gemütlichkeit*, is irritated at being disturbed after having just settled down in his garden to smoke a pipe and enjoy a beer. At first, he takes Plappermann for a traveling clown, to the latter's great dismay. Using the informal address reserved for servants and inferiors, he explains that such performers are no longer welcome in the small town. Just last week, he explains, an "Italian with dogs in hoop-skirts" had entertained the villagers and made off with a good deal of gold.[29] Irritated by the mayor's assumption that he is an "actor on leave" or a "kind of clown," the declamator offers to give an example of his craft. But the mayor declines, telling him that he is "not in the mood" for "jabbering" or "spouting"; instead, he asks if his "troupe" has a passable "Hanswurst."[30] Approached by an itinerant actor, the small-town mayor naturally assumes that a *Hanswurst*, or improvisational comic, cannot be far behind. His expectations are clearly conditioned by his familiarity with the German *Wanderbühne*, or touring company, a type of theater that was rejected by Enlightenment theater reformers but that continued to thrive in some quarters in the

28. See the connection to spatial (geographical and architectural) and social components in Joachim Homann's essay in the current volume.
29. Hess, "Der wandernde Declamator," p.84.
30. Hess, "Der wandernde Declamator," p.84.

early nineteenth century.[31] The mayor's assumption reflects a lack of sophistication, the *Hanswurst* having been long banished from serious German-language theaters. But the mayor's naïve good sense acquires a certain validity when compared with the declamator's pompous self-promotion. Indeed, through this evocation of the *Wanderbühne*, Hess subtly suggests an affiliation between the declamatory concert and primitive or degraded forms of theater, an idea that is reiterated more forcefully in the story's conclusion. Meanwhile, the declamator's outrage at being compared with a traveling circus act inspires Plappermann to defend his craft energetically, characterizing himself and his fellow declamators as traveling "apostles" who glorify the German literary canon just as the Christian apostles proclaimed the good news of the gospel.[32] He adds, heatedly: "What is the cold, dry letter? What is the finest manner of speaking without the coloration of declamation?" Plappermann goes on to suggest that declamation is superior to the theater and may even one day eclipse it, because it focuses solely on the text and needs "no artful setting, no costumes, no decorations, no assistants, nothing sensual. Everything we present is the pure distilled spirit of the poet, the quintessence."[33] Here, Plappermann is interrupted by the mayor, who has figured out that the only way he can put an end to this tedious speech is by granting the declamator his request to perform.

With its half-understood references to aesthetic theory, Plappermann's speech to the mayor mimics the language typical of early-nineteenth-century declamation handbooks or *Deklamierbücher*, which sought to legitimate the new art form, often through overblown evocations of the superiority of oral media over print. Seckendorff was one of the worst offenders in this regard; his *Lectures* evoke in the strongest possible terms the opposition between the "dead letter" and the liveliness of the spoken word, going so far as to describe books as "dead coals" and words as "dead ashes" that the "orator's spirit" could set ablaze.[34] German theorists of declamation such as Seckendorff,

---

31. See, e.g., Claudia Puschmann, *Fahrende Frauenzimmer: zur Geschichte der Frauen an deutschen Wanderbühnen (1670–1760)* (Herbolzheim, 2000).
32. Hess, "Der wandernde Declamator," p.84.
33. Hess, "Der wandernde Declamator," p.84.
34. See Seckendorff, *Vorlesungen*, vol.1, p.9–10; Karl-Heinz Göttert identifies Seckendorff's critique as one of the more vehement ones of the period and traces it back to an oversimplification of Herder's theory of the origins of language. See K.-H. Göttert, "Wider den toten Buchstaben: zur Problemgeschichte eines Topos," in *Zwischen Rauschen und Offenbarung: zur Kultur- und Mediengeschichte der*

H. G. B. Franke, and W. B. Wötzel stressed the pedagogical value of declamation, both as a way of instilling good speaking habits in the young and as a method of conveying knowledge about "classical" German literature, thus casting the declamators in the role of priests or priestesses of the German canon. By having Plappermann compare the traveling "rhapsodes" with the apostles spreading the good news of the gospel, Hess takes aim at the declamatory concert as an outgrowth of the sublimated religious fervor that animated literary culture around 1800.[35] Distilling pure spirit (*Geist*) and converting it into an audible form, the declamatory concert appears here as a kind of absurd literalization of the *Dichterkult* and idealist philosophy. The theory of declamation represented by Plappermann is based on a kind of aesthetic idealism that, if taken to its logical extreme, would obliterate actual aesthetic practices or simply render them irrelevant. But few declamators around 1800 would have claimed that literary declamation was destined to supplant the theater; after all, many if not most of them were actors themselves, a fact that Plappermann seems desperate to conceal.

The rebuttal to Plappermann's defense of the declamatory concert occurs in the coffeehouse scene, in which Freimuth, whose name in German implies an ethos of openness and honesty, attempts to explain what declamation is. The naïve curiosity of the townsfolk about the proposed declamatorium provides the perfect setup for Freimuth's takedown. He begins by remarking that something must be going wrong in the big cities if a declamator is trying his luck in a small town. He does not reject the current fad for declamation on theoretical grounds; rather, the basis for his critique is largely practical, economic, and sociological. While some "virtuosi" exist among the ranks of the declamators, along with critics or connoisseurs who are able to interpret their performances, Freimuth explains, the fad for declamation has also produced a wealth of opportunities for "a bunch of featherless parrots and hairless apes," who practice the art form primarily as a source of extra income. Crucially, he depicts the professional practice of literary declamation as a symptom of an economic slump following the Wars of Liberation, already cited by the mayor

Stimme, ed. Friedrich Kittler, Thomas Macho, and Sigrid Weigel (Berlin, 2008), p.106–107.

35. On the influence of Pietist and Protestant religious traditions on the literary movements of late-eighteenth-century Germany, see Heinz Schlaffer, *Die kurze Geschichte der deutschen Literatur* (Munich, 2008), p.54–63.

earlier in the text. The times have hit the theater particularly hard, and actors are forced to "wander" and recite poems and monologues for money. The result of this is that declamators no longer use their talents for any real purpose but become "'ballad singers' who return us to our childhoods."[36]

While some of the claims about declamation that the story makes via Freimuth are probably true, his perspective is in some ways quite limited. That declamation served a moneymaking function for some performers is undeniable—even Seckendorff writes of rhapsodic declamators filling their pockets with "jingling coins."[37] But such conclusions appear to have been fairly speculative; it is unclear how many declamators, if any, really made a living from their performances alone. It is perhaps female declamators, such as Elise Bürger, Sophie Albrecht, and Henriette Hendel-Schütz, who benefited the most from the declamatory concert as an alternative to acting, once they were considered too old to perform in lead roles; however, "The traveling declamator" does not mention them at all, instead casting its archetypal "declamator" as male. By depicting the present-day culture of declamation as an entirely new phenomenon, symptomatic of a crisis in the theater, "The traveling declamator" also elides the longer history of literary declamation in Germany. In its earlier manifestations, the declamatory concert had been linked closely with quasi-devotional oral practices such as readings of Klopstock's epic *Messiah*. One of the earliest known declamators, Christian Gotthold Schocher, had made a name for himself by performing mostly Christian devotional poetry and excerpts from sermons. By contrast, the adoption of ballads and theater monologues into the repertoire was a later development. In any case, Hess's real target seems to be Seckendorff and his imitators. Indeed, Plappermann mentions him directly, intimating that he is a close friend of the great "man of a thousand talents." By contrasting the clergyman, Freimuth, with the free artist "Plappermann," Hess appears to side with a more conservative approach to declamation; at least in the provinces, he seems to suggest, the privilege of speaking publicly should remain in the hands of those with institutional authority rather than the self-appointed "wandering apostles" of German poetry.

Despite its dismissive attitude toward declamation, Hess's text offers some valuable insights into the history of its practice, insofar

36. Hess, "Der wandernde Declamator," p.85.
37. Seckendorff, *Vorlesungen*, vol.1, p.14–15.

as it locates the declamatory concert within networks of knowledge performance around 1800. Freimuth compares the phenomenon of the traveling declamator with the appearance of "pedagogues, agronomists, chronologists, mnemonics, and other similar apostles," who in a time of reduced book sales, have had to go on the lecture circuit in order to make ends meet.[38] He disputes the informational value of such performances, suggesting that the real models for the traveling knowledge performers of the early nineteenth century are "quack surgeons, worm doctors, and exorcists." Freimuth's assessment of traveling scientists, lecturers, and polymaths recalls the model of knowledge circulation espoused by the late-Enlightenment German intellectual Josias Ludwig Gosch in his 1789 pamphlet *Fragmente über den Ideenumlauf* (*Fragments on the circulation of ideas*).[39] Comparing the circulation of ideas throughout society to the circulatory system of the body, Gosch places special emphasis on the communicative advantages of public speaking situations, in which the flow of "sympathy" between the speaker and the audience allows for knowledge to be produced and retained more effectively.[40] Whereas Gosch assesses the role of oral communication very positively, Hess, via Freimuth, expresses a much more skeptical viewpoint. In his account, declamation can only hold the listener's attention for a limited amount of time; without music or additional visual material, the ordinary people in the audience will quickly get bored, while the educated "man of taste" sneaks away to read the works of his favorite poet in silence.[41]

But Hess perhaps agrees with Gosch after all, insofar as he worries about the impact that listening has on the reception of literature. Having explained the basic concept of declamation to the townsfolk, Freimuth goes on to complain that the declamatory concert has influenced the reception of literature to such a degree that it is no longer possible to read certain works without the imaginary intrusion of the declamator's voice and gestures: "I can no longer read Schiller's 'Song of the Bell' and the majority of his brilliant poems without it happening that the first impression they make on

38. Hess, "Der wandernde Declamator," p.85.
39. See Josias Ludwig Gosch, *Fragmente über den Ideenumlauf* (Berlin, 2006). The notion of the *Ideenumlauf* is also discussed in the foreword to *Performing knowledge, 1750–1850*, ed. Mary Helen Dupree and Sean Franzel (Berlin, 2015), p.1–5.
40. Gosch, *Ideenumlauf*, p.160.
41. Hess, "Der wandernde Declamator," p.85.

me is utterly corrupted by the memory of the facial expressions which the declamator assumed while reeling them off."[42] Whereas Gosch and Seckendorff perceive the auditory dimension as enlivening and even electrifying the "dead letter" of print, Hess describes the oral performance of literature as potentially stultifying and distracting from the printed word, which the story affords a positive, normative status.

In summary, as the most well-traveled of the villagers, Freimuth uses his own position of access to social and knowledge networks in order to decry the influence exerted by declamators and other live performers on those same networks. Yet his critique also illuminates some of the ways in which traveling declamators, as "mutable mobiles," may have helped to promote the circulation of literary knowledge, alongside "immutable mobiles" such as books, journals, and visual images. The problem, Hess suggests via Freimuth, is not so much declamation itself, but rather the times, which cannot provide declamators with an appropriate audience for their performances. To wit, he argues that the "mere declamator" who recites familiar poems "belongs either in a completely uncivilized era, or in a century of absolute refinement"; by contrast, the current era "is composed of both extremes," a chiaroscuro of "light and darkness" that can "bring forth the most fantastic phenomena."[43] The latter is borne out by the story's climax, in which the declamatory concert causes discord and even violence among the townsfolk. The story thus bears out Freimuth's assessment of the current *Zeitgeist*, namely that the aesthetic education of German society has not progressed far enough to allow most audiences to be capable of appreciating the finer nuances of declamation.

By contrast, declamation is depicted positively in "The traveling declamator" when it is anchored within established social institutions or rituals. As an alternative to paid performances by traveling lecturers and declamators, Freimuth advocates establishing "little private lycea" (*Lyceen*) that would educate audiences and particularly young people through enjoyable means, suggesting perhaps something akin to the "lyceum movement" that would flourish in the United States in subsequent decades.[44] Another positive example is offered when

---

42. Hess, "Der wandernde Declamator," p.86.
43. Hess, "Der wandernde Declamator," p.85.
44. On the US lyceum movement see, e.g., Angela G. Ray, *The Lyceum and public culture in the nineteenth-century United States* (East Lansing, MI, 2005).

Freimuth reminisces about a musical salon that he once frequented while he was living in the city. In this "small company" of artists and intellectuals, he recalls:

> There was an arrangement whereby you had generous-minded artists and unpretentious dilettantes who relieved each other by turns and supported each other without demonstrating the least flicker of conceit, envy, jealousy, or other petty passions, whether it was one poem that was yet to be well known or a new and fitting essay that was read, it was the content that counted and the presentation of it was just a vehicle or something extra; or a pretty fragment of a foreign play was performed, or—less frequently and only on holiday weeks—a hymn by the great Klopstock was declaimed—and every member left the meeting feeling deeply moved and transferred the pleasant or solemn mood into the family sphere.[45]

The salon described by Freimuth is nonhierarchical, collaborative, and informally organized. Within its walls, acoustic practices such as music and literary readings create a sense of harmony and a collective emotional experience that the individual participants, both amateurs and professionals, may then carry with them into the private realm of the family. Crucially, Freimuth's salon is free of any kind of professional competition, commercialism, or self-promotion. Meanwhile, its repertoire, which includes readings of works by foreign authors, is both more cosmopolitan and less nationalistic than the declamatory concert. The ritual practice of reading Klopstock's hymns on special occasions mirrors practices associated with the "reading societies" (*Lesegesellschaften*) fostered by Klopstock[46] and perhaps also

---

45. Hess, "Der wandernde Declamator," p.86. "Zwischendurch wurde von liberalen Künstlern, oder unbefangenen Dilletanten, die sich wechselweise ablösten, und harmlos, ohne Eitelkeit, Neid, Rangsucht oder andere kleinliche Leidenschaften, einander unterstützten, entweder ein weniger bekanntes Gedicht vorgelesen, oder ein neuer passender Aufsatz, dessen Inhalt die Hauptsache, der gute Vortrag nur Vehikel und Zugabe war; oder es wurde ein schönes Bruchstück ausländischer Dramatik declamirt, oder seltener, und nur in Feierwochen, eine Hymne des verklärten Klopstock—und immer tief gerührt verließ jedes Mitglied die Versammlung, und trug die freundliche oder hehre Stimmung daheim in seinen Familienkreis über."
46. On Klopstock and the *Lesegesellschaft*, see Johannes Birgfeld, "Klopstock, the art of declamation and the reading revolution: an inquiry into one author's remarkable impact on the changes and counter-changes in reading habits between 1750 and 1800," *Journal for eighteenth-century studies* 31:1 (2008), p.101–17.

the Christian devotional focus of early declamatory performances such as Schocher's; a sophisticated clergyman like Freimuth would have doubtless been inclined to favor such performances over more bombastic, secular ones. Moreover, rather than performing the favorite standbys of early-nineteenth-century declamatory performers—like the Schiller ballads that the declamators have allegedly "ruined"—the participants in Freimuth's salon favor lesser-known poems or topical essays. The private salon described here thus combines elements of the chamber concert with those of the nineteenth-century French *cénacle*, in which literary readings served the purpose of introducing new material to a select, elite audience.[47] At the same time, it functions as a kind of pedagogical public sphere in miniature, where new ideas can be successfully circulated for export into the domestic sphere. Freimuth's speech thus expresses concern about the unchecked proliferation of reading practices and their potential impact on social harmony, particularly in the domestic sphere. However, he also does not dispute the positive aesthetic and pedagogical value that declamation can have when placed in the right hands; in the story's denouement, he promises to read Schiller to the townsfolk from time to time, while declaring that "declamation *ex professo*" is on the way out.[48] He advises Plappermann to return to his former profession as a surgeon, anticipating for him a happy ending not unlike that of Goethe's Wilhelm Meister, if only he will give up his artistic ambitions for a stable middle-class existence.

It is not difficult to see in the character of Freimuth a reflection of Hess's conservative and antirevolutionary stance, insofar as he uses a small-town authority figure to voice fears about the inflammatory effects of certain types of popular art and rhetoric. At the same time, the story's critique of literary declamation may also reflect anxieties about the incursion of the "national" and cosmopolitan into local and regional spaces. This is also highlighted in the follow-up to Freimuth's critique, in which the hapless declamator attempts to demonstrate the value of his craft by declaiming from the newspaper:

> Fabian flipped further. "Here is an article with the headline 'Aus der Schweiz' ['From Switzerland']. Here I will take the liberty of

47. On the distinction between *cénacles* and public readings (*lectures publiques*) in nineteenth-century France, see Jan Baetens, *A voix haute: poésie et lecture publique* (Brussels, 2016), p.26.
48. Hess, "Der wandernde Declamator," p.88.

deviating from our German pronunciation and pronounce the word in the Swiss dialect; I thus say: From the 'Schwitz'! Why?—Because *Schwitz* resembles *schwitzen* (to sweat), and *schwitzen* makes you think of the mountains, which one can only climb in the sweat of one's brow. And once the imagination has grasped the poetic image of the mountains, it follows that the melody of the alpenhorn and the sound of cowbells are naturally evoked along with it."[49]

In addition to satirizing the theoretical pretensions of declamators like Seckendorff, the scene also evokes the popularity of dialect readings, which were sometimes performed as part of the "comic" portion of a declamatory concert. Here, the declamator is depicted as selling a false, misguided image of both the national ("our German pronunciation") and the local/regional. The regional audience proves a stumbling block to the reception of both, as his listeners are not familiar with the "national" repertoire of the declamatory concert and do not have enough distance from their own local culture to appreciate its sentimentalizing representation in the declamatory concert. This is not to say that the story rejects the oral transmission of knowledge through declamation altogether; rather, it critiques a tendency of the networks that linked declamators with each other in the early nineteenth century to produce stereotypical, distorted, or even harmful knowledge about local and regional identities.

To conclude, through the contrast between the failed declamatorium and Freimuth's idealized urban salon, "The traveling declamator" generates both a coherent critique of the declamatory concert as it was practiced in 1816 and a partially sketched vision of how literary declamation might be used to foster harmonious social networks and the circulation of knowledge in both urban centers and the provinces. While the depiction of the archetypal Plappermann as an outcast from the city doomed to wander the provinces in search of an audience is somewhat fanciful, it nonetheless allows the author to make a number of relevant observations about declamatory practice.

---

49. Hess, "Der wandernde Declamator," p.86. "Fabian blätterte weiter. 'Da ist ein Artikel, überschrieben: "Aus der Schweiz." Hier erlaube ich mir, von unsrer deutschen Rechtsprechung abzuweichen, und das Wort in schweizerischer Mundart auszusprechen; ich sage: Aus der Schwitz! Warum?—weil Schwitz an Schwitzen erinnert, und Schwitzen an die Berge, die man nur im Schweize seines Angesichts ersteigt. Und hat die Phantasie einmal das poetische Bild der Berge aufgefaßt, so drängt sich die Melodie des Alphorns und das Geläute der Kuhschellen von selbst auf.'"

Above all, the story conveys a fundamental anxiety about the ways in which orality can transform literature into a popular medium, similar to ballad singing, which the text consistently describes as regressive and childish. Indeed, when the declamator takes the stage, the audience cries out for a rendition of Schiller's "Die Kindsmörderin" ("The child murderess"), a narrative poem that appropriates the generic markers of the broadside or gallows ballad; it is unclear whether they have actually read the poem or are simply tantalized by the promise of a gruesome story. In this scene in particular, Hess's story thus articulates a deep distrust of the small town or village as public sphere as well as of traveling, independent performers. Both are associated with childlike or animalistic regression, buffoonery, greed, manipulation, and even violence. The oral performance of literature is depicted as something with which the broad masses cannot be trusted; its proper place, the story seems to imply, is in larger urban centers where it can be embedded in the practices of elite middle-class sociability. Turning this thesis around, one could also say that Hess recognizes the ambivalent potential of declamation as a popular, sensual medium that could entertain and distract German-speaking audiences from different classes. This potential would eventually be borne out in the nineteenth century—for example, in the proliferation of *Deklamierbücher*, which by the 1890s had led to the mass production of cheap serial pamphlets containing comic poems and cabaret texts written specifically to be read aloud, or in the 1859 celebrations of Schiller's one-hundredth birthday, in which the declamatory reading of Schiller's poems was restaged as a kind of mass event with nationalist overtones.[50] However, more elite, rarefied forms of declamation flourished during this time as well, for example in the *George-Kreis* around 1900. In its acknowledgment of this ambivalence, "The traveling declamator" offers an important and nuanced portrait of the early-nineteenth-century German media landscape and its potential futures.

---

50. On the role of literary declamation in the "Schiller-Feier," see Mary Helen Dupree, "Early Schiller memorials (1805–1809) and the performance of literary knowledge," in *Performing knowledge*, ed. M. H. Dupree and S. Franzel, p.137–64.

Luftschiff der Phantasie: Johann Christian Reinhart, Friedrich Schiller, and artistic networks *c*.1800

JOACHIM HOMANN

Harvard Art Museums

From a legacy in prints to the center of a cultural network: Johann Christian Reinhart and Friedrich Schiller

Art on paper has long been a powerful networking tool. In the years around 1800, the creation and circulation of printed images reflected and indeed contributed to changing patterns of communication and artistic exchange. Related topics are discussed in Sean Franzel's and Renata Schellenberg's essays in this volume, highlighting periodicals and private collections. Prints, especially when produced in larger series, prompted artists to collaborate; they helped foster friendships among artists, with the artists dedicating them to one another and exchanging them as gifts. Through professional printing by publishers and distribution in the marketplace, prints also contributed to the formation of networks that sustained and validated larger circles of members.[1] It is especially intriguing to consider such activities in the intermedial context of publications in word and image, and in the light of the quickly changing political and philosophical parameters in which European intellectuals, whether as artists, writers, or collectors, situated themselves when they formed national and international networks through the creation, dedication, and distribution of prints.[2]

---

1. An exemplary study of networks, created through an early modern print and the benefits and pitfalls of network visualizations, can be found in Stephanie Porras, "Keeping our eyes open: visualizing networks and art history," *Artl@s bulletin* 6:3 (2017), p.41–49; for an assessment of the impact of big data analysis on traditional (art) historical narratives, see Mario Carpo, "Big data and the end of history," *International journal for digital art history* 3 (2018), p.21–35.
2. For the most recent introduction to German prints from the period, see *The*

Figure 4: Johann Christian Reinhart, *Der Sturm, eine heroische, Schillern dedicirte Landschaft* (*The Storm: a heroic landscape dedicated to Schiller*), 1800. Etching on laid paper, 16 × 20 1/2 inches.

The German painter and printmaker Johann Christian Reinhart (1761–1847) is mainly known for his legacy in prints but, during his lifetime, he appears at the center of a network where legacies of things and people intersect and that are at once amplified and obscured by contemporaneous concepts of friendship. This case study therefore elucidates upon the mutual effects—at times destructive, at other times reciprocal and optimizing—that amount to the workings of a network that defy any holistic or complete notions of cultural historiographies.

Reinhart had lived in Rome for more than a decade when in 1800 he dedicated a large etching of a dramatic Italian landscape, crossed by two hurried riders, to his old friend Friedrich Schiller (see Figure 4). The gesture reengaged the writer with the artist, despite the many years that had passed since the two men had last met and the geographical distance between them, as is documented in

---

Enchanted world of German Romantic prints, 1770–1850, ed. John Ittmann (Philadelphia, PA, 2017).

their ensuing correspondence. This essay discusses Reinhart's and Schiller's friendship as one defining bond within a larger network of artists, intellectuals, and collectors that was sustained through the exchange of prints of the Italian landscape circulating in the 1790s and the early years of the 1800s. What qualified these representations of the landscape to serve as a tool of communication that evoked a sense of friendship in their creators and users? The following pages introduce Reinhart's role in the Roman artists' community, trace his and his collaborators' explorations of the landscapes around Rome within the context of the travel patterns of the time, and discuss the changing attitudes toward the landscape in selected artistic and literary representations. Seen against this foil, Reinhart's gesture toward Schiller can be appreciated as an ambitious and intelligent artistic intervention in a network. In the course of this essay, it reveals itself as a foundational gesture in establishing and solidifying the broader artists' network, a noteworthy discursive parallel to their first letters.

Johann Christian Reinhart and his Roman circle: collaboration and networking

From the 1790s to the 1840s, Johann Christian Reinhart was one of the most distinguished artists among the many German expatriates in Rome and a central figure in the international art circles there.[3] Reinhart, a Protestant landscape painter and printmaker from Hof, a town in Upper Franconia, dropped plans to study theology in order to dedicate himself to art, receiving training in Leipzig and Dresden. He first met Friedrich Schiller in 1785 when he spent the summer in Gohlis outside of Leipzig with a close-knit community of friends. After living for three years in the circle of the sympathetic Duke Georg of Saxe-Meiningen, Reinhart received a travel stipend and moved to the Papal State in 1789. He sustained his livelihood through print publication projects, sales of his paintings and drawings, and collaboration on a short-lived almanac in 1810–1811. Through these activities, Reinhart built a reputation throughout Germany and beyond, in spite of his continued absence. Key to his success was his ongoing work with the print publisher and dealer Johann Friedrich

3.   For a brief overview of Reinhart's biography see Andreas Stolzenburg, "Biographie," in *Johann Christian Reinhart: ein deutscher Landschaftsmaler in Rom*, ed. Andreas Stolzenburg and Herbert W. Rott (Munich, 2012), p.101–103.

Frauenholz (1758–1822), since 1790 a leading figure in the German art market who not only maintained a Nuremberg gallery and auction house but also attended fairs and sold on commission to other dealers and private parties.[4] Frauenholz made Reinhart's life in Rome feasible since other sources of income were difficult to tap into.[5] As a Protestant, Reinhart was not eligible for public commissions in the Papal State, and the political turmoil of the era prevented many tourists, whose purchases sustained artists in Rome in previous and following decades, from traveling to Rome. In old age, Reinhart received awards and a pension from the Bavarian King Ludwig I von Wittelsbach (r.1825–1848). Throughout his life, Reinhart remained highly dependent on financial sustenance from German lands and art markets, while his cultural production retained the local signature of Rome.

Here, Reinhart fraternized with other visiting artists and intellectuals, such as the Danish–German painter Asmus Jacob Carstens (1754–1798), art critic and archeologist Karl Ludwig Fernow (1763–1808), painter Joseph Anton Koch (1768–1839), and Danish sculptor Bertel Thorvaldsen (1770–1844). These social activities are well recorded and range from the most informal relations to the organization of annual spring celebrations that galvanized the German arts community in Rome, to the co-founding of a *Kunstverein*, or art club.[6] Reinhart lived successively in several apartments in the neighborhood preferred by many visiting artists,

4. Edith Luther, *Johann Friedrich Frauenholz (1758–1822): Kunsthändler und Verleger in Nürnberg* (Nuremberg, 1988).
5. F. Carlo Schmid lists the art dealers who carried works on paper by Reinhart in his lifetime, such as Johann Friedrich Wenner in Frankfurt, Carl Gustav Boerner and Rudolph Weigel in Leipzig, and Georg Christoph Albrecht Ebner in Stuttgart, in addition to Frauenholz. As Schmid points out, Reinhart also sold to visitors to Rome directly, as was customary for foreign artists residing there. The 1790s, however, were a time of intense collaboration between Reinhart and Frauenholz. See F. Carlo Schmid, "'[…] da mein ganzes Vermögen meine Hände und Kopf sind': Johann Christian Reinhart als Zeichner und Radierer," in *Johann Christian Reinhart*, ed. A. Stolzenburg and H. W. Rott, p.8–25 (8 and 18–19).
6. See F. Carlo Schmid, *Naturansichten und Ideallandschaften: die Landschaftsgraphik von Johann Christian Reinhart und seinem Umkreis* (Berlin, 1998), "Exkurs: Reinhart und seine Künstlerkollegen in Rom: ein geschichtlicher Überblick," p.139–48. For a more multifaceted portrayal of the artists' community in Rome, see *Künstlerleben in Rom: Bertel Thorvaldsen (1770–1844): der dänische Bildhauer und seine deutschen Freunde*, ed. Ursula Peters (Nuremberg, 1992).

around Santa Trinità dei Monti. He often shared apartments with other artists. By all accounts, he was quick to make friends among artists from all over Europe and even got to know the American Washington Allston (1779–1843).[7] Such dynamic communication and social connections added an important layer to Reinhart's life playing out locally while transcending the confines of Rome. His art making, too, served this complex networked existence, as a discussion of two print projects, the *Mahlerisch radirte Prospecte von Italien* (*Painterly etched views of Italy*, 1792–1798) and his *Sturmlandschaft mit zwei Reitern* (*Stormy landscape with two riders on horseback*, 1800), will demonstrate.

Reinhart has been the focus of renewed scholarly interest. Since he published his dissertation on the artist in 1998,[8] F. Carlo Schmid has made new sources available and injected important considerations into many conversations on Reinhart and the graphic arts of his time. Reinhart's 250th birthday in 2011 provided further opportunity to reevaluate this artist's work. A traveling retrospective at the German museums Hamburger Kunsthalle and the Neue Pinakothek, Munich, in 2012–2013 reintroduced the artist to wider audiences and generated a substantial scholarly catalog as well.[9] Another illuminating museum catalog is John Ittmann's *The Enchanted world of German Romantic prints, 1770–1850*, published by the Philadelphia Museum of Art in 2017; it places Reinhart among his German contemporaries. While recent commentators have discussed Reinhart's ability to position his work in the market—he specialized in the classical landscape in painting, drawing, and print and catered to the interests of buyers— the timeliness of his work in political and philosophical terms might still be too little appreciated. The polarizing political events of the

---

7. A catalog of artists connected to Reinhart can be found in Andreas Stolzenburg, "'[...] der redlichste Mann in ganz Rom—fest und unverführbar': Johann Christian Reinhart und die Künstlerschaft in Rom 1790–1847," in *Johann Christian Reinhart*, ed. A. Stolzenburg and H. W. Rott, p.71–91.
8. Schmid, *Naturansichten*.
9. Johann Christian Reinhart's life and work are well researched, and he is beginning to be known beyond circles of scholars specializing in prints of the era. See, works cited elsewhere in these notes by Feuchtmayr, Schmid, Richter, and Richter *et al.* The Hamburger Kunsthalle and Neue Pinakothek Munich dedicated a first retrospective exhibition to Reinhart in 2012–2013. American aficionados of prints and contemporary art took note of a small New York show of Reinhart's prints of the Roman landscape that was installed by the artist Richard Tuttle. It was the exhibition and conversations with Tuttle and curator Christina von Rotenhan, Zurich, that sparked my own interest in the artist.

1790s and early 1800s, especially the French Revolution and its aftermath, including the invasion of Italian lands by the revolutionary troops under General Bonaparte, have only been discussed in a cursory manner. Thinking about Reinhart's prints as a "networking tool" generates new insights, as it broadens the perspective to simultaneously include Reinhart's subject matter, production, and distribution process in the light of the intellectual parameters in which the prints were understood.

The prints

As a printmaker, Reinhart's most ambitious undertaking was the *Painterly etched views of Italy* (hereafter *Views*), a collection of views of the landscapes of Latium that Reinhart conceived and proposed to publisher Frauenholz. The publication, which stretched toward the markets in which Reinhart was active, played to the artist's strength as a painter and draftsman of landscapes and responded to the increased interest in the landscapes and historic sites outside of Rome rather than within the city's walls.[10] Together with his collaborators Albert Christoph Dies (1755–1822) and Jacob Wilhelm Mechau (1745–1808), Reinhart created a portfolio of, in total, seventy-two etchings with an equal number of prints by each artist.[11] Already before the negotiations with the publisher were finalized, Reinhart began to urge friends and benefactors in Germany to subscribe and thereby help finance the undertaking. He proudly reported to Frauenholz in May 1792 that he had successfully enlisted many interested parties, only to come to the realization that the final price for the subscription would have to be twice as high as first envisioned by the three artists, which ultimately forced many of the early backers to reconsider. Nevertheless, the effort demonstrated well Reinhart's understanding of the circulation of prints, as well as his willingness to activate his network of friends and colleagues for his own financial benefit.[12]

10. For a comprehensive discussion of paintings by German artists of the period that respond to the landscapes around Rome, see *Kennst Du das Land: Italienbilder der Goethezeit*, ed. Frank Büttner and Herbert W. Rott (Munich, 2005).
11. Inge Feuchtmayr, *Johann Christian Reinhart, 1761–1847: Monographie und Werkverzeichnis* (Munich, 1975), discusses the portfolio, esp. p.79–82 and 397–401, cat.A, p.52–75. Schmid, *Naturansichten*, discusses the prints, esp. p.161–244.
12. Otto Baisch, *Johann Christian Reinhart und seine Kreise: ein Lebens- und Culturbild* (Leipzig, 1882), p.85–86.

The etchings first appeared in twelve groups of six, with two plates by each artist in each group. The initial schedule of monthly distributions turned out to be too ambitious, however, and the series was completed only in 1798. Frauenholz published a complete set, this time not with a German but with a French title page, in 1799.[13] Leafing through the seventy-two etchings of the *Views* was—and still is—a captivating (and time-consuming) experience for anyone with access to the complete portfolio (see Figure 5). Measuring about sixteen by twenty inches, the sheets are too large to be easily handled and require a sizable clean surface to be spread out for the viewing of several works at a time. It is almost impossible to peruse the images leisurely and to access "favorites" without going through large numbers of prints to find what one is looking for. (The uneven quality of the prints was already a concern for Frauenholz.)[14] This experience is, in fact, intentional and speaks to the artists' goals for this collaborative project. Reinhart and his colleagues required focus and sustained attention. They refused to establish a hierarchy among the works or to privilege some themes over others. Reinhart, Dies, and Mechau effectively produced large quantities of personal views of nature in a demonstration of equality among the artists. This emphasis on cooperation was entirely commensurate with the progressive political leanings of their Roman cohort at the time.[15] But their act of invigorating art consumption through quantity without privilege also proved to be disruptive, as it implicitly questioned convention and precedent.

The innovativeness of their works becomes apparent when compared to contemporary standards. What Reinhart, Mechau, and Dies offer is almost shockingly different from the popular views of Roman monuments by Giovanni Battista Piranesi that, at the time of the first publication of the *Views*, had dominated the Roman

13. Anthony Griffiths, *German printmaking in the age of Goethe* (London, 1994), no.89.
14. And he priced the works accordingly since in "the 1809 catalogue Reinhart's plates were priced at 2 Florins 45 Kreuzer apiece; Mechau and Dies's were only 1fl. 48kr. each." Griffiths, *German printmaking*, no.89.
15. Schmid points out that "Like his friends Carstens, Fernow, and Koch, Reinhart looked with sympathy at the Roman Republic established by the French" (*Naturansichten*, p.143). Carl Ludwig Fernow, in Rome since 1794, was a close friend of Reinhart and lived in the same building with him from 1795 to 1802 (Schmid, *Naturansichten*, p.142).

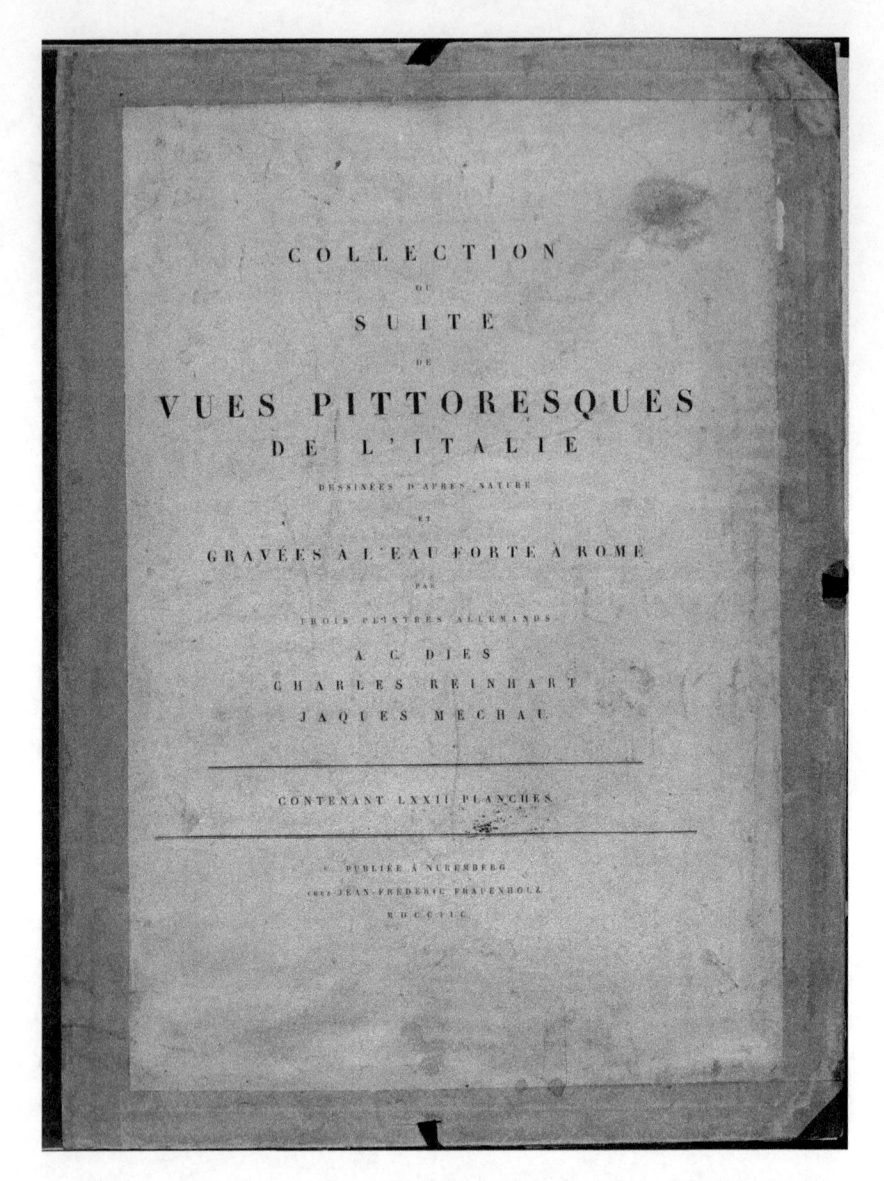

Figure 5: Johann Christian Reinhart, Albert Christoph Dies, and Jacob Mechau, *Collection, ou Suite de vues pittoresques de l'Italie*, 1798. Cover of the portfolio of seventy-two etchings with text pages. National Gallery of Art, Washington, DC, New Century Fund, 2003.86.1-71.

Figure 6: Giovanni Battista Piranesi, *Arco di Costantino*, 1748.
Etching on laid paper, 5 1/16 × 10 5/16 inches (plate). National
Gallery of Art, Washington, DC, Edward E. MacCrone Fund and
the Eugene L. and Marie-Louise Garbáty Fund, 2002.66.1.9.

Figure 7: Giovanni Battista Piranesi, *For di Augusto*, 1748. Etching
on laid paper, 5 1/4 × 10 9/16 inches (plate). National Gallery of Art,
Washington, DC, Edward E. MacCrone Fund and the Eugene L.
and Marie-Louise Garbáty Fund, 2002.66.1.15.

Joachim Homann

Figure 8: Johann Christian Reinhart, *Pallazzola*, 1792. Etching
on laid paper, 11 × 14 3/4 inches (plate). National Gallery of Art,
Washington, DC, New Century Fund, 2003.86.26.

market for visual souvenirs for several decades.[16] Piranesi used
close cropping, forceful perspectival constructions, and dramatic
chiaroscuro effects (see Figure 6). Through fantastical exaggerations
and minute descriptions of archeological details, he kept viewers
looking and learning (see Figure 7). By comparison, most of the
Views present wide-angle perspectives and are classically balanced
and evenly lit (see Figure 8). Bathed in Mediterranean light, the
vistas are made distinct with enough ruins, waterfalls (see Figure 9),
and other features to represent locations recognizable to fellow

---

16. Giovanni Battista Piranesi, *Vedute di Roma: disegnate ed incise da Giambattista
    Piranesi*, vol.1 and 2 (Rome, n.n., 1769). Available at Digitale Sammlungen
    Universitäts- und Landesbibliothek Darmstadt: http://tudigit.ulb.tu-darmstadt.
    de/show/gr-Fol-9-A-41-1 and http://tudigit.ulb.tu-darmstadt.de/show/gr-Fol-9-
    A-41-2 (last accessed June 26, 2023). See also Luigi Ficacci, *Giovanni Battista
    Piranesi: the complete etchings* (Cologne, 2011).

Figure 9: Johann Christian Reinhart, *Sepolcro volgarmente detto degli Orazii e Curiazii a Albano*, 1795. Etching on laid paper, 11 1/16 × 14 15/16 inches (plate). National Gallery of Art, Washington, DC, New Century Fund, 2003.86.20.

travelers (see Figure 10). But topographic accuracy is clearly not allowed to dominate the images.

Reinhart's emphasis is placed not on the faithful recording of archeological sites or natural characteristics; rather, he evokes the aesthetic experience of nature and art in harmony. At a time of unprecedented criticism of the political and hygienic conditions of urban spaces,[17] Reinhart and his consorts left behind a space of privilege and tradition—the city of Rome in which papal might was omnipresent—and collaboratively explored an environment in which, in their idealizing view, equality and a union of natural law and the forces of civilization might be found. Rather than succumbing to enthralled passivity, viewers of their prints were encouraged to roam and arrange, to order, evaluate, and interpret. In subject matter and

17. The politicization of the Italian public and radicalization of many of its members under the influence of the French Revolution is discussed in Harry Hearder, *Italy in the age of the Risorgimento, 1790–1870* (London, 1983), p.19.

Figure 10: Johann Christian Reinhart, *A Subiaco*, 1794. Etching on laid paper, 15 × 11 3/16 inches (plate). National Gallery of Art, Washington, DC, New Century Fund, 2003.86.35.

presentation, Reinhart, Mechau, and Dies impressed on the viewers of their prints the possibility of liberty. To understand the thrust of the artists' argument, it is helpful to consider their work in the context of contemporary debates that were playing out across the arts and had actually found an important precursor or co-producer in German literature.

Emulating Goethe?

The new appreciation for the natural and cultural sights of Latium was expressed, albeit in abbreviated form, in the *Italienische Reise* (*Italian journey*), in which Johann Wolfgang Goethe indicated that his sojourns into the hilly countryside south of Rome offered some of the most joyful experiences of his travels.[18] On December 15, 1787, Goethe reported in a letter from Rome about a hiking tour of several days with friends, which brought him from Frascati across Monte Cavo to Lago Albano, Lago Nemi, and Castel Gandolfo: "I experienced great happiness, which I convey to you from far away. I was cheerful and well."[19] Rather than describing in greater detail what he so enjoyed, he put the reader off until he could show his drawings, "because words and descriptions are nothing."[20] It is this experience of a hike with friends outside the city gates in a Mediterranean landscape saturated with traces of ancient history that Reinhart and his consorts were seeking to replicate in many works of their print series. Like Goethe had implied in the previous decade, images seemed to them better suited than words to convey the sights those excursions offered, along with the emotions they stirred.[21]

18. Interestingly, his perspective on the landscape was shaped in part by his experience of seventeenth-century French landscape paintings of the same area that he saw in Munich and Rome. Stéphane Moses, "Goethes Entdeckung der franzöischen Landschaftsmalerei in Rom (1786–1788)," in *Rom–Europa: Treffpunkt der Kulturen: 1780–1820*, ed. Paolo Chiarini and Walter Hinderer (Würzburg, 2006), p.29–41.
19. "Ich habe grosse Freude gehabt, die ich dir in der Ferne mitteile. Ich war vergnügt und wohl." Johann Wolfgang von Goethe, *Italienische Reise*, in *Sämtliche Werke*, vol.15, ed. Karl Richter (Munich, 1992), p.530.
20. "denn Worte und Beschreibungen sind nichts." Goethe, *Italienische Reise*, p.530.
21. Goethe's own friendship with the internationally celebrated landscape painter Jacob Philipp Hackert (1737–1807), whom he met in Naples in 1786 and whose biography Goethe published in 1811, offered a precedent for such associations. Johann Wolfgang von Goethe, *Philipp Hackert: biographische Skizze, meist nach dessen eigenen Aufsätzen entworfen* (Tübingen, 1811). Coincidentally, Jacob Philipp

Landscape drawings and prints not only aided textual accounts of travel as illustrations, but aimed to offer viewers experiential, visceral access to the landscape. Whereas Goethe may have aspired to emulate visual experience in texts, while clearly insisting on the unsurpassed effect of visual representation, Reinhart's work underscores the uniqueness of visual experience in a more radical way: He sought to capture and proliferate immediacy. Images went beyond reflecting memories—they generated responses in viewers who felt they shared in the experience as travel companions. This nuance becomes apparent in Reinhart's own reservations against illustrations. He explicitly refused to provide captions with the landscape prints that would explain the historic significance of the selected sites, against the stated wishes of his publisher. Reinhart feared that those exposés might end up boring his audiences rather than adding to the allure of the prints.[22] He insisted that the prints had to be understood as artistic responses to the landscape, not pedantic renderings of historically significant sites.[23] He not only sought to liberate artists' encounters with architecture and landscape from existing models but also promoted consumers' freedom and enjoyment in acquiring Italian images.

Authentic artistic expression even trumped conventional standards of artistic quality. Reinhart defended his collaborators, whose work Frauenholz judged as inferior to Reinhart's own:

Hackert and his brother Johann, accompanied by the Swedish sculptor Johan Tobias Sergel (1740–1814) and others, traveled in the spring of 1779 to Frascati, Grottaferrata, Marino, Albano, and Nemi to enjoy the beautiful countryside. Upon their return, they created gouaches and drawings based on the sketches they had prepared during their journey (Goethe, *Philipp Hackert*, p.22–23). This is the same area enjoyed by Goethe and later Reinhart.

22. This refers to Reinhart's letter from May 12, 1794, in which the artist rejects Frauenholz's idea to ask Aloys Hirt for captions. Reinhart wrote: "Wer ihn Ihnen empfohlen, muss ihn entweder nur flüchtig haben kennen lernen— oder seine Menschenkunde war gering. Mit mir sind sehr viele, die ihn seid vielen Jahren kennen, völlig der Meinung, dass Herr Hirt, trotz allen guten Willens ein seichter und langweiliger Schreiber, sehr geschickt sein mag, ein gutes Thema in einem schleppenden, ermüdenden, blümelnden Style schlecht zu geben, der, nachdem er über das Ganze eine trostlose Brühe von stinkender Eigenliebe gegossen, sicher das Vergnügen geniesst, sein Leser mit seinem hundertmal Gesagten als einem unfehlbaren Laudanum in süssen Schlaf zu wiegen." Feuchtmayr, *Johann Christian Reinhart*, p.136–37.

23. Reinhart to Frauenholz, December 29, 1792, Schmid, *Naturansichten*, p.170.

I beg you not to overestimate my work with the eyes of a friend, which would be unfair and would thus be hurtful to me. Every artist works because he enjoys the work and does it for its own sake and for that he needs to be treated fairly. That our works are not similar and will never be is only natural since we differ in our thoughts and feelings.[24]

Reinhart's loyalty to his friends and collaborators, his appreciation of their dedication to the task and the talents they brought to it, is indeed an expression of the project's significance for a "network," understood in the very mundane and pragmatic manner that brought together the temporary Roman communities. It brings together individual actors who form loose and often temporarily confined structures of collaboration or constellation—in this case, the print series—without emphasizing commonality or, for that matter, a central or domineering figure. At the same time, Reinhart intuits what may undo a network by accusing Frauenholz of departing from the works—or things— instead privileging a relation among people or friends. This intuition proves decisive later on.

Years later, under entirely different circumstances, Reinhart emphasized the textual and pictorial confluence that he had vehemently opposed in the 1790s[25] when he co-edited, together with Friedrich Sickler (1773–1836), two volumes of the *Almanach aus Rom* (*Roman almanac*, 1810/1811).[26] Among articles dedicated to ancient monuments and contemporary art and music, biographies of Raphael and Michelangelo, listings of noteworthy archeological discoveries, as well as works produced by artists residing in Rome, several

24. "Worum ich Sie bitte, sehen Sie nicht zuviel bei mir mit den Augen des Freundes, in diesem Fall würde es Ungerechtigkeit sein und dann würde mich's schmerzen. Jeder Künstler arbeitet, weil ihm die Arbeit Lust macht und um ihrer selbst willen und verdient deshalb Gerechtigkeit. Daß unsere Arbeiten nicht einander ähnlich sind und nie werden, ist ganz natürlich, da unsere Art zu denken, unsere Empfindung nicht dieselbe ist." *Heroismus und Idylle: Formen der Landschaft um 1800 bei Jacob Philipp Hackert, Joseph Anton Koch und Johann Christian Reinhart*, ed. Ekkehard Mai and Götz Gzymmek (Cologne, 1984), p.126.
25. F. Carlo Schmid discusses a plan of a portfolio of landscape views of southern Italy and Sicily, which Reinhart proposed to Frauenholz in 1795 as a collaboration with two friends—archeologist and critic Carl Ludwig Fernow and architect Friedrich Weinbrenner. The Revolutionary Wars prevented the realization of this project. F. C. Schmid, "Die Mahlerisch radirten Prospecte von Italien 1792–1798," in *Johann Christian Reinhart*, ed. A. Stolzenburg and H. W. Rott, p.227.
26. *Almanach aus Rom für Künstler und Freunde der Bildenden Kunst* (1810–1811), ed. F. Sickler and C. Reinhart, 2 vols. (Leipzig, 1984).

contributions were dedicated to historic sites in Latium. They were presented in Sickler's descriptions, with a map and Reinhart's etched views. For both the writer and the artist, the remote landscapes offered transformative experiences to the traveler through the remains of the ancient civilization that they preserved and through their natural beauty: "An age-old primeval world of wild battles between frightful forces evokes in us the serious contemplation of a long-lost past filled with heroic deeds, which is transformed by the loving-kindness of ever-fertile beautiful nature—never completely still nor succumbing to the quiet of death—into a gentle elegiac sentiment."[27] Sickler's essay strikes a familiar chord, as it repeats Goethe's admonition that words were unable to do justice to the magnificence of the region:

> Those who have seen this part of the lake and of old Latium, past Nemi, will remember their own feelings and the sight of the landscape, as they look at the enclosed engraving. For those who have not yet been there the following landscape painting [a poem], combined with the viewing of the print, might give a more vivid idea than any description could possibly convey.[28]

Accepting the potential and limitations of words (in poetry and prose) and image, Sickler and Reinhart purposefully employ the three forms of expression in their attempt to create the most immediate experience for their readers that could be printed on paper and circulated. At the same time, they offer a model of a cultural-geographical archive that future written and visual accounts could use as a source of knowledge and experience. Last but not least, they care about their own legacy.

27. "Eine greise, im wilden Kampf schrecklicher Elemente ehemals wirkende Vorwelt, wie eine ruhmerhellte, aber längst entschwundene Vorzeit, wecken uns hier zu ernsten Gedanken, welche nur die liebliche Freundlichkeit einer immerfort bildenden schönen Natur, die keinen absoluten Stillstand oder eine todte Ruhe gewährt, zu sanft elegischen Empfindungen stimmen." Sickler and Reinhart, *Almanach aus Rom*, vol.1, p.75.
28. "Demjenigen, der sie schon gesehen," Sickler wrote, "dem ruft das beigegebene Kupfer, und dem man einen Theil des Sees und des alten Latiums, hinter Nemi aufgenommen, erblickt, diese seine Gefühle, so wie die Gegend selbst sicherlich sehr gut zurück. Wer sie aber noch nicht gesehen, dem verschafft das nachstehende kleine Landschaftsgemälde [a poem] mit der Ansicht des Kupfers verbunden, vielleicht eine lebhaftere Idee, als jede Beschreibung ihm gewähren dürfte." Sickler and Reinhart, *Almanach aus Rom*, vol.1, p.75.

Friendship, competition, network

Even before Sickler and Reinhart united travelogue, poetry, and visual art in their almanac in order to convey not only the knowledge gained but also the feelings stirred by travel through Latium, Reinhart's, Dies's, and Mechau's prints would have been appreciated as contributions to an ongoing exchange among German intellectuals and artists. As the prints intersected existing networks and shifted dynamics within, their effects created a powerful alternative to almanacs (intended to be read like a book, in a more or less linear way). In November and December 1796, Friedrich Schiller's monthly journal *Die Horen* (*The Hours*) published a report by archeologist Aloys Hirt (1759–1837) about his journey into the very same mountainous regions southeast of Rome that were so dear to Reinhart and his peers. Hirt, whom Reinhart knew well, was coincidentally one of the people whom publisher Frauenholz wanted to involve in the *Views*, and whose participation as a commentator and historian he had proposed—to Reinhart's dismay. Whether Hirt's writing was indeed as tedious and sleep-inducing as Reinhart claimed in his rejection of Frauenholz's request was up to the subscribers of *Die Horen* to decide. Perhaps Reinhart feared competition of a different kind rather than a deprival of unfettered visual experience. Indeed, one wonders quite how many readers of Schiller's journal (1795–1797) were concurrently receiving the *Views* and thus were exposed to competing narratives. Reinhart and his team began to send out the first group of six prints in 1792 and concluded the project after a dozen such mailings in 1798. It is therefore tempting to read his *Reise von Grottaferrata nach dem Fucinischen See und Monte Cassino, im October 1794* (*Journey from Grottaferrata to Lake Fucini and Monte Cassino in October 1794*) with the *Views* in mind.

Co-existing, perhaps competing consumer networks were not the only constellations influencing Reinhart's position. Hirt capitalized on stylistic connections when forming his views of Italy. He had been Goethe's cicerone and frequented the same Roman circles in which Reinhart was at home, traveled as a companion to Prince August of England through the regions the three painters drew, and even etched for their portfolio of the *Views*.[29] In his contribution to *Die Horen*, written in letter form and addressed to Duchess Amalia von

---

29. *Die Horen: eine Monatsschrift herausgegeben von Schiller* (1796; Darmstadt, 1959), no.8, p.35–79, and no.12, p.1–20.

Sachsen-Weimar, Hirt complained vehemently about "the impassibility" (*die Unwegsamkeit*) of the area, and found that "the narrow and steep mountain passes of Switzerland, the ridges of the Apennine in Calabria are less arduous and forbidding."[30] The harsh criticism of contemporary conditions sets off detailed descriptions of the feats of civil engineering of ancient Rome—a long-neglected legacy, according to Hirt, that was still visible in the region: "These poor roads are all the more striking, because they connect the most beautiful and fertile regions where daily traffic is a necessity, and almost everywhere they follow the routes of the best known and earliest highroads, of which one can still find in some places understructures and old bridges."[31] Unlike the disgruntled travelers in Germany whose experience of a nation was impeded by such ruins (see Baumgartner's essay in this volume), here the ruins facilitate the identification of an aesthetic network. Such emphasis on the engineering of streets and bridges also characterizes Reinhart's, Dies's, and Mechau's selection of subjects (see Figure 11). The ancient ruins Reinhart and his collaborators recorded are often survivors of public works projects, including viaducts, city gates, aqueducts, fountains, and thermal baths. The imposing substructures of the Colosseum (one of only a few buildings within the city to be featured) and the Villa of Maecenas at Tivoli, among other such examples, add to this focus on functionality rather than monumentality in engineering and architecture (see Figures 12 and 13). Reinhart's *Views* document the decay without attempting to restore the structures or mitigate the impairment that decay creates; his aim is rather to savor the sensory qualities of ruin.

But comparing Hirt's perspective on the landscape of Latium with those of Reinhart, Dies, and Mechau makes even more apparent the latter's willingness to be seduced by their motifs. Hills in sunlight, waterfalls, villages perched on cliffs, dancing peasants under trees, a destination restaurant for leisure travelers, and other such delightful sights caught the artist's attention and were included in the seventy-two *Views* (see Figure 14). Taking the freedom to choose what interested

---

30. "die engen und steilen Pässe der Schweiz, der Bergrücken der Apenninen in Kalabrien sind weniger mühsam und abschreckend." *Die Horen*, no.8, p.36.
31. "Diese elenden Wege sind um so auffallender, da sie die schönsten und fruchtbarsten Gegenden, wo täglicher Verkehr notwendig ist, miteinander verbinden, und man beinahe immer den Linien folget, wo die Alten ihre bekanntesten und fruehesten Heerstrassen durchfuehrten, wovon man noch an manchen Stellen Substructionen und alte Bruecken findet." *Die Horen*, no.8, p.36.

Figure 11: Johann Christian Reinhart, *A Città Castellana*, 1794. Etching on laid paper, 11 × 14 3/4 inches (plate). National Gallery of Art, Washington, DC, New Century Fund, 2003.86.38.

Figure 12: Albert Christoph Dies, *Terme di Caracalla*, 1793. Etching on laid paper, 10 11/16 × 14 3/4 inches (plate). National Gallery of Art, Washington, DC, New Century Fund, 2003.86.7.

In villa Mecenate a Tivoli

Figure 13: Johann Christian Reinhart, *Villa Mecenate*, 1793. Etching on laid paper, 14 7/8 × 11 1/16 inches (plate). National Gallery of Art, Washington, DC, New Century Fund, 2003.86.69.

them, rather than following a prescribed master plan, the artists asserted their subjectivity and in turn allowed viewers to participate vicariously in their travels. Hirt's appreciation of the landscape of

Figure 14: Johann Christian Reinhart, *Aricia*, 1793. Etching on laid paper, 11 1/4 × 14 13/16 inches (proof). National Gallery of Art, Washington, DC, New Century Fund, 2003.86.25.

Latium was not dissimilar to the perspective conveyed in the print project. What caused Reinhart's reservations, however, was clearly the presentation in written and historicizing form, which threatened to introduce a competing narrative and disrupt the network of visual art consumers by enwrapping them in the seduction of journal culture.[32]

In his letters to Frauenholz, Reinhart's immense personal stake is apparent, for example, when he contrasts his painterly views with the more common topographical engravings. Reinhart showed disdain for such descriptive prints, and rejected the notion that his project could be mistaken for such formulaic material.[33] What might have motivated

32. Reinhart's project is markedly different from Grand Tour narratives and guidebooks, discussed in the current volume in the essay by Baumgartner, where aesthetic experience and visual and cartography-like documenting intersect with national intentions.
33. Feuchtmayr, *Johann Christian Reinhart*, p.63, discusses Reinhart's rejection of Wilhelm Friedrich Gmelin as potential collaborator, as Frauenholz had

him and his friends to dedicate years of their lives to this publication? On some level, Reinhart fell prey to the same narrative that he rejected when Frauenholz judged him a superior artist, albeit with a difference. For Reinhart, the superior qualities originated in the artistic method itself: The painterly view reigned above topography. Such a view was trained by an aesthetic rendition of nature, closely resembling what Schiller described as aesthetic experience per se in his own contribution to *Die Horen*, namely *Über die ästhetische Erziehung des Menschen in einer Reihe von Briefen (On the aesthetic education of man in a series of letters)*. Art can serve as an antidote to the specialization and fragmentation of modern life—a liberating power drawn from the holistic experience of nature. The aesthetic transformation is instigated by a visual sensation to which the artist is exposed before he can relate it to his audiences. Aesthetic experience encapsulates the moment when the artist mediates for others, including in future times. Schiller elaborates:

> While the artist is a son of his own times, but it would be terrible if he also was its pupil or even its minion. A benevolent deity needs to seize the infant in due time from his mother's breast, nurture him with the milk of a better era and allow him to grow up under the distant Greek sky until he reaches maturity.[34]

Only as a stranger to his own time could he bring the desired aesthetic purification, Schiller further suggests, and he describes the blessings of the Greco-Roman Mediterranean world with such gusto that his friends and admirers in Rome must have felt vindicated. But the ruins of classical antiquity were not supposed to engender nostalgia; they merely provided a touchstone for imagining the experience of immediacy and the transcendence of time:

> Where a lighter ether opens the senses to the softest touch and luscious matter is enlivened by energy-rich warmth—where the realm

---

suggested. "Was hat der Kupferstecher unter den Malern zu thun?" he asked in a polemic letter from February 6, 1795.

34. Friedrich Schiller, *On the aesthetic education of man in a series of letters*, ed. and translated by Elizabeth M. Wilkinson and L. A. Willoughby (Oxford, 1976), p.56, letter 9, paragraph 4. "Der Künstler ist zwar der Sohn seiner Zeit, aber schlimm für ihn, wenn er zugleich ihr Zögling oder gar noch ihr Günstling ist. Eine wohltätige Gottheit reisse den Säugling bei Zeiten von seiner Mutter Brust, nähre ihn mit der Milch eines besseren Alters und lasse ihn unter fernem griechischen Himmel zur Mündigkeit reifen," *Schillers Werke: Nationalausgabe*, vol.20 (Weimar, 1962), p.333.

of blind mass has already collapsed in the inanimate creation and victorious form is ennobling even the lowliest parts—where in the happy circumstances and the blessed regions, in which only action leads to enjoyment and only enjoyment leads to activity, where life itself becomes a source for holy order and lawful order only produces life—where imagination eternally escapes reality but never loses its connection to the simplicity of nature—only here will senses and spirit, receptive and creative faculties form the happy balance, which is the essence of beauty and the condition of humanity.[35]

This long and riveting statement puts on display the dialectic of Schiller's thinking. Clearly, he appreciated the sensual experience of nature for the impulses it offered to a fertile mind. The reader might wonder, however, to what degree Schiller's educational program implicates the visual perception of nature as a starting point for his deliberations, and whether artistic production could be substituted for the immediate experience of nature.

For visual artists such as Reinhart, the response would have been a positive one. Reinhart, one might argue, was hoping to discover in the mountains of Latium Schiller's ideal of beauty and community. If he did consider his print publication a tool to connect with like-minded souls, "in a few selected circles,"[36] in the making of art as well as in the subscribers' engagement with art, he can be regarded as a co-producer of Schiller's aesthetic vision. Indeed, Reinhart seems to have launched a material tool suited to foster Schiller's program of aesthetic education.

The analogy in Reinhart's and Schiller's aesthetic projects is far more than a serendipitous effect of loosely arranged artists'

35. Schiller, *On the aesthetic education*, p.190, letter 26, paragraph 2. "Da wo ein leichter Aether die Sinne jeder leisen Berührung eröffnet und den üppigen Stoff eine energische Wärme beseelt—wo das Reich der blinden Masse schon in der leblosen Schöpfung gestürzt ist und die siegende Form auch die niedrigsten Naturen veredelt—dort in den fröhlichen Verhältnissen und in der gesegneten Zone, wo nur die Tätigkeit zum Genusse und nur der Genuss zur Tätigkeit führt, wo aus dem Leben selbst die heilige Ordnung quilt, und aus dem Gesetz der Ordnung sich nur Leben entwickelt—wo die Einbildungskraft der Wirklichkeit ewig entflieht und dennoch von der Einfalt der Natur nie verirrt—hier allein werden sich Sinne und Geist, empfangende und bildende Kraft in dem glücklichen Gleichmass entwickeln, welches die Seele der Schönheit und die Bedingung der Menschheit ist," *Schillers Werke*, p.398–99.

36. Schiller, *On the aesthetic education*, p.218, letter 27, paragraph 12; "in einigen wenigen auserlesenen Zirkeln," *Schillers Werke*, p.412.

Figure 15: Johann Christian Reinhart, *Sturmlandschaft mit zwei Reitern*, 1800. Oil on canvas, 14 × 19 3/4 inches.

networks. The analogy is affected by a rhetoric of friendship that had begun to order networked cultural production at the time. Reinhart himself suggested that it may supersede and impair people's judgment, and, in the centuries since then, modern ideals of friendship have cemented legacies and obscured historical incongruities in social relationships. The actual relationship between Reinhart and Schiller bears the markers of alleged equality and disguised hierarchy that shaped eighteenth-century discourses of friendship; the most obvious testimony is a major etching that Reinhart *dedicated* to Schiller with a formal address in Latin in 1800.[37]

The work's idealized, heroic landscape offers a spectacle of contrasts between deeply shaded and brightly illuminated passages (see Figure 15). A thunderstorm is gathering in a mountain range.

37. Reinhart prepared the etching (see Figure 4) with an oil sketch on canvas of the same size as the print, 14 × 19 3/4 inches (see Figure 15). See Stolzenburg and Rott, *Johann Christian Reinhart*, p.323. A pendant, *Hylas, drowned by the nymphs of the stream*, is now lost. According to Ulrike Bühler it signified captivity as the *Stormy landscape* stood for freedom. Mai and Czymmek, *Heroismus und Idylle*, no.54, p.120–21.

Lightening has struck an ancient tower, from which smoke is rising. A turbulent river runs through an open valley. Two knights in armor race on horseback toward the viewer, adding speed and excitement to this stirring image. The dedication (see Figure 4) reads, in abbreviated Latin, "FRIDERICO SCHILLER Ingenio, arte, virtute illustri D.D.D.J.C. Reinhart." It is further signed and dated by Reinhart on the bottom left: "J.C. Reinhart invt. pinxt, et sculpt. Romae 1800."[38] To some degree, these inscriptions follow well-established formulas. For centuries, such notations have distinguished between the author/inventor of the image, the reproductive etcher or engraver who transferred it onto the copper plate, and the publisher who was responsible for the reproduction and distribution of the work. The dedication enshrined the elevated position of the person thus honored, in this case Schiller, indicating in early modernity and all the way through the eighteenth century relationships of patronage and benevolent dependency. It matters little that these dedications had increasingly become a point of decorum in that they no longer always implied social hierarchy and political favors. But Reinhart's dedication stands out in yet another way, one that suggests how rhetoric impacted and solidified ideas about hierarchies among the arts and the role of individuals in art production. He specified that he not only invented and etched but also "painted" the work, a disclaimer that established his authorship with an unusual amount of control over the final product, making it a personal statement. It might not be coincidental that Reinhart's tripartite specification of his role—author, painter, engraver—follows his triple praise for Schiller's genius, artistry, and virtue, all markers of an exceptional individual. These two sets of distinctions are of course aligned, as they are addressing purely conceptual, creative, and practical faculties that echo the Kantian separation of pure reason, aesthetic judgment, and practical reason. Far from being an illustration of a work by Schiller, this etching is a homage and gift that implies a shared vision of both artists—and their equal standing—and thereby claims for Reinhart the elevated cultural status that by the same token he bestows upon

---

38. As F. Carlo Schmid notes, this is the only dedication in Latin that Reinhart added to a print. He dedicated several other works—in his earlier years to benefactors such as Karl-Alexander von Brandenburg-Ansbach-Bayreuth (his *Wassermühle bei den großen Eichen* or *Watermill at the great oaks*, 1788) and later to artist friends, such as Josef Abel (1764–1818) (six Italian landscapes, 1805–1811). See Schmid, *Naturansichten*, p.280–87.

his famous friend. Simultaneously, by resorting to the older rhetoric of dedication with all its decorum, Reinhart signals that Schiller has already achieved a superior standing.

Reinhart's choice of subject matter and the dedication as a formal, interpretative framework offer a stark contrast to the collaborative work of the 1790s. Where the *Views* indicated the Jacobin leanings of Reinhart and his fellow artists, the new work reflected shifting politics and new artistic paradigms. Reinhart's Latin dedication to Schiller falls into the period of the First Consulate in France, during which Bonaparte enjoyed immense popularity for his military successes in Italy (in the battle of Marengo against Austria, June 14, 1800) as well as his legislative and organizational acumen that put an end to the revolutionary chaos of the previous decade.[39] Political and military successes find parallels in art, where we see a turn toward the monument.[40] Reinhart's dedication to Schiller thus not only harked back to an established culture that narrated unequal relationships through the rhetoric of friendship, it also reflected this cult of persona and awareness of the symbolic exchange of honors practiced at this time.

For Reinhart, this gesture accrued "symbolic capital," combining pre- and postrevolutionary value and rhetoric, and emphasizing the rhetorical and conceptual value of friendship as one that did not necessarily circulate within salon culture but is frequently mentioned in scholarly discussions of the eighteenth-century salon. In a more mundane sense, the gesture restored a personal relationship that had been languishing since the artist moved to Rome. Friedrich

39. In Italy, the creation of a French satellite republic in Lombardy caused political uncertainty. For the following years, Italian administrators engaged the French invaders in an exchange of gifts. Celebrating the French victory with enormous festivals and advertising competitions for commemorative monuments dedicated to the French army and their general, Bonaparte, they hoped to assert cultural superiority at a time of political impotence. Mostly in vain, they hoped to receive in exchange for their symbolic gifts a degree of political independence. See Joachim Homann, "Giovanni Antolini's Foro Bonaparte: constitution of public space in Napoleonic Milan," in *The Political economy of art: making the nation of culture*, ed. Julie Codell (Madison, WI, 2008), p.111–23.

40. An example is Antonio Canova's monumental *Napoleon as Mars the peacemaker*. Canova was the most prominent artist in Rome and knew Reinhart personally. See also Susan Jaques, *The Caesar of Paris: Napoleon Bonaparte, Rome, and the artistic obsession that shaped an empire* (New York, 2018); Dieter Richter, *Von Hof nach Rom: Johann Christian Reinhart, ein deutscher Maler in Italien. Eine Biographie* (Berlin, 2010).

Schiller, then twenty-six years old, spent the summer of 1785 in Gohlis, a village near Leipzig, with a group of friends that included the twenty-four-year-old Reinhart. Among others present were Georg Joachim Göschen, who opened his publishing house the same year, and the supportive Christian Gottfried Körner.[41] For Körner, Schiller wrote his "Ode an die Freude" ("Ode to joy") that summer and fall, marking a brief period that is often called the happiest in Schiller's life. It was in a letter to Körner on December 8, 1787 that Schiller expressed how much Reinhart meant to him at the time: "I spent much time with Reinhart, he is still the same old honest guy. Now all his [poetic intention] is directed toward Italy [...] We got to know each other better, I like him a lot."[42] To Schiller, Reinhart was a true friend; any allusion to the deceptive rhetoric of friendship that Schiller had detected elsewhere had given way to an emphasis on equality. Accordingly, Schiller was delighted to hear from Reinhart in a letter dated May 8, 1801, when the artist sent a proof of his heroic landscape. Reinhart evoked the happy days in Leipzig and Gohlis, and assured Schiller that over the past twelve years he had never wavered in his affection and admiration for his friend. He writes:

> Now my friend you are suddenly receiving an invitation to become godfather to one of my black children. I did—as I occasionally like to etch one of my paintings, scratch it onto a copper plate and dedicate it to you—in order to recall in your memory my image [*Bild*], just as yours is fresh and solid in my memory.[43]

Schiller received the letter and the testament in print on June 4 and responded on June 15:

> The proof, my dear old friend, of your memory and your continuing friendship delights me very much; for me, too, the image of good,

---

41. Richter, *Von Hof nach Rom*, p.45–46.

42. Referring to a visit in Meiningen, where Reinhart lived in 1786, Schiller explains to Körner, "mit Reinhart war ich oft zusammen, er ist noch ganz der alte und brave Kerl. Jetzt geht all sein Dichten und Trachten auf Italien [...] Wir haben uns hier noch genauer kennengelernt, ich bin ihm recht gut." Quoted in Feuchtmayr, *Johann Christian Reinhart*, p.139.

43. "Nun mein Freund erhalten Sie mit einmal einen Gevatterbrief zu einem meiner schwarzen Kinder. Ich habe nehmlich,—wie ich mitunder gern etwas radiere eines meiner Gemälde in Kupfer gekrazt, und es Ihnen dedizirt—um auch in Ihrem Gedächtnisse mein Bild hervorzurufen, wie das Ihrige in meinem Gedächtniss Frisch und fest dasteht." Schmid, *Naturansichten*, p.283.

loyal Reinhart has stayed alive, and every traveler from Rome had to report to me about you. [...] Many thanks, old friend, for the beautiful landscape and for the honor you bestowed on me. I had heard that you are using your stay in Rome well and am twice happy to have proof in my hands.[44]

These lines capture a rich layer in the cultural archive of the time. While Schiller holds friendship in high regard (honor), the relationship seems to warrant a token of proof, one that Reinhart provides through the somewhat inversed rhetoric of family (godfather) and, materially, through the etching.

But what qualified Reinhart's landscape to bring back his image in Schiller's memory? Reading Reinhart's dedication letter to Schiller, one wonders why he would not send a self-portrait to his friend. Earlier, Schiller and Reinhart had drawn each other's portraits, and it is known that Reinhart held on to the likeness of his friend until the end of his life. One reason for Reinhart to communicate with Schiller through a rendering of an idealized landscape surely is his specialization in the field. He dedicated an especially splendid example of his work that he considered one of his most important achievements to date to Schiller and sent it to him. In addition, the genre of landscape painting was being revived at the time by artists who found inspiration in the art of the seventeenth-century classicists Nicolas Poussin, Gaspard Dughet, Claude Lorraine, and their Dutch counterparts. Previous generations had ranked landscapes low in the hierarchy of the arts, but a new generation of painters, like Reinhart and his friend Joseph Anton Koch, began to bring more prestige to the field. But it seems even more important to consider what Reinhart chooses not to show as he engages in a conversation with Schiller through visual means. A significant detail in this landscape is the group of two riders, just emerging behind an outcropping as they approach the stage-like foreground of the work. They are bringing an energetic impulse to this gloomy scene without offering any specificity that would advance

---

44. "Wie sehr, mein lieber alter Freund, erfreute mich der Beweis seines Andenkens und seiner fortwährenden Freundschaft; auch mir ist das Bild des guten treuen Reinhart immer lebendig geblieben, und jeder Wanderer aus Rom musste mir von ihm erzählen. [...] Tausend Dank, mein lieber Alter, für die schöne Landschaft und für die Ehre, die Er mir dabei erwiesen hat. Ich hatte schon längst vernommen, dass Er seinen Auffenthalt zu Rom recht gut benutzt hat, und freue mich nun doppelt, den Beweis davon in Händen zu haben." Schmid, *Naturansichten*, p.284.

a narrative. The same is true for the other elements of this view, such as the town—a composite of geometric shapes vaguely reminiscent of classical antiquity without evoking the splendor of ancient Rome, which surrounded Reinhart every day, and the wild landscape that does not exhibit any signs of agricultural use. Reinhart appreciated the Italian landscape for its ability to awaken a longing for the ideal in the viewer, and he omitted details that would have connected his picture to contemporary life. Together with his close friend, scholar Karl Ludwig Fernow, who lived in the same house in Rome, Reinhart must have spent many hours debating the merits of landscape art in the light of Immanuel Kant's philosophy and the aesthetic writings of their mutual friend Friedrich Schiller.[45] They agreed in particular that "Italian nature combined in every regard what favors and elevates the poetic character of a landscape [...] Nature in Italy is by its own merit, its higher degree of beauty and grace, able to make the mind receptive to the sentimental."[46] Among Reinhart's landscapes, this work expresses particularly well the ambition to alleviate the modern viewer's estrangement by encouraging sentimental reflection on the loss of their naïve understanding of nature.[47]

45. Fernow dedicated his influential essay "Über die Landschaftsmalerei" ("On landscape painting") to Reinhart with a letter to the artist published in lieu of a foreword. He declares: "If there is anything truthful and good to be found in this essay, which I dedicate to you as a humble proof of my unwavering respect and friendship, it is primarily the fruit of the many instructive hours I spent in your studio, with your works, studies, and sketches, observing and in conversation" ("Ist in dem Aufsatze, den ich ihnen hier als einen schwachen Beweis einer unveränderlichen Achtung und Freundschaft zueigne, etwas Wahres und Gutes enthalten, so ist dies großenteils die Frucht der vielen lehrreichen Stunden, die ich in Ihrer Kunstwerkstätte, unter Ihren Arbeiten, Studien und Entwürfen in Betrachtung und Gespräch zugebracht habe"). Quoted in Götz Czymmek, "Johann Christian Reinhart und Joseph Anton Koch als Landschafter," in *Heroismus und Idylle*, ed. Ekkehard Mai and Götz Czymmek, p.19–29 (24).
46. "Die italienische Natur vereint in jeder Hinsicht alles, was den poetischen Karakter einer Lanschaft begünstigen und erhöhen kann. [...] Die italienische Natur ist durch sich selbst, ohne die verschoenende Nachuelfe der Kunst, durch ihren edlen Karakter, durch ihre hoehere Schoenheit und Anmuth, faehig das Gemueth sentimentalisch zu stimmen." Schmid, *Naturansichten*, p.294–95.
47. Mildenberger suggests that both Reinhart and Schiller "seem to have secretly harbored hope that the parallels of 'naïve' and 'sentimental' might meet in infinity" ("Sie scheinen von der Hoffnung beseelt zu sein, dass sich die starren Parallelen 'naiv' and 'sentimentalisch' doch noch in der Unendlichkeit treffen könnten"); Hermann Mildenberger, "'Deßhalb bitte ich Ihnen recht sehr, den schönen Vorsatz Italien zu sehn, doch ja nicht wie einen leichten Traum

Meeting in and writing about the aesthetic sphere sustained
Reinhart and Schiller's engagement from here on. They exchanged
letters until Schiller's death in the spring of 1805, but never saw
each other again. The subject matter of their exchange frequently
proved elusive but also aspirational and clearly directed toward the
future, acknowledging the unique status of art and philosophy. One
of Schiller's letters seems emblematic of how they approached their
respective art:

> It means a lot to me that you are still remembering me and you
> preserved your affection for me in spite of our long separation
> and the distance between us, I am thinking of you with heartfelt
> sympathy [...] We will for now visit each other with the airship of
> fantasy [*Luftschiff der Phantasie*], and I will see to it that I can appear
> to you as a ghost in my poetic works.[48]

Schiller followed up on the exchange by asking his publisher Johann
Friedrich Cotta to include works by Reinhart in a new edition
of *Wilhelm Tell*. Reinhart, disregarding the setting and dramatic
structure of the work, submitted six views of landscapes around Rome
and Naples. Again, refusing to consider his art illustrative, Reinhart
proposed "spaces to imagine freedom [*Imaginationsräume der Freiheit*]."[49]
Schiller died before he could see Reinhart's works, and Cotta decided
to disregard them. To publish *Wilhelm Tell* and the Italian views side
by side as independent works of art that resonated with each other
without producing a literal connection would have been daring, to say
the least—akin to an "airship of fantasy."

In Schiller's letters to Reinhart, with their fraternizing and
unreservedly supportive tone, this metaphor stands out for the
complexity of associations it provokes. When Schiller playfully

---

verwehen zu lassen': Johann Christian Reinhart und Friedrich Schiller," in
Johann Christian Reinhart, ed. A. Stolzenburg and H. W. Rott, p.36–46 (45).

48. March 7 (or 14?), 1803: "Wie rührt es mich, Dass Er meiner noch denkt und
mir trotz Zeit und Entfernung Seine Liebe bewahrt hat, auch ich denke Seiner
mit herzlicher Liebe [...]. Wir wollen uns also einstweilen im Luftschiff der
Phantasie besuchen, und ich will sehen, dass ich Ihm zuweilen durch poetische
Werke auf Geisterart erscheinen kann. Kommt einmal wieder eine Gelegenheit,
so gebe Er doch einem Wanderer ein bemahltes Papier von Sich mit, denn Er
soll trefflich mahlen koennen hoere ich von Jedermann, und möchte gern selber
einmal ein Werk seines Pinsels sehen." Schmid, *Naturansichten*, p.285.

49. The term is from Hermann Mildenberger, who traces Reinhart's and Schiller's
friendship in "Johann Christian Reinhart," p.36–46 (43).

proposed something tangible, albeit futuristic—the airship—he not only spoke about the status and potential of the arts but also lifted friendship into the realm of poetic imagination. Indeed, the dual rhetorical move had a particular contemporary appeal. Christoph Martin Wieland, in his description of the first flight of the hot air balloons of the Montgolfier brothers in 1783–1784, closely associated the excitement generated by the new technological invention with the transporting experience of poetic inspiration. Wieland wrote in *Der teutsche Merkur* in the spring of 1784 of the "great, wonderful, spooky, unique spectacle [...] in its first novelty [...] that brings into play simultaneously all the springs of the imagination and of the heart and all kinds of passions, which the experience of the sublime can spark in our souls, [and which every reader was encouraged to feel as intensely] as if he were a poet."[50] When Schiller referred to the *Luftschiff* in 1803, his use of the word would have been understood as a reference to Jean Paul's *Luftschiffer Giannozzo's Seebuch* (*Airship Captain Giannozzo's logbook*, 1801).[51] By evoking the complex character of Jean Paul—who, to say the least, aimed for the skies while counseling those at sea—Schiller acknowledged disparate domains but also doubled down on the book's ease (*Leichtigkeit*). It diffused the tension that Reinhart had built up by insisting that Schiller visit Italy, but nevertheless helped to establish a sense of an elevated artistic discourse in text and images in which like-minded souls communicate with a degree of freedom and intensity not available elsewhere.

50. Christoph Martin Wieland, quoted in Heinz Brüggemann, "Luftbilder eines kleinstädtischen Jahrhunderts: Ekstase und imaginäre Topographie in Jean Paul: *Des Luftschiffers Giannozzo Seebuch*," in *Die Stadt in der deutschen Romantik*, ed. Gerhart von Graevenitz (Würzburg, 2000), p.127–82 (128).
51. Jean Paul, *Titan (1802)* (Frankfurt am Main, 1983).

II

Material cultures

Serial inventories: cataloging the age of paper

SEAN FRANZEL

University of Missouri

A flood of paper

Introducing the first issue of their journal *London und Paris* (London and Paris) in 1798, the Weimar-based editors Friedrich Justin Bertuch and Karl August Böttiger start with the unavoidable question: Why start a new serial publication when so many are already in circulation? "Writing for newspapers [*Zeitungsschreiberey*] is a massive line of business in cultivated states, and it has become the sole notable form of literature in countries like France, and recently in Batavia and Helvetia. The age of paper [*Das papierne Zeitalter*] nearly drowns [*erstickt*] under all the journals and newspapers."[1] Bertuch and Böttiger are as experienced as anyone in adding to the "flood" of print and paper products,[2] having edited leading periodicals of the 1780s and 1790s such as the *Journal des Luxus und der Moden* (*Journal of luxury and fashion*) and *Der teutsche Merkur* (*The German Mercury*). In taking stock of the latest political, cultural, social, and literary trends emanating from these two European capitals, the editors of *London und Paris* are well aware that it is impossible to provide a comprehensive overview of the "age of paper," and yet they hope to provide at least some initial orientation.[3] In this essay, I want to explore one of

---

1. Friedrich Justin Bertuch and Karl August Böttiger, "Plan und Ankündigung," *London und Paris* 1:1 (1798), p.3–11 (3).
2. On the *Bücherflut* metaphor and its relation to library cataloging, see Markus Krajewski, *Paper machines: about cards and catalogues, 1548–1929*, translated by Peter Krapp (Cambridge, MA, 2011), p.8.
3. On the topos of the age of paper, see Christiane Holm, "Goethes Papiersachen und andere Dinge des 'papierenen Zeitalters,'" *Zeitschrift für Germanistik* 21:1 (2012), p.17–40; and Sean Franzel, "The Romantic lecture in an age of paper (money): Jean Paul's literary aesthetics across print and orality," *Romanticism*

the ways in which *London und Paris* seeks, as Bertuch and Böttiger put it, "to disentangle the thousandfold intertwined knot of written and oral traditions,"[4] namely via the attempt to catalog or take inventory of various lead and side players in the print and paper business.

Building readers' capacities for moral and aesthetic judgment (*prodesse et delectare*) was a long-standing goal of most periodicals of the eighteenth and nineteenth centuries. Helping readers navigate various kinds of lists, catalogs, and registries featured less prominently in these journals' stated self-understanding, even if in practice it was integral. Mixing the Enlightenment desire for systematic overview and the pragmatic sense that readers value and enjoy ongoing digests of a range of topics that might not ever reach completion, Bertuch and Böttiger engage in a range of inventorying gestures that warrant closer attention as a key feature of the print and paper landscape around 1800.

The word "inventory" originates in the legal realm, referring to lists of the property of a deceased or detained person,[5] but the word's commercial applications—referring both to products on hand (a store's current inventory) and to the ordered register thereof[6]—apply, in particular, to the realms of politics, culture, manufacturing, scholarship, and so forth, with which Bertuch and Böttiger concern themselves.[7] The lists that readers would encounter in review, fashion,

---

and *Victorianism on the net* 57–58 (2010), https://doi.org/10.7202/1006516ar (last accessed June 27, 2023).

4. Bertuch and Böttiger, "Plan und Ankündigung," p.4.
5. "A detailed list of articles, such as goods and chattels, or parcels of land, found to have been in the possession of a person at his decease or conviction, sometimes with a statement of the nature and value of each; hence any such detailed statement of the property of a person, of the goods or furniture in a house or messuage, or the like." "Inventory, n.," in *OED online*, http://www.oed.com/view/Entry/98981?p=emailA4LQTPDEZ./nE&d=98981 (last accessed June 27, 2023).
6. See "Inuentarium," in *Johann Heinrich Zedlers großes vollständiges Universallexicon aller Wissenschaften und Künste (1731–1754)*, p.14 and 431, https://www.zedler-lexikon.de (last accessed June 27, 2023).
7. Te Heesen argues that there is a shift in the eighteenth-century art collection—in particular, away from the listing and organization of art objects via inventories, i.e., lists of personal property, to catalogs that describe the contents of various private or public collections in more detailed and aesthetically/stylistically specific terms. Anke te Heesen, "Der Ausstellungskatalog als Monographie: über Kataloge und ein neues Format des geisteswissenschaftlichen Publizierens," *Kodex: Jahrbuch der Internationalen Buchwissenschaftlichen Gesellschaft* 5 (2015),

and literary journals range from functional advertising supplements, or *Intelligenzblätter*, to less functional lists that do not rely on readers being able to acquire the products in question. Readers of eighteenth- and nineteenth-century serial print are called upon to digest a range of actual and hypothetical lists, catalogs, and inventories. I want to suggest that these kinds of encounters encourage readers to imagine broader literary, commercial, and scholarly networks that they may or may not be directly part of,[8] and this encourages them to reflect upon how they themselves might create their own inventory-like constellations of products.

This essay examines several different repositories for print and paper, nodal points in the literary and commercial "networks for literary production, dissemination, and reception of the day,"[9] and *London und Paris*'s attempts to take inventory of these sites. I begin with Bertuch's own publishing house, the Landes-Industrie-Comptoir. The term "comptoir" (counter/chamber) that Bertuch used as an umbrella term for his business ventures straddles notions of a concrete physical location and a more diffuse business entity. I then examine articles on the Bibliothèque nationale in Paris, a London used-book store, and a London stationery store. In each case, these locations are profiled as sites where goods are displayed and where stock comes and goes. Moreover, the journal's correspondents linger with open-ended forms of social interaction enabled by these networked nodes, showing the involvement of a range of actors in making their own connections between various print and paper products. My broader argument is that *London und Paris* describes how these sites work by taking partial inventory of them, by performing a kind of cataloging that organizes—and reorganizes[10]—their contents and the kinds of social

---

special issue: *Bleiwüste und Bilderflut: Geschichten über das geisteswissenschaftliche Buch*, ed. Caspar Hirschi and Carlos Spoerhase, p.231–48 (233).

8. Daniel Purdy nicely shows that it is precisely the fact that "eighteenth-century German readers could engage in lengthy discussions and fantasies about products and styles that they could never own" that lends discussions about fashions and the latest trends such imaginary force. Daniel L. Purdy, *The Tyranny of elegance: consumer cosmopolitanism in the era of Goethe* (Baltimore, MD, 1998), p.xiv.

9. See the introduction to this volume.

10. As The Multigraph Collective notes, catalogs "manifest a tendency to unloose objects from their moorings in space and time." See The Multigraph Collective, *Interacting with print: elements of reading in the era of print saturation* (Chicago, IL, 2018), "Catalogs," p.70.

interactions that they promote. In representing and remediating a variety of repositories—scholarly and commercial archives, libraries and warehouses, museums and shops—Bertuch and Böttiger offer readers partial means to "disentangle" the medial landscape in which they find themselves.

This inventorying gesture depends on a double analogy that situates the periodical on the front lines of making partial sense of the world of print and paper. First, as a serial publication, *London und Paris* is akin in certain ways to these storage sites themselves: Like reading rooms or bookstores, periodicals accumulate and store mixed contents, situating individual items or clusters thereof in various modes of proximity.[11] The actuality of serial publications depends on being constantly refilled with new contents—as Bertuch and Böttiger write in their introduction, journals must "renew" and "refresh" themselves serially, "periodically," to keep up with the changing times[12]—but this also contributes to the "drowning" effect of the "flood of books."

Second, the periodical also mimics the print and paper tools used to organize these sites; this includes actual catalogs, lists of contents, as well as various other formats of visual and verbal description. The periodical comes into view as a medium that mirrors and remediates other print and paper products in its medial surroundings. Here it is no accident that these various media often partake in different forms of serial continuation. A good example of this is the catalogs for trade fairs and publishers, with seasonally recurring fairs and recently published titles necessitating new catalogs. (Böttiger even developed an original style of commentary centered on these publications.[13]) The partial or incomplete status of these types of guides, which only feature the most recent publications, is mitigated by the promise that more is

---

11. For work on the periodical as archive, see *Sprache und Literatur* 146 (2014), special issue: *Zeitschrift als Archiv*, ed. Susanne Düwell und Nicolas Pethes, and Gustav Frank, Madleen Podewski, and Stefan Scherer, "Kultur—Zeit—Schrift: Literatur- und Kulturzeitschriften als 'kleine Archive,'" *Internationales Archiv für Sozialgeschichte der deutschen Literatur* 34:2 (2009), p.1–45.

12. "A regularly recurring, *periodic* text renews itself with the renewing, flies with the flying genius of the time, and always offers fresh images, just as it itself is always fresh" ("Eine regelmäßig wiederkehrende periodische Schrift verjüngt sich mit dem verjüngenden, fliegt mit dem fliegenden Genius der Zeit, und liefert stets frische Gemälde, so wie sie selbst frisch ist"). Bertuch and Böttiger, "Plan und Ankündigung," p.7.

13. See Bernhard Fischer, "Poesie der Warenwelt: Karl August Böttigers Messberichte für Cottas *Allgemeine Zeitung*," in *Böttiger Lektüren: die Antike als Schlüssel zur Moderne*, ed. René Sternke (Stuttgart, 2012), p.55–74.

to come. In engaging in quasi-literary, quasi-journalistic, quasi-commercial acts of taking inventory, the editors and correspondents for *London und Paris* are concerned with depicting the cultural techniques that help to organize networks, but they also develop strategies of remediating these techniques, using the periodical to extend or modify various practices of organizing and cataloging.

London und Paris and the Landes-Industrie-Comptoir

Bertuch published *London und Paris* eight times a year from 1798 to 1815, with average runs of 1000–1200 issues. The journal expanded on the model and visual appearance of the *Journal des Luxus und der Moden* (or *Modejournal* for short), which Böttiger also edited in the 1790s, and the editors deemed *London und Paris* the *Modejournal*'s "foreign sister," intending to shift much of the material on England and France from the *Modejournal* into the new venture.[14] Johann Christian Hüttner and Théophile Frédéric Winckler were the journal's main correspondents in its early years, writing miscellaneous short articles about cultural, political, social, and economic life in the foreign capitals, and frequently employing the conceit of the travel guide, the *cicerone*.[15] They also regularly sent back caricatures and other visual images to Weimar, which were then reproduced, reprinted, and hand-illuminated there. Böttiger also served as the main commentator on the English caricatures, situating himself in the tradition of Lichtenberg's Hogarth commentaries.[16] The journal had some luck in starting just as Napoleon was coming to power, and it bore witness to the major political tensions of the day between England and France. *London und Paris* served as a model for other

14. Bertuch and Böttiger, "Plan und Ankündigung," p.9. "*London und Paris* ging aus dem 1786 gegründeten *Journal des Luxus und der Moden* hervor und war duch die farbige Brochur und das Druckbild auch äußerlich als dessen Pendent erkennbar." Werner Greiling, "Kultur aus den 'zwei Hauptquellen' Europas: Friedrich Justin Bertuchs Journal *London und Paris*," in *Europa in Weimar: Visionen eines Kontinents* (Göttingen, 2008), p.138–58 (140).
15. On Hüttner, see Catherine W. Proescholdt, "Johann Christian Hüttner (1766–1847): a link between Weimar and London," in *Goethe and the English-speaking world*, ed. Nicholas Boyle and John Guthrie (Rochester, NY, 2001), p.99–110.
16. See Christian Deuling, "Aesthetics and politics in the journal *London und Paris* (1798–1815)," in *(Re-)writing the radical: Enlightenment, revolution and cultural transfer in 1790s Germany, Britain and France*, ed. Maike Oergel (New York, 2012), p.102–18.

journals, including the *Französische* and *Englische Miszellen* (*French* and *English miscellanea*) founded by J. F. Cotta, which were consolidated into Cotta's influential *Morgenblatt für gebildete Stände* (*Morning paper for the educated classes*).[17] Like the *Modejournal*, *London und Paris* sought both to respond to an emerging desire to be part of the latest trends and to encourage and direct such a desire in the first place.

The title references two overarching commercial and cultural networks, and the editors describe the reach of these networks across Europe in striking imagery: "And all of this information about the world and the time [*all diese Welt- und Zeitkunde*], that pours out into so many larger and smaller canals, flows in fact from two main sources."[18] London and Paris are sources of commercial, political, and cultural innovation, and the journal links up German readers to them via "canals" through which information as well as concrete print and paper matter flow. Such models of flow and circulation were popular in imagining economic life and its various focal or gathering points.[19] Böttiger uses similar imagery in his commentaries on the Leipzig fair, describing how, every half year, Leipzig becomes a center of world trade (*Mittelpunkt des Welthandels*), with crowds of people and products coursing in and out of the city.[20] This is a model of interconnected centers of trade and exchange that wax and wane across time and that reach out to other locations around Europe, a model that imagines the print landscape through intersecting images of the body, the city, and networks of communication.[21] Canalization then serves

17. On the *French* and *English miscellanea* see, respectively, Karin Baumgartner, "Constructing Paris: flânerie, female spectatorship, and the discourses of fashion in *Französische Miscellen* (1803)," *Monatshefte* 100:3 (2008), p.351–68; and Birgit Tautz, *Translating the world: toward a new history of German literature* (University Park, PA, 2018), p.158–61.
18. "Und alle diese Welt- und Zeitkunde, die sich in so viele äußere und kleinere Canäle ergießt, strömt eigentlich von zwey Hauptquellen." Bertuch and Böttiger, "Plan und Ankündigung," p.3.
19. See Joseph Vogl, *Kalkül und Leidenschaft: Poetik des ökonomischen Menschen* (Zürich, 2002), p.223–25.
20. "So ist ein groser Theil von Europa bis an die Grenzen Asiens in den lezten Wintermonaten voll Treiben und Bewegung, um sich auf einem gemeinschaftlichen Sammelplaz, in einer kleinen Mittelstadt des nördlichen Deutschlands an der kleinen Pleiße, zu einem Mittelpunkt des Welthandels zu vereinigen." *Allgemeine Zeitung* 178 (June 27, 1802), p.710.
21. On the intersection of these three metaphors in characterizing the nineteenth-century periodical landscape, see Linda K. Hughes, "*Sideways!* Navigating the material(ity) of print culture," *Victorian periodicals review* 47:1 (2014), p.1–30. See

as a metaphor for managing the flood of information and printed matter (and for avoiding suffocation by drowning), and thus also for activities of serial publications such as *London und Paris*.[22]

One way to regulate information is to organize it into some kind of list, and, like many journals of the time, *London und Paris* contained various partial lists, catalogs, and registers, ranging from inventories of London silver stores or accounts of Italian artworks brought back to Paris to lists of scholars traveling with Napoleon in North Africa or alphabetic catalogs of journals published in Paris between 1797 and 1798.[23] These lists were usually less directly functional than the *Intelligenzblätter*, or advertising supplements, commonly found in the *Modejournal*. These supplements have a relatively straightforward use-value, with specific products being listed along with addresses where readers could obtain them (usually via the name of the publisher, producer, or seller).[24] Review journals performed a similar indexical function, with short reviews of current books accompanied by bibliographical information.[25]

Böttiger was a master of riffing on less immediately functional lists with his witty surveys of book and trade fairs.[26] His articles on the Leipzig fairs for other newspapers started out as commentaries on the book or fair catalog (*Bücherverzeichnis, MeßCatalog*), what he tongue-in-cheek calls the "book of books" (*Buch der Bücher*).[27] This is a playful

also Tautz, *Translating the world*, on the network as a key concept for theorizing the eighteenth- and nineteenth-century city.

22. See Krajewski, *Paper machines*, p.37.

23. On the mediality and aesthetics of the list, see Liam Cole Young, *List cultures: knowledge and poetics from Mesopotamia to BuzzFeed* (Amsterdam, 2017); and Matt Erlin, "Sammlung, Inventar, Archiv: Epistemologien der Liste im Roman des 19. Jahrhunderts," in *Archivfiktionen: Verfahren des Archivierens in Literatur und Kultur des langen 19. Jahrhunderts*, ed. Daniela Gretz and Nicolas Pethes (Freiburg, 2016), p.363–84.

24. See Holger Böning, "Das Intelligenzblatt—eine literarisch-publizistische Gattung des 18. Jahrhunderts," *Internationales Archiv für Sozialgeschichte der deutschen Literatur* 19:1 (2009), p.22–32.

25. On the Enlightenment index and the propensity of texts to constantly point beyond themselves to other texts, see Brad Pasanek and Chad Wellmon, "The Enlightenment index," *The Eighteenth century: theory and interpretation* 56:3 (2015), p.359–82.

26. See Fischer, "Poesie der Warenwelt." See also Ernst Friedrich Sondermann, *Karl August Böttiger, literarischer Journalist der Goethezeit in Weimar* (Bonn, 1983), p.152–76.

27. Karl August Böttiger, "Der Leipziger MeßCatalog," *Neuste WeltKunde* 2:122 (May 2, 1798), p.485.

mode not immediately useful in terms of acquiring specific products, though Böttiger did take specific catalogs as points of departure. At times bordering on annotated advertisements or reviews, such articles include musings on the state of publishing and on various trades and new fashions and technologies more generally, and rely on the conceit of providing a survey or overview (*Übersicht*) of various branches of industry broadly conceived.[28] This informative, entertaining mode catalyzes aesthetic enjoyment in the almost sublime ebb and flow of commerce, in being both overwhelmed by and gaining control over an inundation of goods. This style of article then dovetails with quasi-ethnographic travel writing that comments on stores and shop displays, a topic that would become increasingly popular in literary and fashion journals.

From the editorial perspective, such lists straddle the disinterested description of various markets and commercial networks and the self-interested promotion of one's own products. Cataloging the world of print can be both a valuable public service and a vehicle for casting one's own role therein in a positive light, and Bertuch and Böttiger did not perceive this mixture of disinterestedness and self-interest as any kind of serious contradiction.[29] Moreover, this intersection of fashion journalism, travel writing, and literary critique profits from putting foreignness on display—in the case of the world of print and paper, comparing local and foreign reading and publishing practices and cultivating wonder, awe, and at times disquiet in the "flood of books"—but also from making the foreign familiar, understandable, accessible in both imaginary and actual senses.[30]

London und Paris was published as part of Bertuch's larger umbrella business and publishing house founded in 1791, the Landes-In-dustrie-Comptoir. The semantics of the "Comptoir," "Kontor," or "counter" are revealing in terms of Bertuch's broader interest in shops as physical but also metaphorical locations in commercial and literary networks. The word's original meanings range from a counting table or enclosed box to a writing room where papers and money were

---

28. See Fischer, "Poesie der Warenwelt," p.58.
29. "Bertuch's philosophy of culture [...] relies for justification on a combination of the public good and the individual good." Karin Wurst, *Fabricating pleasure: fashion, entertainment, and cultural consumption in Germany, 1780–1830* (Detroit, MI, 2005), p.131.
30. Or what Tautz in a related context calls "translating the world" for German readers. *Translating the world*, p.158.

stored, and the term came to be a common designation for publishing houses in Bertuch's day.[31] The Landes-Industrie-Comptoir was to function as a kind of overarching private institution (or corporation, in today's parlance) that bundled multiple endeavors, including supporting regional artisans and small manufacturers through loans and credit and promoting economic development and trade in specific principalities (the *Land* in *Landes-Industrie*). In Bertuch's case, this included a paper factory, a paper flower factory, a drawing school, a printing shop, as well as the selling of physical tools, ceramics and baskets, fabrics, chocolate, and wine.[32]

Over the course of his life, though, the Comptoir came to function more as a conventional publishing house. The Comptoir was conceived of as an abstract commercial entity, synonymous with *Handlung*, *Handel*, or *Institut*, but it was also a physical location. As Bertuch devised it, the bundling of different artisanal projects provided a place for various artisans to display their products, a site that "collects their work or patterns in a common magazine [*gemeinschaftliches Magazin*], where the rich enthusiast and buyer can survey with a single glance [*mit einem Blicke überschauen*] and pick something out."[33] An important part of this understanding of the publishing house was thus that it include an open, public shop.[34] Bertuch's mercantile worldview thus involves a keen sense of physical locations that bring together heterogeneous products, as well as the imperative that customers are provided tools for gaining an overview thereof. An underlying logic

31. "Das Contōr, des -es, *plur.* die -e, gleichfalls aus dem Italiän. *Contoro*, bey den Kaufleuten, die Schreibstube. In Ostindien führen auch die Niederlagen und Handlungshäuser der Europäer in fremden Gebiethe diesen Nahmen. Nach dem Franz. *Comptoir*, lautet dieses Wort auch zuweilen im Deutschen Comptor oder Comtor." Johann Christian Adelung, "Das Contor," in *Grammatisch-kritisches Wörterbuch der Hochdeutschen Mundart*, vol.1 (Leipzig, n.n., 1793), p.1348.
32. Gerhard R. Kaiser, "Friedrich Justin Bertuch: Versuch eines Porträts," in *Friedrich Justin Bertuch (1747–1822): Verleger, Schriftsteller und Unternehmer im klassischen Weimar*, ed. Gerhard R. Kaiser and Siegfried Seifert (Tübingen, 2000), p.15–39 (21).
33. F. J. Bertuch, "Über die Wichtigkeit der Landes-Industrie-Institute für Teutschland," *Journal des Luxus und der Moden* (August 1793), p.407–17; (September 1793), p.458.
34. "Auch der tragende Begriff *Comptoir* ging über die kaufmännische Praxis im Warenhandel großen Stils hinaus, wenngleich dies die vorherrschende Wortbedeutung war." Katharina Middell, *"Die Bertuchs müssen doch in dieser Welt überall Glück haben": der Verleger Friedrich Justin Bertuch und sein Landes-Industrie-Comptoir um 1800* (Leipzig, 2002), p.91.

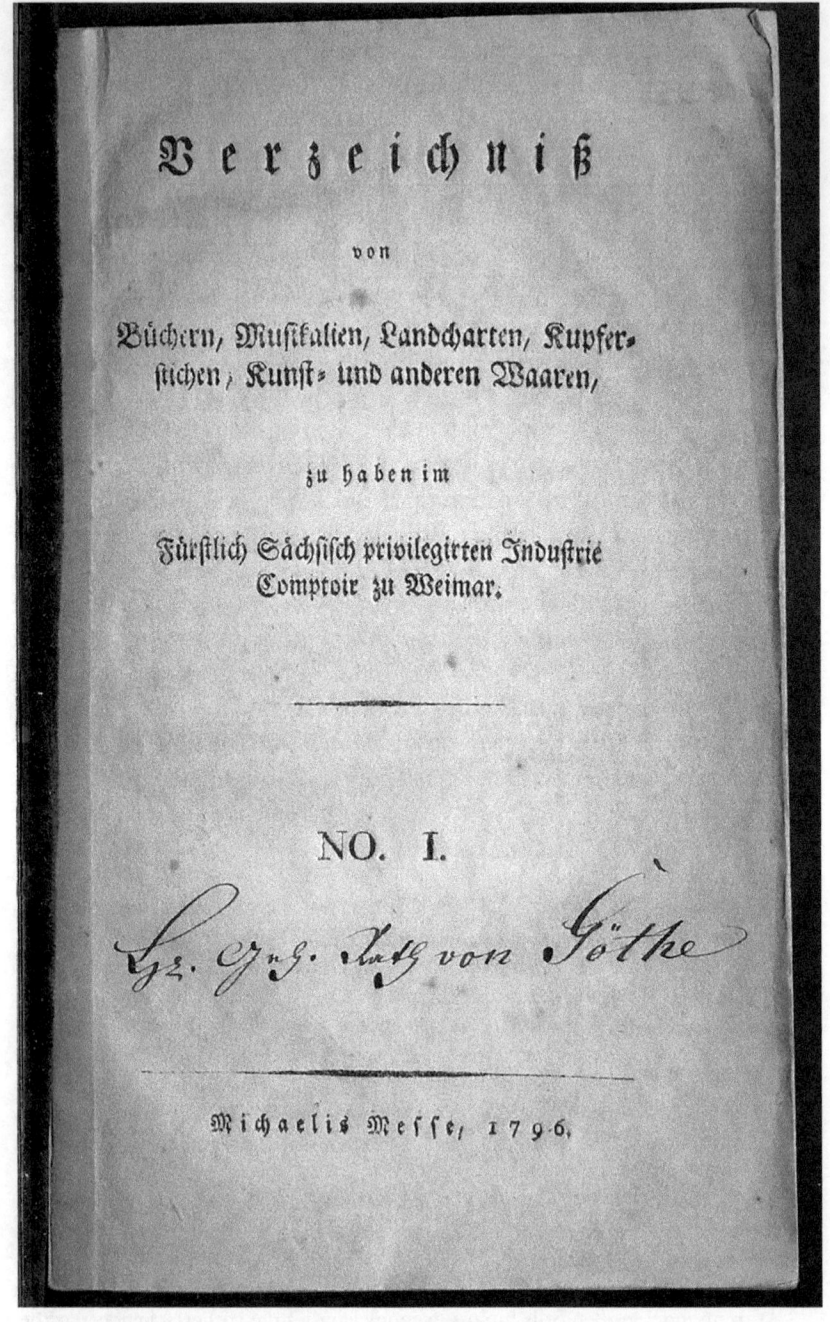

Figure 16: Catalogue of products produced and/or sold by the
Landes-Industrie-Comptoir (1796). Goethe's personal copy. Klassik
Stiftung Weimar.

of publicizing the Comptoir's products cuts across the physical shop and print objects such as journals, books, or catalogs, which all serve to list, preview, organize, and display mixed contents (see Figure 16).

The image shows the cover page of a catalog of the products of the Comptoir—Goethe's own personal copy, in fact—almost certainly produced for the fall Leipzig trade fair, or *Michaelismesse* (noted as its publication date at the bottom). As a tool for this trade fair, it can be considered something of a subcatalog of the larger *Meßcatalog* (Böttiger's "Book of books"), listing the contents of one specific publishing house represented there (one might also assume that an employee of the Comptoir would have had some of these products listed here for sale at the fair). Print and paper tools facilitate a virtual overview that complements physical displays.

The networked library

The second issue of *London und Paris* contains an article entitled "*Thé literaire* with Citizen Millin in the National Library."[35] Louis-Aubin Millin was a curator and professor of antiquities in the French Bibliothèque nationale, and a subsequent article details lectures he gave there.[36] The journal's Paris correspondent T. F. Winckler clearly shows that he is tapping into French scholarly circles, as was Böttiger himself, with Böttiger and Millin maintaining an avid correspondence and Böttiger contributing to Millin's influential journal, the *Magasin encyclopédique* (*Encyclopedic magazine*).[37] Millin also had ties to other well-known German scholars abroad: As noted in the article, visitors to his mixed-gender salon include the von Humboldt brothers, and Karl Friedrich Reinhard and his wife Christine Reimarus, among others. A scholarly (and diplomatic) network comes loosely into view, as does a specific site for accessing that network, the National Library, an important, new, or rather refounded, institution of postrevolutionary France. Subsequent issues of *London und Paris* continue these

35. "Thé literaire beym Bürger Millin in der Nationalbibliothek," *London und Paris* 1:2 (1798), p.184–87.

36. See "Unwissenheit und Stolz der Pariser Künstler: Millins Vorlesungen: das Cabinet der Antiken. Mionets Münzpasten," *London und Paris* 1:3 (1798), p.260–65.

37. See Julia Schmidt-Funke, *Karl August Böttiger (1760–1835): Weltmann und Gelehrter* (Heidelberg, 2006), p.69–72; *Aubin-Louis Millin et l'Allemagne: le Magasin encyclopédique—les lettres à Karl August Böttiger*, ed. Geneviève Espagne and Bénédicte Savoy (Hildesheim, 2005).

discussions of the library, including how it adds ephemera such as newspapers and pamphlets to its holdings, ephemera that *London und Paris* sometimes even reprints and annotates.[38] The National Library is an archive but also a sociable "gathering spot" (*Versammlungsplatz*),[39] and Winckler is both an observer and a participant.

In the process, the article presents a rather standard account of "free sociability" and "urban freedom" (*urbane Freyheit*).[40] The evening salon combines scholarly exchange and musical and literary entertainment, and the article notes that it is free of politics, though its title does refer to the host as "citizen Millin" (*Bürger Millin*), not mentioning his full name, Louis-Aubin Millin de Grandmaison. The article likewise differentiates between two different "salons."[41] The one is dedicated to "literature, scholarship, and friendly discussions,"[42] and is centered around a large table, on which various journals and books and illustrations are gathered for common perusal. The second, larger salon occurs in Millin's own library, where those less concerned with scholarship gather, and where musical instruments for impromptu concerts are stored. I would like to extract one passage from this account of the tea gathering, namely a list presented in a longer footnote (see Figure 17) of the different journals on display there, "in the service of enthusiasts to view and page through."[43]

> I will just name several that come to mind: *domestic French journals*: Magazin encyclopédique. (Because he is the editor, I of course mention it first.) Decade philosophique, Mercure français, Iournal des Mines, Annales de Chymie, Recueil periodique de la Soc. De medicine, Iournal des Muses, Diners du Vaudeville, Iournal typographique et bibliographique by Roux. Le Nouvelliste littéraire des sciences et des Arts by Morin, feuille du Cultivateur; *foreign French* [journals]: Iournal littéraire de Lausanne, Le Nord littéraire by Olivarius; *German journals*: der Deutsche Merkur, Wieland's attisches Museum, Böttiger's Vasengemälde, Jenaer Allg. Litt. Zeit., Zach's Ephemeriden, Meusel's Museum für Künstler und Kunstliebhaber,

38. See Sean Franzel, *"Les Cris de Paris*: Lebendigkeit, Neuigkeit und Intermedi-alität in der urbanen Tableauliteratur um 1800," in *Belebungskünste: Praktiken lebendiger Darstellung in Literatur, Kunst und Wissenschaft um 1800*, ed. Nicola Gess, Agnes Hoffmann, and Annette Klappert (Paderborn, 2018), p.83–103.
39. "Thé literaire," p.187.
40. "Thé literaire," p.187.
41. "Thé literaire," p.185.
42. "Thé literaire," p.185.
43. "Thé literaire," p.186.

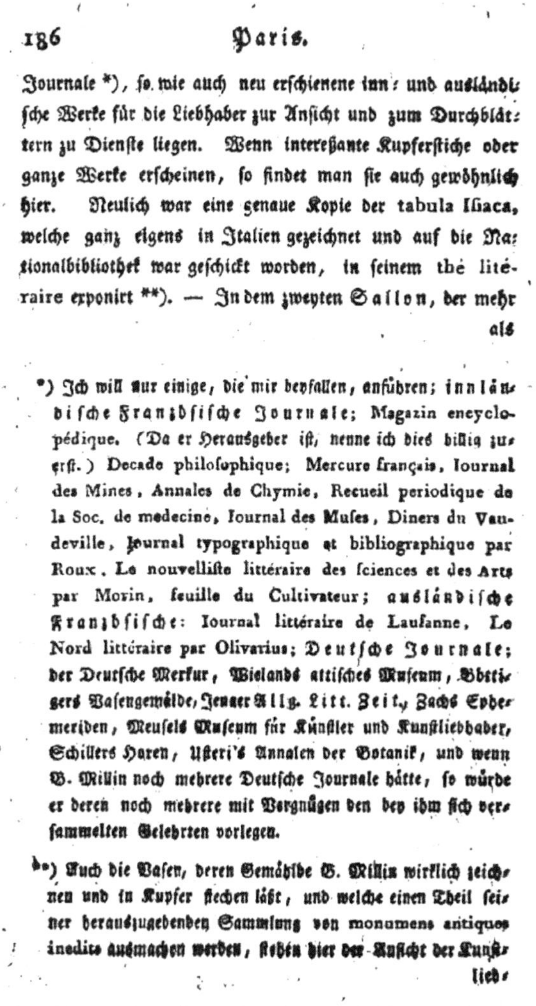

186 **Paris.**

Journale *), fo. wie auch neu erschienene inn= und ausländi-
sche Werke für die Liebhaber zur Ansicht und zum Durchblät-
tern zu Dienste liegen. Wenn interessante Kupferstiche oder
ganze Werke erscheinen, so findet man sie auch gewöhnlich
hier. Neulich war eine genaue Kopie der tabula Iliaca,
welche ganz eigens in Italien gezeichnet und auf die Nationalbibliothek war geschickt worden, in seinem thé lité-
raire exponirt **). — In dem zweyten Sallon, der mehr
als

*) Ich will nur einige, die mir beyfallen, anführen; inn län-
    dische Französische Journale; Magazin encyclo-
    pédique. (Da er Herausgeber ist, nenne ich dies billig zu-
    erst.) Decade philosophique; Mercure français, Iournal
    des Mines, Annales de Chymie, Recueil periodique de
    la Soc. de medecine, Iournal des Muses, Diners du Van-
    deville, Journal typographique et bibliographique par
    Roux. Le nouvelliste littéraire des sciences et des Arts
    par Morin, feuille du Cultivateur; ausländische
    Französische: Iournal littéraire de Lausanne, Le
    Nord littéraire par Olivarius; Deutsche Journale;
    der Deutsche Merkur, Wielands attisches Museum, Böttt-
    gers Vasengemälde, Jenaer Allg. Litt. Zeit., Bachs Epher-
    meriden, Meusels Museum für Künstler und Kunstliebhaber,
    Schillers Horen, Usteri's Annalen der Botanik, und wenn
    B. Millin noch mehrere Deutsche Journale hätte, so würde
    er deren noch mehrere mit Vergnügen den bey ihm sich ver-
    sammelten Gelehrten vorlegen.

**) Auch die Vasen, deren Gemählde B. Millin wirklich zeich-
    nen und in Kupfer stechen läßt, und welche einen Theil sei-
    ner herauszugebenden Sammlung von monumens antiques
    inedits ausmachen werden, stehen hier der Ausicht der Kunst-
    lieb-

Figure 17: Excerpt from T. F. Winckler, "Thé literaire beym Bürger
Millin in der Nationalbibliothek," *London und Paris* 1:2 (1798),
184–87 (186).

Schiller's Horen, Usteri's Annalen der Botanik, and if citizen Millin
had more German journals, he would display more of them with
pleasure for the scholars gathered there.[44]

44. "Thé literaire," p.186.

In effect, the article takes inventory of the reading room, noting specific periodicals available there. The salon is a *Versammlungsplatz* (gathering spot) in a dual sense: for people and print products. This supplemental collection of current journals adjacent to the library proper produces a sense of distinct yet potentially interrelated archives that differ in scope, use, and lasting relevance. The journals mentioned also index transnational scholarly networks that extend to Weimar, Jena, Gotha, and Zurich and to other French-speaking centers of scholarship, as well as the ongoing process of sharing new findings, which is recreated in person in the salon. The German periodical landscape in particular is cast in a positive light. Some of these journals are current, others less so—Schiller's *Horen*, for example, was no longer published in 1798—and most are scholarly/scientific in focus. But a closer look at the contents of this list reveals that it is not entirely disinterested, for it notes several works published by Bertuch's Comptoir, including the *Allgemeine Litteratur-Zeitung* (*General literature magazine*), Zach's *Geographische Ephemeriden* (*Geographical ephemerides*), and Böttiger's *Griechische Vasengemälde* (*Greek vase painting*). Millin's work is promoted, but also that of Bertuch's circle. After all, Böttiger used his frequent contributions to the *Magasin encyclopédique* as something of a "mouthpiece for the propagation of the quality of German culture" in France.[45] What at first glance appears to be a modest form of quasi-ethnographic travel literature comes into view as (self-)advertisement.

This article also seems to advertise the salon as an institution: Should German editors send Millin their periodicals? Should people with means and connections traveling to Paris seek it out? Additionally, in presenting himself as someone with entrée to this network, Winckler promises future reports of its activities in subsequent issues of *London und Paris*.[46] To the extent that the article promises future reports on this salon, it instigates mutually reinforcing patterns of seriality, with future events at the library unfolding in connection with ongoing reports about them, and with the national library and auxiliary

---

45. Sondermann, *Karl August Böttiger*, p.94 and 97.
46. It is striking that Böttiger never traveled to London or Paris and never met Millin in person, even though he became an expert in writing overviews of the literary and scholarly output of France and England. Böttiger thus would seem to represent a successful type of scholarly-journalistic writing akin to a certain type of antiquarianism that can thrive without needing to visit the geographical home of a given culture in person.

archive of the salon also being continuously augmented with new materials. This account of patterns of communication and readership in the salon gives a strong sense of the varied modes through which information is channeled, not merely monodirectionally from Paris back to Germany or out to the French provinces, but in a multidirectional flow. Moreover, the cataloging gesture at work in describing Millin's personal collection certainly diverges from any catalog of the national library, which presumably preserves materials for longer spans of time. This protocatalog functions somewhere in between listing current items for sale (as with the indirect advertisement of Bertuch's products) and archiving items worthy of preservation such as Schiller's *Horen.*

Cataloging the book trade

We encounter a different sort of archival space in the London section of two 1799 issues of the journal, where the famous London bookstore and circulating library of James Lackington are described across several articles and two issues. *London und Paris* was so taken with Lackington's "Temple of the muses" that it reproduced images of it outside and inside, and Bertuch wrote a supplementary article on it, drawing on Lackington's memoirs.[47] The book trade was certainly a topic close to Bertuch's heart, and was in line with the intermittent contributions that he made to the *Journal des Luxus und der Moden* (he rarely contributed to *London und Paris*). The title of the London correspondent J. C. Hüttner's opening article is typical for the journal in how it lists off the topics that will be covered: "English book trade. Comparison with the German trade. Second-hand books. Lackington's Temple of the muses. Trade in completing editions."[48] The comparison of English and German trades opens with an interesting finding: "[O]ne only needs to read the yearly catalogs of new English writings, they are not a sixteenth of the books announced by the Leipzig book fair catalog."[49] Commonly mentioned in German

47. Lackington's memoirs serve as a key source for William St. Clair's history of reading in Britain around 1800. See William St. Clair, *The Reading nation in the Romantic period* (Cambridge, 2004).
48. C. Hüttner, "Englischer Buchhandel. Vergleichung mit dem deutschen. Second-hand books. Lackington's Musentempel. Completierhandel," *London und Paris* 4:7 (1799), p.237–45.
49. "Man lese nur die jährlichen Verzeichnisse der neuen englischen Schriften; sie betragen nicht ein Sechzehnttheil der Bücher wovon Weidmann's Erben in

reports about book fairs, this discrepancy was a minor yet recurrent source of national pride in the face of otherwise dominant British commercial prowess.

Hüttner quickly turns to superlatives in describing Lackington's size and scope: "Everything brought to paper via letters, via stereotypes, via the etching needle, via the graver, old and new, good and bad, expensive or cheap, Lackington's is the most capacious warehouse for it in London."[50] And in an interesting connection to the Paris article quoted above, Hüttner notes that Lackington's reminds the foreign visitor of the "magnificent Bibliothèque du roi or National Library in Paris."[51] However, Lackington's is quite disorganized. Because the store is so popular, its stock constantly shifts, and visitors are in need of more orientation assistance. Lackington does print catalogs twice a year, but they are difficult to decipher if one is not an expert, and even then they are undependable:[52] "[T]here is no chance of finding the excellent, exact, and complete catalogs that our German booksellers carry of their entire stock."[53] This treatment of the English book trade builds on continental tropes about English cultural and scholarly life in circulation at the time.[54] At the same time, though, this lack of organization gives a certain amount of agency back to the reader/customer, who is invited to navigate heterogeneous contents as she chooses.

Bertuch's supplemental article then expands on Hüttner's comparison, contrasting the more diffuse English book trade to the German, which is centered around yearly book fairs. The book fair system leads to a well-organized process of cataloging goods, "the fair catalogs, the exchange and good trade, the correct catalogs of

---

Leipzig und so regelmäßig die Titel im Leizpger Meßkatalog bekannt machen." "Englischer Buchhandel," p.237.

50. "Alles was durch Lettern, durch Stereotypen, durch die Radiernadel, durch den Grabstichel, vorlängst oder neuerlich, gut oder schlecht, theuer oder wohlfeil, zu Papier gebracht worden ist, dafür ist Lackington's Musentempel das weitläufigste Waarenhaus in London." "Englischer Buchhandel," p.241.
51. "Englischer Buchhandel," p.240.
52. "Englischer Buchhandel," p.239–40.
53. "Englischer Buchhandel," p.241.
54. It was common, for example, to lament the British Museum's disorganized appearance "as an immense magazine, in which things have been thrown at random, rather than a scientific collection, destined to instruct and honour a great nation." Barthélemy Faujas de Saint-Fond, *Travels in England, Scotland and the Hebrides*, vol.1 (London, Ridgway, 1799), p.89. Thanks to Noah Heringman for this reference.

products and publishing houses that renew themselves every half year."[55] In German-speaking lands there are many more "aids and tools for gaining a quick overview of the market" (*zur schnellen Übersicht des Marktes*).[56] Bertuch goes on to explain how the English trade is based around individual shops, having developed from stable shops being established by formerly itinerant tradesmen. As he explains, this is how the term "stationery" originated: A stationer is a book and paper seller who has become stationary. English booksellers are less well cataloged, less well networked, if you will, because they do not partake of the travel and exchange and the concomitant need for synthetic inventories characteristic of the German fairs.

That said, Bertuch does remark that he has the latest "London catalog of books" lying in front of him as he writes: It goes "back to September 1799, and costs 4 shillings at [the London publisher] Bent."[57] This catalog is also a kind of serial akin to the half-yearly fair catalogs but much less complete because, as Bertuch explains, much of the English nobility suspiciously looks down on "journalistic scribbling [*Schriftstellerey*]" for the print marketplace, and so their publications are not listed. In particular, the gentleman scholars of the landed gentry prefer to circulate their findings in small circles and not publicize them in the broader marketplace: "[I]t would be a great benefit, especially for the higher sciences, with which the majority of these articles deal, if someone were to make a separate catalog of these cabinet editions [*Cabinetausgaben*]."[58] "Cabinet editions"[59] are semi-private, smaller editions meant for limited circulation; the term introduces an additional archival space to our growing inventory of storage sites,[60] though, as aristocratic private chambers, the "cabinet"

55. "die Meßverzeichnisse, der Tausch- und Sortimentshandel, die richtigen, mit dem Presse versehenen Sortiments- und Verlagsverzeichnisse, die sich halbjährlich erneuern." Friedrich Justin Bertuch, "Zusatz des Herausgebers," *London und Paris* 4:7 (1799), p.242–45 (243).
56. Bertuch, "Zusatz des Herausgebers," p.243.
57. Bertuch, "Zusatz des Herausgebers," p.243.
58. Bertuch, "Zusatz des Herausgebers," p.244.
59. "Of such value, beauty, or size, as to be fitted for a private chamber, or kept in a cabinet. Sometimes more or less technical, as in *cabinet edition*, one smaller and less costly than a library edition, but tastefully rather than cheaply got up." "Cabinet, n.," in *OED online*, http://www.oed.com/view/Entry/25753?redirected-From=cabinet+edition& (last accessed June 27, 2023).
60. On the interest in book cabinets in the *Journal des Luxus und der Moden*, see Wurst, *Fabricating pleasure*, p.164.

is less connected to public, middle-class industry than the *comptoir.*
Bertuch continues:

> To give a very recent example of this, an Englishman, honorable in
> both character and experiences, who for many years now has made
> his house in Weimar a temple of hospitality [*Tempel der Gastfreund-*
> *schaft*], Charles Gore, Esq. has recently had printed a treatise in
> London relevant for the study of shipbuilding: *Result of two series of*
> *experiments towards ascertaining the respective velocity of floating bodies.* 19
> pages in quarto with two engraved plates.[61]

In a peculiar word choice, Bertuch presents a second, Weimar temple
to rival Lackington's "Temple of the muses." Gore's house, though,
fitting with his social class as a gentleman scholar and artist with
access to the Weimar elite,[62] is a private domicile, not a public shop.
Here Bertuch maps a further site of sociable exchange not entirely
unlike Millin's Parisian salon. However, this seeming aside is also
an additional instance of a protocatalog, with Bertuch rising to the
challenge that he himself gave his readers in providing an organized
list of individual, small-run (vanity?) publications of the likes of
Gore's, mimicking, perhaps, the very catalog he has on his desk as he
writes. The bibliographical information provided by Bertuch—which
resembles the information given by a review article or an advertising
supplement—is a protocatalog, a prolegomenon to a future catalog,
a catalog of one item (or rather of three, because his "Editorial
supplement" likewise mentions Bent's catalog and cites Lackington's
memoir), and it is a catalog that calls out for its own serial continuation. At least at this initial stage, the prospect of serial continuation
aligns the catalog with the "small," the partial, the incomplete, rather
than the large, systematic, and self-enclosed.[63]

   Moreover, we see once more how this impulse to catalog also
serves as an indirect form of self-advertisement, with Bertuch putting
his friendship with Gore on display and casting the social scene in
Weimar in a positive light. Gore is an English gentleman scholar, but,

61. Bertuch, "Zusatz des Herausgebers," p.244.
62. He was part of the circle of Duchess Anna Amalia in Weimar, and Goethe even
    drafted a brief biography of him.
63. On the periodical as "small archive," see Frank, Podewski, and Scherer,
    "Kultur—Zeit—Schrift." Pasanek and Wellmon likewise contrast small and
    large indexes, associating the latter with the self-enclosed systematic book ("The
    Enlightenment index," p.362).

perhaps through his connection to Weimar and its mixed social scene, has stepped out of the "cabinet" into more public view, representing a harmonious middle ground between England and German-speaking lands. Bertuch and his correspondent once more open up a tiny window into a social and publication context; they partially map it, suggest that more might be on its way, and invite readers to explore this context in an open-ended manner.

Curiously, the two images depicting the exterior and interior of Lackington's were printed in the issue after the one that contains Hüttner's and Bertuch's articles. A loose serial order of these articles and images comes into view, though it is hard to tell whether the images' placement in the following issue was merely an accident of production; at the very least, these later pieces encourage readers to go back to previous issues. Again, it was common practice for the journal's editors to have French and English images re-etched and printed anew in Weimar (see Figures 18, 19, and 20).[64] Not dissimilar to the account of the Bibliothèque nationale above, the interior view of Lackington's depicts multiple mixed-gender scenes of social interaction playing out across multiple rooms, scenes that are connected to, adjacent to, or inside archives of print and paper. The considerable number of female customers stands out in both original and reproduction, though in each individual scene across both images the figures providing them guidance or orientation are exclusively male. The packages and piles of books in the front left corner are also noteworthy; the German copy has included additional packages, an employee unwrapping them from their packaging, and what appears to be an address label on one of the packages, presenting a compelling visual metaphor of the constantly replenishing stock of this bookseller and the need to put it into some kind of provisional order. Again, the reader gets a sense of multiple adjacent spaces, and of scenes of visitors or customers exploring the repository, looking for different items, without any necessary order of importance imposed on the different scenes. The figure

---

64. The English image appears to have been quite popular, and it was reproduced multiple times over the course of the early and mid-nineteenth century. I was not able to find a copy earlier than 1809, though there obviously must have been an earlier image that was sent back to Weimar in the late 1790s. This image is taken from the April 1809 issue of Rudolph Ackermann's *Repository of arts, literature, commerce, manufactures, fashions, and politics* (London, 1809–1829), a popular periodical not dissimilar in scope and structure to *London und Paris*.

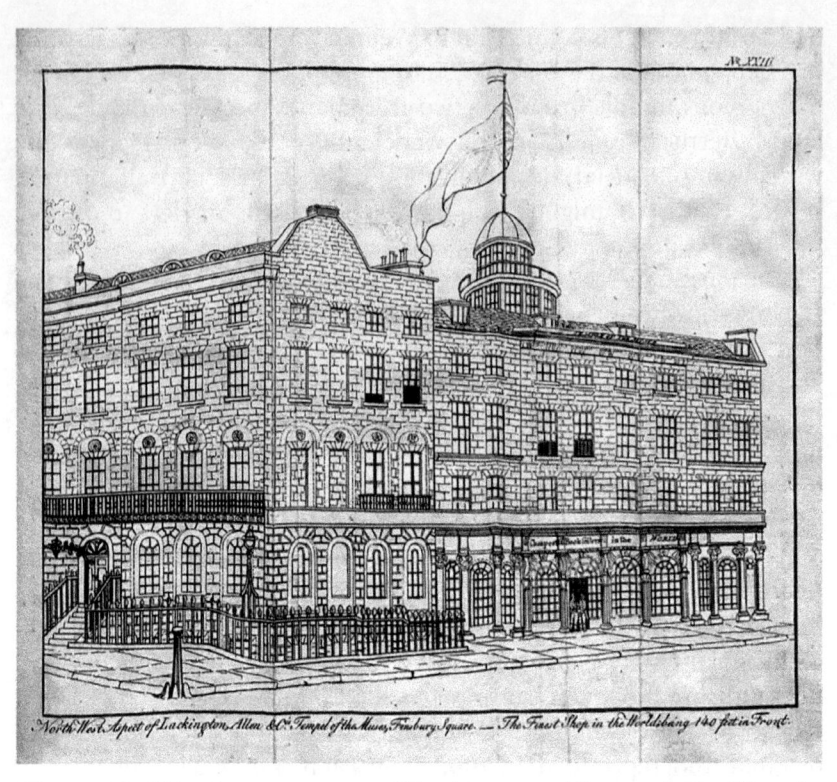

Figure 18: "North-west aspect of Lackington, Allen and Co. Temple
of the muses, Finsbury Square, The finest shop in the world,
being 140 feet in front," from *London und Paris* 4:8 (1799), no.23.
Forschungsbibliothek Gotha.

looking down from the dome might conventionally be associated
with someone taking a position of sovereign overview, but, in these
images, the man with the hat seems to differ little from the other
customers. At most, he observes the diffuse attempts to look around
the shop for print and paper products that we ourselves observe,
gazing down, perhaps, at the man unwrapping the newly arrived
shipment.

We can find further traces of an inventorying impulse, a
Wille zum Inventar, if you will, in several additions in the German
reproduction, for all of the signage present in the German image is
completely missing in the original (see Figures 21 and 22—i.e., details
of Figure 19). The framing decorative draping in the original serves
as a sign in the German copy, helping to gloss the different elements

Figure 19: "Temple of the muses," from *London und Paris* 4:8 (1799), no.24. Forschungsbibliothek Gotha.

of the store—the "lounging room,"[65] "office for binding," as well as sections for "foreing" and "ordre" (apparently the signage was added by artists not fully familiar with current English spelling). These signs also signal the contents of the drawers: "Maps," "Prints," "Plans, Views, &c.," arguably even creating the impression of a printed list with these terms positioned one on top of the other. Though it was not necessarily uncommon for such reproductions to add orienting guides absent in the original, it does stand out how much these additions

65. In the two-page gloss of the image presented as "the visual commentary to the words of our correspondent in the previous issue of this journal," the lounging room is described thus: "Lounging-room heißt ein Zimmer für Faullenzer, die hier plaudern und ihre Gemächlichkeit pflegen wollen." *London und Paris* 4:8 (1799), p.346.

Figure 20: "Temple of the muses" (English original), from
R. Ackermann's *Repository of arts, literature, commerce, manufactures,
fashions, and politics* (1809).

Figure 21: Detail of shelving labels from "Temple of the muses,"
from *London und Paris* 4:8 (1799), no.24. Forschungsbibliothek Gotha.

Figure 22: Detail of drawer labels from "Temple of the muses," from
London und Paris 4:8 (1799), no.24. Forschungsbibliothek Gotha.

capture the inventorying impulse of Bertuch, Böttiger, and their correspondents. This image tracks multidirectional "canalizations," both of print and paper products and of the attention and interests of human actors. Ultimately, journals as inventory spaces condense the tasks of their texts and images, which were to capture and replicate multiple (and multidirectional) layers of material and human action. With this mode of archiving, journals are far more complex than book and print catalogs.

"View of the store of a London stationer"

Bertuch's keen interest in the literary market clearly extends to paper, including the unprinted variety. One of the most successful branches of the Landes-Industrie-Comptoir was a paper flower factory, his journals frequently commented on decorative wallpaper, and he avidly followed developments in paper-making technology, including initial steps to make plant-based paper viable on a large scale. This preoccupation with paper, both self-interested and philanthropic, is reflected in a four-part series of articles about a London stationery shop.

In the first article—entitled "View of the store of a London stationer [*Beschauung des Gewölbes eines Londner Stationar*]. Cordovan. Different sorts and names of the cardboard, cards, parchment, and drawing paper"—the London correspondent Hüttner begins with a problem of travel literature more generally: How to describe the contents of a foreign lifeworld in such a way that communicates the integrated *use* of objects and tools rather than their mere *existence*— these objects' *Zuhandenheit* rather than *Vorhandenheit*? In this case, the correspondent wants to depict the advanced state of English domestic affairs (*Häuslichkeit*) affected by the goods sold by the stationer, which, as he notes, go far beyond basic paper supplies, with stationers playing a role in almost all aspects of the book trade, including binding, operating as lending libraries, and selling writing and office materials.[66] As Hüttner notes, these stationery shops were key gathering spots in literary and commercial networks,[67] and he

66. C. Hüttner, "Beschauung des Gewölbes eines Londner Stationar. Cordovan. Verschiedene Arten und Benennung der Pappen, Karten, des Pergaments, des Zeichenpapiers," *London und Paris* 6:6 (1800), p.110–21.
67. "Sie beschäftigen sich alle mehr oder weniger mit dem Buchhandel, mit Buchdrucken, Buchbinden, mit Lesebibliotheken und mit dem Absatze der

describes their frequently luxurious interiors.[68] However, he suggests that it is difficult to imagine the functionality of a large number of seemingly trivial items without seeing them in action: At stake is the proper representation (*Darstellung*) of the mechanical arts; at stake is imagining—what Hüttner here calls "thinking together" (*zusammen denken*)—how all this heterogeneous material is actually put to use: "So what all, then, does the stationer sell, if one thinks all the scattered articles together?"[69] He therefore proposes the following: "What if one offered the reader a chance to accompany us through multiple London stores and to have the items shown and described to them piece by piece? If we could adequately serve as a cicerone through just six London shops,"[70] then the challenge of representation would be met. Again, it was quite common to position the correspondent as quasi-ethnographic travel guide, with periodical readers being "led" through city parks, museums, collections of antiquities, markets, and more. In effect, the suggestion is that an expert tour through different

---

Schreibmaterialien. Viele nennen sich daher Bookbinder and stationer oder Bookseller and Stationer. [...] Buchführer, Buchdrucker und alle die mit Schreibesachen handeln, gehören noch jetzt zu *einer* Innung, welche die der *Stationers* heißt und ein gemeinschaftliches Versammlungshaus, Stationers-Hall genannt, hat, wo alle Bücher, welche Nachdruck besorgen, ein Privilegium erhalten." "Beschauung des Gewölbes," p.111. Lothar Müller calls the stationer a central node or switching point in literary and commercial circulation (*Schaltstelle der Papierzirkulation*): *White magic* (Malden, MA, 2014), p.165.

68. "Die Stationers verkaufen noch eine Menge anderer Artikel, die nicht eigentlich in ihren Kram gehören. Ihre Läden sind außen und inwendig elegant und die größeren sind öfters prächtig. Ihre meiste Waare befindet sich im Wandschränken mit Glasthüren, und selbst auf den Ladentischen wird alles in Mahagonykasten mit Glasdeckeln bewahrt. Die Auszierung ihrer Ladenfenster ist eine wichtige Angelegenheit. [...] Überhaupt ist das Gewerbe eines Londner Stationers überaus einträglich und hat in einer Residenz, wo so viele Kollegia, Expeditionen, Komptoire, Kaufleute, und große Buchhändler sind, einen fast unerschütterlichen Grund." "Beschluß der Beschreibung des Stationerladens. Quittungsbücher, Lineale, Huswifes und dergl.," *London und Paris* 7:1 (1801), p.26–27.

69. "Was verkauft nun der Stationer alles, wenn man die zerstreuten Artikel sich in einem Laden zusammen denkt." "Beschauung des Gewölbes," p.110.

70. "Wie, wenn man den Leser bäte, uns geradezu in etlicher Londner Gewölbe zu begleiten und sich da die Sachen Stück für Stück zeigen und beschreiben zu lassen? Könnten wir das Amt eines Cicerone nur durch 6 Londner Läden treulich verwalten, so würde uns Niemand wegen des oben aufgestellten Satzes in Anspruch nehmen." "Beschauung des Gewölbes," p.110.

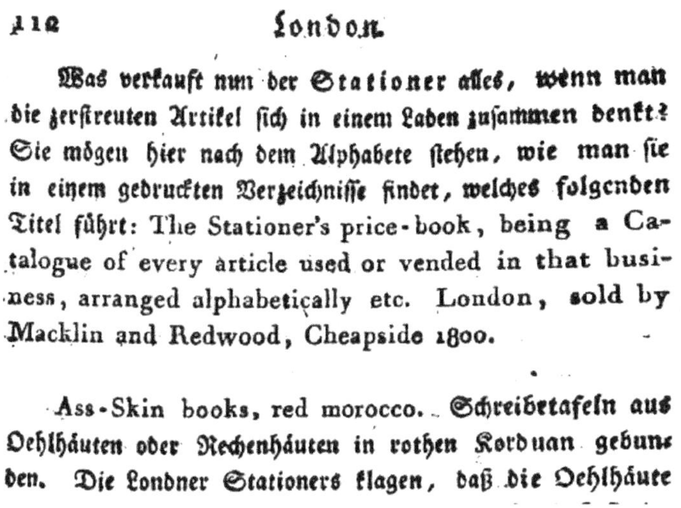

Λ1Q **ƨondon.**

Was verkauft nun ber Stationer alles, wenn man bie jerstreuten Artikel sich in einem Laden jusammen benkt? Sie mögen hier nach bem Alphabete stehen, wie man sie in einem gebruckten Verzeichnisse findet, welches folgenden Titel führt: The Stationer's price-book, being a Catalogue of every article used or vended in that business, arranged alphabetically etc. London, sold by Macklin and Redwood, Cheapside 1800.   —

Ass-Skin books, red morocco... **Schreibtafeln aus Oehlhäuten ober Rechenhäuten in rothen Korbuan gebundern. Die Londner Stationers klagen, baß bie Oehlhäute**

Figure 23: Excerpt from "Beschluß der Beschreibung des Stationerladens. Quittungsbücher, Lineale, Huswifes und dergl.," *London und Paris* 7:1 (1801), 112.

shops can give interested foreigners a sense of the advanced domestic economy of the British in paper-related issues.

In a curious twist, though, the correspondent purports to give this tour by reproducing and annotating a printed catalog entitled "The stationer's price-book, being a catalogue of every article used or vended in that business, arranged alphabetically etc. London, sold by Macklin and Redwood, Cheapside 1800."[71] The ensuing articles, printed across several issues, consist of a translated, annotated, alphabetical wholesale catalog of goods sold by stationers and available for purchase (see Figure 23). Needless to say, it is puzzling that a catalog would be a viable solution for the problem of adequately representing how the English middle and upper classes use paper. This catalog lists an extensive range of items, from high-end paper products to packing paper, from paper for children to paper for libraries. It includes portable desks; varied binding materials and covers; different kinds of containers made of paper that are intended to hold other kinds of paper; "paper cases" for traveling, for carrying sermons, for bankers,

71. "Beschauung des Gewölbes," p.112.

and more; paper wrappings, so-called "outsides" and "dirty" paper to keep expensive paper clean.[72] Recalling the Parisian scholarly networks discussed earlier, Hüttner also notes the importance of cards and flyers in the scholarly world.[73] At least in this respect, the "Republic of Letters" comes into view as a republic of paper.

Hüttner's substitution of the catalog for thick ethnographic description is a strange acceptance of the jolt of remediation. The catalog shifts the supposed focus from a group of "scattered" objects interrelated through use to a mode of alphabetic proximity, as a kind of index, with the accidents of words and names informing the organization of these "scattered" products. This rather peculiar substitution of one form of "thinking together" for another nicely exhibits the kind of "[loosening of] objects from their moorings in space and time" identified by The Multigraph Collective as a key feature of the catalog.[74] The materiality of the paper catalog reproduced by the journal calls to mind the hypermediacy of the paper objects listed—so many varieties of paper, all different to sight and touch—but it also elides certain aspects of these objects' medial function by taking them out of the contexts in which they have their proper functionality.[75]

That said, this account of stationery products does at times arguably shed light on the multiple open-ended uses for paper. I have already mentioned this article's cataloging of the many paper products intended to enclose other paper (which recalls the wrapping paper for the new shipment of books arriving at Lackington's in Figure 19); this kind of paper represents a modular form of placing various sorts of paper products into multiple relations, depending on the needs of the people using them, and the reader is called upon to imagine some of these different relations. Another related instance of

72. C. Hüttner, "Fortgesetzte Beschreibung des Stationers. Outsides, zum Vorsatz-papier der Buchbinder. Parchment-runners, um gleiche Linien zu zeichnen. Leserliche Handschriften der Engländer. Büchschen für Wacholdergummi. Federspulen," *London und Paris* 6:7 (1800), p.195–222 (206).

73. "The scholars, who hold public lectures on all kinds of topics, and the army of private instructors, all have their cards which answer all necessary questions once and for all. The scientific societies: the Royal, the Linnean, the Antiquarian, the Painting Academy and many more all print cards for the use of their members, so that they are aware of conference and meeting days." "Beschauung des Gewölbes," p.117.

74. The Multigraph Collective, "Catalogs," p.70.

75. On the dynamic of "hypermediacy" and simulated immediacy characteristic of remediation, see Jay David Bolter and Richard Grusin, *Remediation: understanding new media* (Cambridge, MA, 1999).

this can be found in the catalog entry on "Files," which describes the eighteenth-century sense of the file as a thread or wire used to keep documents or paper in order:

> *files* refer to a row of loose papers connected by means of a wire, thread, or leather cord, etc. Most commonly this refers to newspapers hanging slackly down from the thin piece of wood to which they are connected [...] The stationer sells either mere wires connected to wood, or wires connected to cardboard maps [*mapfiles*] or to plates set on cardboard [*printfiles*], or one just uses quite thin string [*laces*].[76]

Files are an additional technique for bringing temporary order to print and paper products, and, once more, this technique is connected to the intersecting worlds of periodicals and sociability. These strings represent a key element of the infrastructure of the age of paper, as they offer the means for connecting things to one another, for putting them in physical proximity, not just for "thinking them together."

This catalog article is also affected by the seriality of the journal itself. *London und Paris* reproduces the piece across multiple articles and issues, with the last article appearing over a year after the first, and broken up by an issue that does not contain any continuation of the piece.[77] In addition, the third article in the series directly follows the second in the same issue, causing the reader to wonder why the editors introduced a new article number and did not simply continue the list of the second article without any additional paratextual markers. To be sure, irregular continuation is rather conventional in serialized periodical literature, but here we are dealing with nonnarrative continuation, the continuation of a list, a cliff-hangerless sequel, and one in which the list's use-value seems to decrease the more time intervenes between articles. Spacing out the reproduction of the shop catalog in serialized articles breaks with the list's orientation to the present moment,[78] and introduces a different temporality according to which the reader is "guided" through the shop (this is also a feature of Böttiger's trade fair reports, which are published several months after

---

76. C. Hüttner, "Fortsetzung der Materialen welche ein Stationer verkauft. Verzierte Papiere, Rechnungszettel. Papierfiligran. Forell. Falzbeine. Dintenpulver," *London und Paris* 6:7 (1800), p.202–203.

77. After the second to last article, one reads "the conclusion as soon as possible [*den Beschluß ehestens*]," rather than something like "the conclusion in the next issue," though it is unclear what would be holding up the editors from being able to print the last section. *London und Paris* 6:7 (1800), p.211.

78. See Young, *List cultures*, p.33.

the fair and are often spaced out irregularly across several months in sometimes more than twenty installments).

One might also link these disarticulated parts of the catalog up to the titles of the articles themselves, which provide even more partial, selective lists of certain key products.[79] Are these the potentially most interesting, most desirable, most unusual goods—the highlights, if you will? Again, this listing is somewhat analogous to signage that one might encounter on or behind the counter or in printed advertisements, but here the primary function is not to sell the items. We are presented with strange transpositions from one repository to another: from the shop display to the catalog, from the catalog to the periodical. In the meantime, the opening conceit of visiting the store falls ever more by the wayside: Would an actual visitor to the stationer not be worried that products listed by this outdated catalog were no longer available? Be that as it may, these articles help to map ongoing patterns of circulation and to visualize the journal's ongoing status as a dynamic archive, via analogy both to the stationer's shop and to the remediated catalog.

Conclusion

If it is plausible to suggest that Bertuch and Böttiger display a pronounced impulse to take stock of "the age of paper" and to promote a certain inventorying competency that complements practical as well as aesthetic judgment, then we might conclude by reviewing once more the several inventories that their journal offers to readers. In the case of Millin's salon, *London und Paris* takes a snapshot of its contents at a given moment, cognizant of the fact that they are being potentially replenished. This essay shows both how print and paper archives facilitate certain kinds of sociability and how more stable repositories such as a national library interact productively with auxiliary spaces whose contents are more in flux. The salon provides a loose model for thinking about different types of print products across the spectrum of books, manuscripts, or documents housed more permanently in the library and more present-oriented serial material: The world of periodicals operates as a valuable supplement associated with a necessarily ongoing social and scholarly exchange.

---

79. "Beschauung des Gewölbes"; "Fortsetzung der Materialen welche ein Stationer verkauft"; "Fortgesetzte Beschreibung des Stationers"; "Beschluß der Beschreibung des Stationerladens."

The articles and images depicting Lackington's "Temple of the muses" amplify the notion of a shifting archive, and reinforce the sense that the utopian horizon of systematic overview exists only in its absence. Bertuch uses the difference between England and Germany to performatively envision a more perfect inventory of the publishing world: Commerce and scholarship will both benefit from such inventorying, which is held back by accelerated commerce and social prejudice. By listing his friend's publication—an inventory of one—Bertuch enacts the absence of a proper catalog, but he also envisions the possibility of an inventory to come. In turn, the images of the interior of Lackington's depict scenes of nonhierarchical and provisional, multidirectional movement through a loosely arranged archival space, modeling potential ways of orientation in the absence of more extensive organization. And the final example of the stationer's catalog is characteristic, one might say, of the broader aims of Bertuch's and Böttiger's fashion journalism, which is faced with the challenge of imagining certain lifeworlds on the basis of product description. Readers are encouraged to make the leap from individual products to aspirationally envisioning a whole way of life, a domestic economy enhanced by luxury items. This essay makes clear the disjunctive nature of the middle-class imaginary based around goods, for it avoids producing any unified, holistic representation of the lifeworld promised at the outset. In each case, we might also conclude that, through a gesture of cataloging, *London und Paris* gives a (foreign) site that collects heterogeneous items a certain amount of familiarizing (German) order. In the last case, though, the catalog is both part of the foreign site and part of *London und Paris*, both internal to the storage site being described (as an aide for stationers' shops) and external to it, as an artifact remediated through translation, reprinting, and serialized redistribution.

All of these articles (and the images of Lackington's as well) present us both with inventories and with meta-inventories, inventories that have been put into a frame and that readers have been directed to regard at a certain aesthetic or ethnographic distance, rather than ones that have mere use-value. This status of being a meta-inventory, of being a remediated version of an inventory, is in part what allows Bertuch and Böttiger to rely on and generate the desire for more, for serial installments of other inventories that are, to a greater or lesser degree, severed from direct application. They train readers to view themselves in a network, even to become an agent in said network, though not necessarily through direct use of the catalogs on offer. Imagining oneself in a network by being on the lookout for the next installment—this, after all, is one of the key tasks of the consumer in "the age of paper": *die Fortsetzung folgt...* This sequel *builds on* the dynamic archives and serialized tools that organize the "age of paper" and helps us to reimagine the relationship between digital media and their predecessors.

Cultivating contacts: collectors, critics, and the public in eighteenth-century German-speaking Europe

Renata Schellenberg

Mount Allison University

Absent infrastructures

The decentralized configuration of Germany in the eighteenth century provided a challenging backdrop upon which to develop a coherent understanding of a national art. The complexities inherent to the operation of a country consisting of more than 360 principalities made it difficult for many common sociocultural connections to take place, providing a veritable obstacle for cross-national contact and affiliation. Author Christoph Martin Wieland summarized well the predicament of cultural interconnecting in eighteenth-century Germany by linking two framing challenges: the geographical breadth of the nation and its dearth of communicative media. According to his assessment, Germany lacked the infrastructure for a network of influence, exchange, and conversation. He made the following statement in the foreword to the first issue of his journal *Der teutsche Merkur* (*The German Mercury*), justifying the new publication through its potential solution for the problem at hand:

> We have no state capital, which would stand as the universal academy of virtuosos of the nation or provide the norm of (good) taste. We have no permanent national theater and our best actors, as our best writers, poets, and artists, are dispersed throughout the German empire and, for the most part, thus robbed of close interaction and the confidential communication of their thoughts, reproaches, and judgment, which would contribute so greatly to the perfection of their work.[1]

---

1. "Wir haben keine Hauptstadt, welche die allgemeine Akademie der Virtuosen der Nation, und gleichsam die Gesetzgeberin des Geschmacks wäre. Wir haben

Wieland presented his journal as a means of aggregating the disparate strains of national cultural creativity and a way to counter the fragmentation of communication. *Der teutsche Merkur* is but one example of the efforts undertaken by German authors to overcome this state of isolation and disconnectedness, but it does exemplify the key role print culture played in creating cultural cohesion in the eighteenth century. As this essay argues, this publication effort was both varied and manifold, resulting in many prolific forms of writing, the consumption of which created communities of readers but also a strong sense of national belonging.[2]

Print proved to be the perfect medium with which to devise and express a unified national artistic identity in Germany. The periodical press was particularly conducive to this task, as it was capable of propagating information quickly to a wide audience of readers, engaging the public in a way that was not only direct but also constantly changing. In the long eighteenth century, there were more than 1000 different journals circulating through German-speaking Europe, an astonishing quantity of publications that provided a ready platform for the dissemination of news while also initiating opportunities for social contact and networking.[3] Reading was, moreover, a popular national pastime, something that further facilitated the active exchange of cultural news. Although there were few journals explicitly dedicated to matters pertaining to material and aesthetic culture, the collecting and display of material culture did become a popular topic

---

kein fest-stehendes National-Theater, unsre besten Schauspieler, so wie unsere besten Schriftsteller, Dichter und Künstler, sind durch alle Kreise des deutschen Reiches zerstreut, und größtenteils der Vortheile eines näheren Umgangs und einer vertraulichen Mittheilung ihrer Einsichten, Urtheile, Entwürfe, u.s.w. beraubt, welche zur Vollkommenheit ihrer Werke so viel beytragen würde." Christoph Martin Wieland, "Vorrede des Herausgebers," *Der teutsche Merkur* 1 (1773), p.iii–xxii (vi).

2. This essay complements Karin Baumgartner's contribution in the current volume in that both rethink the question of national belonging, albeit with different trajectories. Collecting is an accumulating, local activity, whereas travel and mapping emphasize expansiveness.

3. For more on this, see Helga Brandes, "The literary marketplace and the journal, medium of the Enlightenment," in *German literature of the eighteenth century: the Enlightenment and sensibility*, ed. Barbara Becker-Cantarino (Rochester, NY, 2005), p.79–102. For more on the conditions prevalent in general reading culture in eighteenth-century Germany, see Matt Erlin, "Useless subjects: reading and consumer culture in eighteenth-century Germany," *The German quarterly* 80:2 (2007), p.145–64.

of discussion in many German journals and featured prominently in their pages. Collections were described, analyzed, and shared in literary form by the public, all of which helped position collecting as a viable and acceptable social practice. This, in turn, legitimized and substantiated collecting as a cultural practice, providing an accessible forum in which it could be known.

Within this publishing context, collecting emerges as an inherently social endeavor that openly initiated contact and directly emboldened communication. As a leisure and social activity, it helped bridge some of the patent obstacles of the general sociopolitical divide in Germany by creating vibrant networks of cultural interactions that focused on the procurement and enjoyment of material culture. And it did so mostly by cannily operating through print rather than through direct community contact and by using popular forms of print media to make its case known.

In eighteenth-century Germany, the network of contacts that ensued from collecting practices fostered various forms of sociability in addition to encouraging an engaged form of interaction among those who participated. This community of collectors proved to be not only articulate but also determined to document their collecting experience in fixed form, leaving a clear trace of their activities and interactions in print. Regardless of national context, collecting is invariably contingent upon curiosity and the articulated interest of those involved, which posits it as a necessarily social activity that is meant to be shared throughout society. Considering the particular conditions of eighteenth-century Germany, it is fruitful to examine the manner in which these collecting contacts were promulgated, while paying attention to the means by which their connectivity was sustained.

Print collections as national networks

Wieland's *Teutsche Merkur* lent itself well to discussions pertaining to collecting and the enjoyment of material culture because it was keen to investigate issues related to contemporary aesthetic culture. It therefore readily accepted and published material on *Kunstsachen* (art objects/matters), as well as presenting official *Kunstkritik* (art criticism) itself. Among the many other sociocultural contemporary topics covered, the *Merkur*, for example, contained numerous factual accounts of visits to smaller regional collections, publicizing the existence of these items to the reading public. These items would frequently be published as part of a letter or a personal travelogue, relaying the existence of a collection as a significant part of the journey. The journal integrated such reports into the other mainstream topics it covered, thereby presenting collecting activities as a significant source of interest and news.

By publishing these articles, *Der teutsche Merkur* created clear links between critics, connoisseurs, and a general public interested in collecting. It altered the public's perception of art collections by making them seem communicable through print and therefore entirely accessible to a wide general audience. To this end, it published reports by recognized authors on well-known galleries, proclaiming the relevance of these established collections to the nation and its art aficionados. One of the more prominent examples of this is certainly Wilhelm Heinse's fictionalized account of the famous Düsseldorf Gallery, "Über einige Gemälde der Düsseldorfer Galerie" ("On a few paintings of the Düsseldorf Gallery"), which was published in the journal between 1776 and 1777 and drew a great response from the reading public.[4] Written in epistolary form and addressed to the popular contemporary poet Johann Wilhelm Ludwig Gleim, this article extols the virtues of the Düsseldorf collection, offering a descriptive inventory of the picture gallery, while placing special focus on the Rubens paintings for which the gallery was known. Rather significantly, through his text, Heinse transforms the visual display into a verbal account, deliberately shifting the visual experience into lexical form, thereby expanding the accessibility of the gallery to a reading rather than purely viewing public. This verbal transformation should be understood as more than mere ekphrasis, as it not only allowed this art collection to be viewed beyond the immediate physical space of the display, but also created an enthusiastic forum of knowledge sharing that people read and actively considered while formulating their own views of the gallery.[5]

In addition to chronicling the existence of various art collections throughout Europe and disseminating this information to the reading

4. Wilhelm Heinse, "Über einige Gemählde der Düssendorfer Galerie," *Der teutsche Merkur* 4 (1776), p.3–14, 106–19; *Der teutsche Merkur* 3 (1777), p.117–35; *Der teutsche Merkur* 2 (1777), p.60–90.
5. The impact of Heinse's text on the public has been well documented in Sabine Koch's critical commentary on the CD appendix of "Über die Düsseldorfer Gemäldegalerie," in *Tempel der Kunst: die Geburt des öffentlichen Museums in Deutschland 1701–1815*, ed. Bénédicte Savoy (Cologne, 2015), p.151–95 (151).

public, Wieland's journal also carried articles that delineated and prescribed modes of behavior expected from the visitor in the display space. A rather famous fictionalized account of the gallery experience published in *Der teutsche Merkur* was, for example, Johann Heinrich Merck's "Ueber die letzte Gemälde Ausstellung in **" ("About the last exhibition of paintings in **"), which appeared in the journal in 1781. Here Merck describes the protocol that accompanies the viewing of such exhibitions, designating this social etiquette as "ein angenehmes Schauspiel" ("a pleasant spectacle") due to its many peculiarities and the gross artificiality of conduct on display.[6] In his text, Merck makes fun of traditional but clearly recognizable forms of *Salonkritik* (criticism of and in salons), taking particular note of the contrived and fake interest of the public viewing the art and thereby criticizing their dilettante approach.[7] Merck positions himself as an astute observer of the space in which the exhibition is taking place, but, rather than focusing on the art, he summarizes the social exchanges he is experiencing. It is relevant to note that Merck's article is construed as a conversation and, as such, it highlights the discourse customarily used in these spaces, documenting, if slightly exaggerating, the characters, dialogue, and expressions associated with contemporary art viewing. By recording this protracted *Galeriegespräch* (gallery conversation), he ridicules social convention while also capturing ephemeral aspects of those conversations associated with art—a valuable preservation of information that is not usually documented in traditional forms of critical literature.

In some cases, the editor of the journal—while discussing *Kunstsachen*—was eager to facilitate a type of cultural contact with the reader, emphasizing this mediating role as a key editorial function. Johann Georg Meusel certainly communicated an effervescent enthusiasm when articulating his purpose as editor of the influential *Museum für Künstler und Kunstliebhaber* (1787–1792). Unlike *Der teutsche Merkur*, this magazine focused exclusively on artistic content, a subject that Meusel believed required a specific commitment on the part of its publisher. Reflecting on his role as editor, Meusel viewed his

6. Johann Heinrich Merck, "Über die letzte Gemälde Ausstellung in **," *Der teutsche Merkur* 4 (1781), p.167–78 (167).
7. At one point, Merck caustically speculates on the presumed sophistication of the visitors to the gallery, stating: "Indessen thaten sie doch alle, als wenn sie in der Jugend zeichnen gelernt hätten" ("Whereby they all behaved as if they learned drawing in their youth"). Merck, "Über die letzte," p.168.

primary responsibility to act as a mediator, someone capable of negotiating with stakeholders within a larger framework of contacts in order to facilitate social interaction and collaboration. He wrote: "I enjoyed the pleasure of making artists and connoisseurs familiar with each other, by giving the former reward and payment, and the latter the opportunity to acquire the possession of wonderful works."[8] As becomes evident, within this context, the *persona* of the editor was as important as the information communicated, because it was the editor who ensured that this news would be relayed to an interested audience. Throughout Meusel's publication, there is a strong sense of pedagogical duty driving his editorial work, as he understood that the information he published was used not only to entertain but also to educate readers who came into contact with it.

These editorial activities created a journalistic practice that firmly anchored collecting within popular culture. This development encouraged public interest and investment in these matters, and shaped the general perception of collecting activities within eighteenth-century German society. There appeared to be a tacit consensus that careful literate expression should accompany the presentation of objects, and that print could be used demonstratively to further the aims of collecting practices in society. The close association forged between print and the display of material culture helped these two things become intertwined in the popular imagination, making them appear as if they were acting in complementary fashion. As a consequence, reading, rather than direct viewing, became an acceptable means of learning about collections and a legitimate way of experiencing these objects from afar. Both authors and editors used print media as the persuasive means to communicate collected artifacts, and manipulated their rhetoric in deliberate ways to achieve this aim and draw people to collections.[9] Rather significantly, the use of popular print media to promote collecting positioned these undertakings as

8.   "Ich genoß das Vergnügen, Künstler und Kunstfreunde auf mehr als eine Art mit einander bekannt zu machen; jenen Belohnung und Absatz, diesen den Besitz herrlicher Werke zu verschaffen." Johann Georg Meusel, "Vorbericht," *Museum für Künstler und Kunstliebhaber* 1 (1787), p.1–4 (1).
9.   Certain techniques were used to motivate readers to explore these items in person. Critics like Chloe Chard have described this technique as the hyperbole of representation, whereby the author of an article renders the object ineffable, and encourages readers not to read, but to see it for themselves; see *Pleasure and guilt on the Grand Tour: travel writing and imaginative topography 1600–1830* (Manchester, 1999), p.64.

a legitimate intellectual activity, worthy of the public's attention. It appealed to a mental rather than purely visual engagement on the part of the reading public, and, more importantly, authors and editors trusted their ability to engage in this way, believing them able to process information past the immediacy of the page.

Inventories of collectors, collecting, and collections as canon

Some authors devised tangible inventories of collected artifacts, creating large, printed compendia of collecting practices and artists in Germanophone Europe and thereby generating an independent research resource for those interested in this subject matter. These textual collections summarized the scattered artistic activity taking place across Germany and gave a comprehensive presentation of German art to readers. For example, amateur art historian Heinrich Sebastian Hüsgen published his *Nachrichten von Franckfurter Künstlern* (*News about Frankfurt's artists*) in 1780 with a thoroughly researched appendix that claimed to contain all art items worthy of being seen in Frankfurt's public buildings and private residencies.[10] Hüsgen's publication wanted to produce a veritable provenance of cultural activity, establishing Frankfurt, a traditional mercantile city, as an important artistic center. Hüsgen considered it imperative that such an archival record be created in his city, and encouraged others to write testimonies about other German collections and to gather and preserve data on artifacts. He justified the need for accumulating such information by characterizing Germany as an exemplary and fruitful place for the production of arts—"[die] von den Künsten fruchtbare Nation"—and therefore a place worthy of this type of documentation.[11] Hüsgen himself exerted considerable personal effort in creating his publication, stating that the work was produced as the result of "vieljährige[n] Fleiß," long-standing and vigilant diligence.[12] It is of no small importance, of course, that Hüsgen himself was a collector and that, in putting pen to paper and accumulating this data, he was

---

10. Heinrich Sebastian Hüsgen, *Nachrichten von Franckfurter Künstlern und Kunst-Sachen enthaltend das Leben und die Wercke, aller hiesigen Mahler, Bildhauer, Kupfer- und Pettschier-Stecher, Edelstein-Schneider und Kunst-Gieser, nebst einem Anhang von allem was in öffentlichen und Privat-Gebäuden, merckwürdiges von Kunst-sachen zu sehen ist* (Frankfurt am Main, n.n., 1780), title page.
11. Hüsgen, *Nachrichten*, p.viii.
12. Hüsgen, *Nachrichten*, p.ix.

motivated to a certain degree by self-interest—wanting to legitimize his own involvement in collecting.

A more comprehensive compendium of art news was created by Karl Heinrich von Heinecken, who was the director of the engravings cabinet in Dresden from 1746 until 1763. He was a recognized connoisseur, someone who knew art and who, by virtue of his profession, understood the edifying and cultural value of displaying art in public spaces. Between 1768 and 1786, he wrote a three-volume text, *Nachrichten von Künstlern und Kunst-Sachen (News about artists and artistic matters)*, in which he aggregated information on art and artists and expounded on the importance that collected artifacts have within contemporary society.[13] In the early stages of the project, Heinecken used information from an established inventory and merely cited existing archival resources on the subject, republishing historical records compiled by his predecessors. Later he expanded the registry to reflect his own Germanophile views, adding information on German artists and their work to this source. He did not see the existing record as complete without including this information, insisting that German art must have proper representation within official archival registers. Hüsgen wanted German artists' efforts to be chronicled alongside those of their European counterparts so that they could be understood and physically experienced by the reading connoisseur. His amalgamated inventory should consequently be seen not only as an effort to generate and disseminate knowledge about collecting, but also as the practicable means with which to legitimize this entire endeavor within German society. With his compendium, he was moreover creating an accessible database for others to use, and by documenting these things in language, he was trying to give authoritative permanence to this information.

There were other, more practical publications that similarly propagated collecting among the general public while indirectly creating networks of contact and exchange. The catalogs did not neatly align with other narratives about nation that were teleologically driven. As unlikely as it may seem, sales catalogs adopted a distinct way of articulating the aesthetic and social value of objects, even though they were ostensibly produced for commercial purposes

13. Karl Heinrich von Heinecken, *Nachrichten von Künstlern und Kunst-Sachen* (Leipzig, Kraß, 1768); *Nachrichten von Künstlern und Kunstsachen: zweiter Theil* (Leipzig, Kraß, 1769); *Neue Nachrichten von Künstlern und Kunst-Sachen* (Leipzig, Breitkopf, 1786).

alone. Art dealers went to great lengths to augment the appeal of the catalog and, in some cases, enlisted known writers to compose the sales inventories because of their ability to illuminate the object for the buyer on the commercial market.[14] This involvement ascribed a certain degree of literacy to the economic transaction and expanded the readability of the sales catalog. However, the accumulation of such sales data is valuable for other noncommercial reasons as well. Namely, the information relayed in these trade publications offers a surprising amount of insight into the lifestyle of the eighteenth-century public, and can be used as an authentic ethnographic tool. These inventories reliably showcase what people owned in their homes, and chronicle both their aesthetic and their practical needs. By reading these inventories, one can learn about the prevalent tastes and trends in society because the items for sale were assigned not only a commercial value but a clear cultural value as well. Sales catalogs conveniently preserve this information. By grouping sales inventories together, one can easily discern patterns of consumption that inform the modern reader and researcher about what items were fashionable in eighteenth-century society, thereby disclosing some of the hidden domestic stylistic choices made by people in their day-to-day lives.[15]

With the emergence of the first public museums and galleries, another specialized publication appeared on the scene. In the late 1700s, the first official museum inventories began to appear, a literary novelty on the market that was completely dedicated to the displayed and publicly viewed object. A famous example of this is Christian von Mechel's *Verzeichniß der Gemälde der Kaiserlich Königlichen Bilder Gallerie in Wien* (*Catalog of paintings in possession of the imperial gallery in Vienna*), a catalog that was produced in 1780 and summarized the objects displayed in the Belvedere gallery. Mechel prioritized the accessibility of the collection, and went to great lengths to make this display space visibly comprehensible to the public, implementing

14. This information is relayed as part of the online Getty Provenance Index; Sale Catalog D-A42, Auction house Juncker; Kaller. This, like other historical sales records, can be accessed here: https://piprod.getty.edu/starweb/pi/servlet.starweb?path=pi/pi.web (last accessed July 5, 2023).

15. In 2002, Thomas Ketelsen and Tilmann von Stockhausen compiled a directory of sales catalogs of paintings in the early modern period in the Germanophone context. One of the things that can be deduced from parsing this information is the popularity of Dutch (rather than German) landscape paintings. For more on this, see Burton Fredericksen and Julia Armstrong, *Verzeichnis der verkauften Gemälde im deutschsprachigen Raum vor 1800*, 3 vols. (Munich, 2002), vol.1, p.22.

some literary innovations to his text to achieve this aim. He arranged
the text of the catalog to correspond to the walls of the gallery,
thereby mirroring the content of the collection and mimicking the
physical layout of the display space within the text. The objective, in
Mechel's words, was to create a "sichtbare Geschichte der Kunst," a
visible history of art, in both the catalog and the Belvedere gallery
that would be available for readers and the actual visitors of this
display space.[16] The catalog thereby acquired a twofold purpose
as a publication: It was a repository of gallery information and an
educational guide for uninitiated third parties. The entire publication
was positioned toward the public, rather than toward the imperial
owners of the collection. Its printed summary of artifacts facilitated
the inclusion of the public into the spectacle of art: not only by
ascribing cogency to the display of the artifacts but by providing the
visitor with an informed and ultimately more pleasant experience.

A case study: Weimarer Kunstfreunde

A notable and key consortium combining connectivity, contacts,
and collecting within eighteenth-century German society is certainly
the Weimarer Kunstfreunde (Weimar Friends of Art), or WKF for
short, a group of recognized art connoisseurs operating in classical
Weimar. The WKF was formed in 1799, and was a small and
engaged group of like-minded art lovers that posited its existence
as both defender and enforcer of good taste. Members of the group
were traditionally trained neoclassical experts from a wide range of
disciplines: art critic Ludwig Fernow, writer Friedrich Schiller, art
historian Johann Heinrich Meyer, and, of course, that most famous
of Weimar residents, author Johann Wolfgang Goethe. As the name
of the group suggests, the essential momentum of the Kunstfreunde
group was consensus and collaboration. Together, members of the
group espoused a collective stance toward art, and their opinions were
formulated in such a way as to indicate that the views of the group
were the result of a harmoniously reached agreement rather than
polemical debate. In fact, Goethe envisioned the entire project as a
type of conversation in which proper communication alone would

16. Christian von Mechel, *Verzeichniß der Gemälde der Kaiserlich Königlichen Bilder
    Gallerie in Wien verfaßt von Christian von Mechel der Kaiserlich. Königlich Mitglied
    nach der von ihm Allerhöchsten Befehl im Jahre 1781 neuen gemachten Einrichtung*
    (Vienna, n.n., 1783), p.xi.

elucidate WKF members' views and achieve their goals. He seemed to believe that clarity, transparency, and harmony among friends—or, as he expressed it, "harmonisch verbundener Freunde"[17]—had a certain potency, which, once accepted and recognized, would eventually prevail in greater society.

By grouping their expertise together, members of the WKF believed that they were creating a consortium that others should emulate. They believed that the development of their group was organic, and viewed it as a naturally progressive collaboration. The notion of a self-sustained, self-perpetuating community fueled by good will was a core belief of the group, as demonstrated by the following citation:

> When a group of people live together in such a manner that they can call themselves friends, having a shared common interest in progressively educating themselves and committing to shared objectives, they can be sure that they will again come together in manifold ways, and that even a direction that appears to separate them will, in fact, bring them happily back together.[18]

Consensus was seen as a motivating principle for an ever-expanding alliance that would grow freely from its formative core of several individuals to include many more. It would appear that, in presenting this type of accord, the WKF was interested in creating a template of conduct for others by providing a concrete example of how to navigate an increasingly changing world. The WKF wanted to inspire readers on an individual basis, encouraging them to aspire to a higher level of communication and interaction. Indeed, when discussing the objectives of the group, Goethe was quite adamant about emphasizing the nurturing intentions of the WKF, asserting that, on the whole, they were a malleable group, interested primarily in mentoring a younger generation of artists rather than mandating a singular theoretical platform. As Goethe noted in his private correspondence

17. Johann Wolfgang von Goethe, *Sämtliche Werke: Briefe, Tagebücher und Gespräche*, 40 vols. (Frankfurt am Main, 1985–2013), vol.18, p.458. All subsequent references to this edition are given as "FA" followed by the volume number.
18. "Wenn mehrere vereint auf diese Weise zusammen leben, daß sie sich Freunde nennen dürfen, indem sie ein gleiches Interesse haben, sich fortschreitend auszubilden, und auf naheverwandte Zwecke losgehen, dann werden sie gewiß sein, daß sie sich auf den vielfachsten Wegen wieder begegnen, und daß selbst eine Richtung, die sie von einander zu entfernen schien, sie doch bald wieder glücklich zusammen führen wird." Goethe, FA 18, p.459.

on the matter: "Our intention thereby is to inspire and excite, not to determine and create."[19]

The group operated cannily within the realm of print, utilizing the publication format of the periodical, in particular, to champion their classicist cause and recruit new members. They were, however, careful to publish in journals already agreeable to their views. They limited themselves to specialized publications such as *Propyläen* and, later, *Kunst und Althertum* (*Art and antiquity*)—journals where Goethe exercised editorial control over content and in which there was no opportunity for rebuttal or contestation. The articles published in *Propyläen* were thus largely programmatic in nature, as they were presented from the viewpoint of an experienced connoisseur and titled in such a way that suggested they were offering complete guidance to uninformed readers in their understanding of art. They provided a collective and indisputably finalized perspective on a wide range of topics rooted in artistic practice, espousing a tried and trusted neoclassical approach to art. In so doing, they believed they were addressing theoretical and practical concerns shared by their readers, delivering an authoritatively set prototype of artistic taste for the general public to follow.

The WKF took their outreach activity one step further by organizing a series of art exhibitions entitled the Weimarer Kunstausstellungen (Weimar art exhibitions), which began in 1799 and continued until 1805. The stated intention of these exhibitions was to move past the theoretical ruminations on art and to create real, physical artifacts that could objectively manifest the aesthetic intentions of the group. In their statement to artists submitting work to this art competition, Goethe and Meyer explained the endeavor as a concerted means of delving into art, noting that the awarded prize was meant to serve as an incentive (and not a reward) for this activity. The organizers, however, also explicitly stated that their intent was to mingle directly with the artists as a means of focusing their creative activity and bringing their talent together into a single forum. Identifying themselves as editors of the printed medium (and not as organizers of the displayed space), they explained: "[A]nd thus the editors of the Propyläen want nothing more than to delve into the practicalities of art and to unite with engaged artists in creating

19. "Unsere Absicht dabei ist, aufzuregen und zu wirken, nicht festzusetzen und zu bauen." *Berichte des freien Deutschen Hochstiftes zu Frankfurt am Main*, vol.11 (Frankfurt am Main, 1895), p.201.

good work."[20] These exhibitions were meant to mimic the mode of sociability that Goethe had encountered in Italy among the many *Kunstkolonien* (artists' colonies) he had associated with in the 1780s, in which the discussion of art was focused and immediate, which consequently dissolved any possibility of caustic exchange between art creators and critics.[21] Members of the WKF were diligent in documenting the efforts of the artists participating in their events, and following each exhibition they published a detailed inventory (*Verzeichnis*) of all the exhibited work, leaving concrete and summative textual evidence of the event.

It may appear as if these exhibitions achieved success in bridging some of the patent physical and knowledge gaps on the German art scene. The exhibitions were, however, particularly constructive insofar as they assisted artists in a practical fashion by providing support, reward money, and an actual museum space in which their work could be viewed. By drawing on literary themes and making these themes visual, there was, moreover, a deliberate performative aspect to the Weimar exhibitions, as text was used beyond the written page to stimulate cognate artistic creativity. The overall intention of the exhibitions was to correlate literary themes with a stark and faithful visual representation and bring these literary themes to life. When elaborating on the purpose of the exhibition, Heinrich Meyer focused on the intellectual curiosity associated with the event. He noted that its primary objective was "that the audience participate more vigorously,"[22] meaning that the audience assume a more *proactive role* in Weimar art affairs, and he hoped to establish a more fluid relationship between spectator and artist, removing some of the misconceptions one may have of the other. Following the competition, the art was reviewed and promoted in select publications (*Propyläen, Jenaer Allgemeine Literaturzeitung* [*Jena's general literary magazine*]), an act that led to the additional distribution of this information, garnering awareness of these activities outside of the immediate display space. By engaging in this practice, the WKF clearly bridged an important gap between print and practice, bringing the entire interaction full circle.

20. "so wünschen die Verfasser der Propyläen nichts mehr als recht bald ins Praktische der Kunst einzugreifen und sich mit wackern Künstlern zu mancherlei guten Werken zu vereinigen." Goethe, FA 18, p.650.
21. For more on the motivating factors driving the Weimar art exhibitions, see Goethe, FA 18, p.1279–80.
22. "daß das Publikum lebhafteren Teil daran nimmt." Goethe, FA 18, p.818.

They also created a transmedial platform from which to communicate with their audience. They connected a literary theme derived from text to an intelligible image and then reintroduced that image back into a critical text, creating a cohesive interface between two very different types of artistic production. However unintentional this may have been, this cross-disciplinary rapport presumed a connection in terms of message, as well as a strong intellectual commitment on the part of their audience to this message. Crucially, by delivering this content via different modalities, they appealed to separate modes of perception (and cognition) from their readers, asking them to engage with this information in a twofold manner and to view the content of their artistic message through both text and image.

This intermediality was, however, undermined by the strict prescriptive focus adopted by the WKF. They would not/could not stray from their narrow selection of classical themes, restricting the artists' creativity to predetermined criteria and making these competitions purpose-oriented and geared toward a particular interpretation of classical literature. The negative reaction of the public to the Weimarer Kunstausstellung and their vitriolic rejection of the principles of the WKF baffled Goethe and Heinrich Meyer, who saw their activities in an entirely different light.[23] They believed the WKF was doing a necessary public service by creating cultural cohesion and by establishing a normative understanding of art for the fragmented art scene of eighteenth-century Germany, centering these activities for future connoisseurs. When they wrote about the exhibition, they repeatedly stressed the collaborative effort of those who participated, noting that the event provided a national overview of cultural activity in Germany: "A general overview of all the competing art pieces, received from different parts of Germany, allows us an overview of intellect, culture, and talent of the nation"[24]—something not found elsewhere in the disparate cultural conditions of Germany at the time. This positive point was corroborated in the popular press. In the journal *Der teutsche Merkur*, an anonymous author praised the efforts of

---

23. Romantic painter Philipp Otto Runge criticized the direction and purpose of these exhibitions. He believed that the organizers were "auf einem ganz falschen Weg" ("on an entirely erroneous path") and could not recognize the merit of these competitions. For more on this discussion, see Goethe, FA 18, p.104–106.

24. "Ein nochmaliger allgemeiner Überblick über alle, aus verschiedenen Gegenden Deutschlands eingegangene, Konkurrenzstücke gewährt uns zugleich den Überblick über Geist, Kultur und Talent der Nation." Goethe, FA 18, p.804.

the group in creating a true national art competition, opening doors to the discipline to anyone who wanted to apply.[25] Yet the disconnect with the public prevailed, and, in 1805, following the death of Friedrich Schiller, the activities of the group all but halted.

Before dispersing and dissolving their collaborative alliance, members of the group did participate in a final project, drawing on their existing complementing expertise to produce *Winckelmann und sein Jahrhundert* (*Winckelmann and his century*), which was published with the Cotta press in 1805. The motivation underlying the publication of these essays has been argued and elaborated on by many critics, some asserting that the publication was a final *Parteifest* (manifesto) of the WKF, others stating that the publication was, in fact, a corrective measure, meant to address some of the mistakes made by the WKF during their exhibition days.[26] In any case, what is significant here is how this collection was presented to the reading public. Rather than focusing on the corpus of Winckelmann's famous academic work and extolling the virtues of his classicist approach to art, the collection focused on Winckelmann the person, accumulating a variety of perspectives on both his life and his work. This small volume consequently encompasses an intentional medley of notably different types of information about Winckelmann—a mixture that includes personal letters as well as several carefully crafted essays written by members of the WKF—and is meant to be read precisely as an uneven blend of different genres and texts. This assortment of writing is presented as an intertextual collective homage to Winckelmann and is intended to celebrate the complexity of the person in addition to his neoclassical viewpoint. There is agreement among the contributors that this composite mix of writings is directed to a singular goal and that, despite their disparate appearance, all texts originate from this uniform intent, "out of the same spirit."[27] Unlike previous endeavors in which the WKF futilely attempted to create an authoritative, abstract theory of art, the intention here appears palpably different. With this volume, Winckelmann is effectively monumentalized by the WKF, marking a decisive turn away from the creation of more theory and a move toward the concrete, visible object.

25. "Neue Preisaufgabe an die Künstler Teutschlands," *Der neue teutsche Merkur* 1 (1800), p.33–44.
26. For more on the possible rationale for creating this text, consult the critical commentary in Goethe, FA 19, p.624–25.
27. "aus eben demselben Geiste." Goethe, FA 19, p.12.

Objects: collection, cohesion, and the future

But, even after this symbolic gesture, members of the WKF did not disappear entirely. After a decade of independent projects, Goethe and Meyer resurfaced under a common name to co-edit another journal, *Über Kunst und Alterthum* (*About art and antiquity*), which was published between 1816 and 1828. It too focused on matters of aesthetic culture, but did so differently from *Propyläen*, shifting its attention from theoretical treatises to a more deliberate focus on the manifestation of material culture. The journal was initially commissioned as an official government *Denkschrift* (commemoration) to chronicle the damage caused by the Napoleonic Wars in the Rhein and Main regions, and thus had in its origins a rather patriotic intent.[28] Goethe was tasked with compiling an inventory of destroyed artistic sites, and traveled through this area to create this report. In time, this literary project grew into a more expansive national publication dedicated to the preservation of various forms of creative output and activity. Notably, many articles in the journal continued to offer information on exhibitions and collections throughout Germany, chronicling, as it were, sites and objects worthy of being seen. There is manifest effort on the part of the editors to systematize this information for readers and to make it useful in their own investigations of these sites. Goethe saw this aggregation of information as an impetus for future sociability as well as future projects, endorsing the systematic method of gathering data as an invariably positive development. As he noted, "each methodic composition of dispersed elements contributes to a form of intellectual sociability, which then becomes our highest aspiration."[29]

Goethe's inclination to designate these activities as a form of sociability may seem an odd choice, but it does communicate something important about the underlying canonical intentions of the *Kunst und Alterthum* project. Envisioned as a publication that could bring structure and order to the German cultural landscape in the aftermath of the Napoleonic Wars, it succeeded in creating an authoritative record of general cultural productivity in the region. It

---

28. For more on this, see Friedmar Apel and Stefan Greif, "Über Kunst und Altertum," in *Goethe Handbuch*, ed. Bernd Witte *et al.*, vol.3 (Stuttgart, 1997), p.619–39.

29. "Jede methodische Zusammenstellung zerstreuter Elemente bewirkt eine Art geistiger Geselligkeit, welche den das Höchste ist, wornach wir streben." Goethe, FA 20, p.40–43.

did so by chronicling both the literary and the artistic work that was created within this national space for over a decade and, rather importantly, by showing the social and cultural interconnectedness of these activities. By being presented with this information together as a compact whole, readers were encouraged to adopt a synthesized understanding of these matters and to see them as a legitimate form of a common national cultural production. Goethe's determination to preserve these activities as a unified body of work thus speaks directly to the preservation of a national cultural legacy as well as to the building of a community cognizant of the value that culture plays in the construction of identity.

The cumulative and representative tendencies adopted by Goethe and Meyer in their approach to both material and literary culture in *Über Kunst und Alterthum* correspond well to preceding trends practiced by literary peers in the German-speaking society of the long eighteenth century. The activities outlined in this essay attest to a larger, collective, cross-national effort to create cohesion and coherence in the disparate circumstances of eighteenth-century Germany, and to do so by collecting and preserving this data through the medium of print. Despite differences in approach, there was obvious agreement that this culture of writing was the right methodology with which to counter the piecemeal sociopolitical landscape in Germany, and literary activity emerged as the viable corrective structure to facilitate and cultivate the necessary cultural contacts. Collectors, in particular, seemed to benefit from this trend, as it supported their activities—not only by stimulating interest in the acquisition and ownership of objects in society, but by creating a discourse that substantiated their presence and purpose. They readily capitalized on the availability of print to promote collecting as an acceptable social practice while also adhering rather closely to the notion that, by grouping and organizing things together, one can make good sense of the outside world.

An eighteenth-century New England library in its European, material context

CRYSTAL HALL

Bowdoin College

A personal library reflects a deliberately constructed meeting place of authors, printers, publishers, editors, patrons, materials, and ideas.[1] While, as a body, these collections of books may reflect what has later come to be understood as a canon, as Sean Franzel and Renata Schellenberg have shown elsewhere in the current volume, the discerning merchant and customer often brought together materials that ran counter to those interpretations of value and cultural priorities. At the turn of the nineteenth century, for an elite statesman in Massachusetts, that meeting place of objects was an aggregate of North American, transatlantic, and European knowledge networks: an assemblage of national histories, Enlightenment thinking, and aspirational cultural traditions. For James Bowdoin III, who developed his library as a planned donation to Bowdoin College, such a collection required attentive work with objects such as booksellers' catalogs, which offered local attempts to mediate the chaotic print market (described by Franzel in his contribution to this volume). A network of ideas mediated by agents interested in promoting sales and circulation, James Bowdoin III's personal library is also a sample of the ways in which medium, genre, and language shape the bias, exchange, and appropriation of cultural objects across national discourses and languages. Close readings of passages, quantification of the material features of the texts, network visualization and analysis of subject headings, and probabilistic modeling of title groupings together show media-specific levels of cultural identities in the collection in order to

---

1. This work would not have been possible without the generous support of staff at the George J. Mitchell Special Collections and Archives of Bowdoin College: Marieke Van Der Steenhoven, Meagan Doyle, Roberta Schwartz, and Caroline Moseley.

argue that early students at Bowdoin College would have confronted at least two different understandings of European culture in their library.

The personal book collection of James Bowdoin III (1752–1811) represents the accumulation of useful knowledge, as defined primarily by the eighteenth century, to be transmitted to the students of the nineteenth century in the spirit of informed democracy. The library includes over 2000 pamphlets, plus more than 2050 volumes that represent 780 titles in sizes that range from folio to duodecimo.[2] Working with the best information available, the historian Kenneth Carpenter summarized: "The library of James Bowdoin III was essentially a creation of the 1790s and the first decade of the nineteenth century."[3] Moreover, 90 percent of the authors in James Bowdoin III's collection of books and pamphlets died after 1700, and 50 percent died or stopped being active after 1789. These calculations indicate that much of the work was written by Bowdoin's contemporaries. Based on marginalia and print dates, scholars are confident that very few of the books belonged to family members. James Bowdoin III collected an ambitious and broad-ranging donation of books for the young Bowdoin College. As part of his bequest of acreage and money to the college upon its founding in 1794, he asked that the college be named for his father (1726–1790), the influential politician and naturalist, and, upon James Bowdoin III's death in 1811, his library passed to the college, which some historians have estimated doubled, if not tripled, the holdings at the time.

The collecting patterns on topics such as international law and politics in some ways parallel Bowdoin's life events, while in other ways the emphasized subjects in the collection seem unusual for a gentleman's library of the period. As a graduate of Harvard and Oxford who completed his Grand Tour of continental Europe in the early 1770s, James Bowdoin III became involved in colonial politics during the early years of the Revolution and continued in roles related to international relations with the United States. The library emphasizes French and particularly Parisian influences related to his diplomatic efforts involving the Louisiana Purchase prior to 1803 and his participation in negotiations with Spain over West Florida around 1805–1807. Attempts to reconstruct its appearance used

2. See Kenneth Carpenter, "James Bowdoin III as library builder," in *The Legacy of James Bowdoin III* (Brunswick, ME, 1994), p.84–126 (84).
3. Carpenter, "James Bowdoin III," p.94.

the inventories of the crates that arrived at the college, under the presumption that the books were packed with shelf mates, resulting in a presumed organization similar to the topical arrangement of the reference collections in the Bibliothèque nationale's reading room in Paris.[4] The similarity may arise from the fact that nearly 400 volumes (one fifth of the collection) were purchased during Bowdoin's stay in Paris in 1806. While the curricular subjects are represented, the collection focuses on topical concerns of the new nation: recent history, law, and politics. Although not as large as Thomas Jefferson's private library, Bowdoin's was nonetheless respected, valuable, and assembled with intentionality.

Assembling such a collection required leveraging resources in social as well as mediated networks of texts. The use of social capital and international connections was relatively straightforward. Correspondence reveals that Bowdoin relied on familial and professional connections in old England as well as a New England ship captain, who was responsible for, among other things, acquiring a complete copy of Diderot's *Encyclopédie*.[5] His letters report that many such requests went unanswered either because books could not be found or because they were lost in transatlantic shipments. French books were likely bought in Boston, if not in Paris, and letters regarding new purchases often repeated the catalog of authors that Bowdoin already owned, as though he needed to demonstrate to the bookseller that he was a knowledgeable buyer. Accordingly, the collection that Bowdoin was able to assemble was determined by what his network of agents allowed him to see of the print world through their own selection and priorities.

The books, journals, and pamphlets were further mediated by networked sites of advertising and inventory: booksellers' catalogs. This medium participates in the acts of documenting possessions for sale and after purchase that we see in Franzel and Schellenberg's essays. The catalog is a site of unstable inventory and the articulation of desired objects of cultural value to the purchaser. The care with which Bowdoin assembled his collection through this medium can be seen in the dog-eared pages or the ink-filled margins of his copies of book catalogs from sellers, printers, and established libraries. The extant Bowdoin Collection includes eight examples of this genre, representing local institutions such as Harvard and the Boston

4.   Carpenter, "James Bowdoin III," p.114.
5.   This is documented extensively by Carpenter, "James Bowdoin III," p.94–102.

Library, as well as stationers and booksellers in London and Paris.[6] The sales lists that contain dashes, underlines, and other indications that Bowdoin paused over a title will inform much of the context for this essay. Yet his copy of the *Catalogue of books in the Boston Library, May 1, 1797* has several uncut pages, suggesting that it was never thoroughly consulted. The same is true for his copy of the *Catalogue of books in the library of the American Academy of Arts and Sciences* (1802). More than providing suggestions for where Bowdoin acquired these books and pamphlets, the booksellers' lists offer a window onto the selection of authors, languages, and subjects that were available to readers and collectors at the turn of the nineteenth century.

The same mediation applies to the electronic data that today describes Bowdoin's personal library and will be used here to complement the examination of individual objects. Data for the quantitative and distant reading analysis of this library are based on the bibliographic records for those titles, held by the George J. Mitchell Special Collections and Archives and spanning 351.8 linear feet. The records represent the documentation of the original catalogers in 1811, interventions of special collections librarians during their work with James Bowdoin III's library, and metadata development for discoverability in today's electronic catalog of Bowdoin College Library.[7] The result is an opportunity to explore questions of national construction of identity and transatlantic knowledge transfer in this largely symbolic collection by considering the relationships that are apparent from material properties of the volumes, their content, and their bibliographic metadata.

---

6. The dog-eared copy of *A Catalogue of several libraries and parcels lately purchased, containing several thousand volumes of valuable and curious books in almost all languages, arts, and sciences* lists titles and print dates of pieces "Which will begin to be sold very cheap […] on *Monday, Jan. 22, 1759*" by George Keith (London, n.n., 1759).

7. Like any data with a long history, this data needed cleaning to be standardized for a quantitative and digital humanities-based analysis. For example, the "country" heading in the records frequently included abbreviations for states in which a title was printed; the imprint information needed to be separated into city, printer, and year; and the publication date needed to be standardized. Books often resist even these simple, standard categories, which can lead to their exclusion from analysis due to their irregularity. Every attempt was made to be as inclusive as possible with the available information.

Quantifying and contextualizing material properties

Counting and sorting the characteristics of the material history of the books and pamphlets in the collection can offer one way to access the international connections and perspectives to which an early Bowdoin student or faculty member would have had access. Publication location, language, and year of printing all contribute to the sense of the European, transatlantic, or emerging United States identity represented by the titles. Although quantity alone brings attention to English and French titles from Boston, London, and Paris, this section will explore the place of German and Italian authors, titles, and printers for a better understanding of the limits of knowledge networks represented by the collection.

The predominance of texts written in French and English is unsurprising. Working with the physical copies of the books (not pamphlets), the historian Kenneth Carpenter documented that 54 percent of the titles in the collection are in English.[8] According to his calculations, when considering volumes instead of titles, the majority of the volumes (56 percent) are in French. Multivolume sets with twenty or more volumes, such as the *Memoirs* of the Institut national des sciences et des arts, or the complete set of the *Gazette nationale* (considered the record of the French Revolution), account for much of this difference in quantity. But the digital representation of the library through the bibliographic records poses a challenge to confirming Carpenter's observations about linguistic representation by treating pamphlets and books as the same material. It clearly displays the dominance of English (see Figure 24). The digital representation also opens the door to a new question that challenges the privileged position of books as priority objects of cultural exchange: the notable linguistic difference between short- and long-form titles. The language of the medium is as much an indicator of the value of English as a site of monographic authority as it is the language of plurivocality of short, often ephemeral publications on ultracontemporary topics.

The absence of books or pamphlets in German, in particular, fits a trend in the pre- and postrevolutionary learned society of the period. Even though the first Bible to be printed in the colonies in a European language was in German, print overwhelmingly focused on English

---

8.   See Carpenter, "James Bowdoin III," p.94.

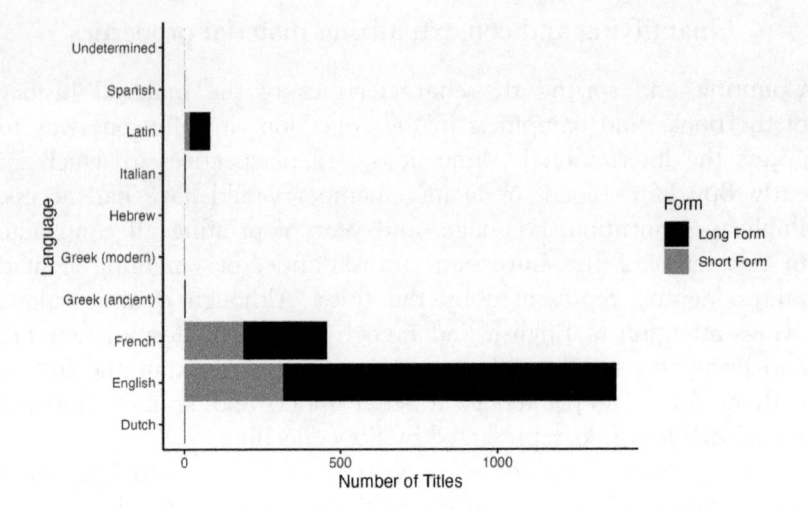

Figure 24: Bar plot of the languages represented in the titles in James Bowdoin III's library collection. Titles published in fifty pages or fewer are considered short form (bound volumes of serial publications are treated as long form since they are organized by an editor). Created by Crystal Hall.

documents.[9] Kirsten Belgum has explored the question of book provenance as a proxy for cultural transfer in her work on German books in the collections of prominent Americans and educational institutions in the United States in the first decades of the nineteenth century. As she states about these early years, "a young scholar in New England had a hard time even finding a book in German to learn the language."[10] The self-representation of the long-form contents of Bowdoin's library confirms her findings.[11]

In a similar vein, there are only three books written in Italian and two Italian linguistic texts in the collection. These titles are related to architecture and plants, volumes full of nontextual information for a

9. Russell L. Martin, III, "North America and transatlantic book culture to 1800," in *A Companion to the history of the book*, ed. Simon Eliot and Jonathan Rose (Oxford, 2007), p.259–72 (264).
10. Kirsten Belgum, "Distant reception: bringing German books to America," in *Distant readings: topologies of German culture in the long nineteenth century*, ed. Matt Erlin and Lynne Tatlock (Cambridge, 2014), p.209–27 (211).
11. A subsequent project for the interested scholar would be to examine the contents of serial publications and bound volumes of multiple texts to examine the multilingualism that pervades nonbook forms in the media of the period.

reader unfamiliar with the language. Bowdoin did purchase a copy of Giuseppe Baretti's popular English–Italian dictionary, English–Spanish dictionary, and Italian grammar. Baretti was one of the more prolific Italian authors in Anglophone circles during this period. His two-volume *Account of Italy* was listed for sale in the same marked catalog and others, although it is not part of Bowdoin's collection.[12] His Italian dictionary is listed in one of Bowdoin's dog-eared book sale catalogs for 2 pounds 2 shillings and at the slightly better price of 1 pound 10 shillings in another.[13] It would seem to have beaten out the equally popular dictionaries and grammars by Palermo (the linguistic resource of choice for Harvard).[14] Baretti's English–Italian dictionary represents one of seventeen linguistic families for which Madison suggested resources for Congress.[15]

Was Bowdoin conscientiously turning away from languages other than French and English, or was there simply a limited supply of books in German, Italian, or Spanish for sale through his network of buyers and sellers? His catalogs tell the story. Bowdoin's copy of the seemingly plurilinguistic *Supplement au catalogue de livres françois, latins, etc.* lists primarily French and Latin titles, with the exception of five Italian books, two in English, and one German title related to horseback riding.[16] The English books are an English–French dictionary and a work on Athenian antiquities. The Italian titles are translations of Virgil's *Aeneid*, a selection of Ovid's letters, and Lucretius's *De rerum natura*, along with Benedetto Varchi's histories, and a series of *disegni* completed in Rome. Bowdoin owned two copies

---

12. John Almon, *A Catalogue of books, with the prices: to be had at J. Almon's, bookseller and stationer, opposite Burlington-House, in Piccadilly* (London, J. Almon, 1774), p.8.

13. Almon, *A Catalogue*, p.6; G. G. J. Robinson, *A Catalogue of books printed for and published by G. G. J. and J. Robinson* (London, Paternoster-Row, 1790), p.15. For perspective, the "Translation of part of the 23rd canto of Ariosto's Orlando Furioso" was listed for 1 shilling, 6d (Almon, *A Catalogue*, p.7).

14. Palermo's *Italian Grammar* (Almon, *A Catalogue*, p.15) was also in Harvard's 1773 catalog of frequently consulted titles, *Catalogus librorum in Bibliotheca cantabrigiensi selectus, frequentiorem in usum Harvardinatum, qui gradu baccalaurei in artibus nondum sunt donati*.

15. Information about Madison's proposed library can be found in Robert A. Rutland, *"Well acquainted with books": the founding framers of 1787, with James Madison's list of books for Congress* (Washington, DC, 1987).

16. *Supplement au catalogue de livres françois, latins, etc. a Amsterdam, sur l'oude Turfmarkt & a Leipzig unter dem hohmannischen hausse auf der Peter-strasse* (Amsterdam, Chez Arkstée et Merkus, 1767).

of the similarly multilingual *Catalogue de livres anglais, allemands, italiens, espagnols, portugais, hollandais, russes, et de langues orientales* (Paris, 1806), but he retained only the first part, the English books.

Nonetheless, the catalogs offer a window into what works were available in translation at the time. Without devolving into a list of lists, the survey of Italian titles in Bowdoin's pamphlets of booksellers' holdings reveals remarkably little overlap in offerings. Even the 1773 catalog of frequently used books in the Harvard library lists few Italian titles: five in Italian, two in translation, and two in Italian with the English translation.[17] The five books in Italian range broadly in topics from two works based on the archeological finds at Herculaneum (rediscovered in 1706) to the first encyclopedia of Italian authors by Giusto Fontanini and the works of Francesco Algarotti, the Newtonian expert who was an active correspondent with French intellectuals in the Republic of Letters. Cesare Beccaria's seminal work on criminal justice (1764) appears here and in many catalogs, unsurprising given its influence on thinkers like Jeremy Bentham and the development of the US Constitution and Bill of Rights.[18] The Bowdoin Collection also includes a translation of Cesare Beccaria's *Essay on crimes and punishments*, with commentary attributed to Voltaire (translated from the French). In 1783, James Madison proposed to Congress a legislative library with the heaviest emphasis on the histories of the United States and Britain; eight titles are in Italian (none in German), including Beccaria on crime and Machiavelli's complete works.[19] Thomas Jefferson's collection showed a similar emphasis on Italian treatises on

17. The translations are Angeloni's *Letters* and Veneroni's *Italian master*. Available in both Italian and English translation are: Cornaro's *On long life* (translation bound with original) and Tasso's *Gerusalemme liberata*.

18. In one of the few instances of two Italian works on the same topic, Bowdoin owned a translation of an edict from the grand duchy of Tuscany, printed after the state had abolished capital punishment. The *Edict of the grand duke of Tuscany, for the reform of criminal law in his dominions* (London, n.n., 1789) announces at the bottom of the title page that the pamphlet was not for sale, but meant to be "had gratis of Messrs. Cadell, Johnson, Dilly, and Taylor." The editor explains why he has paid for a translation and made the work public: "from a general admiration of the *just* and *benevolent* principles by which it was dictated." He goes on to say that the Tuscan system cannot compare to the English, "but at the same time, he is fully persuaded that there are many things in it which are well deserving of *notice* and *imitation*; and that whenever a revisal of our own penal laws shall take place, many useful hints may be derived from this code for their *improvement*" (p.i, recto; italics in the original).

19. See Rutland, *"Well acquainted with books."*

personal rights such as Beccaria's.[20] Importantly, the Harvard catalog also has marginalia from the period, but none of the marks points to titles related to Italy or Italian authors.

The availability of translated work follows the same pattern, or lack thereof, in thematic unity as the advertised books for purchase in Italian. Booksellers offer canonical authors such as Petrarch "translated by Mrs. Dobson" as well as titles that are lesser known today or were written in English by Italians abroad.[21] Perhaps the most curious, and certainly the shortest, example of the latter in Bowdoin's collection is the eight-page pamphlet of self-promoting observations on oral hygiene for children by the Italian-born dental surgeon Bartholomew Ruspini. In this wide-ranging multilingual context, the works translated from Italian in the Bowdoin Collection find an easy home. Subjects span dancing, electricity, literature, natural history, politics, and religion, each represented by, at most, two titles. These include Machiavelli's works as well as unsigned works such as *The nurse: a poem*, both of which were offered for sale in catalogs.[22]

Travel narratives feature most prominently in the Bowdoin Collection, reflecting the commercial and cultural trends of the Grand Tour.[23] Bowdoin amassed a variety of national and professional perspectives on European countries including Italy and Germany (in spite of the challenges to navigating the landscape documented by Karin Baumgartner in her contribution to the current volume). These books include the English naturalist John Ray's *Travels through the Low Countries, Germany, Italy and France* (1738); a reprinting of the Scottish Bishop Burnet's *Travels through France, Italy, Germany, and Switzerland* (1750), of which Bowdoin's fellow statesman John Adams owned a first edition; German archaeologist Johann Georg Keyssler's *Travels through Germany, Bohemia, Hungary, Switzerland, Italy, and Lorrain* (1760); the French astronomer Joseph Jérôme Lalande's *Voyage d'un*

20. See Linda Carroll, *Thomas Jefferson's Italian and Italian-related books in the history of universal personal rights* (New York, 2019).
21. See Almon, *A Catalogue*; Pelham's Circulating Library, *Catalogue of Pelham's Circulating Library, no. 59, Cornhill: consisting of a chosen assortment of books in the various branches of literature* (Charlestown, MA, 1802); and James White, *A Catalogue of books in various branches of literature* (London, n.n., 1797).
22. See Robinson's *Catalogue* for Machiavelli's works, translated by Ellis Farnsworth in 4 volumes, and Pelham's Circulating Library (*Catalogue*, p.38) for "Nurse; an Italian poem, translated by Roscoe."
23. See Harvard University Library, *Catalogus*; Almon, *A Catalogue*, p.14; and Pelham's Circulating Library, *Catalogue*, p.8–9.

François en Italie (1769); French archaeologist Abbot Barthélemy's *Travels in Italy* (1802); and the more general *Guide des voyageurs en Europe* (1807) by the theater director Heinrich August Ottokar Reichard.[24] As Joachim Homann documents in his contribution in the current volume, the export and translation of Italian landscapes was part of a larger aesthetic project, and one that aligns with the literary and linguistic findings presented in the second half of this essay. Although not present in today's collection, Bowdoin's marginalia in a book catalog indicate an interest in two further titles: "*Misson*'s celebrated voyage to *Italy*, recommended by Mr. *Addison*" and *Sentimental letters on Italy by President Dupaty*.[25] The perspectives also include an interest in military expeditions related to the Napoleonic Wars.

Examining the place of publication tells a different story from the examination of the languages in which the works were printed. The books and pamphlets in Bowdoin's collection were printed overwhelmingly in London, Paris, Boston, and Philadelphia. Yet the smaller printing sites tell an important story of the work at the margins to transmit knowledge. For example, by the early 1800s, Bowdoin had collected over 500 books and pamphlets from thirty printing locations in the US.[26] By 1765, German presses had recovered from the devastation of the Thirty Years War of the prior century, but continued political fallout, the lack of foreign knowledge of German, and the challenges of infrastructure limited the materials' wider circulation.[27] Thomas Jefferson, who had a library three times the size of James Bowdoin III's, owned twenty-three titles printed in Germany; Bowdoin had fifteen.[28] Kristen Belgum's work has nicely shown both that German books were rare in American libraries at the turn of the nineteenth century and that the contents of these libraries were typically written in classical Latin. Bowdoin's books from Germany were in French and Latin on subjects as diverse as lexicography and grammar, criminality, histories of the Egyptians and the Chinese, herbaria and plant cultivation, treaties and alliances,

24. See the John Adams Library holdings at Boston Public Library.
25. See *Books of entertainment, &c.* (London, n.n., 1773), p.56, and White, *A Catalogue*, p.26.
26. The first press had been established in the American colonies by 1639, and, a century later, there were fifteen printers operating in nine locations. See Martin, "North America," p.263.
27. Rietje van Vliet, "Print and public in Europe 1600–1800," in *A Companion to the history of the book*, ed. S. Eliot and J. Rose, p.247–58 (249).
28. Belgum, "Distant reception," p.211.

and the complete works of Voltaire in a 1785 edition printed in Kehl. The five books printed in Italy came from Venice (the Italian title on natural history and Lalande's French travel narrative) and Rome (the previously mentioned titles on art and architecture in Italian). The difference between German titles and books produced in Germany, in particular, draws attention to a question raised by Erlin and Walsh in their research on the journals of the German Enlightenment corpus: Who was physically producing the knowledge available for transmission?[29]

When seen as the sum of their material attributes, Bowdoin's non-English and non-French European books represent a culture of consumption without deep engagement in any aspect of national or other identities beyond destinations for travel. Access to non-Anglophone or non-Francophone cultures occurs through translation and transit. While the broad topical coverage would seem to limit possibilities for the narrowing of engagement or stereotyping, the lack of specialization points to a lack of perceived defined identity by foreigners. However, this result is only apparent from a consideration of the material history of these books and pamphlets, understood as institutional, intellectual symbols. This is not an assessment of James Bowdoin III or the early faculty at the college.[30] These are observations based on one kind of evidence. The electronic records associated with James Bowdoin III's collection offer other ways to access and assess the content of the books and pamphlets in order to evaluate this claim.

Networks of ideas

While printing locations and years as well as the dates of activity of authors can provide a certain insight into the collection, they minimally indicate the network of ideas represented by the texts. We know that book usage defies even these categorizations: Readers

29. Belgum, "Distant reception," *passim.*
30. For instance, Parker Cleaveland was academically indebted to and then revered by the French and German mineralogists. Goethe frequently revisited mineralogy and corresponded with one of Cleaveland's pupils. However, that he honored Cleaveland in a poem in 1830 ("Den Vereinigten Staaten") is perhaps an overstatement. On the poem, see Charles C. Calhoun, *A Small college in Maine: two hundred years of Bowdoin* (Brunswick, ME, 1993), p.101–102; for a more extensive discussion, see Thomas Riley, "Goethe and Parker Cleaveland," *PMLA* 67:4 (1952), p.350–74.

make what use they desire from the texts they read. For example, concerning Voltaire's history of the life of Peter the Great, Bowdoin wrote to a young protégé: "[D]ont deceive yourself upon this point thro[h] Juvenile ideas that commercial enquiries cannot be consistently made by British officers, you will find Voltaire's History of Peter y[e]. Great & y[e]. Abbé Raynal's History of the two Indias will assist you in these enquiries."[31] Digital tools allow us two ways to approximate these connections, although both are dependent on the accuracy and the completeness of the data that we utilize. Taken together, these connections can represent a network, which can offer an approximation of the breadth and depth of the collection.

Since we lack details about how Bowdoin would have read (or would have recommended that students read) most of the works that he collected, an extant proxy exists in the Library of Congress subject headings for these works. These are problematic in their own right since they represent a scholarly interpretation of a work and historical bias from their own cultural moment, but they do reflect the organization of the volumes into an intellectual arrangement via keywords for discovering associated records in the library. Of the 1938 entries in the digital catalog of James Bowdoin III's library, only forty-three lack Library of Congress headings, including nine Bibles. The subject headings are not used here as a complete representation of the materials that early students would have found in the volumes that Bowdoin bequeathed to the institution. Instead, the network of connected headings and subheadings offers a way to see a preliminary, albeit imperfect, interpretation of each text.

At the scale of the entire library, all of the interconnections of ideas are visible (see Figure 25). Unsurprisingly, the collection is dominated by the history and politics of France, Great Britain, and the United States. The network allows us to immediately see the emphasis on the American Revolution, biography, commerce, descriptions, and foreign relations (the largest, purple nodes in the online figure). Another highly interconnected set of subject headings relates to Massachusetts, with the heaviest emphasis on sermons (in blue). This is closely related to the brown cluster of subject headings on the Church of England, Catholicism, theology, and ecumenical matters. Finally, natural philosophy, including illustrations, represents the third-largest subject cluster (in green). This group is closely related to classical subjects of Rome, antiquities,

---

31. As cited in Carpenter, "James Bowdoin III," p.88.

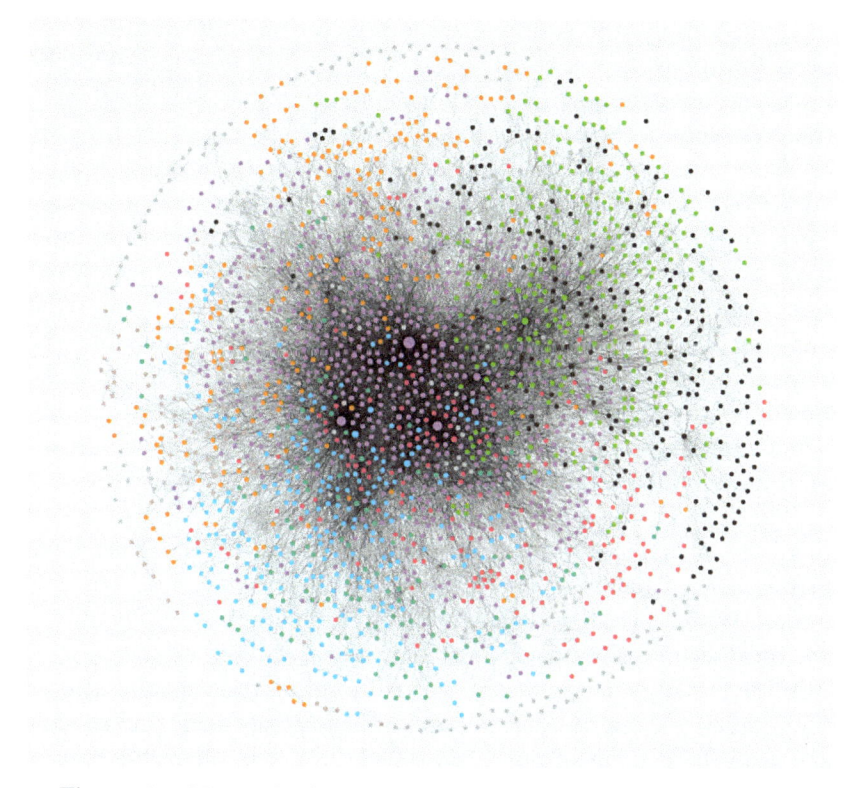

Figure 25: Network visualization of Library of Congress subject headings in James Bowdoin III's library collection. Nodes are subject headings; edges indicate co-appearance in a book's metadata. Color indicates modularity (highly interconnected groups of subject headings). Node size indicates degree (number of connections to other subject headings). Edge thickness indicates relative number of times that connection appears in the collection. An interactive version of this network visualization and a high resolution of this figure can be found online. Created by Crystal Hall.

architecture (in orange), and science periodicals and their coverage (magenta). While these three thematic clusters and their related subtopics account for nearly 80 percent of the subject headings in the collection, the remaining 20 percent are so unconnected to one another and the rest of the graph that they skew the measurements of this network of ideas.

Quite simply, the result is a remarkably unconnected network for a library that was constructed with such intentionality.[32] The visualization captures that Bowdoin's intention was breadth. Rather than densely interconnected specialization, we find a network of ideas that explores the boundaries of late-eighteenth-century knowledge. If we return to the historian who has done the most work on the library, Carpenter, he concludes that Bowdoin "may have been the first American to form a library to give away," since the collection seems comparatively "heterogeneous and unfocused."[33] According to his research, the bequest looks like the acquisition lists of the Harvard Corporation during the years when Bowdoin was a member. He was collecting the types of books that benefactors typically did not donate: reference works, periodicals, and multivolume sets.

The network analysis adds to this understanding by suggesting that this is a collection with wide-ranging content coverage in addition to the type of medium. The peripheral subjects (in gray) represent unique works like Bartholomew Ruspini's pamphlet on dentistry, chemical studies of toxicology and pharmacology, and mathematics.[34] Admittedly, this representation is an artifact of the indexing practices of the Library of Congress, but the subject headings provide preliminary access to the content of hundreds of titles that are otherwise among the great unread by modern scholarship. Although many of these subjects and associated titles have escaped an academic lens, and their status as reading material for early students at the college may have been symbolic at best, they represent a part of this collection that was developed with intentionality and years of work that involved the activation of a network of book buyers. When we consider that Bowdoin intended to donate these volumes to the college, the role of the bequest as foundational takes on new meaning. It was clearly meant for investment—providing not only the seed of the library but also an incentive for further purchase, donations, and collecting for the benefit of a community of future learners, administrators of

32. Available in the digital collaboration hub for the current volume. The undirected graph has a diameter of 8, overall modularity of 0.457 (Louvain algorithm), and density of 0.004. There are 2301 nodes and 13,547 edges.
33. Carpenter, "James Bowdoin III," p.115.
34. A close reading of Ruspini in this context is available in the online supplement to the current volume.

knowledge, and creators, rather than for one's own enjoyment and proof of learnedness.

But where are European cultures in this model of the intellectual contents of the library? By reducing the graph to only the nodes (subject headings) that contain the names or adjectival forms of European countries, we can see the distribution of these countries throughout the topical communities in the network. This approach privileges a post hoc understanding of the nation-state, but is used here to highlight how these nations are connected to the larger conversations seen in the overall network about history, theology, natural philosophy, and so on. Given the predominance of French and British texts, authors, and topics, the diagram in Figure 26 focuses on the other European nations. While most of these subjects are part of the largest cluster on history (purple in Figure 25), Italy, Germany, and Austria are associated with art and architecture (orange). That is, while Sicily, Mount Etna, and Florence exist predominantly in historical subject networks, Italy as a nation is most closely affiliated with art and architecture. Brandenburg stands out for its connection to scientific journals (magenta). Italian and Spanish are part of a smaller group centered on dictionaries (teal, about 5 percent of the nodes). The countries are not heavily interconnected with each other but are instead distributed across the topical coverage of the collection. Consequently, in this twentieth-century mapping of the coverage of the bequest, national identity begins to feel topical, while history seems multinational. The figure is a provocation to explore the nodes in the digital exhibit, for example, to investigate the subject connections to "Germanic peoples" and "Andalusia (Spain)" to see how they are represented if they are not directly connected to nations or historical subjects.

Because this view of transatlantic thought and identity relies on the imposed organizational schema of the Library of Congress,[35] I will now turn to an analytical approach that is more generative, allowing the books and pamphlets to speak for themselves, in a way,

---

35. For a discussion of changes to headings and inclusivity of library science practitioners in the development of these headings, see Alva T. Stone, "The LCSH century: a brief history of the Library of Congress subject headings, and introduction to the centennial essays," *Cataloging & classification quarterly* 29:1–2 (2000), p.1–15. For a deeper engagement with challenges of bias in the schema, see Sara A. Howard and Steven A. Knowlton, "The Library of Congress Classification and subject headings for African American studies and LGBTQIA studies," *Library trends* 67:1 (2018), p.74–86.

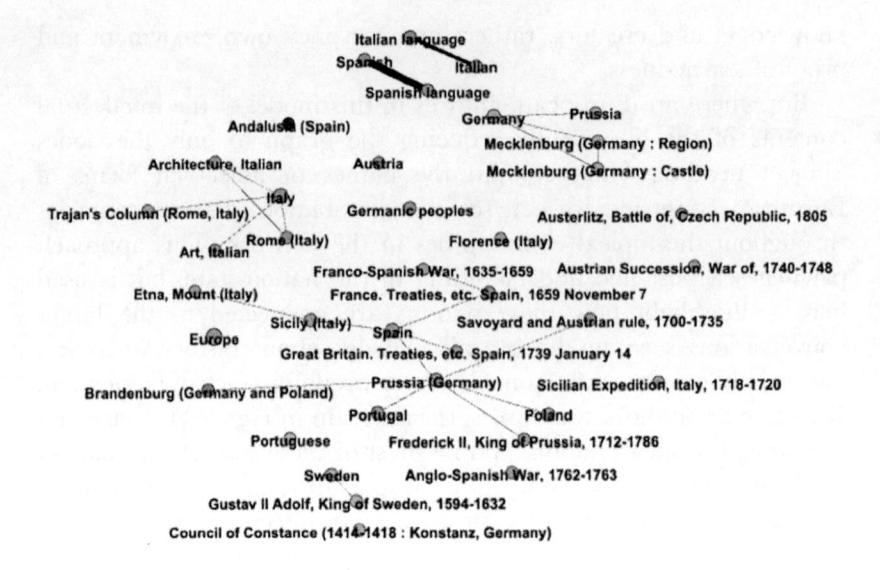

Figure 26: Subset of the network of Library of Congress subject headings in James Bowdoin III's collection. Includes nodes that use nominal or adjectival forms of European countries. Color version of this figure available online. Label size and node size have no symbolic value. The layout was created manually for legibility. Created by Crystal Hall.

through topic modeling. Because the full text of the works in James Bowdoin III's collection is not available, this approach focuses on the title alone. Topic modeling is a method of text analysis usually applied to content, but title pages are rich with descriptors that can help to reveal patterns of advertising to readers—particularly given the lengthy, descriptive titles of the eighteenth and early nineteenth centuries. The approach of prioritizing the title (i.e., the information that was on the first page to reach a reader or in the bookseller's catalog) adds another layer of understanding of how an early Bowdoin student might have encountered European identities in the new collection.

A model of title topics

This final pathway of analysis allows us to see these questions of European cultures in the library from a perspective of distant reading that is similar to what booksellers were trying to achieve with their catalogs of titles. This approach offers a means of seeing the place of translation in the library as well as the narrowing of the media representation of the subjects. Topic modeling presumes that texts, in this case titles, are composed of terms selected from groups of words that are frequently used together. Using a bag-of-words model, the computational process infers the groups from the data provided (the titles); then, human readers of both the texts and the groups of words (topics) in the resulting computational model infer a human-readable label, or topic label, for the "bags of words."[36]

I applied this approach across James Bowdoin III's library with an exploratory goal, not as an attempt to establish an optimized model of the titles.[37] For the titles, topic modeling indicates both attributes that are expected and those that add new information to the analysis of the symbolic and functional values of the collection. Table 5 lists the ten most important terms for assigning a topic to a title in order of importance. This means that, after calculating which words occur together in all of the titles, if a title contains "histoire" (from topic 1 in table 5), the title is more likely to be associated with that topic than with others. Each list of words in Table 5 is a topic, and we can infer names for these topics such as history, literature, religion, book catalogs, governance, trade regulations, and so on.

36. The analyst must also determine the number of topics presumed to be in the collection of texts. After creating models of different sizes, I settled on fifty. Models with more topics were overly specific (e.g., histories written by men named Thomas and histories written by men named James). Models with fewer topics were too general (e.g., modern and ancient history or principles of nature, law, and religion). All work was done in R, with the lda package using a collapsed Gibbs sampler at 5000 iterations. A more detailed explanation of this method can be found in the digital collaboration hub for the current volume.

37. Since the goal was exploratory, not descriptive, I chose a range of topic numbers for the models: 5 (zoomed out, far too general), 25 (driven by language more than topic), 50 (reported here), 100 (too narrow to add to the understanding of national identities for this essay).

Table 5: Most prominent topics in fifty-topic model of titles in James Bowdoin III's library.

	Top ten words in topic	General label
1	histoire vie louis jusqu france lettres langlois paix lhistoire joseph	history
2	magazine london review time british literary universal entertainment monthly doctrine	literature
3	death george esq james sermon church occasioned bowdoin boston washington	religion
4	catalog books various philosophical plantarum boston printed london sold genera	book catalogs
5	law nations french treatise treaties principles rights english government affairs	government
6	commerce trait fran droit code notes leurope nature pr principaux	trade

Quite notably, most of these topics also indicate a format for the topic: letters, magazines, sermons, catalogs, books and treatises, and notes and codes, respectively. Therefore, the inferred label cannot just be French history or British literature, for example, but letters on French history and magazines of British literature. Further refinement would allow us to say with more precision what proportion of the titles fall into these categories, which would be a valuable next step for comparative work. As it stands, this model already adds a new layer of understanding to what Bowdoin was collecting and how driven by format and genre it would appear to be. The results also raise the question of the formats in which these ideas were available generally, so that we may better appreciate what was being transferred across the Atlantic at the turn of the century in terms of ideas packaged as objects. In spite of the long-standing privileged status of the book, the model emphasizes a semantic network for titles that is dependent on self-presentation as something other than a book. It also challenges an understanding of knowledge networks that relies only on one material form of dissemination of that knowledge.

The model is built from evidence from a historically and culturally situated decision about appeal to potential readers: the title. The results draw our attention to some of the features of both *translatio studii* (the imperialistic transfer of loci of cultural importance) and translation within the collection that were not captured by the language of publication, printing location, identity of the author, or subject headings. To explore this further, Table 6 presents topics related to language, with a focus on translation.

Table 6: Topics related to translation in fifty-topic model of James Bowdoin III's library.

	Top ten words in topic	General label
14	english use grammar latin dictionary words language languages spanish new	bilingual English dictionaries
15	english notes translated testament history greek critical bible new latin	biblical translation
18	translated english french written monsieur mr latin thomas greek originally	classical translation
23	fran dictionnaire french ois nouveau latin ais traduite traduction remarques	bilingual French dictionaries
24	translated french plates travels history illustrated copper original natural general	translated travel volumes

The linguistic attributes of the collection are complicated by these results. We could call topics 14 and 23 bilingual English and French dictionaries, respectively. Topics 15, 18, and 24 outline different translation priorities: biblical notes, classical essays and works, and illustrated travel volumes, respectively. So, while material history suggests a broad range of subject matter coming from non-Anglophone, non-Francophone, and non-Latin sources, the role of declaring a translation for promoting or identifying a work carries other connotations. We have lost the granularity of distinguishing the translation of Italian texts on dance, electricity, and politics that we saw in the collection with other tools, but have gained a window onto how a majority of translators and publishers in this collection positioned their works in a larger context.

The translators offer the best evidence for what is implied by their work, whether it be bringing along the ideas into a new language or appropriating those ideas within a new cultural system expressed in that language. For example, the collection includes an English translation from the French translation of Ludovico Muratori's Italian *Relations of the missions of Paraguay* (1759), written about a country with its own multilingual identity. In this long chain of *translatio*, there is no statement about the liberties the English translator may have taken with the French text. The English preserves the admission of the French translator from the Italian about adding roughly six pages of explanatory material while having "taken a greater liberty in cutting off some things" that seemed "useless" and transposing sections of text that seemed "misplaced" in the original version.[38] Even language books such as dictionaries and grammars partake in the interpretation of materials in this liminal space between two cultures. In the final section of his popular *Grammar of the Italian language,* Joseph Baretti offers sentences from his "friend and instructor" Samuel Johnson as a form of supplemental education for "youth, whom experience has not yet taught the ways of the world, I have added to it a Praxis of sentences, collected from the works of my friend and instructor Mr. Samuel Johnson."[39] The "Praxis" appears as the last section of the volume, after the "Grammar of the English language / Grammatica della lingua inglese" that offers a short introduction to English for Italian speakers. Presented as "Thoughts on various subjects / Pensieri sopra vari soggetti," the 135-page section offers facing-column translations from English to Italian of passages ranging in length from a single sentence to two pages. Given its location in the volume, the "Praxis" seems intended for native speakers of both languages. Baretti samples heavily from Johnson's *The Rambler,* in which the noted English author wrote, for example: "There is nothing more dreadful to an author than neglect; compared with which, reproach, hatred, and opposition, are names of happiness; yet this worst, this meanest fate, every one who dares to write has reason to dread."[40] Baretti reorganizes the quotation (with certain liberties) and eliminates the context for this seemingly harsh understanding of happiness: "Reproach and hatred are names of happiness when compared with neglect / I rimproveri e l'odio altrui ci dogliono a un gran pezzo meno che non l'altrui dispregio."[41] These

38. Ludovico Muratori, *A Relation of the missions of Paraguay: wrote originally in Italian, by Mr. Muratori, and now done into English from the French translation* (London, J. Marmaduke, 1759), p.vi. See Girolamo Imbruglia, *The Jesuit missions in Paraguay and a cultural history of utopia (1568–1789),* translated by Mark Weyr (Leiden, 2017), for the political and theological implications.

39. Joseph Baretti, *A Grammar of the Italian language* (London, Hitch *et al.,* 1762), p.i.

40. Samuel Johnson, "No. 2: the necessity and danger of looking into futurity," *The Rambler* (March 24, 1750), https://www.johnsonessays.com/the-rambler/no-2-the-necessity-and-danger-of-looking-into-futurity/ (last accessed June 28, 2023).

41. Baretti, *A Grammar,* p.154.

are but two examples of a larger project of translation, *translatio studii*, and transport occurring across national, continental, and temporal divides. James Bowdoin III was able to collect portions of this project at different levels.

Thus, we can say that there are Italian authors in the collection and an interest in the Italian language, and the topic model can even point us toward the predominance of translations in the collection. Yet the work of making the connection between languages and, by extension, between cultural milieus, via translation, is more complex than its representation as an edge in a network diagram would suggest. The edge—the indication of a potential structure for transfer, movement, and relationality—is necessarily a site of selection and modification. Digital humanities tools offer a way to envision those sites of potential exchange in their totality; digital humanities methods offer the iterative and nonlinear understandings to emerge; and close reading brings the varieties of transatlantic, European identities in James Bowdoin III's library into relief: the mainstream, book-driven *translatio studii* and the peripheral genres and voices that underwent transformation prior to being identified for inclusion in the collection.

Conclusion

The College Library was an early priority of the trustees, with an initially greater symbolic value than the practical, educational purpose that it would later serve. When President Joseph McKeen opened the college in 1802 to its first class of eight students led by one professor, the library was housed in what was then a wooden chapel. Samuel Deane, a member of the first board of trustees, used his personal library to seed the collection, which was supplemented by small, individual donations.[42] The trustees defined the role of the college librarian in their 1795 meeting prior to having books, a space to house them, or even a site for the college! One historian has pointed out that this meant Bowdoin "had a library before it had a president, faculty, buildings, or students."[43] Yet consultation was limited to the hours of 12:00–1:00, one day per week.[44] To claim that its items, individually or collectively via their embedded networks,

---

42. See Calhoun, *A Small college*, p.105; and Louis C. Hatch, *The History of Bowdoin College* (Portland, ME, 1927), p.9.
43. Calhoun, *A Small college*, p.105.
44. Calhoun, *A Small college*, p.105–106.

structured students' engagement with disciplines or interdisciplinary endeavors or even fostered knowledge of other cultures would be an overstatement. The library's overt investment was more modest, though its effects were more far-reaching.

Following closely upon the institutional models of Harvard and Brown, a collection of books was an important structure to represent intellectual and cultural capital, but there was little demand for the content in the early decades of the college's history. Moreover, James Bowdoin III's bequest arrived in Brunswick in 1811, only one year after the opening of the University of Berlin, which offered the first example of the Humboldt model for an academic research library that would change the nature of higher education.[45] In a pre-Humboldt era of the value of a library for an institution, students and faculty were able to take advantage of circulating libraries and private, family collections to meet their scholarly and entertainment needs. Inadvertently, James Bowdoin III was ahead of his time. He sponsored and encouraged a model of collection and sharing that became exemplary as academic libraries began to model themselves on par with their European counterparts.

Nonetheless, Bowdoin and his network of agents were operating in the decades during and after the American and French Revolutions and the Napoleonic campaigns in order to establish this collection of materials. In a way that is heavily associated with medium and genre, the library collection represents unspecified and varied interests that rarely go further than the individuals and authors who had already penetrated British and French cultural concerns. It is worth bearing in mind that Bowdoin's donation of his art collection, built in part from his Grand Tour in the early 1770s, reveals a completely different approach to intercultural exchange. Given the limited availability overall, the library bequest nonetheless offers multiple pathways to explore German and Italian topics. National and international perspectives are spread across a breadth of subjects in the books and pamphlets. Translation reflects *translatio studii* as much as it does an assimilation or incorporation of ideas across borders.

Now, if this all sounds too smooth or utopian, without the messiness of the conflicts that occurred throughout these decades, we can turn to the periodicals in the collection for another perspective. Periodicals are underrepresented in the approaches used so far, but Bowdoin's

---

45. See Wayne Bivens-Tatum, *Libraries and the Enlightenment* (Sacramento, CA, 2012).

collection balances the two hierarchies of knowledge represented by periodicals and nonserial publications. As James Wald has outlined, the book-length volumes carry the venerable permanence of the knowledge of an individual, while the periodicals present a collective of voices, often on ephemeral but recent topics.[46] The index for a journal or magazine can offer a window into its contents akin to the Library of Congress subject headings, albeit one contemporary to the material and with little or no claim to neutrality. Summarizing from the index of the *London magazine* (a periodical present in the collection), Italy appears in the publication both for its cultural offerings (dancing, opera, singing, and travels) and also for its pitied role in European conflicts.[47] In this way, Italy is most similar to ancient Greece, albeit primarily the ancient culture that has since lost its power while retaining its interest to tourists. Germans are treated much more roughly: as a populace subject to criticism, as nobility under question, and as a political threat to England. Given the political relationship between England and Spain, the similarly critical, war-focused treatment of Spain is unsurprising. As Erlin and Walsh highlight elsewhere in this volume, we want our data to point to accepted knowledge about the period (the index is an additional reliable witness in our historiographical toolkit) and to open new roads of research (the journals will capture an aspect of European cultures absent from the curated advertising and inventory of booksellers).

These topics, in the difference between what can be gleaned from the books and pamphlets, shift the questions of transatlantic cultural transfer into a realm in which medium is of the utmost importance but also must be considered heterogeneously in order to formulate a comprehensive understanding of cross-cultural exchange around 1800. As part of an ultracontemporary gift for the foundation of a liberal arts college in the early nineteenth century, these volumes represent the phases of national identity formation of the eighteenth century, with all of the implied conflict, anxieties, and ambitions.

46. James Wald, "Periodicals and periodicity," in *A Companion to the history of the book*, ed. S. Eliot and J. Rose, p.421–33.
47. *General index to twenty-seven volumes of the London magazine, viz. from 1732 to 1758 inclusive* (London, n.n., 1760), Eighteenth Century Collections Online, Gale, Bowdoin College Library. Pages are unnumbered, but the headings for all subjects mentioned here are, respectively: IR-IT, GR-GU, GE-GE, SP-SP.

III

Reading

First letters

NACIM GHANBARI

University of Siegen

The first letter

On April 28, 1761, thirty-nine-year-old Anna Louisa Karsch wrote a letter to Johann Wilhelm Ludwig Gleim. Not much older than Karsch, Gleim—in contrast to the letter writer, who was raised in poverty—had published several volumes of poetry and was known for his German odes. Karsch thus addressed her letter to the poet, the *Dichter*, and registered that she had revered him "not only since yesterday [...] no, but for a long time."[1] This first letter is written by a long-term devoted female reader speak but also someone who (albeit only over the last few months) has found herself torn from the "darkness" and "tumult of oppressive worries" ("Tumult niederdrükender sorgen")[2] and thrown into the whirlwind of literary Berlin. Her mention of Berlin *Gesellschafften*, "societies,"[3] serves as an introduction to a period of poetic productivity; after all, while experienced as hostile, the environment is what induces Karsch to

1. This essay was translated by Joel Golb. The German version of this essay, titled "Erste Briefe," can be found in *Goethe medial: Aspekte einer vieldeutigen Beziehung*, ed. Margrit Wyder, Barbara Naumann, and Georges Felten (Berlin, 2021), p.9–25. The current essay is largely similar to the German version, other than the remarks on Anna Louisa Karsch, and is published here with permission from De Gruyter.
   "nicht erst seit gestern [...] nein schon lange"; *"Mein Bruder in Apoll": Briefwechsel zwischen Anna Louisa Karsch und Johann Wilhelm Ludwig Gleim*, vol.1, ed. Regina Nörtemann (Göttingen, 1996), p.5. This discussion is connected to a book project treating patronage and eighteenth-century German literature. The project has been organized under the auspices of the Media of Cooperation collaborative research center 1187, funded by the German Research Foundation.
2. Nörtemann, *"Mein Bruder,"* vol.1, p.5.
3. Nörtemann, *"Mein Bruder,"* vol.1, p.5.

write, for the sake of, as she cryptically puts it, "Beßer mein zu sein" ("being myself better").

What Karsch describes as "efforts" emerging from convivial hubbub was not presented to Berlin's society but rather (as far as we can gather from her narrative) meant to find a public among select friends—a privileged circle. Hence, Karsch begins by introducing a "friend" who has delivered Gleim's greeting and "encouragement" to her and is in possession of Karsch's work (the unnamed friend was Karl Wilhelm Ramler). The reference to the friend here serves as a kind of door opener; he will turn out to be the godfather of a relationship that will endure for over thirty years. Although, as the deliverer of Karsch's writing to Gleim, Ramler is mentioned as a possible mediator, Karsch seizes the opportunity to address Gleim directly in an unmediated way and spontaneously pass on a poetic "trifle":

> for the sake of being myself better, I often pick up the pen and write amidst all the surrounding noise, and my indifferent friend will be able to send you two efforts of that sort. I believe that I do not have enough sweep for the ode; however, our emulator of Horace tells me that you are requesting several songs from me that you will find suitable to entitle odes; here is one such trifle.[4]

The letter from Karsch to Gleim can be read in various ways. The obvious context for understanding this short text is, above all, the complete correspondence consisting of the thousand-plus letters that Karsch sent to Gleim and Gleim's about two hundred answers, archived in the Gleimhaus in Halberstadt.[5] Regina Nörtemann's two-volume edition of the letters contains only a third of them, but nevertheless offers a good idea of the long-lasting epistolary partnership: a partnership that, as Nörtemann observes in the

---

4. "offt ergreiff ich um Beßer mein zu sein die feder und schreibe mitten untter den Geräusch was um mich her ist, und mein gleichgülltiger freund wird Ihnen zweene Versuche von dieser Art senden können, ich glaube nicht Schwung genug zur Ode zu haben, indeßen sagt mir unßer Nachahmer des Horaz daß Sie mehrere Gesänge von mir verlangen denen Sie den Tittel Einer Ode zu geben vor gut finden, hier ist Eine sollche Kleinigkeit"; Nörtemann, *"Mein Bruder,"* p.5–6.
5. Ute Pott, *Briefgespräche: über den Briefwechsel zwischen Anna Louisa Karsch und Johann Wilhelm Ludwig Gleim: mit einem Anhang bislang ungedruckter Briefe aus der Korrespondenz zwischen Gleim und Caroline Luise von Klencke* (Göttingen, 1998), p.7.

edition's afterword, frustrates standard categories of friendship, love, and working relations.[6]

In this essay, I present an additional interpretive framework by removing Karsch's letter of April 28, 1761 from the context of the epistolary exchange and aligning it differently. Even before being answered by Gleim and becoming part of a long communicative process, Karsch's letter is a "first letter." Its status and value are unique. Here, I would like to sketch the systematic value of "first letters" for the study of social networks around 1800 and comment on a series of them. Such an approach offers a new perspective within eighteenth-century studies: In this framework, epistolary communication emerges as more than a transmission of exclusively private documents, rather constituting an important medium for overcoming hierarchic and cultural borders. Conceiving these letters as a network-creating textual form allows for a correction of the established literary-historical narrative that aligns letters with the personal and private sphere. In the case of Karsch's literary work, this perspective allows us to free her oeuvre from being narrowly defined by Gleim and his circle, and consequently circumscribed within the cult of friendship-enthused *Empfindsamkeit*. "First letters" draw our attention to medial practices of patronage and the dependence of networks on material objects.

A youth awaiting patronage

A number of recent publications make use of the concept of social networks to describe and analyze medial and literary history. In these publications, the network is sometimes used as a metaphor for a mesh of informal ties and sometimes inherits the concept of the egalitarian social circle or—to use the German term—*Sozietät*, which has been crucial for research on the Enlightenment.[7] If we consider the conceptual history of the term "social network" to better understand the network metaphor's currency in this context, one thing becomes abundantly clear: Network is being used, first and foremost, to describe asymmetric relationships developed outside of

---

6. Regina Nörtemann, "Nachwort," in *"Mein Bruder in Apoll": Briefwechsel zwischen Anna Louisa Karsch und Johann Wilhelm Ludwig Gleim*, vol.2, ed. Ute Pott (Göttingen, 1996), p.523–55.

7. Nacim Ghanbari, "Netzwerktheorie und Aufklärungsforschung," *Internationales Archiv für Sozialgeschichte der deutschen Literatur* 38:2 (2013), p.315–35 (323–26).

established institutional frameworks.[8] The question of eighteenth-century networks thus leads directly to that of social relations, which were asymmetric and nonbinding (i.e., not contractually or institutionally secured), as Melanie Conroy, among others, shows for networks on either side of the French Revolution.

In the eighteenth century, in contrast to the binding contract, the relationship between patron and client was defined as a form of "incomplete obligation."[9] The relationship was the outcome of an exchange of mediatory services and protection or financial support. The exchange could but did not necessarily have to imply reciprocity. On the side of the donating party, those participating in the exchange were designated as patron, benefactor, or friend; on the side of the receiving party, they were referred to as client or, again, friend.[10] Friendship was thus the concept that held the two positions together in a semantically fluid process, often disguising dependencies. The medium of friendship and, as we shall see, that of patronage, was first and foremost the letter.

A "first letter" aims at establishing this relationship of patronage. But what are the defining features of such a letter? When we read eighteenth-century letters, we may be struck by the preponderance of epistles that could not possibly be first letters: Often without salutations, these letters begin abruptly, *in medias res*, with thanks for received mail or a complaint about not receiving a response to a letter. Most of the extant letters, then, refer to already established correspondence. In contrast, "first letters" maintain an ambivalent relationship to the sphere of written communication. They may refer to the author's written or desired correspondence with other people, which may even have motivated the "first letter," and, frequently, one's own or a third name appears in the letter of a still unfamiliar, "absent" person. In any case, the first letter refers to a space outside of the existing network, a bridge that is yet to exist. Moreover, "first letters" remind us of a world outside of written communication whenever they seek to legitimize their effort to establish contact through the

8.   Ghanbari, "Netzwerktheorie," p.326–30.
9.   "Patron," in Johann Heinrich Zedler, *Grosses vollständiges Universal-Lexikon*, vol.26 (1740; Graz, 1961), col.1400–1402 (1401).
10. The term "patronage" is mainly used in a generic sense: Although the Latin root word, *patron*, is derived from *pater* and is a masculine noun, the patronage relationship includes female benefactors and clients. In eighteenth-century German-language literature, the *Patronin* is a well-known figure.

letter by referring to personal contact with a friend in common. To be sure, the first sentences of such letters often do not reveal whether the mediating reference belongs to the spoken realm of personal contact or to the written sphere of an established correspondence; however, they do make clear that seeking out epistolary communication is justified.

This understanding of a "first letter" thus needs to be distinguished from an author's first *transmitted* letter. Nevertheless, the two definitions are interrelated. In fact, literary studies owes one of the few close readings of a "first letter" to the intersection of the two definitions: In a 1976 essay, later republished in an essay collection, *Der Briefschreiber Goethe* (2015), Albrecht Schöne discusses Goethe's letter to Ernst Carl Ludwig Ysenburg von Buri,[11] dated May 23, 1764. This was the first of three letters that the fourteen-year-old Goethe sent to the seventeen-year-old Ysenburg von Buri; it is also the first letter by Goethe that has been preserved.[12] With his letter, Goethe was following a clearly defined goal: acceptance into the literary Arcadian Society of Phylandria, presided over by Ysenburg von Buri. Schöne deciphers the different references and allusions and the letter's form as elements of a rhetorically schooled, polite "application letter."[13] These elements include the following: making sure that "I" does not appear in the first sentence; social distance, which Goethe expressed by leaving a distinct empty space between the salutation and the start of the letter proper; the date placed at the end of the letter; the compliment extended to Ysenburg von Buri that opens the letter; and, finally, a self-presentation consisting exclusively of literary allusions. Schöne refrains, however, from defining the letter as standard or, in Ysenburg von Buri's words, as *artig*, since, to paraphrase Buri further, according

11. Albrecht Schöne, *Der Briefschreiber Goethe* (Munich, 2015), p.43–71. First published as "Soziale Kontrolle als Regulativ der Textverfassung: über Goethes ersten Brief an Ysenburg von Buri," in *Wissen aus Erfahrungen: Werkbegriff und Interpretation heute—Festschrift für Herman Meyer*, ed. Alexander von Bormann (Tübingen, 1976), p.217–41. Ernst Carl Ludwig Ysenburg von Buri (1746–1807) published a group of comedies and tragedies between 1778 and 1793 that have been largely forgotten by German literary history. In civic life he became a soldier. *Deutsches Literatur-Lexikon: biographisch-bibliographisches Handbuch*, ed. Bruno Berger and Heinz Rupp, vol.2 (Bern, 1969), col.381.

12. As Albrecht Schöne notes, strictly speaking, two earlier epistolary poems by Goethe to his grandparents would have to count as well. Schöne, *Briefschreiber Goethe*, p.48.

13. Schöne, *Briefschreiber Goethe*, p.52.

to all the rules of art, the letter sets up its constructive principle in an all too refined, even polemical, manner. On various occasions, it takes a commentating or even explanatory position vis-à-vis itself, as if the letter writer wishes the addressee to understand that he knows exactly how to write a formally perfect letter.

Schöne's reading of Goethe's "first letter" addresses the rhetorical and social challenges of establishing communication across institutional and cultural borders by relying on an apt literary-historical anecdote. The reading draws on a metaphor that alludes to an increasingly popular custom in eighteenth-century houses of bourgeois Germans: employing tailors as servants in order to keep household costs as low as possible. Those suffering under this beautiful new idea contrived by inventive household heads were, above all, the tailors themselves, finding their art demoted to a pure service function in a household; however, the sons of such households, intent on elegant presentation, were also thus deprived of access to select tailors. In the year of his "first letter," 1764, Goethe was such a son and, in Schöne's words, was also "oddly" dressed, which is to say "swathed" in old-fashioned attire.[14] Laying aside old clothes and styles had to wait until he left the paternal household and moved to Leipzig.

Schöne's reading of Goethe's "first letter" is itself elegantly "swathed" in observations of a vestimentary sort—observations suggesting adherence to a corporative vestimentary order, although the self-reflective elements they contain point to a sense of fashion or an awareness of one's own unfashionable appearance. But, moving beyond this, it is clear that this "first letter" articulates a sense of an already existing social network with which the letter writer would like to establish contact.

How to write a first letter

According to Schöne, the corporative vestimentary order requires correspondence according to "letter-writing guides" (*Briefsteller*), which prescribe epistolary rhetoric, formal structure, and appearance. In his reading of Goethe's epistle, Schöne refers to Christian Weise's letter-writing schemata in the *Neu-Erleuterten Politischen Redner* (*Political orator, newly commented upon*) of 1684 and the *Curiösen Gedancken Von Deutschen Brieffen* (*Curious thoughts on German letters*) of 1691. Goethe's letter here follows Weise's prescription of a five-part chreia (or

14. Schöne, *Briefschreiber Goethe*, p.46.

anecdote), which takes the two basic epistolary elements of *Vorsatz* and *Nachsatz* (i.e., the preliminary and concluding material or, transposed from the Latin *antecedens* and *consequens*, the "premises" and "results") and added to them a *connexio* (transition) and then initial and final compliments.[15] The epistolary examples that Weise weaves into his discussion are almost entirely from the sphere of patron–client relations. Many of the letters begin with the salutation *Mein Patron* and conclude with the formula *Meines Herrn Dienstergebenster*, which roughly translates as "In my good sir's most respectful service." The examples are a treasure trove for cultural-historical exploration of the phenomenon of patronage, as they open up the broad field of services, connections, and objects for which a client could call upon a patron.[16] When it comes to an inquiry into "first letters," Weise's book, *Curiöse Gedancken*, represents a peculiar phenomenon—in that it does not contain a single example of a "first letter." The social world reflected in the enclosed sample letters is one of already existing patron–client relations, maintained through congratulatory, invitational, and beseeching communication.

These omissions notwithstanding, we do find one epistolary schema that is very similar to the idea of a first letter: "*Initial-Compliment.* I take the liberty, / despite his numerous duties / to write

15. Reinhard M. G. Nickisch, *Die Stilprinzipien in den deutschen Briefstellern des 17. und 18. Jahrhunderts: mit einer Bibliographie zur Briefschreiblehre (1474–1800)* (Göttingen, 1969), p.108–11.

16. The pattern at work in most of the guides is that those speaking are nearly exclusively future male clients. The rare letters "from a woman's hand" are stylized replies to contact initiations of an erotic nature. The replies are first and foremost rejections and evasions dictated to the virtuous females. *Des Galanten Frauenzimmers kluge Hofmeisterin* directly advises female readers that this instruction book is meant not to write letters—apparently, the possibility of letters to both female friends and female patrons was not even considered. The book draws its female readers' attention to a problem seen as inherent in the very form of the letter itself, even when serious business matters are being addressed: "At the letter's opening and closing, certain pleasant forms of speech are used / called compliments; but she cannot choose the words so well / that they cannot be wickedly appropriated and interpreted very badly" ("man bedient sich allezeit im eingang und zu ende der briefe einiger angenehmen redens=arten / die man *compliment*en nennet; sie kan aber die worte nicht so wohl auswehlen / daß man denselben nicht eine schlimme auslegung boßhafftig zueignen möge"). If writing a letter cannot be avoided, the recommendation is to make it "very short" ("gantz kurtz"). *Des Galanten Frauenzimmers kluge Hofmeisterin aus dem Französischen ins Teutsche übersetzt* (Leipzig, J. Thomas Fritsch, 1696), p.196–97.

him. | *Antecedens.* I would be very interested in becoming acquainted with the patron. | *Connexio.* Now I know | that the same person stands in good relationship with him: | *Conseqvens.* I thus request | that he should not refrain from his recommendation. | *Final-Compliment.* I intend to expiate this with at least a pious prayer."[17] Weise furthermore devotes a section to letters that are *weitläuffig,* "expansive" or, as he implies, "needing amplification." For him, the letter's purpose is the search for a patron. Using and amplifying himself as an example, he equips the speaking "I," who now has the audacity to speak up, with a brief story: "I have now continued my studies to the point | where generous friends have advised me | that I should look about for a patron | through whose gracious *cooperation* the path to advancement might prove somewhat easier."[18] The letter's addressee is a friend, who "during his important *expeditionibus* at an aforementioned illustrious court made an acquaintance of no insignificant nature,"[19] and who may be helpful to the letter writer. Acquaintance with the potential patron needs mediation by a friend; direct contact by the potential client seems inconceivable in Weise's epistolary universe. This makes clear why this sort of letter has to remain a lacuna in Weise's book.

If we consider the status of the "first letter" across German letter-writing guides from the seventeenth and eighteenth centuries, then our suggestion is confirmed: Authors consistently argue from within an already existing network of patronage relationships. In these guides, entry into a patron–client relationship appears to be problematic, and

17. *"Initial-Compliment.* Ich nehme die Kühnheit | bey seinen vielfältigen Verrichtungen an ihn zu schreiben. | *Antecedens.* Ich möchte gerne mit dem Patron bekandt seyn. | *Connexio.* Nun weiß ich | daß derselbe mit ihm in guten Vernehmen stehet: | *Conseqvens.* Als bitte ich | Er wolle mir seine *Recommendation* nicht versagen. | *Final-Compliment.* Ich will solches zum wenigsten mit einem andächtigen Gebet verschulden." *Christian Weisens Curiöse Gedancken von Deutschen Brieffen wie ein junger Mensch, sonderlich ein zukünfftiger Politicus, die galante Welt wohl vergnügen soll; in kurtzen und zulänglichen Regeln so dann in anständigen und practicablen Exempeln ausführlich vorgestellet; erster und andrer Theil* (Dresden, Johann Christoph Mieth, 1691), p.86.
18. "Ich habe mein Studieren nunmehro so weit fortgesetzet | daß ich mich | auff Einrathen vornehmer Freunde | nach einem Patron umsehen sollte | durch dessen gnädige *cooperation* der Weg zur Beförderung etwas leichter möchte gewiesen werden." *Christian Weisens Curiöse Gedancken,* p.87 (italics in the original).
19. "bey seinen wichtigen Expeditionibus, an gedachten Hochfürstl. Hofe nicht eine geringe Bekandtschafft erworben hat." *Christian Weisens Curiöse Gedancken,* p.87.

the guides underscore this verdict in many different ways; sometimes the entry occurs only as if it were en passant. The silence (or even the void) of the "first letter" calls for an explanation. The guides clearly show a certain familiarity with what Johann Christoph Stockhausen includes in his *Grundsätze wohleingerichteter Briefe* (*Principles of well-designed letters*) of 1751: the "enlistment letter" (*Anwerbungsschreiben*), "in which a person asks for the friendship of another."[20] But, although Stockhausen lists the *Anwerbungsschreiben*, he neither explains how to write them nor considers them relevant: "I here find little worth mentioning."[21] Such (seemingly) absent attention to "enlistment letters" is not restricted to one guide; Christian Fürchtegott Gellert's collection of 1751, *Briefe, nebst einer praktischen Abhandlung von dem guten Geschmacke in Briefen* (*Letters, alongside a practical treatise on good taste in letters*) contains only a single "first letter" displaying all the genre features.[22] While some examples in the preface and many of the seventy-three letters recommended for imitation can be placed in the context of patronage,[23] we again have letters addressed to clients in order to confirm already existing patronage relationships by communicating thanks.[24]

Despite this, Gellert's collection is of great importance when it comes to understanding the complexities of the patron–client relationship, as it is the first book to explain the apparently insecure status of the "first letter" by spotlighting the fragility of the relationship itself—thus leaving behind the prevailing assumption of the letter-writing guides that the drafting of "enlistment letters" was a self-evident process hardly needing explanation. Gellert was the first to define letters to patrons and benefactors as a liminal phenomenon that cannot easily be aligned with the ideal of the "natural letter," which he describes as a "free imitation of good conversation,"[25] because the relationship

20. "worinn man sich die Freundschaft eines andern ausbittet." *Johann Christoph Stockhausens Grundsätze wohleingerichteter Briefe, nach den neuesten und bewährtesten Muster der Deutschen und Ausländer; nebst beygefügten Erläuterungen und Exempeln* (Helmstädt, Christian Friederich Weygand, 1751), p.190.
21. "Hiebey finde ich wenig zu erinnern." *Stockhausens Grundsätze*, p.190.
22. Christian Fürchtegott Gellert, *Gesammelte Schriften: Kritische, kommentierte Ausgabe*, ed. Bernd Witte, vol.4 (Berlin, 1989), p.175–76.
23. Gellert, *Gesammelte Schriften*, p.111–12, 116, 166–67, 190–91, and 207–208.
24. Gellert, *Gesammelte Schriften*, p.199–200, 202, and 211–12.
25. "freye Nachahmung des guten Gesprächs." Gellert, *Gesammelte Schriften*, p.111. The topical nature of this definition is highlighted in Diethelm Brüggemann, "Gellert, der gute Geschmack und die üblen Briefsteller: zur Geschichte der

between nonequals at work here is an obstacle to just that candor attributed to spoken discourse and, by extension, to epistolary form: "One should not speak with important gentlemen freely, and what is more likely then speaking with them fearfully?"[26] The impossibility of approaching "important men," *große Herren*, is manifest in the reluctance of many letter-writing guides to offer polished examples of "first letters."

But this insecurity is not only grounded in patron–client asymmetry. It calls attention to a problem already examined by Mark S. Granovetter, one of the first theorists of networks, in a broadly discussed 1973 essay entitled "The strength of weak ties."[27] Granovetter here makes the empirical observation that close relatives and friends ("strong ties") are virtually never responsible for the circulation of important information; that role falls on rather distant acquaintances ("weak ties"). This observation implies that social networks are unpredictable, which also holds for access to these networks and developing ties within and among them. While novel at the time, today this observation strikes us as self-evident because any idea of a regulated network with a clearly defined origin and clear rules for expansion is basically a self-contradiction. Most importantly, Granovetter's idea challenges well-worn assumptions about eighteenth-century communication networks as well as the role that guidebooks played in engineering epistolary exchange. In their tendency to wrap themselves in silence when it comes to exemplary "first letters," de facto leaving the drawing up of such letters to the inventiveness of those striving for acceptance, the guides confirm a central assumption of network theory: brokerage.

A patron/client in action: Goethe's first letters

Schöne's reading of Goethe's first letter directly takes up the problem of the impossibility of addressing "important gentlemen" in that it deciphers self-reflective references and self-commentary as a sovereign

---

Rhetorik in der Moderne," *Deutsche Vierteljahrsschrift für Literaturwissenschaft und Geistesgeschichte* 45:1 (1971), p.117–49 (145).

26. "Man soll mit großen Herrn nicht frey reden; und was ist alsdann möglicher, als daß man ängstlich spricht?" Gellert, *Gesammelte Schriften*, p.141.

27. Mark S. Granovetter, "The strength of weak ties," *American journal of sociology* 78:6 (1973), p.1360–80.

distancing from the instructions of letter-writing guides. To be sure, the young Goethe does bow to the rules of the guidebooks, but, by having them appear in somewhat "costumed" form, he prepares his emancipation from them. I would like to discuss this interpretation by comparing Goethe's first epistle with other "first letters" he wrote.

Taking this approach makes sense to me since Schöne's reading suggests a kind of exceptional status for the letter in question, interpreting it as an irreversible shift in style. In addition, Schöne doubles down on Goethe's stylistic emancipation, as well as his actual actions, through the letters he includes and comments upon in this edition. By leaving Frankfurt behind with the second letter discussed, Schöne underscores the role of spatial distance and its mediation in Goethe's life and writing. Schöne follows Goethe to Leipzig, where the young poet anticipates *The sorrows of young Werther* through his letters to his private tutor Ernst Wolfgang Behrisch.[28] In the essay collection, references to letter-writing guides are almost completely limited to the context of Goethe's letter to Ysenburg von Buri; Schöne's approach to the guides thus exemplifies the common literary-historical way of treating the genre: The guides are seen as belonging (in the best case) to an early phase of German-language epistolary convention, and a letter's literary qualities are, first and foremost, manifest in their deviations from the letter-writing guides' instructions. Only then does a letter stand the chance of becoming part of literary tradition. In this manner, the factual youth of the letter writer and the metaphoric youthfulness of the German-language literary letter mirror one another.

An initial sampling from Goethe's letters between 1764 and 1804 reveals at least six "first letters."[29] With a cursory comparison of these texts, one letter in particular stands out—to be precise, it is the draft of a letter to Johann Gottfried Steinhäuser, published in the fourteenth volume of the Weimar edition of Goethe's correspondence. I will begin with this text as a basis for commenting on the five other letters. Steinhäuser was a physicist and mathematician, known to

28. Schöne, *Briefschreiber Goethe*, p.73–122.
29. Here are the addressees, in chronological order: Gottfried August Bürger (Frankfurt, February 12, 1774); Friedrich Gottlieb Klopstock (Frankfurt, May 28, 1774); Elisabeth Charlotte Constantia von der Recke (Weimar, May 30, 1785); Johann Gottfried Steinhäuser (Jena, September 17, 1799); Georg Wilhelm Friedrich Hegel (Jena, November 27, 1803); Johann Adam Schmidt (Jena, December 23, 1803).

Goethe because of his publications on "magnetic phenomena." The letter's first sentence refers to their shared scientific interest and to the addressee's "outstanding knowledge in this discipline," justifying the wish to "establish ties"—or, more literally, "enter into relations," *in Verhältniß kommen,* with Steinhäuser.[30]

The letter's penultimate sentence, consisting solely of questions regarding Steinhäuser's "magnetic magazine," in turn makes clear that the "relations" are meant to take the well-known form of a scholars' correspondence: "I ask for a favorable reply and for permission then to continue a correspondence concerning this subject."[31] The striking quality of the letter consists in the fact that, here, Goethe is really trying to initiate a correspondence—where his remaining "first letters" leave an impression of wishing to actually prevent such epistolary interchange and instead to transfer communication into the field of the spoken word.

Goethe's letter to the Vienna doctor and surgeon Johann Adam Schmidt is closest in spirit to the letter to Steinhäuser because Goethe again begins by alluding to shared "scholarly" interests. Simultaneously and importantly, the letter deviates from the communicative model of scholars' correspondence, since here Goethe's writing is both invoked and immediately retracted in favor of the superseding wish for personal contact, underscored by substituting Vienna for Schmidt's home:

> Not being able to know your disposition toward my work, I will consider my work in your sense then and look forward confidently to the time when I may send it or preferably bring it to you—that last hope being something I cannot fully abandon, all the less so as I have heretofore irresponsibly neglected seeing the great imperial city.[32]

30. "Da mich die magnetischen Erscheinungen seit einiger Zeit besonders interessieren, so wünsche ich mit einem Manne in Verhältnis zu kommen, der in diesem Fache vorzügliche Kenntnisse besitzt. Dieselben sind mir als ein solcher bekannt geworden, ich nehme mir daher die Freiheit einige Anfragen zu tun." Johann Wolfgang von Goethe, *Sämtliche Werke: Briefe, Tagebücher und Gespräche,* 40 vols. (Frankfurt am Main, 1985–2013), vol.31.1, p.726. All subsequent references to this edition are given as "FA" followed by the volume number.
31. "Ich bitte um gefällige Antwort und um die Erlaubnis alsdann über die Sache selbst einen Briefwechsel fortzusetzen." Goethe, FA 31.1, p.727.
32. "Ohne daß ich Ihre Gesinnungen über meine Arbeiten vernehmen kann, betrachte ich alsdann meine Arbeiten in Ihrem Sinne, und sehe getrost der Zeit entgegen wo ich sie Ihnen dereinst senden oder lieber bringen möchte, welche letzte Hoffnung ich mir nie ganz nehmen kann, um so weniger als ich bisher

A similar dynamic is at work in Goethe's (presumed) first letter to Hegel. The laconic epistle accompanies one of Goethe's texts, sent to the philosopher with a request for reading and critique. At the same time, it contains a recommendation concerning the form that the exchange is meant to take: "I would most appreciate your looking at the accompanying text and letting me know your thoughts about it when we meet."[33] The frequent references to the oral sphere are ambivalent: They open simultaneously the prospect of an intensified relationship and the possibility of dodging the relationship. Goethe knew too well that an actual meeting would probably not be forthcoming, but there was something about the first letter that called upon unmediated contact and that both revealed and concealed Goethe's attitude toward the recipient—as well as himself.

"First letters" format relationships, assign correspondents' roles, fix positions, or maintain mobility. Through these letters, the correspondents' status is both marked and masked. Goethe's first letter to Friedrich Gottlieb Klopstock marks such a negotiating process while casting light on the practice, well known from letter-writing guides, of indirectly mediating a relationship of patronage through befriended third parties. In essence, with his letter to Klopstock, Goethe rejects the prevailing conventions of social triangulation and thus the client's role that was earmarked for him. Familiar to literary historians today, the rift between the two authors is foretold in this first letter through Goethe's omission of the invitation to collaborate or participate in the development of new material.

In the letter, Gottlob Friedrich Ernst Schönborn and Heinrich Christian Boie are invoked as mediating third parties, but their services are then spurned in favor of addressing Klopstock directly. The reasons Goethe offers for the rhetorical freedom, not to say overreach, are astonishing: "Shall I not address the living man to whose grave I would make a pilgrimage?"[34] Through the mingling of funeral and pilgrimage images, Goethe seems to offer something

---

die große Kaiserstadt zu sehen unverantwortlich versäumte." Goethe, FA 32.2, p.429–30.

33. "Möchten Sie wohl beikommende Schrift durchsehen und mir bei gelegentlicher Zusammenkunft Ihre Gedanken darüber sagen." Goethe, FA 32.2, p.415.

34. "Schönborn in einem Briefe aus Algier den ich gestern empfangen habe, schreibt mir: 'Klopstock wird sie durch Boie um einige ihrer Arbeiten ersuchen lassen'. Und warum soll ich Klopstocken nicht schreiben, ihm selbst schicken was es auch sey, und was für einen Anteil er auch dran nehmen kann! Soll ich

morbid to Klopstock akin to a burial object. The pilgrimage metaphor removes the potential patron and mentor from the sphere of shared creation, stylizing Klopstock as a figure from the past: an impression reinforced by the vagueness of Goethe's reference to additional works and pieces ("some things") he intends to send the poet in the future. "Here, then," writes Goethe to the older master, "you have a piece that probably will never see print and which I ask you to return to me straightaway."[35]

The "piece that probably will never see print" symbolizes a relationship that probably will never come about. Goethe's manuscript can hardly be considered the stuff of intimate communication.[36] It is meant neither to generate exclusive fellowship between the correspondents—it is merely briefly presented before being, as it were, "straightaway" withdrawn—nor to initiate a collaborative situation, since the request for a reading and critique is missing. Indeed, this "first letter" excludes precisely the prospect of shared improvement of the text leading up to its printing. Furthermore, with the formula "or at least I'll let you know," referring to eventually sending Klopstock published material (or rather not doing so), Goethe also underscores possible neglect on his part in the course of future epistolary exchange: in short, an acknowledgment in this "first letter" that he will perhaps not be able to honor his offer.

As a clear contrast to Goethe's first letter to Klopstock, we have its epistolary counterpart in a letter to Gottfried August Bürger. The vagueness of the references to the included manuscript and to future "things" in the letter to Klopstock stands in contrast to a concrete reference to the gift of a book sent to Bürger: "I am sending you the second edition of my *Göz*" (the reference is to Goethe's play *Goetz of*

---

den Lebenden nicht anreden, zu dessen Grabe ich wallfahrten würde." Goethe, FA 28, p.367–68.

35. "Hier haben Sie also ein Stück das wohl nie gedruckt werden wird, das ich bitte mir gerade zurückzusenden. Sobald einige Dinge von mir die fertig liegen gedruckt sind, schick ich sie Ihnen oder meld es wenigstens, und wünsche dass Sie empfinden mögen mit welch wahrem Gefühl meine Seele an Ihnen hängt." Goethe, FA 28, p.368.

36. Christian Benne, *Die Erfindung des Manuskripts: zur Theorie und Geschichte literarischer Gegenständlichkeit* (Berlin, 2015). A brief outline of the thesis is presented in Christian Benne and Carlos Spoerhase, "Manuskript und Dichterhandschrift," in *Handbuch Literatur & materielle Kultur*, ed. Susanne Scholz and Ulrike Vedder (Berlin, 2018), p.135–43.

Berlichingen).[37] What, in the letter to Klopstock, is a pilgrimage evoking a pace conceived of as rather slow has its counterpart in the letter to Bürger in an striking image of breaking down a "paper partition." At several points, the letter emphasizes things held in common between Goethe and Bürger; it contains a clear offer of mutual exchange and does not hesitate to repeat such points: "If you're working on something, send it to me. I'll do the same. [...] You're only showing it to your heartfelt friend; I'll do that as well." The manuscripts Goethe mentions in this letter are precious objects meriting protection and control over circulation: "And promise never to copy anything."[38]

Goethe's use of "first letters" mirrors the variety within the genre; they are difficult to subsume into a single typological concept. The process of waiting for a favorable opportunity for initiating contact emphasized in the letter-writing guides from Weise to Gellert has its textual correspondence in the formal variety of the letters, which, depending on the occasion, are drafted as cover letters, invitations, supplications, or commendations. The letters to Klopstock and Bürger are striking in their brevity. They are cover letters, of the sort often accompanying sent objects or another main letter.

Goethe's "first letters" are stamped by a contradiction that also applies to his general attitude toward letters: While he recognizes their value, he also treats them as disposable. Hence, in the course of his life, Goethe often strives for the most complete possible preservation of his own letters and those from others sent to him. He also edits the epistolary collections of befriended authors, demonstrating his awareness of the historical and biographical significance of letters.[39] At the same time, on various occasions, he destroys large collections of his letters rather than seeing them become part of his legacy.[40]

---

37. "Ich schicke Ihnen die zweyte Auflage meines Göz. Ich wollt Ihnen schon lang einmal schreiben, und die Paar Stunden die ich mit Ihrem Freunde Destorp zugebracht habe haben mich determinirt. Ich thue mir was drauf zu gute, dass ich's binn der die Papierne Scheidewand zwischen uns einschlägt." Goethe, FA 28, p.349.

38. "Wenn Sie was arbeiten schicken Sie mirs. Ich wills auch thun. Das giebt Muth. Sie zeigens nur den Freunden ihres Herzens, das will ich auch thun. Und verspreche nie was abzuschreiben." Goethe, FA 28, p.350.

39. *Winkelmann und sein Jahrhundert: in Briefen und Aufsätzen*, ed. Johann Wolfgang von Goethe (Tübingen, 1805); *Briefwechsel zwischen Schiller und Goethe in den Jahren 1794 bis 1805*, 6 vols. (Stuttgart, 1828–1829).

40. Ernst Beutler, "Goethes Jugendbriefe," in *Wiederholte Spiegelungen: drei Essays über Goethe* (Göttingen, 1957), p.5–30 (6–8).

Horst Fleig thus speaks of a kind of "negative autobiography"[41] emerging from such conscious annulment of the documentation of his life. Similarly, articulating itself in "first letters" is knowledge of the genre's binding force—they are, after all, traditionally meant to establish a tie of patronage. Likely aware of the transgressive potential of "first letters," especially when it came to reading and interpreting biography and the networks enwrapping and being centered around him, Goethe tries to establish distance from the start. As a rule, his "first letters" do not open any perspectives for the future in the manner of Karsch, instead almost anticipating the end of the scarcely begun relationship: this by trying out rhetorical strategies "to let the curtain fall."[42] Goethe, it seems, first and foremost sought to stay in control of his life's narrative.

One of Goethe's six "first letters" has not yet been commented on but offers a final frame for understanding the challenges of Karsch's letter to Gleim. This is the letter to Elisabeth von der Recke, which combines elements of letters of attendance, supplication, and commendation into an artful whole.[43] Goethe's opening, with his request to welcome the countess "in writing," contains a possible reference to the letter's status as a "first letter." Mention of the written greeting suggests that Goethe was already acquainted with the countess beyond this written introduction. The crossing of a threshold, needing justification in a "first letter," is here tied to the distinction between oral and written communication.

The letter's beginning evokes a scene of sociable hubbub—a confusing coming and going of various friends whose names do not need spelling out by Goethe. He announces his arrival and raises the prospect of other friends arriving later. But already in the second paragraph, the image of an unclouded welcoming celebration is retracted, in that Goethe—seemingly casually—slips in news of the death of a man known to the countess, the mayor of the neighboring town of Lobeda. What then follows is a brief history of the mother of the suddenly deceased mayor's widow, a woman who at a manifestly old age now faces the task of caring for the widowed daughter and seven orphaned children. The letter, which begins as a letter of attendance, shifts into a supplication, expressing Goethe's wish to financially support the dead man's survivors. At the letter's end, the

41. Goethe, FA 37, p.636.
42. Beutler, "Goethes Jugendbriefe," p.27.
43. Goethe, FA 29, p.581–82.

convivial friends mentioned at the beginning are brought together in a kind of "supportive fraternity"; the supplicant confirms that "our most gracious rulers"[44] have taken over part of the costs, but indicates that something "still remains" for friends to do.[45]

An additional rhetorical parenthesis contained in the letter is the striking mention of "healing" as a metaphor. In the first paragraph, we read of the "salutary spring"[46] near which the friends wish to bid the countess welcome; in the letter's last sentence, the countess appears to have herself been transformed into the healing spring— she is asked "to heal the wounds inflicted by fate."[47] The request for financial support is wrapped in an organic metaphor, thus being freed from the economic realm. Evidently, economic questions cannot be directly addressed; the semantics of patronage allow an embedding of material questions in a naturally conceived system of gift exchange.

As indicated in his letter to Elisabeth von der Recke, Goethe exploits the various possibilities inherent to a "first letter": the polite inquiry to wait on the countess, the request for financial support for the family—with Goethe verbally cloaked as a messenger simply conveying news of the misfortune of strangers—and, finally, the heart of the letter, a commendatory section, meant to move the countess to act.

The letter's novella-like second paragraph, where the death of the Lobeda mayor serves as the starting point of Goethe's story, can also be read as a miniature edition of a female vita—one that has been restricted in a socioeconomic sense. The client for whom Goethe is supplicating, and who is initially introduced exclusively in terms of her relationship to the dead man, is first and foremost a "grandmother" who, even before the sudden death of her son-in-law, "had no wish other than to reach the end of her life decently and honorably in very limited economic circumstances."[48] Once again, like in the letter to Klopstock, we find the figure of an anticipated end—death— doubling as a vanishing point of the initiation of contact: Not life, but the client's "evening of life" is what needs protecting. Goethe only moves to a compliment in the letter's third paragraph, for the sake

44. Goethe, FA 29, p.582.
45. Goethe, FA 29, p.582.
46. Goethe, FA 29, p.581.
47. Goethe, FA 29, p.582.
48. "keinen Wunsch hatte als, bey einer sehr eingeschränckten Haushaltung, ihr Leben anständig und ehrbar zu endigen"; Goethe, FA 29, p.581.

of commending his client: She is "truly an unusual sort of woman."[49]
She is special for one striking reason: Alongside her modest, decent,
honorable life—a life that could look toward its own end in "peaceful
confidence"—she has been active as an author. With her polemic
piece "Winde und Männer: Antwort eines Frauenzimmers auf Dr.
Sheridans Wolken und Weiber" ("Wind and men: answer of a woman
to Dr. Sheridan's 'Clouds and women'"), which appeared in 1782 in
Christoph Martin Wieland's journal *Der teutsche Merkur*, Johanne
Susanne Bohl became famous overnight. Goethe thus recommends to
von der Recke someone who is far from being unknown: At the time
of the letter's writing, Bohl was a colorful figure in the literary sphere
in which both the countess and Goethe moved. We can thus read
Goethe's "first letter" to Elisabeth von der Recke as the documentation of two practices not yet common in the eighteenth century:
the commendation of female authors and the masking of female
authorship for the sake of such commendation.

Authorial self-staging: Karsch to Gleim

In conclusion, I would like to approach the question of the extent
to which close readings of "first letters" and a study of patronage
informed by social theory cast light on each other, returning once
more to the first "first letter" I discussed here. If we reconsider Anna
Louisa Karsch's letter to Gleim in light of the various interpretive
facets developed above, the following picture emerges: A potential
client (Karsch) is writing; she knows how to commend herself—
in at least a twofold sense of the word. On the one hand, she
does so through presentation of exact knowledge of the rhetorical
requirements imposed on any letter aimed at a potential patron: The
letter initially offers an expression of thanks for the attention that
Gleim has apparently paid to Karsch's literary efforts (which others
have told her about). Karsch explains why she has now contacted
Gleim. She states that she has been familiar with his writing for a
long time and expresses her admiration for his writing through her
use of the only hyperbolic sequence in the letter ("but I ask you to

---

49. "Ich weis daß Ew Gnaden, bey Ihrem Aufenthalte in Jena, Sich grosmütig
erkundigt, ob dieser, würcklich in ihrer Art seltnen Frau irgend eine Hülfe
nötig sey. Damals konnte sie mit einem ruhigen Vertrauen auf ihren Zustand
sehn und mit danckbarer Beschämung Ew Gnaden Grosmuth ablehnen. Wie
verschieden steht es ietzo mit ihr!" Goethe, FA 29, p.581.

believe that it is not since yesterday that I highly esteem, admire, and revere you, and—what goes beyond all that—feel great fondness for you, no, this has been so for a long time now").[50] She also weaves numerous figures of self-diminution into the letter ("my memory is not so faithful"; "I believe that I do not have enough sweep for the ode"; and so on).

On the other hand, Karsch commends herself through a sovereign approach to her life history. Very much aware of the fact that Berlin's society considers her a literary novice of low origins at best, she transforms this society in her narrative. Berlin's society appears as a sensation-hungry clique that merits no mercy in her eyes. The absence of a bookish vocabulary, which for many eighteenth-century epistolary theorists rendered the so-called "women's letter" worthy of emulation, also proves to be a biographical advantage: Because women like Karsch were excluded from the republic of savants, the typical serial listing of university studies and Grand Tours was necessarily missing and thus other, new motifs and rhetorical staples had to be supplied. In this respect, Karsch's letter to Gleim constitutes an interesting literary source. It invites comparison with other biographies of female authors and erudite men, especially biographies bound into "first letters." A close reading of appropriate individual letters[51] makes clear that a precise, artful self-staging as a female client—especially one aware of the fragile and "incomplete" status of patronage relationships who knew how to use this knowledge—could be a strategy for both appearing as an author and controlling one's own visibility. We can trace this form of self-staging in Karsch's letter through the movement of the unnamed "friend," who surfaces a total of five times and whose position changes significantly in the course of the letter's writing.

At the beginning, the "friend" appears as a typical friend in "first letters," one who had evidently transmitted a greeting and with whom the author has regular personal contact. The letter reports that this friend is increasingly becoming a figure in the public literary sphere— one who not only sees to the dissemination of news and shares smaller poetic experiments but who is also subject to assessment. Decisive

50. "aber ich bitte Ihnen zu glauben daß ich Sie nicht erst seit gestern hochschäze, Bewundre, verEhre, und was diß alles übertrifft liebhabe, nein schon lange"; Nörtemann, *"Mein Bruder,"* vol.1, p.5.
51. This way of focusing on individual letters is presented in *Der Brief: Ereignis & Objekt*, ed. Waltraud Wiethölter and Anne Bohnenkamp (Frankfurt am Main, 2010).

here is the letter's final section. After Karsch has proffered the poet she venerates rhetorically schooled politesse in the letter's first part, entered her life history in the second part, and ushered in her request for critique and help improving her "songs" in the third part, she finally formulates her invitation: "[A]llow the spring to entice you; travel to Berlin."[52] Following the invitation, she refers to the "many people familiar with the charm of your lively conversation" and is presumably joyfully awaiting Gleim's visit to Berlin. Here, Karsch has the "friend" surface once again, changing his status once and for all. To begin with, the letter reports that the friend is among the "many" awaiting Gleim's visit who are anxious to bask in Gleim's attention and "acclaim"[53]—but, later in the sentence, Karsch dismisses the friend from the circle of admirers, displacing him to the position of an author judged by Gleim and Karsch together: "[A]nd I congratulate myself for considering his two odes 'To the king's enemies' and 'Upon the artillery piece,' as you yourself do, to be the most beautiful of the odes. We are both right, for our feeling—that incorruptible judge—is decisive here, and her judgment holds."[54]

With this added sentence, Karsch succeeds in inverting the relationship structure at work here: At this point, the friend is no longer the friend from the beginning of the letter. It is not the friend who bestows compliments and commends Karsch; rather, Karsch is the one who knows herself to be in accord with Gleim in judging the friend's writing. Hence with this letter, Anna Louisa Karsch not only requests critique and assistance in improving her poetic efforts in a way typical for many "first letters," but goes beyond that to transmit to Gleim the image of a critical dyad: "[O]ur judgment holds"—the mediating friend has been removed from the picture. The literary strategy through which letter writer Karsch approaches this friend, the way she has him enter as a mediator and withdraw from the stage,

---

52. "laßen Sie sich doch den frühling verloken, reisen Sie nach berlin," Nörtemann, *"Mein Bruder,"* vol.1, p.6.

53. "hier erwarten Ihnen vielle die mit denen Anmutigkeiten Ihrer lebhafften Gespräche Bekant sind und / die auch in der entfernung Ihre freunde bleiben müßen mein freund ist Einer von den Ersten, Er thut Stollz auff Ihrem beyfall." Nörtemann, *"Mein Bruder,"* vol.1, p.6.

54. "und ich wünsche mir Glük daß ich wie Sie, Seine zwey Oden, die an die feinde des Königes, und die auff daß Geschüz vor die schönsten erkenne, wir haben Beyde recht, denn unßere empfindung diese unbestochne Richterrin entscheidet hier, und Ihr Außspruch gillt"; Nörtemann, *"Mein Bruder,"* vol.1, p.6.

defines this "first letter" as the articulation of a playful distancing from the status of a client. In this case, then, the "first letter" accomplishes two things: It is a "ticket into the network,"[55] but, at the same time, Karsch here tries out the role of an author forging a bridge in a network, based on the exchange of critical notes and corrections.

In a comparative reading of "first letters," Karsch emerges as an author eminently suited for the study of patronage and networks of correspondence: She is a highly eloquent (and grateful) client. Her letters offer us the image of a female poet stemming from modest circumstances who can step onto the literary stage thanks to patronage, using the literary stage and her communication with a public to acknowledge the work of her former patrons. In Karsch's self-interpretation, her status as a client and authorial pride are inseparable. In addition, we may presume that her self-staging as a female author, which was exceptional in the eighteenth century, both contains and has as a precondition her sometimes ironic self-description as a client.

55. Erdmut Jost, "Eintrittskarte ins Netzwerk: Prolog zu einer Erforschung des Empfehlungsbriefs," in *Briefwechsel: zur Netzwerkbildung in der Aufklärung*, ed. Erdmut Jost and Daniel Fulda (Halle an der Saale, 2012), p.103–43.

Mapping the nation: foreign travel in Germany 1738–1839

Karin Baumgartner

University of Utah

A moment in space and time

In the last three decades of the eighteenth century, as the German nation began to take shape in the minds of German elites, travel reports helped fill a geospatial void since Germany, unlike France, had not been mapped yet.[1] Descriptions of the territory encompassed by this putative German nation were generally vague, and Peter Ambrosius Lehmann's popular travel guide *Die vornehmsten Europäischen Reisen* (*The noblest European journeys*) from 1767 could not give accurate geospatial information (longitude and latitude). Rather, the guide resorted to describing Germany in terms of its size (11,124 German square miles) and in relation to the territory of other nations (Prussia, Poland, Hungary, United Netherlands) and natural borders (the North Sea, the Baltic Sea, the Alps).[2] Within these amorphous boundaries, foreign and

---

1. The Cassini family—primarily César-François Cassini de Thury (Cassini III) and his son Jean-Dominique Cassini (Cassini IV)—surveyed France between 1756 and 1789 and published 181 partial maps between 1756 and 1815. The Cassini map is also known as the "Map of the Academy" and was the most accurate map available at the time. Only in 1828 did George IV of England commission Carl Friedrich Gauss to undertake the first geodesic surveys of the kingdom of Hanover, the first such comprehensive survey in Germany. See John Noble Wilford, *The Mapmakers* (New York, 2000), p.136–47.
2. *Die vornehmsten Europäischen Reisen: wie solche durch Deutschland, die Schweiz, die Niederlande, England, Frankreich, Italien, Dännemark, Schweden, Hungarn, Polen, Preussen und Rußland, auf eine nützliche und bequeme Weise anzustellen sind; mit Anweisung der gewöhnlichsten Post- und Reise-Routen, der merkwürdigsten Oerter, deren Sehenswürdigkeiten, besten Logis, gangbarsten Münz-Sorten, Reisekosten etc., auch einer neuen Sammlung von Post- und Bothen-Charten, Post-Verordnungen, Post-Taxen etc.*, ed. Gottlob Friedrich Krebel, vol.1 (Hamburg, Herold, 1767), p.498–99. The book was originally published by Peter Ambrosius Lehmann in

German travelogues about *Teutschland* (Germany) created a new layer of perception that shaped the narratives of German national identity. As expected, this process would be fragile and uneven, and borders remained contested throughout the nineteenth century.[3]

Textual networks of space

Jean Baudrillard famously claimed that maps precede territory,[4] or, in the words of Geoff King, "to be included on the map is to be granted the status of reality or importance. To be left off is to be denied."[5] National maps and nationalism are inextricably linked, as maps do not just express a preexisting sense of the nation but help create nationalist sentiment.[6] In the absence of a national map with clearly delineated territory, imaginary space—or in David Bodenhamer's terminology "place"—comes to fill in the gap.[7] While "space" is an abstract geometrical concept defined by latitudes and longitudes, "place" is the temporal expression of this space and is imbued with cultural meaning. The genre of travel literature, *ars apodemica*, addresses both terms: Travel routes are linked to territory in a concrete way—travelers move in real space—while the descriptions assembled in *apodemica* (travelogues) present the cultural and temporal expression of space. For this reason, travel accounts contribute to the cultural saturation of space, making it concrete in the minds of their readers.

Travel reports, as I will show below, were grafted onto earlier knowledge networks such as commercial travel routes, aristocratic

---

Hamburg. Gottfried Friedrich Krebel took over the editorship with the eleventh edition in 1767. This German tome saw fifteen editions between 1703 and 1801, when it was discontinued.

3. See Ernst Moritz Arndt, *Der Rhein, Deutschlands Strom, aber nicht Deutschlands Grenze* (1813; Dresden, 1921), p.33–34. Arndt too had to describe Germany with recourse to the borders of other nations. This made it particularly torturous to claim the Rhine as Germany's river.

4. Jean Baudrillard, "Simulacra and simulations," in *Selected writings*, ed. Mark Poster (Stanford, CA, 1988), p.166–84 (166).

5. Geoff King, *Mapping reality: an exploration of cultural cartographies* (New York, 1996), p.18.

6. King, *Mapping reality*, p.25.

7. For the distinction between space and place, see David J. Bodenhamer, "Narrating space and place," in *Deep maps and spatial narratives*, ed. John Corrigan, Trevor M. Harris, and David J. Bodenhamer (Bloomington, IN, 2015), p.7–27 (14–15).

travel networks and familial connections, mathematical and geographic tractates, and local knowledge by drivers, cicerones (tour guides), and innkeepers. Sometimes travel reports were in tension with previous knowledge networks; sometimes they extended and popularized these networks. Overall though, the network of roads and cities described in travelogues about Germany came to bind together in the minds of their readers what in reality was a dizzying array of entirely separate political and ecclesiastic entities. Indeed, *Die vornehmsten Europäischen Reisen* expended over thirty pages to inventory all political units within Germany proper (excluding Bohemia, Moravia, Silesia, Courland, etc.).[8] Travelogues thus turned fragmented "real" space into a unified textual construct that appeared more cohesive than it really was. In other words, Germany, as a national construct avant la lettre, was fixed in space through travel routes and specific places that came to define and determine what counted as Germany in the public imagination.

While both foreign and German travel narratives contributed to inscribing the German nation onto territory, foreign leisure travelers, especially the British, traveled across Germany much earlier and in larger numbers than other travelers, owing to their economic resources and the British penchant for the Grand Tour. Many of these foreign travelers would subsequently publish their reminiscences in journals and newspapers at home from where they filtered back into the German imagination through translations. Published in leading German periodicals, these translated travelogues provided a textual reference for German writers and thinkers to view—and describe— their version of the German nation.[9]

This multifaceted knowledge and publishing context provides the background for this article, which will concentrate on the "footprints" established by foreign travelers in Germany. What were the routes traveled and the sights seen? What kind of Germany arose in these travelogues from the layers of postal routes, cartography, aristocratic connections, and the priorities of local tour guides? Since German travel in the late eighteenth century was rudimentary and mostly geared toward Italy,[10] the corpus comprises mostly British and French travelogues between 1738 and 1839.

8. Krebel, *Die vornehmsten Europäischen Reisen*, p.502–31.
9. Hagen Schulz-Forberg, "European travel and travel writing: cultural practice and the idea of Europe," in *Unravelling civilisation: European travel and travel writing*, ed. Hagen Schulz-Forberg (Brussels, 2005), p.13–42 (30).
10. A notable exception is Friedrich Nicolai, whose unfinished twelve-volume work

The British generally traversed German-speaking central Europe on their trip home from Italy or Switzerland. Most prominent among these are John Moore's descriptions of his travels with the duke of Hamilton, Ann Radcliffe's journey along the Rhine River, and Mary Shelley's miserable and underfunded foray into Switzerland.[11] In contrast, French travelers were mostly interested in the Prussian military maneuvers in Silesia and the Hapsburg court in Vienna.[12] Among these travelogues, Mme de Staël's book stands out for its cultural approach, complete lack of geographic description, and an idiosyncratic route through Germany.[13] What is, however, apparent in mapping the travel routes laid out by British and French authors is the consistency of the itinerary over the time period. While travel "off the beaten path" was possible with advanced planning and determination, most travelers chose to stick to the established postal routes and therefore would see the same sights and visit the same places. The relationship between the preexisting imaginary space— acquired through the consumption of earlier travelogues—and the actual travel routes taken remained consistent over time, and there is little evidence that British and French tourists sought to expand their horizons regarding the German territory. Rather, the main concern of these travelers was ease of movement and a functioning

---

describes his travels through southern Germany and Switzerland. Christoph Friedrich Nicolai, *Beschreibung einer Reise durch Deutschland und die Schweiz, im Jahre 1781, nebst Bemerkungen über Gelehrsamkeit, Industrie, Religion und Sitten*, 12 vols. (Berlin, Nicolai, 1783).

11. John Moore, *A View of society and manners in France, Switzerland, and Germany, with anecdotes relating to some eminent characters* (London, Strahan & Cadell, 1783). Ann Radcliffe, *A Journey made in the summer of 1794, through Holland and the western frontier of Germany, with a return down the Rhine: to which are added, observations during a tour to the lakes of Lancashire, Westmoreland, and Cumberland* (London, printed for G. G. and J. Robinson, 1795). Mary Shelley, "History of a six weeks' tour through a part of France, Switzerland, Germany, and Holland: with letters descriptive of a sail round the lake of Geneva, and of the glaciers of Chamouni [1817]," in *Women's travel writing: 1750–1850*, ed. Caroline Franklin, vol.2 (London, 2006), p.295–483.

12. C. W. Thompson argues that eighteenth- and early-nineteenth-century French writers tended to avoid Germany as a subject of their travel narratives. The Rhine River, for example, did not come to French attention until the middle of the nineteenth century, when Romantic writers such as Alexandre Dumas, Victor Hugo, and Gérard de Nerval traveled in Germany and Switzerland. C. W. Thompson, *French Romantic travel writing: Chateaubriand to Nerval* (Oxford, 2012), p.139–60.

13. Mme de Staël (Anne-Louise-Germaine), *Germany* (London, 1813).

and interlocking system of inns, postal stations where fresh horses could be procured, and easily accessible sights. As a consequence, infrastructural conditions were most crucial in terms of how travelers traversed Germany, what they saw, and how they were able to contextualize their observations. This is true for both British and French travelers: Routes for all travelers were based on much older travel infrastructure that served pan-European medieval trade routes or military invasion routes rather than a sightseeing itinerary.[14]

Rewriting the Grand Tour: Thomas Nugent's travel guide

Travel in Germany, then, took place within preexisting knowledge networks, the most important being the Grand Tour, an educational and ideological journey for British aristocrats to the continent that arose in the sixteenth century and reached its pinnacle in the eighteenth century.[15] Commonly, the journey took two years, and the young lords and their mentors would visit France, Italy, Germany, and the Netherlands. Sometimes the journey was extended into Spain, Scandinavia, or Russia, although the heart of the journey was always an extended sojourn in Italy. Accurate numbers of travelers are hard to establish, but estimates speak of 10,000 to 15,000 British travelers over a twenty-year period in the late eighteenth century.[16] The aristo-

14. French travelers followed routes drawn up by French cartographer Cassini, who established an invasion route from Strasburg to Vienna. Cassini had been commissioned by Louis XV in 1745 to survey the Palatine, Württemberg, Swabia, Bavaria, and Austria in order to produce accurate maps. Traveling under the pretense of observing the passage of Venus on the Sun, Cassini was received enthusiastically at the court in Württemberg, and thus able to produce accurate measurements of southern Germany. See César-François Cassini, *Relation d'un voyage en Allemagne: qui comprend les opérations relatives à la figure de la terre & à la géographie particulière du Palatinat, du duché de Wurtemberg, du Cercle de Souabe, de la Bavière & de l'Autriche: fait par ordre du roi: suivie de la description des conquêtes de Louis XV, depuis 1745 jusqu'en 1748* (Paris, Imprimerie royale, 1775), p.vii–xiv.

15. John Towner, "Literature, tourism and the Grand Tour," in *Literature and tourism*, ed. Mike Robinson and Hans Christian Andersen (London, 2002), p.226–38 (227). Also see James Buzard, who argues that the Grand Tour served the ideological goal of cementing the solidarity of the British ruling classes and providing them with a "pseudo-historical legitimation" as the heirs of Rome. See James Buzard, *The beaten track: European tourism, literature, and the ways to culture, 1800–1918* (New York, 1993), p.121.

16. T. C. W. Blanning, "The Grand Tour and the reception of neo-classicism in Great Britain in the eighteenth century," in *Grand Tour: Adeliges Reisen und*

cratic Grand Tour came to an end with the Continental Blockade in 1806. When travel to the continent resumed after the Napoleonic Wars, bourgeois travelers and, shortly after, mass tourism had taken over continental travel. Within the framework of the Grand Tour, Germany—loosely defined through its language—was a European backwater that offered neither classical history like Italy nor political drama like the French Revolution nor the marvels of manufacturing of the Low Countries. Only the British interest in Rhine tourism after 1814 brought western Germany more fully into a pan-European travel network.[17]

Scholars have tended to view the Grand Tour in monolithic terms—a pleasure tour on the continent dedicated to classicism and aesthetic purposes.[18] There existed, however, significant variation in the *purposes* of the tour, if not in the itinerary. For example, John Ray's travelogue *Journey through part of the Low-Countries, Germany, Italy, and France*, first published in 1673, describes the author's two-year travels through much of the European continent for scientific rather than political or aesthetic purposes.[19] Joseph Marshall, another British traveler, focused mostly on agricultural methods when, in 1768–1770, he took his journey off the beaten track to Holland, Flanders, Germany, Denmark, Sweden, Lapland, Russia, Ukraine, and Poland.[20] French emigrants, in turn, tended to travel east (rather than south to Italy) in fear of the Directory and later Napoleon, when large parts of Europe became inaccessible to them.[21]

---

europäische Kultur vom 14. bis zum 18. Jahrhundert, ed. Rainer Babel and Werner Paravicini (Ostfildern, 2005), p.541–52 (541–42).

17. The Rhine route became the dominant itinerary through Germany in 1836 through Murray's *Hand-book*, staking out a route from Dutch and Belgian ports to Switzerland along the Rhine River. See John Murray, *A Hand-book for travellers on the continent: being a guide through Holland, Belgium, Prussia, and northern Germany, and along the Rhine, from Holland to Switzerland* (London, 1836).

18. Katherine Turner, *British travel writers in Europe 1750–1800: authorship, gender and national identity* (Aldershot, 2001), p.60.

19. John Ray, *Observations topographical, moral, & physiological made in a journey through part of the Low-Countries, Germany, Italy, and France: with a catalogue of plants not native of England, found spontaneously growing in those parts, and their virtues* (London, Printed for John Martyn, 1673), p.iii.

20. Joseph Marshall, *Travels through Holland, Flanders, Germany, Denmark, Sweden, Lapland, Russia, the Ukraine, and Poland: in the years 1768, 1769, and 1770: in which is particularly minuted, the present state of those countries, respecting their agriculture, population, manufactures, commerce, the arts, and useful undertakings*, 3 vols. (Dublin, printed for H. Saunders *et al.*, 1772).

21. See Mme de Staël's preface to her *Germany* (p.i–xv), in which she describes the

The Grand Tour as a pan-European endeavor was underwritten by a number of guidebooks and timetables, the most prominent being Thomas Nugent's genre-defining work *The Grand Tour, or a Journey through the Netherlands, Germany, Italy and France. [...] by Mr. Nugent*, first published in 1749.[22] Nugent's four-volume work maps the most common travel routes through the continent. While this information had long been available locally for traveling merchants, Nugent was the first to assemble this pan-European travel grid in one place. The monumental handbook also includes lists of accommodations, currencies, measurements; an overview with political, statistical, geographic, and climatic information; and, most important of all, an extensive alphabetical appendix with all cities and post stations listed and cross-referenced to the corresponding page number in the book.[23] This guide, with its extensive summary of existing postal routes, points to the well-developed infrastructural grid that facilitated travel in the eighteenth century, particularly the Calais–Paris and Venice–Rome

---

difficulties imposed on her movements.

22. Thomas Nugent, *The Grand Tour: containing an exact description of most of the cities, towns, and remarkable places of Europe: together with a distinct account of the post-roads and stages, with their respective distances [...] likewise directions relating to the manner and expence of travelling from one place and country to another, as also occasional remarks on [...] each respective country*, 4 vols. (London, Printed for S. Birt, D. Browne, A. Millar, and G. Hawkins, 1749). John Towner lists several other earlier guidebooks to the Grand Tour. These are Andrew Boorde's *The Fyrst boke of the introduction of knowledge* (1542), Richard Lassels's *The Voyage of Italy* (1686), and Maximillian Misson's *A New voyage to Italy* (1691). Towner, "Literature," p.228.

23. Nugent outlines his approach as follows: "Tho' most gentlemen are presumed to have some knowledge of geography, yet as this is not always the case, a general description of the several countries is prefixed to each volume, with an account of their situation, extent, climate, soil, seas, rivers, and mountains. From the country we proceed to the inhabitants, describing their persons, manners, customs, language, learning, arts, and religion. Commerce is the next subject; under which article we consider its rise, progress, and present state of prosperity or decline, commonly adding, for the sake of such as travel for business, a list of the principal fairs, and of the chief commodities of each town and province. Next comes the manner of travelling; where care has been taken to insert whatever we could possibly collect either from our own or other people's observation, in regard to the different carriages as well by water as land, with their hours of setting out, and respective prices. The knowledge of the several coins being a necessary thing for travellers, we have therefore been very exact upon this head and hope that such accounts as are here given of foreign monies and of their reduction to English standard, will be of some use and satisfaction" (Nugent, *The Grand Tour*, vol.1, p.iv–v).

routes. With its list of departure days and times, mileage information and duration of travel segments, the handbook made traveling plannable and predictable. Nugent was fully aware of the paradigm-changing nature of his work, and stated in the preface to the first volume: "If […] the following work should happen to prove of any use to the public, it will be owing as much to the novelty of the method, as to any merit the author pretends to claim from new discovery of matter."[24] The book, as the author recognized, was part of a larger push toward more reliable travel guides that described factually what travelers could expect once they arrived at their destination.[25]

Increased touristic interest in Europe coincided with the rise of such factual travel information. Nugent recognized that, even though a myriad of travelogues had been written during the previous two centuries and "very few things have escaped [the] observation" of eager travel writers, those travel narratives "are generally insufficient for the direction of those who consult them for real use, and as instructive companions."[26] Rather than "brilliant tales of faraway lands," Nugent promised factual information on "the difference of roads and accommodations, the nature and price of carriages, the knowledge of various coins, with several other articles absolutely necessary in foreign peregrinations."[27] The book was immensely successful and saw two more print runs over the next three decades, certainly owing to the accuracy of Nugent's information, which, he claimed, was based on his own travels and extensive research in geographical publications.[28] Nugent was most innovative in his systematic approach to the travel grid: Each route is briefly introduced, and keywords are printed in the margins to allow travelers to quickly thumb through the book in search of information (see Figure 27). The four volumes are of "small size" (octavo) to make them portable in a gentleman's luggage and therefore have no maps.

---

24. Nugent, *The Grand Tour*, vol.1, p.iii.
25. John Edmund Vaughan, *The English guide book, c.1780–1870: an illustrated history* (Newton Abbot, 1974). Vaughan describes the birth of the guidebook in the middle of the eighteenth century, which went hand in hand with the revitalization of cartography in Great Britain on the one hand (p.81) and the commercial interest of publishers on the other (p.99).
26. Nugent, *The Grand Tour*, vol.1, p.iii–iv.
27. Nugent, *The Grand Tour*, vol.1, p.iv.
28. Nugent, *The Grand Tour*, vol.1, p.v.

« Exit   **The grand tour** – Thomas Nugent

122   *The* TRAVELLER'S GUIDE

thing upon the road, till he comes the next day to *Oldenburg*.

XII. GROTSANDER.

Grotsander.   The road from *Leer* to *Grotsander*, and from thence as far as *Oldenburg*, is through a fandy barren country, which affords a very difagreeable profpect. *Grotsander* is only a hamlet, confifting of a few huts and the poft-houfe. Here the *Pruffian* poftilion changes horfes, and is relieved by the *Danifh* poftilion, who fets out with the poft-waggon in about an hour after for *Oldenburg*, which belongs, with the whole county, to the king of *Denmark*.

XII. BLEXHUSE.

Blexhufe.   This is alfo a hamlet, but has no poft-houfe, only a miferable dirty inn, where the poftilion arrives towards midnight, and refrefhes himfelf and his horfes for about three hours, during which time the paffengers are allowed to take a little fleep; and the next morning early they arrive at *Oldenburg*.

XIV. OLDENBURG.

Oldenburg.   *Oldenburg* is the capital city of the county of that name, in eaft longitude 7. 32. latitude 53. 35. fituated twenty-five miles weft of *Bremen*, on the river *Hund*, which falls into the *Wefer* a little below where there is a cuftom-houfe, and fhips pay toll to the king of *Denmark*. This is a good looking old town which was formerly well fortified, but the works are now fallen to decay. The houfes are old fafhioned and moft of them built with wood, which gives it a very antique afpect. The country round about

through GERMANY.   123

about is marfhy and barren, which renders the inhabitants induftrious, and makes them apply themfelves to trade. Here the counts of *Oldenburg* formerly kept their refidence, from whom the houfe of *Denmark* is defcended. The principal things worth a traveller's notice are, the count's palace or caftle, which is a handfome old building, the town-houfe, the pleafure-garden, and the king's ftables. There was formerly a very good library here with feveral other curiofities, but they have been all tranfported to *Copenhagen*. They have a governor appointed by the king of *Denmark*, who is fovereign of this and the adjacent county of *Delmenhorft*.

The principal inns at *Oldenburg*, are the *White-horfe*, the *Lion*, the *Englifh arms*.

XV. DELMENHORST.

Delmenhorft.   *Delmenhorft* is a fmall town of *Germany* in the circle of *Weftphalia*; in eaft longitude 8. 12. latitude 53. 25. It is fituate on the river *Delm*, about five miles weft of the city of *Bremen*. The place itfelf is very inconfiderable, confifting of little more than one long ftreet, with poor looking houfes, and is only remarkable for being the capital of a county, which gives a title to his *Danifh* majefty. There was formerly a good caftle here, where the Counts held their refidence, but it is now fallen intirely to decay.

XVI. BREMEN.

Situation of Bremen.   *Bremen* is the capital of the dutchy of that name, fituated in a great plain on the river *Wefer*, in eaft longitude 8. 20. latitude 53. 25. feventy miles northweft of *Zell*, and as many fouthweft of

G 2   *Hamburg.*

Figure 27: Excerpt from Thomas Nugent, *The Grand Tour: containing an exact description of most of the cities, towns, and remarkable places of Europe: together with a distinct account of the post-roads and stages, with their respective distances [...] likewise directions relating to the manner and expence of travelling from one place and country to another, as also occasional remarks on [...] each respective country*, 4 vols. (London, Printed for S. Birt, D. Browne, A. Millar, and G. Hawkins, 1749), vol.2, p.122–23.

Those, Nugent decided, should be large and rolled onto a round stick for portability.[29]

The second volume of Nugent's work is dedicated to Germany, and the handbook describes a grid of about 800 cities and postal roads crisscrossing central Europe, including Germany, Poland, Bohemia, Moravia, Austria, with side trips extending to Moscow and Stockholm. In his descriptions of Germany, Nugent relied extensively on Lehmann's *Die vornehmsten Europäischen Reisen*, the German apodemia first published in 1703. Incidentally, the German apodemia was published in Hamburg, a city that features prominently in

29. Nugent, *The Grand Tour*, vol.1, p.vii.

Nugent's *Grand Tour*. A comparison of the two apodemias shows that Nugent borrowed freely and extensively from *Die vornehmsten Europäischen Reisen*, for example in his summary of Germany's geographic boundaries and its political organization. The format of Nugent's handbook hewed closely to the German original by reproducing the extended index of city names and the book's organization according to travel routes (see Figures 28a and 28b). A closer inspection reveals that Nugent mostly translated the information in the older guide, as is evident in this entry for the small post station Zollenspicker (on the road from Hamburg to Magdeburg). The German version reads: "ZOLLENSPICKER, ist ein Haus an der Elbe, noch zu den vier Landen gehörig allwo man nach dem Hoop ins Lüneburgische überfähret. Die in der Elbe liegende Winser-Schanze gehöret zum Lüneburgischen."[30] Nugent translated this as "Zollenspicker is a house on the Elbe belonging to the two districts of Lubec and Hamburgh where there is a ferry to cross the Elbe and carry you in to the duchy of Luneburg. There is a fortress here in the Elbe which belongs to the elector of Hanover as duke of Luneburg."[31] Here, Nugent clarified information that would be unfamiliar to his readers, such as "vier Lande" (four lands), and added information important for British travelers, namely that the elector of Hanover, at that time George II of Great Britain, owned the fortress in the Elbe in his role as duke of Luneburg. The close comparison makes apparent that Nugent overlaid his travel routes on a much older transportation grid.

What is significant here is that he departed significantly from the routes used by aristocratic travelers in the late seventeenth and early eighteenth centuries. Those had focused on aristocratic connections—for example, beginning in 1714, the need to curry favor with the new Hanoverian king and learn German, or the desire to see the Prussian military reviews in Silesia.[32] The route from Hamburg to Magdeburg described in this excerpt skirts Hanover by about 90 miles and leads the traveler directly to Leipzig, the commercial center of Saxony, from where travelers would proceed to Dresden and then to Prague and Vienna. Nugent thus opened up German-speaking Central Europe in terms of both geographic reach and the social class of the traveler by replacing aristocratic networks forged by family

---

30. Krebel, *Die vornehmsten Europäischen Reisen*, p.4.
31. Nugent, *The Grand Tour*, vol.2, p.262.
32. Jeremy Black, *The British and the Grand Tour* (London, 1985), p.9–10.

Figure 28a: Excerpt from *Die vornehmsten Europäischen Reisen*, ed. Peter Ambrosius Lehmann (Hamburg, Lehmann, 1703), p.4–5.

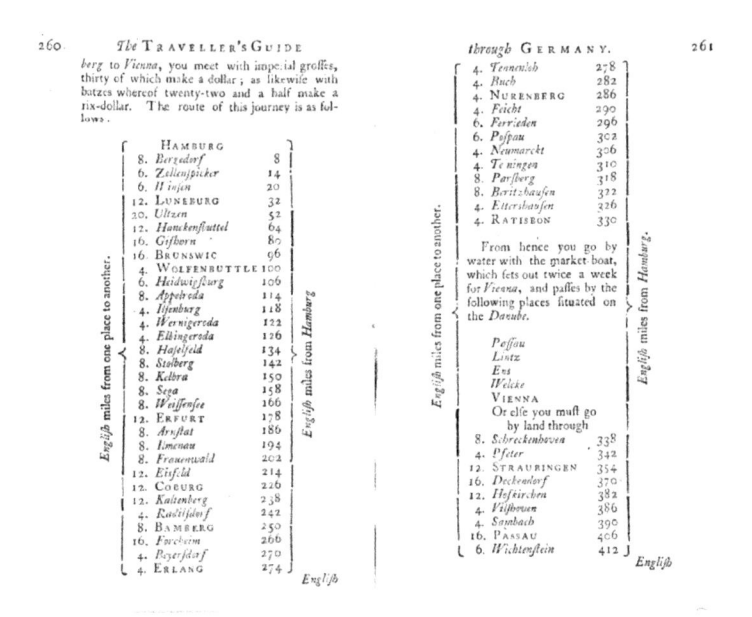

Figure 28b: Excerpt from Thomas Nugent, *The Grand Tour*, vol.2, p.260–61.

ties or political allegiances with geographic and cultural information about the destination that could be used by anybody with the money and time necessary to travel. Handbooks such as Nugent's *Grand Tour* made large-scale travel possible and ushered in modern tourism.

Nugent's entry point into Germany was the Hanseatic city of Hamburg, which had a long history of trade relations with Great Britain. The city is mentioned seventeen times as either a departure or arrival point—more than any other German city—and Nugent seems particularly familiar with Hamburg. His descriptions of Hamburg and its sights span seven pages in comparison to the five pages that describe Vienna and Leipzig, the three pages devoted to Berlin and Dresden, and the one page dedicated to Munich. Overall, Nugent closely copies *Die vornehmsten Europäischen Reisen* and, accordingly, traditional commercial centers such as Hamburg, Leipzig, and Frankfurt and their fairs receive more attention than the sights of the Bavarian capital, which, according to Nugent, hold little interest for those traveling for business.[33] Like the earlier handbook, Nugent's descriptions focus on buildings, grand boulevards, historical sites, religious buildings, libraries, military installation, and trade fairs. These accounts are enumerative and statistical, and tell readers very little about Nugent's personal impressions.[34] Natural beauty is seldom mentioned, and Nugent's intended travelers are expected to visit the main cities and interact there with an educated German middle-class population.[35]

Traveling through cartographic voids

In 1745, the cartographer Cassini was shocked by the impenetrability of Württemberg and the general lack of roads and transportation infrastructure in southern Germany, and wrote: "The interest they took in [the project] made me forget all the problems I was having

---

33. Nugent, *The Grand Tour*, vol.2, p.299.
34. Cologne, for example, is praised for the number of its steeples and gates: "'Tis very rare to see so many steeples anywhere at once, as appear to travellers upon approaching this city. There are twenty-four gates, thirteen to the land, and eleven on the Rhine. The streets are large and well paved in the middle of the town, where there are two spacious market-places. Though the town is pretty populous, yet the walls inclose a considerable space of ground, which is not built upon, and particularly three hundred acres planted with vines" (Nugent, *The Grand Tour*, vol.2, p.292).
35. Nugent, *The Grand Tour*, vol.2, p.93.

in a country where I couldn't discover the direction of the road, and where I found only barren mountains covered in forests."[36] In comparison to France, the Low Countries, Great Britain, and Italy, the German lands were behind in both infrastructural and economic development. The advice provided by Nugent (and his German predecessor) was therefore crucial for a region that had not yet been extensively mapped. Very few accurate topographical measurements were available to travelers, as German publisher and traveler Friedrich Nicolai discovered on his journey through Germany. In volume 9 of his monumental twelve-volume oeuvre *Beschreibung einer Reise durch Deutschland und die Schweiz, im Jahre 1781 (Description of a journey through Germany and Switzerland in 1781)*, he groused:

> An example of this mess is that the author [of the guidebook] talks at length about the location of the city yet does not give cartographic specifics. According to the Berlin collection of astronomical tables, […] the city of Ulm is situated at 27° 37' longitude und 48° 24' latitude; however, in the Berlin Astronomical Ephemera for the year 1785, […] the longitude is fixed at 27° 36' 15" and latitude at 48° 23'.[37]

As he traveled, he found that maps, if they existed at all, were often insufficient and out of date, and neither rivers nor towns or roads were correctly recorded.[38] Cartographic knowledge proved lacking, particularly when he decided to leave the postal road and venture off the beaten track. At this point, he discovered that local, embodied knowledge was crucial. On a journey from Stuttgart to the Abbey of St. Blasien in the southern Black Forest, Nicolai was forced to rely on a number of local coachmen who took his carriage further

---

36. "L'intérêt qu'ils y prenoient, me faisoit oublier toutes les contrariétés que j'éprouvois dans un pays où je ne découvrois dans la direction de la route que je devois suivre, que des montagnes sans objets, couvertes de bois, entassées les unes sur les autres." Cassini, *Relation d'un voyage*, p.xiv.
37. "Ein Beyspiel der Unordnung ist, daß der Verfasser [of the guidebook], welcher umständlich von der Lage der Stadt redet, nicht ein Wort von der geographischen Lage derselben sagt. Nach der Berliner Sammlung Astronomischer Tafeln […] liegt die Stadt Ulm unter 27° 37' Länge und 48° 24' Breite; hingegen in den Berlinischen astronomischen Ephemeriden für das Jahr 1785 […] wird die Länge auf 27° 36' 15" und die Breite auf 48° 23' angegeben." Nicolai, *Beschreibung einer Reise*, vol.9, p.4. Note that Nicolai is referring to the Ferro meridian (prime meridian) located at 17° 40' W, which dominated cartography until 1884, when it was replaced by the Greenwich meridian. See Wilford, *The Mapmakers*, p.257–59.
38. Nicolai, *Beschreibung einer Reise*, vol.12, p.171–72.

and further into the unknown over unimproved trails.[39] Geographic information within this local knowledge network was rendered not in geospatial data (miles) but rather in time increments (30 hours), and local knowledge and cartographic knowledge often conflicted. For example, the local guide took Nicolai on a circuitous and "terrifying route" from St. Blasien to Schaffhausen in Switzerland despite the map showing a direct route. The captive Nicolai could only speculate that his guide might have wanted to visit a secret lover in another town along the way.[40] The terrifying journey shows, however, that geodetic penetration of Germany was so rudimentary that travelers were forced to rely on local advice.

Nicolai's journey through Germany was successful only because he, as a famous Berlin publisher, could call on an extended network of correspondents on his way through the unfamiliar south. Local expertise thus provided an important layer of information. Informants in Stuttgart and later Tübingen who knew the area referred Nicolai to their local contacts: "In Stuttgart, I was referred to Consul Schwalb, who (if memory serves me right) managed the monastery's transactions in Württemberg."[41] This correspondent network supplied Nicolai with practical information about where to stay, what to see, and whom to meet. While modern readers have criticized the tedious nature and didacticism of Nicolai's travelogue, with its volumes of ancillary materials, these twelve volumes must be viewed within the context of Nicolai's attempt to render German territory more transparent and accessible through cartographic accuracy and factual advice. In effect, he is engaged in an effort to discredit and replace local knowledge in favor of supraregional knowledge networks calibrated to an educated and affluent readership ready to explore. Lack of such information forced travelers—especially those not proficient in the German language—on established postal roads, and the foreign travelogues show that there were indeed only a limited number of ways to cross Germany.

39. Nicolai, *Beschreibung einer Reise*, vol.12, p.3–4.
40. Nicolai, *Beschreibung einer Reise,* vol.12, p.147.
41. "Man hatte mich in Stuttgard [*sic*] an den Herrn Konsulenten Schwalb [in Tübingen] gewiesen, welcher (wenn ich mich recht erinnere) die Geschäfte des Stifts im Wirtembergischen zu besorgen hat." Nicolai, *Beschreibung einer Reise*, vol.12, p.147.

On the beaten path

For the most part, travelers followed the routes laid out by Nugent's handbook, although the entry point into the German empire moved from the north to the southwest, meaning that travelers entered Germany through Strasbourg or Basel on their return from either Switzerland or Paris (see Figure 29). The traditional Grand Tour then proceeded up the Rhine to Frankfurt. From there, travelers crossed through Hesse and the kingdom of Hanover toward Berlin. Later travelers would skip Hanover in favor of Weimar and Erfurt, and head toward Berlin. After several weeks in Berlin, travelers turned south toward Dresden, Prague, and Vienna. Most travelers spent the bulk of their time in Vienna before they traveled toward Venice through Styria and Slovenia. The sojourn in Vienna was often punctuated by extensive trips through Silesia, Bohemia, Moravia, and sometimes side tours to Hungary. The single objective of these eastern travels was to visit the battlefields of the Thirty Years War or the Seven Years War, and to verify with their own eyes the Prussian military advantages over Austria. Another, more direct, route was the one mapped by Cassini along the Danube toward Vienna, a favorite of French travelers (see Figure 30). Later travelers, most notably the British Romantics, added the route south along the Rhine River, entering Germany through Kleve and Aachen (Aix-la-Chapelle), particularly after the French Revolution in 1789 (see Figure 31). The final destination was not necessarily Germany but the mountains of Switzerland, as had been Ann Radcliffe's plan. Similarly, John Owen, on the Grand Tour with a young unknown gentleman, traveled down the Rhine River to reach Geneva, where they spent a significant amount of time. This Grand Tour was interrupted, when Owen and his charge were attacked by a revolutionary mob in Lyon. At that point, Owen separated from his employer and proceeded from Switzerland along the southern route toward Vienna— the German empire was perceived as the safer travel destination.[42] The Romantics added not only the Rhine route to Nugent's itinerary, but also routes along the Giant Mountains in modern-day Poland, an area without prosperous commercial centers and therefore not mentioned in Lehmann's *Die vornehmsten Europäischen Reisen* (see Figure 32). While Nugent had mapped the route from Salzburg (or Innsbruck) to Italy

---

42. John Owen, *Travels into different parts of Europe, in the years 1791 and 1792: with familiar remarks on places-men-and manners*, vol.2 (London, Printed for T. Cadell, jun. and W. Davis, 1796), p.349.

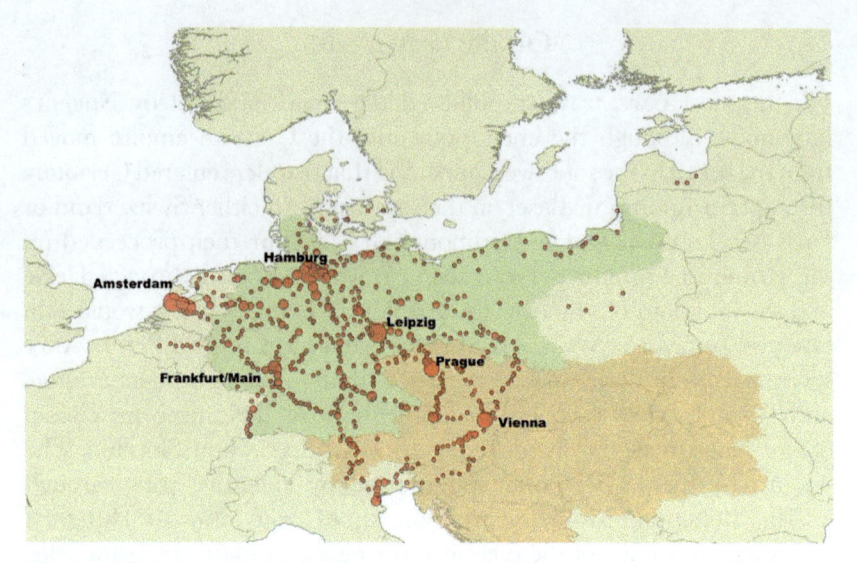

Figure 29: Map of cities along routes in Thomas Nugent's *The Grand Tour*. Size indicates number of routes that include the city. Visual created by Karin Baumgartner.

across the Brenner Pass—a popular road for German travelers on their way to Italy—few later foreign travelers would choose it. Rather, the more popular route for English travelers would lead from Graz to Slovenia and from there to Venice. The most significant differences between Nugent's travel advice and travelers' actual routes arose in the chosen itineraries of French travelers. These travelers, more interested in military conquest than in trade and commerce, traveled to see battle-fields, which took them significantly further into Bohemia, Moravia, and Silesia, often bypassing the towns mapped in *Die vornehmsten Europäischen Reisen.*

Overall, these side trips were exceptions to a travel network that remained consistent over the hundred-year time period described here. Few foreign travelers dared to veer off the beaten track—increasingly so, as the time spent on the journey shortened from two years to just a few months. As Edward Wilkey's travelogue from 1839 indicates, the rapid journeys of the nineteenth century relied on the established travel grid and the accompanying infrastructure (hotels and inns) even more strongly.[43] Despite the increasing popularity of

43. Edward Wilkey, *Wanderings in Germany: with moonlight walks on the banks of the Elbe, the Danube, the Neckar, and the Rhine* (London, 1839).

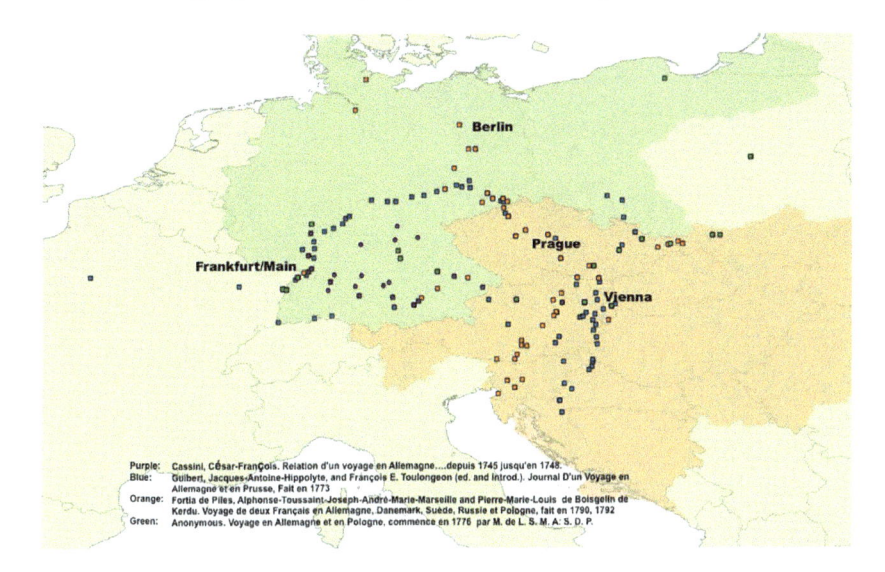

Figure 30: Map of cities along routes in four different French travel
guides: César-François Cassini, *Relation d'un voyage en Allemagne* [...]
depuis 1745 jusqu'en 1748 (Paris, Imprimerie royale, 1775) (purple);
Journal d'un voyage en Allemagne et en Prusse, fait en 1773, ed. Jacques-
Antoine-Hippolyte Guibert and François E. Toulongeon (Paris,
1803) (blue); Alphonse-Toussaint-Joseph-André-Marie-Marseille
Fortia de Piles and Pierre-Marie-Louis de Boisgelin de Kerdu,
*Voyage de deux Français en Allemagne, Danemark, Suède, Russie et
Pologne, fait en 1790, 1792* (Paris, Desenne, 1796) (orange); and the
anonymous *Voyage en Allemagne et en Pologne, commencé en 1776 par M.
de L.S.M.A.S.D.P.* (green). Visual created by Karin Baumgartner.

the western route along the Rhine River, there is significant overlap
in British travel routes between 1772, when John Moore traveled with
the duke of Hamilton, and 1822, when John Russel undertook the
same tour with his charge, Viscount Lescelles (see Figure 33). Even
though later (Romantic) travelers tended to privilege nature over
buildings and cities, their paths through Germany did not diverge in
any measurable way from those who had gone before them, and the
overlap in travel routes draws attention to the lack of advancement in
travel infrastructure in large parts of Germany.

Overall, travelers kept to the existing roads and to places that were
easily accessible by coach. This was true for all travelers, including
those in search of the picturesque, such as Ann Radcliffe, Mary Shelley,

Figure 31: Map of cities along routes in travel guides written by British Romantics: Ann Radcliffe's *A Journey made in the summer of 1794, through Holland and the western frontier of Germany, with a return down the Rhine: to which are added, observations during a tour to the lakes of Lancashire, Westmoreland, and Cumberland* (London, printed for G. G. and J. Robinson, 1795) (red); and Charles Dodd, *An Autumn near the Rhine, or Sketches of courts, society, and scenery in Germany, with a tour in the Taunus Mountains in 1820* (London, 1821) (blue). Visual created by Karin Baumgartner.

John Carr, and John Owen. What we do not find in these travelogues are walking tours similar to the one Samuel Taylor Coleridge and William Wordsworth undertook in the Lake District. The Shelleys had attempted to walk across France, but gave up soon enough when the obstacles mounted and food was hard to procure away from the infrastructural grid.[44] In Germany, scenery was viewed from the coach or the boat; Romantic side excursions, to an overlook for example, were infrequent and difficult to organize due to the need for a local guide.[45] Travel in northern Germany was particularly arduous because

---

44. Shelley, "History of a six weeks' tour," p.314–20.
45. See Annegret Pelz, *Reisen durch die eigene Fremde. Reiseliteratur von Frauen als autogeographische Schriften* (Cologne, 1993), p.78 and 114. Here, she argues that the coach made travel possible for women, as it allowed them to keep the illusion of domestic space alive during their travels. While male travelers

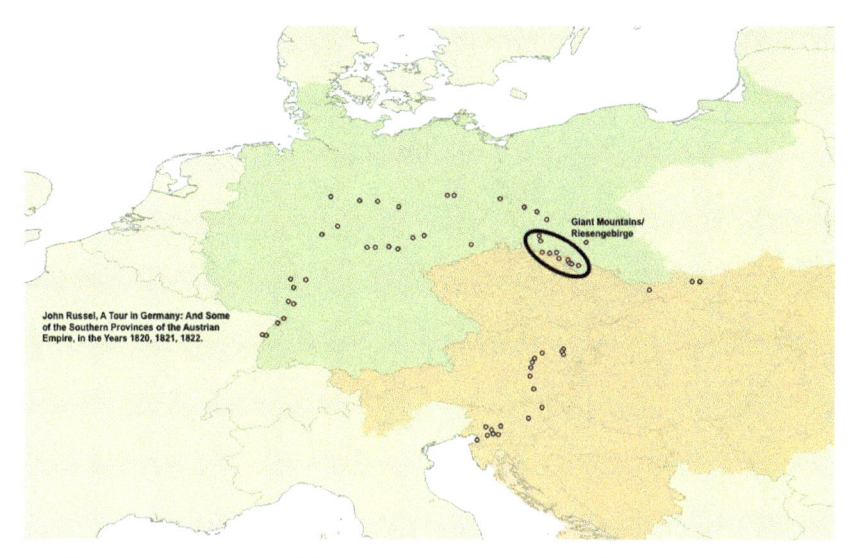

Figure 32: Map of cities along routes in John Russel's *A Tour in Germany, and some of the southern provinces of the Austrian empire, in the years 1820, 1821, 1822* (Edinburgh, 1824), with Giant Mountains circled. Visual created by Karin Baumgartner.

of the sandy soil that made traveling by coach extremely slow, and few travelers followed Nugent's advice to enter Germany through Hamburg. Many simply avoided going north from Berlin. Overall, the majority of all travelers aimed for Vienna and Austria. One reason might be that English and French travelers, thinking within the familiar territorial structures of the nation-state, were simply looking toward the capital of the empire to understand Germany. Another more prosaic explanation had to do with the well-maintained roads the Austrians built, which were featured in Nugent's and many other travelogues. While expensive, the roads in the Austrian empire were well built and protected from bandits and highwaymen, and post stations were strung along the road at predictable intervals, providing travelers with horses, food, and shelter.

---

certainly had more access to exterior space, the travelogues consulted for this essay reveal that both male and female travelers tended to stick to coaches or boats for sightseeing.

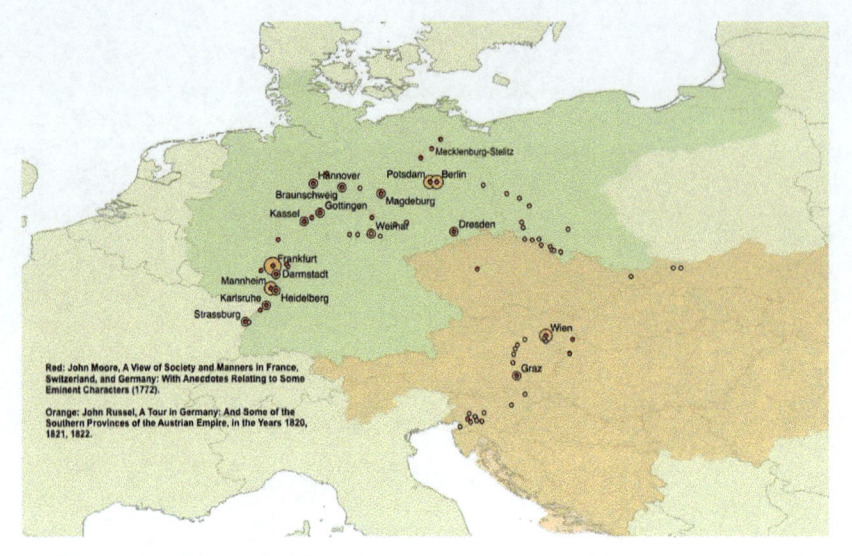

Figure 33: Map of cities along routes in John Moore's *A View of society and manners in France, Switzerland, and Germany, with anecdotes relating to some eminent characters* (London, Strahan & Cadell, 1783) (red; the map indicates the year in which the trip took place: 1772); and John Russel's *A Tour in Germany* (orange). Size indicates the number of times a city is mentioned. Visual created by Karin Baumgartner.

Foreign descriptions of Germany

The general impression evoked by travel in Germany overall was one of extreme poverty, a lack of infrastructure related, in particular, to lodging and sustenance, and a gruff and uneducated population. Nugent, for example, advised travelers to carry their own food and bedding on any trip. Early travelers such as Marshall (1768) recounted the challenges involved in traveling across Westphalia, a particularly impoverished part of Germany. On his trip from Duisburg to Minden, Marshall was forced to stay overnight in a one-room hovel that served both humans and animals, and no food could be procured in this part of Germany.[46] While aristocratic travelers like Moore and the duke of Hamilton, who had access to German court society, could escape the public inns, the table d'hôte, and the vicissitudes of traveling post, middle-class travelers had to make do with the inferior infrastructure

46. Marshall, *Travels through Holland*, vol.2, p.52.

available to Germans. Accordingly, Ann Radcliffe's travelogue describes many German towns as slums not fit for entertaining foreign visitors, and traveling as arduous. In a final summary, she wrote:

> Without this journey of eleven or twelve hundred miles we should have considered Germany, as its position in maps and description in books represent it, to be important, powerful, and prosperous; or, even if it had been called wretched, the idea would have been indistinct, and the assertion, perhaps, not wholly credited. The greatest and, as it is reasonable to believe, the best part of Germany we have now seen, and, in whatever train of reasoning it is noticed, have an opinion how it should be valued. Those, who cannot guess at causes, may be sure of effects; and having seen, that there is little individual prosperity in Germany, little diffusion of intelligence, manners, or even of the means for comfort, few sources of independence, or honourable wealth, and no examples of the poverty, in which there may be pride, it was not less perceptible, that there can be no general importance, no weight in the balance of useful, that is, peaceful power, and no place, but that of an instrument, even in the desperate exercises of politics.[47]

John Russel, traveling in 1822, was equally scandalized by the poverty, dirt, and grime he observed in Westphalia: "The villages [...] display, externally at least, the utmost squalor. The only tolerable dwelling is generally that of the postmaster; the others are wooden hovels, dark, smoky, patched, and ruinous. The crowds of begging children that surround you at every stage, [...] prove that there must be poverty as well as slovenliness."[48] The fact that earlier travelers complained less about the inferiority of German infrastructure than later travelers certainly points to the fact that Germany had developed a relatively efficient transportation system very early, as shown in Lehmann's *Die vornehmsten Europäischen Reisen*, yet was not able to keep up with the rapidly increasing expectations of its foreign travelers, who had honed their observational powers in Great Britain, France, and Italy. In particular Italy, as impoverished and fragmented as Germany, had managed to develop an interlocking system of transportation, accommodation, provisions, knowledgeable guides, and travel agents that successfully catered to the needs of foreign tourists.[49] By 1839,

---

47. Radcliffe, *A Journey*, p.342.
48. John Russel, *A Tour in Germany, and some of the southern provinces of the Austrian empire, in the years 1820, 1821, 1822*, 2 vols. (Edinburgh, 1824), p.231.
49. See Mariana Starke, *Letters from Italy: between the years 1792 and 1798, containing*

Germany was beginning to catch up with international standards of comfort, and Edward Wilkey's tour through Germany was generally a pleasant one, although complaints about food and accommodation are present here too.[50]

Travelers were baffled by Germany's political fragmentation, which they experienced in the many border crossings and examinations they endured. The French aristocrat Fortia de Piles gives a vivid description of such an examination on his entry into Hapsburg territory:

> The village where the luggage gets inspected is two miles from Passau in a forest, in an extremely dreary location. This is all the more arduous for travelers, because the boats, if they are very laden, must wait here for twenty-four, thirty-six, even forty-eight hours. The search is strict and necessary: Each traveler receives a paper, wherein it is stated that he has been inspected, and he can travel on to Vienna without further searches except when the officials are in a bad mood. This bad mood can, however, be mollified with a twenty-kreutzer coin.[51]

After the Napoleonic Wars, these complaints translated into more explicit political analysis. Charles Edward Dodd, who traveled through the western part of Germany in the entourage of Robert

---

a view of the revolutions in that country, from the capture of Nice by the French republic to the expulsion of Pius VI. from the ecclesiastical state: likewise pointing out the matchless works of art which still embellish Pisa, Florence, Siena, Rome, Naples, Bologna, Venice, &c: with instructions for the use of invalids and families, 2 vols. (London, 1800).

50. Wilkey wrote: "By way of supper we had, at a road-side inn, the most execrable apology for a meal I ever partook of, consisting of sour bread, rancid butter, and slices of sausage strongly flavoured with garlic. The beer which accompanied this repast was decidedly the most bitter I ever tasted, and the whole reminded me strongly of Italian vetturino fare"; Wilkey, *Wanderings in Germany*, p.64.

51. "Das Dorf, wo das Gepäk visitirt wird, liegt zwei Meilen über Passau mitten im Gehölz, in einer äußerst traurigen Lage. Dies ist um so beschwerlicher für die Reisenden, weil die Schiffe, wenn sie sehr beladen sind, vier und zwanzig, sechs und dreißig, bisweilen acht und vierzig Stunden hier liegen bleiben müßen. Die Visitation ist streng und nothwendig; jeder Reisende erhält einen Zettel, worauf bezeugt wird, daß er visitirt worden, und mit diesem Zettel kann man nach Wien kommen, ohne aufs neue visitirt zu werden, ausgenommen, wenn die Vistators übler Laune sind, aber auch diese Laune läßt sich, mit einem Zwanzigkreuzerstük leicht besänftigen." Alphonse-Toussaint-Joseph-André-Marie-Marseille Fortia de Piles and Pierre-Marie-Louis de Boisgelin de Kerdu, *Voyage de deux Français en Allemagne, Danemark, Suède, Russie et Pologne, fait en 1790, 1792* (Paris, Desenne, 1796), p.21.

Stewart, Viscount Castlereagh, the British architect of the post-Napoleonic political order and the Congress System, wrote: "The Continent is as likely to suffer from being overrun by two or three immoderately sized sovereigns, as from the miserable stagnation of intellect and frittering of character in the principalities of three leagues by two."[52] John Russel, traveling in 1822, found that the German Confederation (the legal framework negotiated at the Vienna Congress) "serves no purpose other than enabling Austria and Prussia to rule all Germany [...] One-third of the votes, belongs to Austria, Prussia, England, Denmark, and the Netherlands."[53] The Germany that emerged from these travelogues was and remained puzzling and practically difficult to navigate. What bound these Germans together into a unified German nation—these travelogues claimed—was their backwardness, their lack of education, and the political instability Charles Dodd sensed wherever he went. These attributes allowed Radcliffe, Russel, Dodd, and later Wilkey to represent Germany as a primitive, albeit pastoral, place that provided the greatest possible contrast to industrialized and modern Britain.

German reactions to foreign travelogues

German readers eagerly absorbed many of these foreign reports about Germany, but bristled at the descriptions they read. In 1786, for example, a reviewer in the *Allgemeine Literatur-Zeitung* (*General literature journal*) grumbled that such travelogues gave too superficial an impression—in particular if written by the English, a nation, the reviewer noted, given to traveling for entertainment rather than edification.[54] The reviewer of Jacques-Antoine-Hippolyte Guibert's *Journal d'un voyage en Allemagne et en Prusse, fait en 1773* (*Journal of a journey to Germany and Prussia, undertaken in 1773*) in the *Allgemeine*

---

52. Charles Dodd, *An Autumn near the Rhine, or Sketches of courts, society, and scenery in Germany, with a tour in the Taunus Mountains in 1820* (London, 1821), p.505.
53. Russel, *A Tour in Germany*, vol.1, p.32.
54. The reviewer referred to *A Descriptive journey through the interior parts of Germany and France including Paris: with interesting and amusing anecdotes by a young English peer of the highest rank, just returned from his travels* (1786), *Allgemeine Literatur-Zeitung* 273 (1786), p.313–16 (316). Criticism of dandy lords and their vile behavior abroad was common in Great Britain, where aristocratic travel memoirs were viewed with moral and aesthetic suspicion. The German reviewer tapped into this pan-European sentiment. See Turner, *British travel writers*, p.58.

geographische Ephemeriden (*General geographical ephemerides*) was equally unenthusiastic about the posthumously published travelogue, comparing it to a picked-over corpse.[55] John Moore's travelogue was more positively reviewed, after it appeared in a German edition in the fall of 1779,[56] but Charles Dodd's *Autumn near the Rhine* found little approval. Sections of the book were translated and published in the *Morgenblatt für gebildete Stände* (*Morning paper for the educated classes*), one of the more liberal journals in Germany. Yet an extensive footnote in the *Morgenblatt* informed the reader,

> We are going to point out for our readers that the views of this Englishman are of particular interest, because they mostly diverge from our own. It is good for us to see how others err in their judgment of us; first, in that it shows us a new aspect of ourselves, and second, because we might become more delicate in our judgment of others. All readers are free to disprove this Englishman; preferably in the English press and not in the German papers.[57]

What is particularly interesting about Dodd's travelogue is that the German translation was a veritable rewrite of the English original with many political passages excised and softened, yet not even this redacted version found favor in the German press. When Germans finally began to travel the homeland, the travel advice and itineraries available to them seemed puzzling and rudimentary, and many German writers would have felt like pioneers as they explored Germany. Still, the itineraries of French and British travelers left their mark on the German imagination, as is apparent in *Das*

55. Review of Jacques-Antoine-Hippolyte Guibert and François E. Toulongeon, *Journal d'un voyage en Allemagne et en Prusse* (1803), *Allgemeine geographische Ephemeriden* 19 (1803), p.203–207 (204).
56. Henry L. Fulton, "An eighteenth-century best seller," *Papers of the Bibliographical Society of America* 66 (1972), p.428–33 (428 and 432).
57. "Wir bemerken unsern Lesern ein für allemal, daß die Ansichten dieses Engländers grade deßhalb ein besondres Interesse haben, weil sie von den unsrigen in den mehrsten Fällen ganz abgehen. Es ist uns gut, zu sehen, wie Andre sich irren, indem sie uns beurtheilen; einmal, in dem es uns eine neue Ansicht unsrer selbst zeigt, und zum Andern, weil wir in unserm eignen Urtheil über Andre dadurch behutsamer werden können. Diesen Engländer zu widerlegen, steht Jedem frey; doch vor dem englischen, nicht dem deutschen Publikum müsste dieses geschehen." "Skizzen eines Engländers aus den deutschen Rheingegenden," translated by Christian Moritz Engelhardt, *Morgenblatt für gebildete Stände* 274 (1818), p.1093–95 (1093). It is unclear whether the translator or the editor authored this footnote.

malerische und romantische Deutschland, in zehn Sektionen (*Picturesque and Romantic Germany in ten volumes*), a comprehensive and prescriptive travel handbook published in 1836 that inventoried the accumulated geographic and cultural knowledge constituting the German nation. The handbook singled out principally the places and sights visited by earlier British and French travelers as particularly representative of this nation.[58]

Conclusion

Foreign travel narratives about Germany remained largely stable over a hundred-year period, pointing to the fact that Germany did not see much investment in infrastructure until the 1830s. The consistency of routes, cities, and sights, and even popular inns and rest stops, contributes to a certain ennui palpable in these foreign travelogues, with many writers copying from earlier travelogues. Over the time period described, travel continued to take place within an infrastructural network originally geared toward merchants and trade. This meant that large trading centers were (and remained) relatively well connected while other parts of Germany were barely accessible to travelers, such as the routes from Berlin to the north or the Baltic Sea and all of Westphalia. In comparison, the duchies of Hesse-Darmstadt and Hesse-Kassel were overrepresented, especially in British travelogues, as these smaller courts were actively courting British travelers to raise their own prominence. Vienna, famous for its creature comforts, remained a popular destination, even though the British and French disdained the archaic and corrupt political system of the Hapsburg Empire and the loose morals of its population. Often writers would take their impressions of Vienna and apply them to all of Germany, not sufficiently understanding the local differences in the vast geographic territory. The itineraries of foreign travelers (and later the itineraries of German travelers following in their footsteps) remained circular, and allowed for a reading of Germany as unified and singular, even if those descriptions summarily dismissed this Germany as impoverished or politically delayed.

Taken together, the travelogues under discussion created a spatial imaginary that could be anchored in geometric space when calls for

---

58. *Das malerische und romantische Deutschland, in zehn Sektionen* (Leipzig, 1836–1842) had a different author for every volume. Authors included Gustav Schwab, Nicolaus Lenau, and Carl Simrock.

a unified German nation became prominent during the Napoleonic Wars. Yet, as Jason Hansen has shown, data collection and mapping lagged significantly behind the ideological calls for this nation.[59] Coherent visual images of the nation, such as accurate maps that would give readers a bird's-eye view of the nation, were lacking until late in the nineteenth century. Travel narratives thus filled these cartographic gaps. The many travelogues published in the late eighteenth and early nineteenth centuries transformed what were limited and fragmented local experiences of place into a textual overview of the whole that prepared readers for the geographic and cartographic projects that began to emerge in the 1830s.[60]

59. See Jason D. Hansen, *Mapping the Germans: statistical science, cartography, and the visualization of the German nation, 1848–1914* (Oxford, 2015), p.53.
60. Hansen, *Mapping*, p.50–53.

A call for a concert of eavesdroppers: Beethoven's conversation notebooks

PETER HÖYNG

Emory University

Introduction

Despite the continuous flow of books on all aspects of Ludwig van Beethoven (1770–1827) and his music––which has certainly been accelerated by the composer's 250th birthday in 2020[1]—scholars have overlooked a remarkable, even unique, primary source: the so-called *Konversationshefte*, or conversation notebooks, which span the last decade of the composer's life, from February 1818 until his death in March 1827. As will be shown, the notebooks hold the key to this part of Beethoven's life.

In 1798, at just twenty-seven years old, Beethoven, already celebrated for both his virtuosity at the piano and his inventive compositions, realized that his precious sensory organ, his auditory instrument, was beginning to falter. This impending loss of hearing

---

1. The German government agreed in 2013 to devote special funding to celebrating Beethoven's 250th birthday. The public funding mirrors and accentuates the cultural capital that the German government has assigned to the composer despite the fact that he lived most of his life in Vienna, Austria, and composed all his significant music there. The creation of a Beethoven Jubiläums Gesellschaft GmbH in 2016—a subsidiary of the Beethoven-Haus in Bonn—which coordinated all the efforts to celebrate this particular birthday underlines the tension of making Beethoven local ("Steigerung der Bekanntheit Bonns als Beethoven-Stadt" ["increase of Bonn's fame as Beethoven-city"]), while proudly claiming that the entire world is celebrating his birthday. See https://www.bthvn2020.de/ueber-uns/ueber-bthvn2020 (last accessed June 30, 2023). These deliberate promotion efforts marketing the composer at the local and national level as an international icon barely skirt the efforts to make traditional German musical aesthetics seem, once again, superior, demonstrating how the arts are used to promote a national if not nationalistic agenda in times of globalization.

not only shook Beethoven as a private person but also destabilized his well-crafted public persona. Three reference points illustrate the agony that this situation inflicted. When Beethoven acknowledged his disability while flirting with suicide in the fall of 1802—as documented in a letter that eventually acquired mythical proportion as the so-called "Heiligenstädter Testament"—he admitted his fear of revealing any of his embarrassment in public.[2] Twelve years later, however, when Beethoven could no longer hide his disability, Johann Nepomuk Mälzel, an engineer best known as the inventor of the metronome, proudly designed "ear trumpets" just for Beethoven. But by 1818, Beethoven's hearing had become so poor that even this device was no longer of much use to him for communicating with others. Now, everyone in the audience could witness his deafness firsthand because his movements while conducting were disconnected from the orchestra's performance. Nevertheless, in 1824, Beethoven conducted his Ninth Symphony in front of a full house.[3] From then on, Beethoven's deafness actually became an integral part in providing the nexus between his personal and artistic life, for it demonstrated the prevalent paradigm of "anguish becoming triumph"—as encapsulated, for example, in the subtitle of a recent biography.[4]

Hence, writing became imperative and was the only option remaining for Beethoven's circle of family and friends to continue interacting with him. As for *Aufschreibesysteme* (Friedrich Kittler), or writing tools, those used in conversation with Beethoven comprised a "slate and a slate pencil" and "a conversation book made by folding and stitching a large sheet of writing paper into octavo format, along with a pencil for conversing with the deaf invalid."[5] While both of these utensils sufficed for basic and daily communication, they differed categorically in terms of archiving the written notes. Whereas the slate allowed for easy erasure of any jotted messages, the small

2. "I was soon compelled to withdraw myself, to live alone. [...] It was impossible for me to say to people, 'Speak louder, shout, I am deaf.' Ah, how could I possibly admit an infirmity in the one sense which ought to be more perfect in me than in others." Quoted according to Maynard Solomon, *Beethoven*, 2nd ed. (New York, 1998), p.152.
3. Thomas Forrest Kelly, *First nights: five musical premiers* (New Haven, CT, 2001), p.143.
4. Jan Swafford, *Beethoven: anguish and triumph* (Boston, MA, 2014).
5. Gerhard von Breuning, *Memories of Beethoven: from the house of the black-robed Spaniards*, ed. Maynard Solomon (Cambridge, 1995), p.90.

books preserved the conversations both then and, eventually, for us today. These penciled conversations are of greatest value as cultural documentation of the first part of the nineteenth century, not despite their transience and quotidian prosaic qualities but precisely because of these traits.

No other source allows us to eavesdrop on day-to-day conversations that are as unfiltered and as unedited as these random notes, intended for no purpose beyond the immediate communicative needs of the parties involved. The value of this premodern recording of daily discourse is only partly diminished by the fact that the disabled composer most often responded verbally and not in writing. As Jan Swafford correctly summarizes: "Of the entries he wrote in the books, most were items for himself: musical sketches [very few], marketing schemes, shopping lists, addresses, book recommendations."[6] But, aside from Beethoven's personal notes, the textual fragments document people, concerns, and objects in Beethoven's close network. They map the intersection of the public and private in ways that looking only at individual, one-on-one encounters cannot. Furthermore, the documented text corpus has become the only evidence of this network's actual existence and the place that continues to harbor these exchanges.

In 1846,[7] Anton Schindler, Beethoven's somewhat dubious secretary late in the composer's life (1822–1824 and 1826–1827), sold 137 (out of a total of 139) of these notebooks to the Royal Archive in Berlin, today's Staatsbiliothek zu Berlin (and, with this sale, the process of the composer's renaturalization to Germany and his transformation back into a German composer began).[8] Even though all major biographers since the late nineteenth century have quoted from or published parts of the notebooks, it was only from 1963 on that Beethoven scholars began scrutinizing them using the latest forensic innovations and the

---

6. Swafford, *Beethoven*, p.698.
7. Ludwig van Beethoven, *Ludwig van Beethovens Konversationshefte*, ed. Karl-Heinz Köhler *et al.*, 11 vols. (Leipzig, 1972–2001), vol.1, p.7. All subsequent references to this edition are given as "BKh."
8. This nationalistic appropriation was also aided by the fact that, throughout his life, Beethoven maintained an ambivalence toward the city and the Hapsburg court (as his various plans for leaving the city altogether indicate), even though he received honorary Viennese citizenship in 1815. Today, Vienna proudly celebrates Beethoven's presence throughout the city through museums, street names, and memorials, while making no mention of his misappropriation as an Austrian. See Solomon, *Beethoven*, p.116 and 177–78.

highest standards of editing possible at the time. Previous attempts had been hampered by the Cold War, but, in 1968, the first volume was finally published. The strenuous and tedious nature of this work is evidenced by the fact that the last volume was only published thirty-three years later, in 2001. This German edition forms the core of Theodore Albrecht's monumental endeavor to provide an updated edition of the *Konversationshefte* in English; the first of the projected twelve volumes has recently been released.[9]

To the best of my knowledge, neither musicologists nor biographers have attempted to analyze or interpret this set of eleven volumes in a comprehensive manner.[10] Naturally, scholars like to quote from the conversation notebooks, often recycling the same tidbits of information. This or that cherry-picked observation or brief context thereby becomes paradigmatic of a given aspect of the composer's life. Such an approach often replicates the flippant, volatile, and fleeting character of the original daily discourse, thereby pushing aside any attempt to make holistic sense of the exchanges. What we do not yet have is a single, quantitative—and, more importantly, qualitative and comprehensive—study or sophisticated interpretation of these jotted and more or less accidentally archived conversations. Digital humanities is increasingly enabling the translation of quantitative analysis into qualitative analysis, allowing us to, for example, better understand the role of individuals within Beethoven's network.

Scholars' relative disregard for Beethoven's conversation notebooks provides an example of a disciplinary split or compartmentalization in the research of a given topic—or even a single artist, in this instance. The fact that the notebooks have received, at best, partial attention derives, of course, not from ignorance but from the challenge these notebooks pose for all types of readers. For musicologists, the notebooks are far less significant than Beethoven's musical sketchbooks; for biographers, the conversations, as a whole, are too tedious to read and hence serve, at most, as a confirmation of a singular aspect; and, if cultural historians are aware of the notebooks at all, they simply

---

9. Ludwig van Beethoven, *Beethoven's conversation books*, ed. and translated by Theodore Albrecht, vol.1, no.1–8 (February 1818 to March 1820) (Woodbridge, 2018). All subsequent references to this edition are given as "BCB."

10. A notable exception to this statement can be found in Sanford Friedman's *Conversations with Beethoven* (New York, 2014), a novel based on the reading of the notebooks and narrated through a variety of genres and by filling in the gaps of the existing notebooks.

outsource this rich trove as something that Beethoven scholars do, with the result that the text corpus has become none of their business.[11]

If we think of academic disciplines in social terms as functioning networks, this relative research gap regarding Beethoven's conversation notebooks then also provides us with some initial insight into such social networks: They can function (the implications of the term notwithstanding) in (relative) isolation to one another (e.g., German studies scholars typically do not converse with those studying Beethoven's life and music). Nevertheless, I will draw on the field of social network theory as far as it is part of the emergent field of digital humanities. Here, the conversation notebooks may pose a worthwhile challenge to (among other things) facilitate a better understanding of the rise of an ego network and its relevance for the formation of tradition and legacy. Since engaging with digital humanities as a novice presents as much an opportunity as a challenge,[12] I hope to utilize social network theory both as a topic and as a method, seeking to effectively leverage the latter by limiting my endeavors to only three aspects when exploring the treasure trove of the conversation notebooks.

First, I will emphasize the dual character of these unfiltered records: While they present an opportunity for an unusually "thick description" of daily life, the notebooks can also be challenging for today's readers

---

11. The relative scholarly negligence of Beethoven's conversation notebooks reminds me of the dilemma that W. Daniel Wilson encountered in the 1990s when he began exploring the extensive files produced by Goethe in his various positions as minister in Saxony-Weimar. The *Germanisten* thought of these administrative and policy documents as unworthy of *their* attention since the files presumably contained no sophisticated thought or aesthetic merit, rendering them worthy only for historians. Historians, however, ignored these documents altogether because Goethe fell under the domain of the *Germanisten*. Hence, despite extensive research on the German poet since the late nineteenth century, the policy and legal documents that Goethe read and signed in his various administrative positions remained unknown, only to finally be exposed by someone trained—God forbid—in German studies from the US. This previous research gap serves as a cautionary tale, underscoring how poorly the humanities fare when disciplines function in isolation without collaborative exchange or a network. See W. Daniel Wilson, *Das Goethe-Tabu: Protest und Menschenrechte im klassischen Weimar* (Munich, 1999).

12. Having perused a number of introductory books, I settled on and follow mainly the sociologist Charles Kadushin's introduction to social network theory. Charles Kadushin, *Understanding social networks: theories, concepts, and findings* (Oxford, 2012).

because of their authentic richness and twined messiness. For heuristic reasons, I will briefly contrast these fragmented snippets to Benjamin's historical *Passagen-Werk* (*Arcades project*), which will allow me to argue why social network theory can serve as a method for overcoming hermeneutic shortcomings.

Second, I will discuss Beethoven's records of daily communication as a document of his immediate social network and will briefly outline a *qualitative* analysis of this network. In this regard, my thesis is twofold: (1) Beethoven's network remained small, especially when considering his growing international recognition and the fact that he never met many of the people he mentioned in conversation; and (2), along with his circle of trusted friends, he found himself in the midst of the nascent network of a bourgeois market economy and its vagaries, and thereby departed from a system of aristocratic patronage and the relative safety of his first decade in Vienna.[13]

Third, the field of digital humanities provides a rich opportunity for creating a diverse network of scholars in the humanities that could work to develop a full digital edition of the notebooks using Text Encoding Initiative (TEI) standards, as has been done, for example, for Shakespeare's texts. Based on such a digitized text corpus, this collaborative effort would eventually ease the exploration of the meaning and complexities of the notebooks, both in quantitative and in qualitative terms, and would enable a fuller analysis of Beethoven's social network. The network visualizations in this essay preview the scope of future analysis.

What to do with fragments of daily life?

At first, we abandon the desire to mediate and interpret the renowned composer's public and personal life, and hence ignore every biographer's primary objective. Instead, we treat the notebooks' recordings simply as a set of oral communications among (predominantly) men in post-Napoleonic Vienna. This proposition is made easier by the fact that Beethoven almost never offers remarks about his artistic work, making it feasible to disregard any immediate bearing that the notebooks might have on his music.

Following this plan, we are then faced with notes that contain an array of assertions or a variety of speech acts (i.e., very different genres

13. For the latter, see Tia DeNora, *Beethoven and the construction of genius: musical politics in Vienna 1792–1803* (Berkeley, CA, 1995), ch.4 and 6.

within daily discourses). The notebooks include, for example, oral reports, brief dialogues, minor and major observations and remarks, references to and judgments of various individuals, expressions of interest in material goods, shopping lists, personal comments jumbled with political ones, notes from newspapers (all of which were censored), and thoughts (including philosophical ones), all interspersed with brief monologs. Each of these genres requires different contexts, knowledge, assessment, and reading techniques, and each also allows for new insights into the life of the highly repressive Metternich era from the perspective of the center of the Hapsburg Empire.

Precisely because these written records served no other purpose than meeting the demands of a given moment and day (i.e., with no posterity in mind), the first step of decoding them can be compared to the work of an anthropologist. As Clifford Geertz writes: "Doing ethnography is like trying to read (in the sense of 'construct a reading of') a manuscript—foreign, faded, full of ellipses, incoherencies, suspicious emendations, and tendentious commentaries, but written not in conventionalized graphs of sound but in transient examples of shaped behavior."[14] In other words, ethnography, in Geertz's view, very much resembles the hermeneutics for dealing with a fragmented text.

What, then, do we have before us when reading from Beethoven's notebooks? Most of the time, the concerns of daily life and errands:[15] The winter is so cold that one's feet begin to freeze, and one looks for an appropriate heater while the latest fashion of an iron furnace is declared insufficient.[16] Where does one get clothing, and how long will it last?[17] Which apartment should be rented for the summer, and what price is feasible? Which furniture is necessary—and affordable— if renting outside of Vienna? Which dentist would be best to consult?[18] Which methods and means exist to fight deafness?[19] How can one protect oneself against sexually transmitted disease?[20] Where does one find good but inexpensive wine? One drinks too much of it and

---

14. Clifford Geertz, "Thick description: toward an interpretive theory of culture," in *The Interpretation of cultures: selected essays* (New York, 1973), p.3–32 (10).
15. The following two paragraphs contain excerpts that I have translated from the indicated points in the notebooks.
16. Beethoven, BKh, vol.1, p.96, 120, and 122 / BCB, vol.1, p.84, 109, and 111.
17. Beethoven, BKh, vol.1, p.358.
18. Beethoven, BKh, vol.1, p.376.
19. Beethoven, BKh, vol.1, p.190 / Beethoven, BCB, vol.1, p.187.
20. Beethoven, BKh, vol.1, p.55 / Beethoven, BCB, vol.1, p.34.

not everyone can handle it.[21] The notebooks contain no shortage of shopping lists, often followed immediately by rather important matters: "At the next meeting, declare my nephew to Dr. B[ach] as my heir—shaving brush, juniper, broom, [...], sealing wax, ink."[22]

The eating of oysters is frequently mentioned; they are simultaneously appreciated as a sign of luxury and dismissed as a "fancied delicacy."[23] Since the oysters are shipped from Italy, they trigger references to the country. To travel there, however, is only possible for wealthy aristocrats, such as Beethoven's private pupil. If oysters are seen as indicative of a luxurious lifestyle, it is only because financial worries and considerations are often a topic of great concern. How can one secure a living and profitably invest one's money? "If you get bank shares again, you must spend all of the money that you've gotten. / Everything else is uncertain; don't get taken in by any speculation. Your money is earning you at least 8%, you cannot hope for. Leave the buying and selling to the Jews. We will not have luck at it; that is my advice."[24]

In short, we learn much about the fundamentals of daily life in Vienna from the notebooks: the living conditions of a bourgeois group of men, eating and sleeping habits, personal and public health, social and religious hierarchies, racial and gender differences, and information about the incipient financial market. In addition, we also learn about nascent modern recording techniques: Jotting down quotidian notes seems so erratic that it resembles a modernist-styled stream of consciousness, resulting in the quest for order, which before long was fulfilled through a more or less definitive written biography.

These highly detailed conversational notes create their own density, especially if one reads the complete record along with the endnotes.[25] (The endnotes reflect the stupendous and collaborative work of a small network of scholars across the Cold War divide between East Berlin and Vienna, and make for an interesting sidenote.) Yet despite this compact and complex range of information, the notes fail to amount to what Gilbert Ryles terms "thick description," a methodological

---

21. Beethoven, BKh, vol.1, p.154 and 355.
22. Beethoven, BKh, vol.1, p.373.
23. Beethoven, BKh, vol.1, p.124 / Beethoven, BCB, vol.1, p.113.
24. Beethoven, BKh, vol.1, p.239 / Beethoven, BCB, vol.1 p.239.
25. The English edition of the notebooks thankfully places the footnotes on the same page of the text passages to which they refer.

approach that—thanks to Clifford Geertz—has achieved recognition beyond anthropology.[26] Geertz defines its foundation as follows:

> The concept of culture I espouse [...] is essentially a semiotic one. Believing, with Max Weber, that man is an animal suspended in webs of significance he himself has spun, I take culture to be those webs, and the analysis of it to be therefore not an experimental science in search of law but an interpretive one in search of meaning.[27]

If we understand culture as social interaction that constantly produces and negotiates meaning, those social interactions demand an interpretive description. Geertz uses his theoretical framework of "thick description" to fend off reductionist behavioral structures or generalizations when observing different or foreign cultures. He instead aims at understanding subjects according to their own premises, including their misunderstandings, writing that "[t]he whole point of a semiotic approach to culture is [...] to aid us in gaining access to the conceptual world in which our subjects live so that we can, in some extended sense of the term, converse with them."[28]

Geertz's plea for a cultural hermeneutic, which gained wide coinage through Stephen Greenblatt's cultural poetics in the early 1990s, translates, in our specific context, to the question: How can an accumulated recording of daily fragments of one-on-one conversations provide us with an understanding of a city or culture at a given historical moment? To answer this question, I turn, for heuristic reasons alone, to Walter Benjamin's *Das Passagen-Werk* (*Arcades project*).[29] Benjamin viewed Paris as "The metropolis of the nineteenth century" (a title he gave to his project in an outline from 1935),[30] thereby turning it into an object of a study of modernity fueled by capitalism, which, in his view, reveals itself as a phantasmagoria,[31] thus disrupting the

---

26. Geertz, "Thick description," p.6.
27. Geertz, "Thick description," p.5.
28. Geertz, "Thick description," p.24.
29. Walter Benjamin, *Das Passagen-Werk*, in *Gesammelte Schriften*, ed. Rolf Tiedemann, vol.5 (Frankfurt am Main, 1982); Walter Benjamin, *The Arcades project*, translated by Howard Eiland and Kevin McLaughlin, prepared on the basis of the German volume edited by Rolf Tiedemann (Cambridge, MA, 1999).
30. Irving Wohlfarth, "Die Passagenarbeit," in *Benjamin Handbuch: Leben, Werk, Wirkung*, ed. Burkhard Lindner (Stuttgart, 2006), p.251–74 (257–58).
31. Timo Skrandies, "Unterwegs in den Passagen-Konvoluten," in *Benjamin Handbuch*, ed. B. Lindner, p.274–84 (279).

idea of history as the constant flow of bourgeois progress.[32] Instead, in the words of Susan Buck-Morss, Benjamin envisioned "a Marxian retelling of the story of Sleeping Beauty."[33] To this extent, Benjamin became an observer and flaneur of everyday life and a collector of massive "notes scattered through a series of files organized or 'convolutes' organized under diverse headings such as 'boredom, eternal return' or, more straight forward, 'the stock exchange,'" with the result of an unmanageable amount of notes on material culture.[34] Benjamin's aesthetic response in assembling these convolutes for such a philosophical retelling was to resort to the technique of montage, creating, in the words of Simon Gunn, "the assemblage of fragments of theory and concrete historical detail, quotation and interpretation, arranged on a principle of dis/association."[35] In short, Benjamin intentionally sought to disrupt a linear interpretation and opposed a unifying hermeneutic position à la Geertz.[36]

While Beethoven's conversation notebooks unintentionally provide us with a corpus of fragments that offer insights into early-nine-teenth-century daily life in a still aristocratic society, Benjamin's *Arcades project* intentionally presents fragments of daily life in Haussmann's redesigned Paris as the crystallization and phantas-magoria of capitalism. Divergent in their intentions, both text corpora share a lack of wider reception (though for very different reasons), not least due to the challenges of both reading the vast corpora and making meaning of them.

My reasons for invoking two collections of fragments of daily life through their text corpora is not so much that the status of a text as fragment can be very different—intentional versus unintentional, mediated versus authentic, artistic versus casual, philosophical versus pedestrian—but also because the goal of extracting the meaning of daily life through fragments is largely independent of the text's intentions and that of its authors. For these reasons, the two divergent

32. Simon Gunn, "The city of mirrors: the *Arcades project* and urban history," *Journal of Victorian culture* 7:2 (2002), p.263–75 (266).

33. Susan Buck-Morss, The Dialectics of seeing: Walter Benjamin and the Arcades project (Cambridge, MA, 1993), p.271.

34. Gunn, "The city of mirrors," p.265.

35. Gunn, "The city of mirrors," p.265.

36. While scholars recognized Benjamin's *Arcades project* after its first publication in 1982 as salient for grappling with alternative histories, according to Irving Wohlfarth, its scholarly reception to date has not realized its potential. Wohlfarth, "Die Passagenarbeit," p.269 and 271.

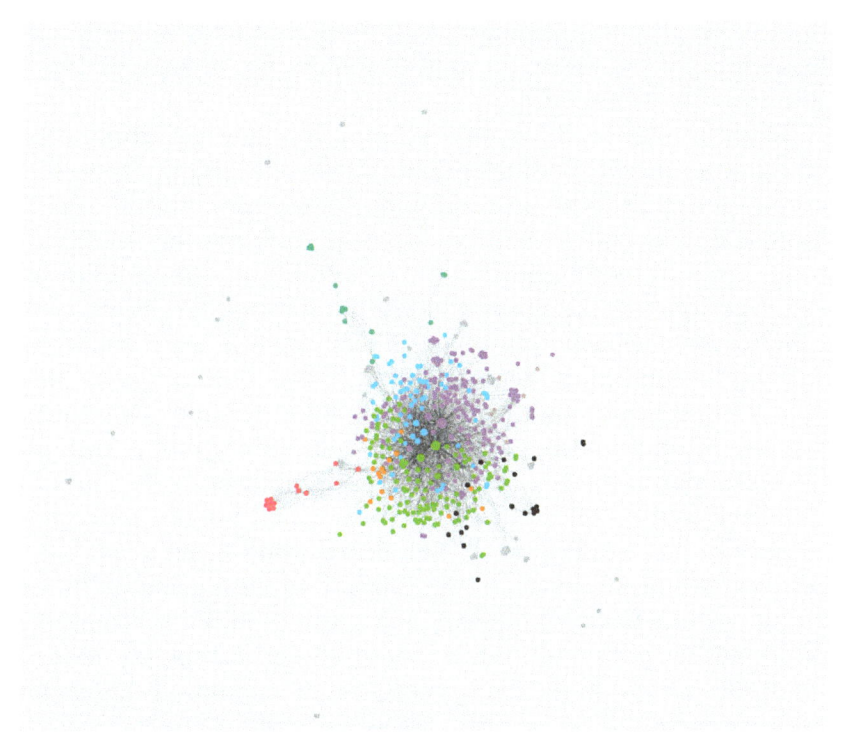

Figure 34: Network visualization of connections in volume 1 of
the critical edition of Beethoven's conversation notebooks. Nodes
represent individuals who are named or identified as scribes; edges
indicate that the two individuals appear on the same page of the
edited volume. Color indicates modularity (interconnectedness of
people). Size indicates degree (number of connections). Data from
Ludwig van Beethovens Konversationshefte, ed. Karl-Heinz Köhler *et
al.*, 11 vols. (Leipzig, 1972–2001), vol.1. An interactive version of this
network visualization and a high resolution of this figure can be
found online in the digital collaboration hub for this volume.
Visual created by Crystal Hall.

text corpora help to modify Geertz's hermeneutic desires by creating
webs of meaning. I argue that, rather than conversing in solitude with
past actors as strangers, creating a web of meaning out of fragments
can best be accomplished through a social web of scholars and
disparate yet complementary knowledge. In other words, I argue that
creating meaning out of the (limited) agents or small groups whose

fixed records of oral communication from the 1820s we serendipitously inherited represents a challenge too great to be addressed by a single scholar or discipline.

Restoring this social web requires more than the coexistence of text corpora whose similarity in difference suggests model-like capabilities. It is here that social network theory functions as a catalyst and method to map how to best proceed in comprehensively exploring the dispersed remarks that we find in the notebooks. Driven by the project itself (i.e., understanding the text corpus of Beethoven's conversation notebooks), one should gather a diverse network in terms of expertise, generation, gender, and professional status. I argue that such a montage at the social and scholarly level enables the creation of a meaningful understanding of the text corpus that is itself an (unintentional) montage. Using just the information in the index of volume 1 of the edited conversation notebooks, we can see such a network emerge (see Figure 34). This network documents a link (edge) between two people (nodes) if they appear on the same page in the edited volume. It is a preliminary attempt to capture the complexity of Beethoven's private life. While only a proof of concept, the network graph offers a way to test the hermeneutics, and ultimately argues for the development of a tool that reflects the original structure of the notebooks. In my analysis, I will refer to network graphs for volumes 1 and 11 of the notebooks.

A glimpse of a qualitative and quantitative analysis

An initial reading of the draft network, using the more conventional framework of social network theory, offers an important observation that vindicates the theory's usefulness as an analytical tool (see Figure 34). It also opens up more complex lines of inquiry that can be pursued through sophisticated tools of digital network analysis. Readers are invited to search for the individual names in the analysis in the online network representation.

When the conversation notebooks started, in February of 1818, not only was Beethoven a well-known person in Vienna but he was becoming increasingly recognized as a composer internationally. In December 1815, in the wake of the Vienna Congress, for which Beethoven premiered a number of new symphonies and other musical compositions,[37] he was granted honorary Viennese

---

37. Solomon, *Beethoven*, p.286–87.

citizenship. His popularity within the city had grown so much that, to send Beethoven a letter, it was supposedly sufficient to simply write his address as: "Beethoven, Vienna," despite his numerous moves and address changes.[38] One such piece of mail, clearly a sign of Beethoven's international regard, reached him in 1816, when the "British publisher Birchall [...] requested variations of folk songs, and Thomson [a Scottish publisher who earlier commissioned from Beethoven arrangements of folk songs] subsequently commissioned variations on sixteen melodies."[39] One year later, in 1817, Beethoven was invited by the Philharmonic Society of London to compose two symphonies. Beethoven asked for more than the 300 Guinean francs offered, but ultimately declined the commission.[40] The same year, the leading music journal in German-speaking countries, the *Allgemeine musikalische Zeitung* (*General music magazine*) in Leipzig, published Beethoven's wishes for the tempi—initiated by the newly invented metronome—for his by then eight symphonies, and thereby presented the set of symphonies for the first time as a canonical unit, or *Gesamt-kunstwerk*. Last but not least, in early 1819, Anton Diabelli, a composer, music teacher, and music publisher, wrote a short waltz and solicited fifty Austrian composers to compose variations on it.[41] His plan was intended as a marketing coup for his and his friends' publishing house; they planned to issue all the variations for the patriotic purpose of raising money on behalf of the orphans and widows of the Napoleonic Wars. Supposedly, Beethoven was initially not amused at being thrown in with such a heterogeneous and relatively undistinguished group of composers and being asked to contribute a variation on a trivial composition.[42] As shown in Figure 34, based on the first volume of the notebooks, Diabelli remained peripheral to the core of routine

---

38. *Das Beethoven-Lexikon*, ed. Heinz von Loesch and Claus Raab (Laaber, 2008), p.851 and 853.
39. William Kinderman, *Beethoven*, 2nd ed. (Oxford, 2009), p.221–22.
40. Kinderman, *Beethoven*, p.221. See also *Beethovens Tagebuch*, ed. Maynard Solomon (Mainz, 1990), p.103 (entry no.119).
41. To place this number of composers in context, beginning in 1808, the archduke of Austria, a student of Beethoven's, cataloged his music library, including the number of composers and their works: "By 1818, it had reached 6,700 pieces and 1,075 composers." David Wyn Jones, *Music in Vienna 1700, 1800, 1900* (Woodbridge, 2016), p.78.
42. Instead of contributing one variation as requested, Beethoven instead began a large-scale project and completed no fewer than twenty-three variations a few months later of what would in 1823 eventually become his last grand piano work, the so-called "Diabelli variations," op.120. Kinderman, *Beethoven*, p.233.

visitors, appearing with other individuals who have very few identified conversations in the notebooks. Yet another look at volume 11 of the notebooks (see Figure 35) reveals that Diabelli appears in the network representation on pages with family members, friends, assistants, and doctors, documenting the mundane context in which the Italian composer's grand plan was received.

Despite indices of an increase in fame and international recognition, the notebooks show that, in relative terms, Beethoven remained isolated—not least because of his disability. After all, one notices only a small number of friends and acquaintances who communicated with the deaf artist by writing notes. If going by the quantitative analysis of the names index of the first volume, these individuals are: his nephew Karl, as well as his (male) friends Carl Bernard, Joseph Czerny, Franz Janschikh or Janitschek, Franz Oliva, Karl Peters, and Heinrich Seelig.[43] (Beethoven's mother disrupts this order; she is the fifth most popular person named in the notebooks or featured as a scribe.) None of these friends were relevant to Beethoven as a composer, and, with the exception of Carl (Joseph) Bernard, editor of the state-sanctioned *Wiener Zeitung*, none of these individuals could claim social or cultural capital placing them in the leading networks chronicled in Vienna's— or, for that matter, Beethoven's—cultural legacy.

This disconnect—intensifying international recognition versus the private life of a relatively isolated social network of close friends—hints nevertheless at a larger issue: While Beethoven's artistic recognition was independent of his immediate social network, it thrived due to a relatively small network of musicians and their link to institutions—for example, Ferdinand Ries (1784–1838), a locally and internationally well-connected musician. Like Beethoven, Ferdinand Ries was born in Bonn and his father Franz Anton, like Beethoven, was a member of the Bonn Hofkapelle. In fact, Franz Anton taught the young Beethoven violin. When his son Ferdinand eventually made it to Vienna in 1803, he became Beethoven's piano student while also studying composition with Johann Georg Albrechtsberger (whom Beethoven had also contracted as his teacher when he arrived in Vienna about a decade earlier). However, Ferdinand Ries not only became Beethoven's student—he temporarily also functioned as his secretarial assistant (in 1804–1805 and again in 1808–1809). Ries's wandering lifestyle as a composer and pianist eventually took him to London, where he made friends with another friend of his father, Johann Peter Salomon, who was also a member of

43. Beethoven, BKh, vol.1, p.515–29.

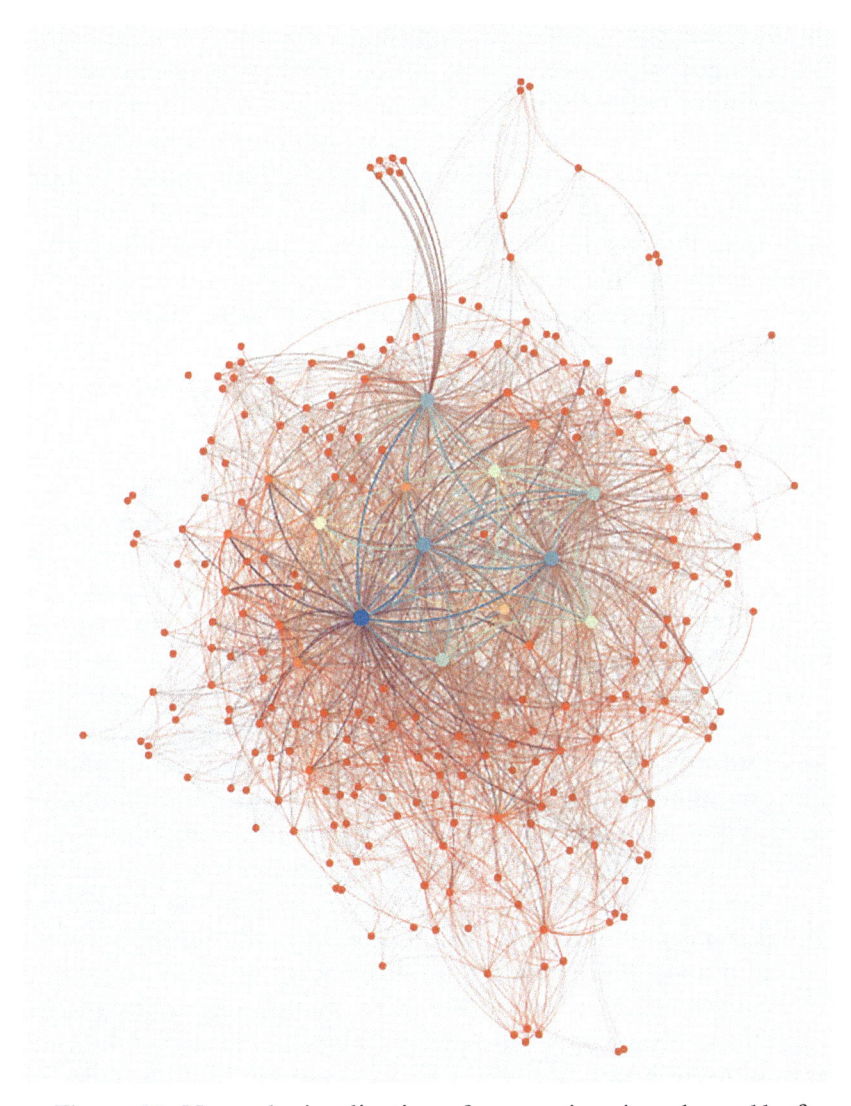

Figure 35: Network visualization of connections in volume 11 of the critical edition of Beethoven's conversation notebooks. Nodes represent individuals who are named or identified as scribes; edges indicate that the two individuals appear on the same page of the edited volume. Data from Köhler *et al.*, *Ludwig van Beethovens Konversationshefte*, vol.11. See the interactive visualization for volume 11 in the digital collaboration hub for this volume. Visual created by Peter Höyng and Emory Center for Digital Scholarship.

the aforementioned orchestra in Bonn and a violin teacher of his father. Salomon not only helped to invite Joseph Haydn to London twice but also became a member of the London Philharmonic Society, which Ries joined in 1815, eventually becoming one of its directors. It was in this capacity that Ries invited Beethoven to visit London and compose symphonies for them in 1817.[44] Notably, Ries occupies a different space from Diabelli in the notebooks' network; he bridges the public–private divide in Beethoven's life and his connections, and his mere presence in two networks supports Beethoven's growing reputation despite greater social confinement (see Figure 34).

How does this change the interpretation of the relationship among these professional connections through personal associations and the use of networks such as Beethoven's various music publishers (mainly accessed through letter writing) versus the small circle of friends that we encounter in the notebooks? For starters, the various networks— whose different affiliations and identities are illustrated in the graph's different colors—appear somewhat unstable in Beethoven's notes.

Beethoven's initial reliance on aristocratic patrons, especially in his first fifteen years in Vienna, was increasingly replaced by a bourgeois music market. As Tia DeNora states regarding Beethoven's first decade in Vienna: "At a time when aristocratic connections were still crucial to a musician's economic survival, Beethoven was exceptionally well placed."[45] In the spring of 1809, Beethoven secured the assurance of aristocratic support one last time when three young members of the high nobility promised a large annuity after Beethoven threatened to leave Vienna for a position with King Jérôme Bonaparte in Kassel, Westphalia. In return for the generous annual income, Beethoven had to pledge to remain in Vienna or in Hapsburg lands.[46] The devaluation of the annuity due to the inflation that followed Napoleon's occupation of Vienna in the fall of the same year was one reason why Beethoven successively began looking for ways to secure greater economic self-reliance—he sought to increase his entrepreneurial ventures while maintaining his artistic ethos and

44. See https://de.wikipedia.org/wiki/Ferdinand_Ries (last accessed June 30, 2023).
45. DeNora, *Beethoven*, p.61. A page earlier, DeNora also remarks on the close-knit network of the higher aristocracy when she writes: "Austro-Hungarian aristocrats were interrelated through numerous family links which transcended geography and which overlapped with the diplomatic and administrative positions in which family members served." DeNora, *Beethoven*, p.60.
46. Solomon, *Beethoven*, p.193–94.

artistic independence. Although the Vienna Congress coincided with the peak of Beethoven's economic success and popularity, it is often also seen as his artistic low point, best symbolized by the "Battle symphony," *Wellingtons Sieg, oder die Schlacht bei Vittoria (Wellington's victory, or the Battle of Vittoria)*, which he composed in 1813 after Mälzel commissioned it with an eye toward popular (i.e., commercial) success. It received an enthusiastic reception before and as part of the musical festivities of the Vienna Congress.[47]

The extent to which this gradual shift from patronage to self-entrepreneurial existence occupied Beethoven's mind becomes obvious, for example, in the recurring conversations with his close friends about investing in stocks. Indeed, the notebooks provide a great deal of insight regarding Beethoven's concerns about financially maintaining and managing his lifestyle. Figures like Mälzel fade into the background—he does not even appear in volume 11 of the notebooks. Questions and discussions about food habits, travel, moving, and buying books and (music) paper (both were relatively expensive), and many other concerns related to daily life, provide ample clues about the social status of an independent composer who was concerned about securing his income and wanted his artistic status to be mirrored in success and financial security.

In short, whereas Beethoven relied on his limited but effective network of professional musicians, friends, associates, and publishers to enumerate the income for his compositions as best he could, his conversation notebooks reveal a vulnerability regarding his status as a largely independent artist who simultaneously wished to secure his social status through economic means.

Collaborative opportunities

As promising as these first steps toward an index-based qualitative analysis are, they are, at best, just that: promising (i.e., providing an initial and partial glimpse of the opportunities that lie ahead in the interpretation of a full-text corpus). The first step is making the eleven volumes available in a fully searchable, digitized version, as has been done, for example, with the works of Heinrich Heine and Friedrich Nietzsche. Their digitized texts are accessible online, based on editorial works meticulously prepared and published as *historisch-kritische Gesamtausgaben* (critical editions of collected works); in

47. Solomon, *Beethoven*, p.285–87.

that way, they are comparable to the eleven volumes of Beethoven's conversation notebooks.

As discussed above, we currently have eleven critically edited volumes of the original 137 notebooks; the first is about 400 pages long and has no fewer than 932 well-researched footnotes, adding another 100 pages to its length. Unsurprisingly, the eleven volumes have several indexes that enable checking cross-references of both individual persons and terms, which we used to begin a preliminary data-driven analysis simply by visualizing Beethoven's network. To call cross-checking cumbersome is nothing less than an understatement. Even Theodore Albrecht, translator and editor of the English edition, seems to surrender when stating that "a cumulative index for the entire set of *Conversation Books* is almost unthinkable."[48] These volumes simply prevent scholars from probing the text corpus further in ways that allow for the quantification of qualitative analysis. And, while this edition resembled the state of the art until the late 1980s, forty years later—and twenty years into the digital age—it has fallen behind in terms of what digital humanities can offer.

The eleven volumes included in the Hathi Trust digital archive can only be searched in a limited way: One can enter terms or names, and the search results indicate only the page(s) of a given volume without providing any further statistical data for a given number of questions.[49] Copyright restrictions fully apply.[50] As a result, one can, for example, look up the term "Aktien" (stocks) for each of the eleven volumes, but one cannot even pursue a Boolean search such as "Aktien" AND the person attached to that conversation. Likewise, one can look up Beethoven's dubious secretary and associate "Schindler" or Beethoven's nephew "Karl," but not search for where "Schindler AND Karl" show up together, and so on. In other words, it is not possible to fully search the network of friends and their ties to other individuals or their ties to each other.

For example, we can peruse what scholars have done with the presentation of texts of the leading Western author—to whom Beethoven

48. Beethoven, BCB, vol.1, p.xxxv.
49. See https://catalog.hathitrust.org/Record/000011973 (last accessed June 30, 2023).
50. As of spring 2018, I had not received any response from the Breitkopf & Härtel publishing house when I inquired about the status of the copyrights. They now hold the copyrights to what was previously published by VEB Deutscher Verlag für Musik, Leipzig, during the German Democratic Republic (vol.1–9), subsequently the Deutscher Verlag für Musik Leipzig (vol.10 and 11).

as the iconic Western composer has at times been compared—namely, William Shakespeare.[51] Shakespeare's works are presented not only in a digitized format (like those of the aforementioned German authors) but as part of a larger understanding of the digital humanities and its opportunities. As Holly Gilbert explains regarding the Shakespeare edition as part of the Folger Shakespeare Library: "Folger Digital Texts is a project undertaking a very traditional humanities aim—preserving, organizing, and making available Shakespeare's collection of works—but breaks newer ground with digital tools and a great contribution to the collaborative, open source nature of digital humanities initiatives."[52]

One key element in presenting Beethoven's conversation notebooks in a similar manner—and the prime catalyst enabling more sophisticated research of their text corpus—will ultimately be preparing the corpus as a digital edition using the schema of the Text Encoding Initiative (TEI).[53] A search of "Projects using the TEI" quickly shows both how active this area of digital humanities has become and how many voids still exist.[54] Preparing such a TEI corpus amounts to providing significant resources in personnel, knowledge, and technology, which thus explains why so few are available to date. Making the conversation notebooks fully available as a digital text would allow scholars to more readily explore sets of correlations and

51. See Peter Höyng, "'Shakespeare's Bruder': Beethovens Shakespeare-Rezeption und ihre unerhörten Folgen," in *Shakespeare im 18. Jahrundert*, ed. Roger Paulin (Göttingen, 2007), p.119–39.
52. Holly Gilbert, "Folger Digital Texts," *Digital humanities at Geneseo* (2017), http://dh.sunygeneseoenglish.org/2017/09/20/folger-digital-texts/ (last accessed June 30, 2023). This introduction to the technological aspects of Folger Digital Texts is highly recommended for novices like myself since it strikes a balance between general goals and greater technical details that require computer literacy. The result of this concerted effort can be seen as part of the Folger Shakespeare Library: www.folger.edu/shakespeare (last accessed June 30, 2023). Likewise, the Emily Dickinson Archive (http://www.edickinson.org, last accessed June 30, 2023) also presents a state-of-the-art example of modern digital humanities.
53. "Die Vorzüge elektronischer Editionen als Hilfsmittel für Literaturwissenschaftler sind evident: die schnelle Suche von Zeichenketten über große Textkorpora und die Visualisierung komplexer Textbeziehungen z.B. in historisch-kritischen Ausgaben sowie die Möglichkeit einer weiteren Optimierung der Edition ohne Neusatz des Textes." Fotis Jannidis, "TEI in der Praxis," *Jahrbuch für Computerphilologie*, http://computerphilologie.digital-humanities.de/praxis/teiprax.html (last accessed June 30, 2023).
54. <Text Encoding Initiative>, "Projects using the TEI," https://tei-c.org/Activities/Projects/ (last accessed June 30, 2023).

would enable data analysis that could begin to make meaning out of this unique resource—including network analysis that would capture more than networks that are based on the traditional edition-based index. The network diagrams presented in the digital collaboration hub materials for this essay (see Figure 35) represent only a portion of the rich data contained on the pages of the notebooks, and do not yet capture the metadata about the individuals and their relationships to Beethoven.

In conclusion, I return one more time to the idea of a social network as a mode of collaboration—not just among Beethoven's contemporaries but also among scholars today. If such a network can be defined as a set of interactions among groups or people, and their relationships to one another,[55] then, in line with social network theory, a network of scholars should be created that avoids homophily and propinquity (i.e., it should be diverse in terms of geography, nationality, and expertise, for example).[56] Instead of a scholarly network guided mainly by mutuality and reciprocity, such a network should be complex and diverse in terms of how the scholars know each other and should create various professional constellations. This scholarly network would ideally consist of linguists; historians with knowledge of musical, social, political, and legal history; scholars of disability studies, book markets, and media studies; and, last but certainly not least, digital scholars. The point of departure for Beethoven's group would be the notebooks (after they have been fully digitized, as outlined at the end of this essay), which would thus (at least initially) make Beethoven their center of inquiry by heuristic default. Where the notebooks capture Beethoven's networks during his lifetime, an interdisciplinary network of scholars could work toward reexamining Beethoven's legacy and revising existing disciplinary accounts, which often privilege linear stories and histories.

This suggestion insinuates nothing less than a paradigm shift from the often incited and requested interdisciplinary work within the humanities. The latter model implies that a specific discipline acts as a supreme authority, not only seemingly devoid of agents but also making them subjects to succumb to the given rules and borders that have evolved over time within the given discipline. After all, there is a reason why a field of inquiry is called a discipline: it indeed can restrain its actors if one does not adhere to the standards

55. Kadushin, *Understanding social networks*, p.14 and 26.
56. Kadushin, *Understanding social networks*, p.18–21.

of that field. Each discipline carefully supervises who is included and who is excluded, independent of how porous these borders might become over time. Each discipline governs how each individual scholar can or should mediate disciplines. More often than not, new fields emerge precisely because a certain discipline begins, through growing narrowness or specialization, to enforce its mechanism of exclusion. Hence, one can historically observe how disciplines have not only unfolded but multiplied and morphed into an ever-increasing multitude of specialized fields, each establishing its own professional networks. This development calls for a reversal that is similar to a quasi-natural law: The more the fields of specialization increase, the greater the call for interdisciplinary work—often without having networks to support such claims. Interdisciplinary work seems to be the remedy for fragmentation, and bringing at least two (or presumably more) disciplines together assumes that the combined strengths of the disciplines involved will be more adequate for a given topic.

Instead, I argue, drawing on social network theory allows for a small but significant shift in this dilemma of an ever-growing fragmentation of knowledge and its inadequate repair by alleged interdisciplinary work. After all, network theory—without reflecting on itself or commenting on its own networks and interdisciplinary history—can shift its focus not onto a given institution or discipline but rather onto the actors that actually create the institution or discipline by conceptualizing how they relate to one another. I furthermore maintain that utilizing a network as a shell or method can help to replace an authoritative approach in which the discipline acts as the mastermind, thereby creating a more diverse mindset in which agency is given to the scholars and specialists working on a given project.

For Beethoven's conversation notebooks, scholars, data, and technologies might be best unified under the sponsorship of an institution such as the Beethoven-Haus in Bonn and carried forward in a truly collaborative manner. Beethoven's conversation notebooks certainly deserve to be shepherded into the age of digital humanities, since they present a text corpus that can only be explored as a network and through a network.

IV

Expansive networks

Social and conceptual networks in eighteenth-century German periodical literature

MATT ERLIN

Washington University in St. Louis

MELANIE WALSH

University of Washington in Seattle

We tend to think of the late eighteenth century as a highly connected age. With regard to the networks of the German Enlightenment and German Romanticism more specifically, scholars have often focused on the categories of societalization (*Vergesellschaftung*) or sociability (*Geselligkeit*), pointing to the emergence of new arenas of social interaction, from secret societies to literary salons to spa tourism, and showing how they fostered unprecedented levels of contact between genders and among different status groups.[1] Another line of inquiry has sought to uncover contemporaneous *discourses* of connectivity, that is to say, the emergence, in the eighteenth century itself, of the idea of the network as a conceptual category for understanding the structure and function of the modern world.[2]

As fruitful as previous discussions of the topic have been, they have often remained at a general level, emphasizing the sheer fact of connectivity or its overall intensity rather than addressing precisely

1. As the editors of a recent essay collection put it: "Während des 18. Jahrhunderts führt ein rasanter Diversifizierungsprozess zu immer neuen Formen des geselligen Miteinanders." Günter Oesterle and Thomas Falk, "Einleitung," in *Riskante Geselligkeit: Spielarten des Sozialen um 1800*, ed. Günter Oesterle and Thorsten Valk (Würzburg, 2015), p.9–24 (9).
2. Jeanne Riou, Jürgen Barkhoff, and Hartmut Böhme, for example, have explained how "circulation" becomes a leading metaphor in the period in fields ranging from biology to economics to literature and anthropology. See Jeanne Riou, Hartmut Böhme, and Jürgen Barkhoff, "Vorwort," in *Netzwerke: eine Kulturtechnik der Moderne*, ed. Jürgen Barkhoff, Hartmut Böhme, and Jeanne Riou (Cologne, 2004), p.7–16.

how the elements in a particular network are connected. For the past two years, we have been engaged in a project that employs the tools of network science in order to enhance our understanding of this area. Networks, after all, come in a multiplicity of forms. Techniques and vocabularies have been developed in sociology and mathematics for analyzing and talking about these forms and their properties, and literary and cultural studies scholars are beginning to make use of these techniques and vocabularies in order to extend the valuable insights that they have already generated into issues of connectivity and relationality in cultural history.[3]

While some of this work has focused on patterns of character interaction in literary texts, other cultural historians, taking their cue from existing sociological studies on scientific and scholarly networks, have turned their attention to periodicals and especially the topic of citation or co-publication networks.[4] These latter studies captured our interest as a result of the prominent role of periodical literature in the German-speaking world around 1800. This role has been well documented, not least with regard to the central debate in the *Berlinische Monatsschrift* (*Berlin monthly*) about the meaning of the term "Enlightenment." But the medium has a significance that goes far beyond this specific and localized interrogation of the concept. An explosion of new publications meant that journals served as a key channel for the reception, evaluation, and dissemination of new knowledge, as well as the establishment and consolidation of intellectual cohorts.[5]

3. For an overview and application from the German-speaking world, see Peer Trilcke, "Social network analysis (SNA) als Methode einer textempirischen Literaturwissenschaft," in *Empirie in der Literaturwissenschaft*, ed. Philip Ajouri, Katja Mellmann, and Christoph Rauen (Münster, 2013), p.201–47. See also the introduction to the present volume.

4. Especially significant for our project has been the work of Hoyt Long, e.g., "Fog and steel: mapping communities of literary translation in an information age," *The Journal of Japanese studies* 41:2 (2015), p.281–316, as well as that of Kurt Beals, e.g., "Redefining Dada: the avant-garde as network," talk delivered at the annual conference of the German Studies Association, San Diego, CA, September 2016.

5. According to Helga Brandes, more than 7000 unique German-language titles were in circulation in 1830. Helga Brandes, "The literary marketplace and the journal, medium of the Enlightenment," in *German literature of the eighteenth century: the Enlightenment and sensibility*, ed. Barbara Becker-Cantarino (Rochester, NY, 2005), p.79–102 (81). See also Gustav Frank, Madleen Podewski, and Stefan Scherer, "Kultur—Zeit—Schrift: Literatur- und Kulturzeitschriften

The study of eighteenth-century periodical literature, moreover, has been greatly facilitated by the creation of the Zeitschriften der Aufklärung (Journals of the German Enlightenment) collection, a full-text electronic database of articles from—at the time we began our work—161 eighteenth-century journals.[6] The articles themselves, which are available as individual page scans, constitute a one-of-a-kind resource for scholars of the period. But, with regard to quantitative analysis, the bibliographic information, or metadata, proves equally valuable. It provides an unparalleled, if far from complete, documentation of Germany's journal publication network between 1750 and 1815. After extracting this metadata and compiling it in tabular form, we have pursued two distinct but related avenues of inquiry. The first is an investigation of authorial co-publication networks, undertaken with the aim of better understanding the collaborative and collective practices that shaped intellectual life in this period. Our starting assumption was that co-publication in periodicals can serve as a proxy for certain types of loose affiliation (whether actual personal relationships, aesthetic or ideological commonalities, or geographical proximity), and that such affiliations can, in the aggregate, be understood to represent informal "cohorts" that occupy particular positions in the intellectual field, if only temporarily.[7] Our initial question was a fairly simple one. We wanted to know how much cross-publication existed across journals and disciplines and which authors were key players in such cross-publication.

Our second set of analyses entailed a shift from social to semantic networks—that is, networks in which the nodes are words or concepts, rather than individuals or institutions, and the edges between them represent some kind of linguistic or logical connection.[8] Since we

---

als 'kleine Archive,'" *Internationales Archiv für Sozialgeschichte der deutschen Literatur* 34:2 (2009), p.1–45 (5–6).

6. The Zeitschriften der Aufklärung database is hosted by the University of Bielefeld and has since been expanded to include 189 journals; see http://ds.ub. uni-bielefeld.de/viewer/collections/zeitschriftenderaufklaerung/ (last accessed July 3, 2023).

7. Hoyt Long, "Toward a sociology of modernism: network analysis and avant-garde poetry in Japan," talk delivered at the annual conference of the American Association for Asian Studies, San Diego, March 1, 2013; Katherine Giuffre, "Mental maps: social networks and the language of critical reviews," *Sociological inquiry* 71:3 (2001), p.381–93.

8. See John Sowa, "Semantic networks," http://www.jfsowa.com/pubs/semnet.htm (last accessed July 3, 2023).

focused on the bibliographic information, or metadata, from these journals—and not the full text of articles—we used article *titles* to create semantic networks in which two words appear as linked if they co-occurred in a single title, such that each article title generates what is known in network theory as a "clique."[9] We felt that article titles were particularly well suited to serve as the building blocks for a cognitive map, inasmuch as the inclusion of a word in an article title suggests a higher degree of intentionality and self-awareness about an object of inquiry than does its mere appearance in the body of an essay. Words that appear in multiple titles serve as points of contact between the cliques, and those words that connect the highest number of these cliques can be seen as conceptual anchors, at least with regard to the periodical literature of the period. One of the foundational insights of network analysis is that "meaning emerges from relations among cultural elements rather than inhering in the elements themselves."[10] When constructed on the basis of a large number of source texts, semantic networks can foreground this relational meaning, shedding valuable light on the conceptual topography of a particular individual thinker or, in our case, a particular historical moment.

In this set of analyses, our specific interest has been in the evolving relationship between science and literature, and between scientific and literary discourse more specifically, as it takes shape in the periodical literature included in our dataset. This relationship has been at the center of a number of important recent studies of the period. Such scholars as Joseph Vogl and Nicolas Pethes have argued that both science and literature around 1800 must be viewed in the context of a broader epistemological framework or discursive order.[11] With regard to periodical literature in particular, contributors to the volume *Naturkunde im Wochentakt* (*Science in weekly installments*) have addressed the popularization and dissemination of scientific knowledge in and

9. A clique is defined as a graph (or part of a network) in which all of the nodes are connected to all of the other nodes.
10. Paul DiMaggio, "Cultural networks," in *The Sage handbook of social network analysis*, ed. John Scott and Peter J. Carrington (Los Angeles, CA, 2011), p.286–301 (294).
11. Nicolas Pethes, "Serial individuality: eighteenth-century case study collections and nineteenth-century archival fiction," in *Distant readings: topologies of German culture in the long nineteenth century*, ed. Matt Erlin and Lynne Tatlock (New York, 2014), p.115–32; Joseph Vogl, *Kalkül und Leidenschaft: Poetik des ökonomischen Menschen* (Zürich, 2002).

through eighteenth-century journals.[12] These and other studies have enriched our understanding of the knowledge ecology of the period, and they also raise the question of whether this understanding might be further enhanced by a shift in scale. With this question in mind, we constructed a subset of the journal titles that appeared in either literary or scientific journals.[13] The resulting table of 19,794 titles from the two categories served as the foundation for the creation of our semantic network.

Our project is ongoing, but preliminary results have already opened up new research perspectives. In the case of co-publication networks, for example, we have begun to identify structurally analogous positions occupied by different actors within the network, such as a subset of what might be termed Enlightenment "grinders" (J. H. Campe and D. H. Hegewisch are two examples), whose high connectivity results from dispersed publication in multiple journals rather than affiliation with a particular journal (as with J. G. Herder). With regard to our semantic networks, we have been able to establish which operations and modes of knowing are more likely to be associated with either literary or scientific objects, and which should be understood as "concepts that transcend one particular discourse and whose definition cannot be limited to one 'culture' or the other; they do not fit neatly with either literature or science."[14] Even in the case of operations that seem to fall squarely into one arena or the other, moreover, the network-based approach reveals the rare instances of cross-pollination.

The interview that follows emerged out of the discussion inspired by our presentation of some of these results.

1. Crystal Hall and Birgit Tautz: Do you feel that your work represents digital humanities research as process-driven rather than results-oriented? That is, what new understandings of the

---

12. *Naturkunde in Wochentakt: Zeitschriftenwissen der Aufklärung*, ed. Tanja van Hoorn and Alexander Košenina (Bern, 2014).
13. Our categorization was based on Joachim Kirchner, *Die Zeitschriften des deutschen Sprachgebiets von den Anfängen bis 1830* (Stuttgart,1969), which classifies over 6600 journals into twenty-three different thematic groups.
14. "diskursübergreifende Konzepte, deren Definition nicht auf eine der beiden 'Kulturen' Literatur oder Wissenschaft beschränkt werden kann." Nicolas Pethes, "Verfahren und Formen," in *Literatur und Wissen: ein interdisziplinäres Handbuch*, ed. Roland Borgards *et al.* (Stuttgart, 2013), p.229–98 (229). Translation by Birgit Tautz.

materials have arisen from creating a network model of their connections?

Matt Erlin:

The question of what counts as "results" in computational work in the humanities is a big one, and has been around since digital humanities first captured the attention of the scholarly public. Tom Scheinfeldt, in his contribution to the 2010 edition of *Debates in the digital humanities*, referred to it as the "where's the beef" question: "What questions does digital humanities answer that can't be answered without it?"[15] More common is the reference to the "so what" question, conceived as a kind of litmus test that will establish whether the insights generated by a particular analysis are trivial or simply reiterate (or, at best, empirically validate) things we already know about literary and cultural history.

Personally, I am a strong believer in results-oriented, argument-driven scholarship that participates in ongoing debates in one's field. That said, I can think of at least a couple of ways in which our research into Enlightenment publication networks has been more process-driven than is the case in traditional literary and cultural studies work. One is that our starting point was a corpus (the Journals of the German Enlightenment database) that had never been scrutinized in its entirety and a method (network analysis) that has only recently begun to feature in humanities research. For better or worse, we did not begin the project with a particular hypothesis in mind. Instead, we set out with a basic idea of how network analysis had been used in other contexts, especially in studies of citation networks, and with a general sense of the arguments that have been made about the print culture of the German and European Enlightenment.

Initially, we were very focused on author networks and what they might tell us about structural roles in the journal network—that is to say, we were interested in whether we could identify a subset of authors who, for example, helped bridge other, more close-knit communities that were overwhelmingly associated with a specific journal. Could we characterize a particular type of Enlightenment intellectual based on publication practices? This question remains to be answered fully, but we have already generated some promising preliminary results.

15. Tom Scheinfeldt, "Where's the beef? Does digital humanities have to answer questions?," in *Debates in the digital humanities*, ed. Matthew K. Gold (Minneapolis, MN, 2010), p.56–58.

Only as we began to create the network visualizations did we become aware of other intriguing features of the data, such as the relative percentages of anonymously published articles in different journals, or the relative frequency with which foreign versus German authors appeared in article titles. And it was only on the basis of this iterative process that we came up with the idea—borrowed from work done in the natural sciences—of looking at semantic networks of words from article titles rather than limiting ourselves to networks of journal authors.

Melanie Walsh:
Yes, our project has been very process-oriented, and even exploratory, in that way. But ultimately, even if and when you begin with a firm hypothesis, I don't think you can have honest, interesting results without an open, recursive reflection about methods. I also think our project has been process-oriented in a different way, which stems from the nature of our collaboration. Since my primary contribution to the research is network analysis and visualization (though I'm a literary scholar, my subfield is postwar American fiction), my first investment has usually been in the process: How can we computationally identify semantic connections between journal articles? How can we incorporate and visualize the discipline of each journal? How does network analysis compare to other possible computational approaches, such as mapping word embeddings with Word2vec?[16] Then, collaboratively, we think through the resulting networks together. How do these networks corroborate, challenge, or provide new insights into previous scholarship written about the Enlightenment? These discussions send us back to tweak our process once more.

2. Crystal Hall and Birgit Tautz: The humanities thrive on the inclusion of multiple perspectives, both of the actors and producers of the objects that we study and of scholarly approaches. Can you speak to how (or if) the process of creating or exploring the layers of a network model augments our capacity to embrace these multiple points of view?

---

16. Developed by Tomas Mikolov at Google, Word2vec is a popularly used algorithm that places words from a corpus in a vector space, such that related words should be situated closely together in that space.

Matt Erlin:

When modern network analysis first came to prominence in sociology in the 1980s, it was greeted by some as a welcome corrective to attempts to explain human behavior exclusively in terms of individual or collective attributes and norms, from class membership or party affiliation to age and gender.[17] In contrast to approaches that stress such attributes, as well as to the individualism of rational choice theory, network analysis shifts focus to the structured relations among actors or "nodes," and insists that these relations, and the shape of the network as a whole, are the key to understanding the behavior of the nodes. In the case of works of art, for example, research on cultural networks has argued that collaborative networks or "artworlds" are what produce both art and the meaning of art, and that these artworlds, rather than the works themselves, are the proper objects of analysis.[18]

With regard to our general interest in the Enlightenment, this has meant a shift from ideas contained in central texts (Kant's famous essay, for example) to a focus on interpersonal and interinstitutional relationships on a more macro scale.[19] With regard to our specific investigation of the relationship between literary and scientific discourse, in my mind, the most striking example of multiple perspectives pertains to the very basic question of how we frame this relationship. Much of the previous work on the topic takes a discourse-analytical approach, looking at literary and philosophical works and identifying shared conceptual structures or epistemological presuppositions. As soon as one starts thinking about nodes and edges in the context of periodical literature, however, new, more concrete perspectives on the links between science and literature open up.

Melanie Walsh:

As a concrete example of such links, scientific and literary journal articles were often connected by genre words such as "Nachricht(en)"

---

17. For an overview, see Mustafa Emirbayer and Jeff Goodwin, "Network analysis, culture, and the problem of agency," *The American journal of sociology* 99:6 (1994), p.1411–54.
18. Paul DiMaggio, "Cultural networks," p.286.
19. Our efforts can be understood as one variant of a more general trend in Enlightenment scholarship, as exemplified by the recent volume edited by Clifford Siskin and William Warner, *This is Enlightenment* (Chicago, IL, 2010). Also significant in this context is the work of Brad Pasanek and Chad Wellmon, e.g., "Enlightenment, some assembly required," in *The Eighteenth centuries*, ed. David Gies and Cynthia Wall (Charlottesville, VA, 2018), p.14–39.

and "Bemerk(ung)(en),"[20]—news and notes—seemingly mundane words that played surprisingly important structural roles in the network (we're going to address this issue more fully later, so I'll leave that as a teaser for now).

Another one of the things that makes network analysis so valuable, in my opinion, is that it allows us to see "brokers" within a network. Brokerage is a concept that has been theorized at length by sociologists like Ronald Stuart Burt, who have used it to describe the individuals in a social network who help bridge otherwise closed-off groups of people. Brokers are gatekeepers. The concept of brokerage can be quantified, in network science, by a metric called "betweenness centrality," which calculates the extent to which a given node falls on paths between other nodes.[21] Betweenness centrality reveals more than simply which nodes have the most number of outright connections (a metric called "degree centrality"), by indicating which nodes *connect* the most other nodes in the network. Often this metric will help reveal concepts (in the case of the semantic network) or people (in the case of the social network) who have been previously overlooked, such as noncanonical or marginal authors, whose work we can now see in a new light for its structural contribution to the Enlightenment network.

Finally, I don't feel like we can talk about new perspectives or points of view without also mentioning the scale of our project. We're working with thousands of Enlightenment authors, hundreds of journals, and tens of thousands of articles over a roughly sixty-five-year period. Computational methods and network analysis allow us to see patterns across this massive archive that would be difficult if not impossible to see with traditional humanistic research alone.

Matt Erlin:
Melanie's two specific examples point to a very fundamental way in which network analysis encourages multiple perspectives. It forces us to think explicitly about what we mean when we refer to shared "discursive frameworks" or a common "epistemological formation." Explaining how new theories of probability (Rüdiger Campe,

---

20. To consolidate our semantic network, we have reduced all title words to their stemmed forms, e.g., "Bemerkung" to "Bemerk." After the first mention of a word with its inflected forms included in parentheses, we subsequently refer to the word by its stemmed form.

21. For a more detailed definition, see M. E. J. Newman, *Networks: an introduction* (Oxford, 2010), p.185–93.

Joseph Vogl) or natural-scientific experimentation (John Bender) inform the eighteenth-century novel offers one perspective on this topic.[22] Identifying specific terms or concepts that co-occur in titles from both literary and scientific journals, or the frequency with which authors publish in both types of journals, addresses the topic from a different angle. Answers to questions about the interpenetration of literary and scientific discourse in the period depend largely on the perspective we adopt, or, to borrow a phrase from Fredric Jameson, on "focalizations on distinct levels of abstraction."[23] If traditional close reading reveals that Schnabel's *Insel Felsenburg* (*Rock castle island*, 1731) is deeply indebted to the diagrammatic imagination of Enlightenment science (Vogl), but network analysis shows that the number of authors who published across disciplines is vanishingly small, what are we to make of these two data points?[24] I think we have a richer and also a more complex picture of the relationship between literature and science than we would have with just one of these results. The next step would be to develop a conceptual model that makes sense of both levels.

3. Crystal Hall and Birgit Tautz: Literary and cultural scholars often problematize features of their materials as a way to better understand their relationships in different contexts. Where did your *Network@1800* visualizations immediately draw your attention? What features of the graph provoked further questions?

Melanie Walsh:
Although visualization is definitely one of the most intuitively appealing aspects of working with networks (the aesthetic spectacle first drew me to the field, for sure), network visualizations can often be tricky to produce in an effective, readable way, especially when they get to be of a certain size. For this reason, the first few visualizations that we produced weren't really drawing our attention anywhere at all. In fact, the early visualization stages pretty perfectly exemplify

---

22. Rüdiger Campe, *Spiel der Wahrscheinlichkeit: Literatur und Berechnung zwischen Pascal und Kleist* (Göttingen, 2002); Vogl, *Kalkül*; John Bender, "Novel knowledge: judgement, experience, experiment," in *This is Enlightenment*, ed. C. Siskin and W. Warner, p.284–300.

23. Fredric Jameson, "Marxism and postmodernism," *New Left review* 1:176 (1989), p.31–45 (41).

24. Vogl, *Kalkül*, p.192–94.

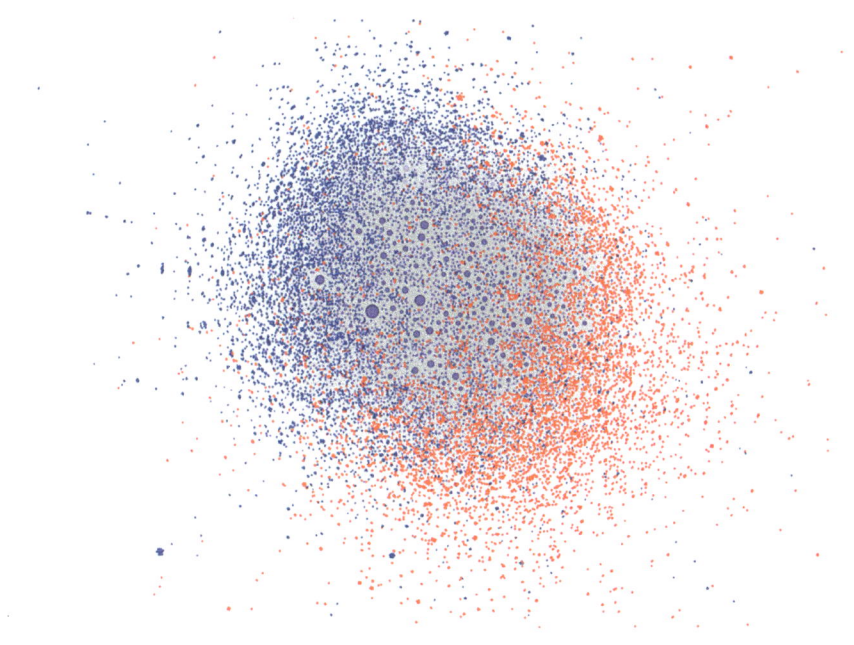

Figure 36: Network diagram of non-stop word terms used in article titles in the database Journals of the German Enlightenment, 1750–1815. Color coding indicates terms used only in literary journals (red) and only in scientific journals (blue). Size indicates degree (number of connections to other terms). Visual created by Matt Erlin and Melanie Walsh.

the process/results dialectic that we were talking about earlier. Take our 1750–1815 science–literature semantic network, for example, which consists of all non-stop words from journal article titles that were classified as either scientific or literary. This network contains tens of thousands of nodes (words) and tens of thousands of edges (connections between words that appeared in the same article title). When visualized with a basic force-atlas algorithm (a commonly used algorithm for drawing networks and the default in the Gephi software package) without modifying any other parameters, the resulting network looks like, as Matt and I have joked, a giant hairball. (The "giant hairball" is indeed a pervasive problem and thus a pervasive joke within the wider network visualization community.)

To produce a network visualization that actually offered insights into the scientific and literary discourses of the Enlightenment, we had to readjust our methodology to emphasize the things we ultimately wanted to explore, even if we didn't know exactly what those results would reveal. So we color-coded the nodes, making words that only appeared in scientific journal articles blue, words that only appeared in literary journal articles red, and words that appeared in both scientific and literary journal articles purple. We also sized the nodes by degree, making the nodes with the most connections in the network appear the largest.

These adjustments helped give us a series of baseline networks that were much more legible. In the now color-coded and size-adjusted network pictured in Figure 36, we can see that there are two distinct groups of scientific and literary concepts connected by a smaller group of bridge words and concepts. Those bridge concepts were definitely something that we wanted to explore further, especially because this macro view doesn't allow us to see the concepts or the concepts they help connect with any real granularity.

Matt Erlin:

One additional feature of the dataset quickly becomes apparent upon reviewing this visualization. Overall, we have more exclusively literary (red) than scientific (blue) terms, which reflects the skew in the number of literary titles as a proportion of the total number of titles. We have no reason to believe that this imbalance invalidates our claims, but we would like to create a more evenly distributed corpus for future analyses. Setting this point aside for the moment, as Melanie mentioned, the visualization also makes clear that the majority of terms that occur in the titles of articles from literary or scientific journals only occur in one of the two categories. That is to say, it appears that some version of the famous 80–20 rule (also known as the power law) also applies with regard to the bridge words that became our primary focus. In other words—and oversimplifying quite a bit—the impression one gets from the visualization is that a majority ("80 percent") of the bridging work is done by a minority ("20 percent") of the terms. This asymmetry appears in even more striking form in a related visualization, one where we have reconfigured the network as bimodal with each of the two primary categories (literary and scientific) serving as the anchoring nodes of the network.

Much can be said about the visualization in Figure 37 (1750–1815), in which the shared terms appear between the two large journal category nodes. But, for the moment, I would just like to underscore its methodological significance. Our initial explorations ultimately led us to what I think is a pretty innovative application of the idea

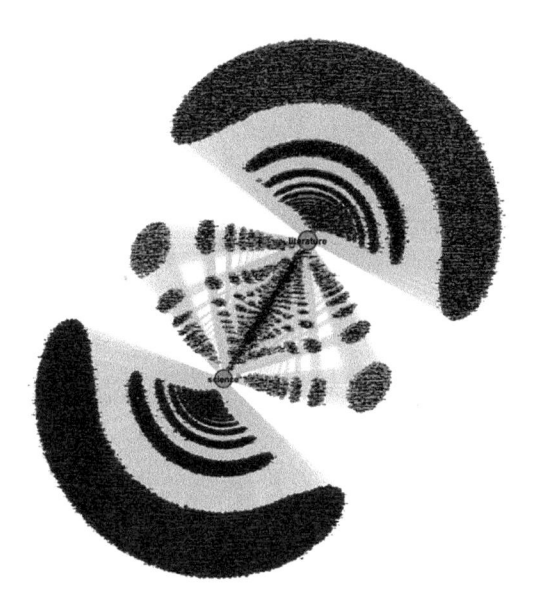

Figure 37: Network diagram of non-stop word terms used in article titles in the database Journals of the German Enlightenment, 1750–1815. Size indicates degree (number of connections to other terms). As opposed to Figure 36, this graph is formatted to emphasize bridging terms, those used in article titles in both scientific and literary journals. Visual created by Matt Erlin and Melanie Walsh.

of brokerage from social network analysis, the inspiration for which came from a group of computer scientists working in Brazil.[25] Instead of brokerage understood in terms of human actors who mediate between groups, we are trying to identify examples of semantic brokerage, that is to say, key terms that serve as connection points between articles from literary and scientific journals. Drilling down to investigate what these terms are and how they function in titles has led to some intriguing results that push us to think about discursive interpenetration—maybe we can simply say "interdisciplinarity" as a kind of shorthand—in a new way.

25. H. B. B. Pereira, I. S. Fadigas, V. Sennaa, and M. A. Moreta, "Semantic networks based on titles of scientific papers," *Physica A* 390 (2011), p.1192–97.

4. Crystal Hall and Birgit Tautz: On a related note, did you see a relationship (even an antithetical one) between features that might have been unexpectedly emphasized and those that were surprisingly absent? Can this be a productive tension?

Melanie Walsh:
As I mentioned earlier, there were some unexpectedly dominant words in our scientific-literary semantic network, such as "Nachricht" (news), "Bemerk" (notes), "Abhandl(ung)(en)" (treatises), "Brief(e)(n)" (letters) and "Betracht(ung)(en)" (observations and/or considerations). These are essentially genre markers, in the sense that they describe the category of the journal article that follows the title. We were surprised by the relative prominence of these words—over and above more substantive nouns such as "Bildung" (education), "Geschmack" (taste), "Vernunft" (reason), or "Mensch" (human)—because they have not traditionally been considered major conceptual players in Enlightenment discourse. But this unexpected emphasis helped us better understand our methodological approach and the unique contribution that we think this methodological approach makes to Enlightenment scholarship.

Matt Erlin:
I would just add here that we were *initially* surprised. Upon further reflection, we realized that the regular inclusion of genre indications in titles makes sense. But this feature of the corpus is not one that we would have even considered if it had not been foregrounded by the network-analytical approach. The fact that it makes sense, in other words, in no way detracts from its significance as a research finding, since the prominence of these terms opened up an entirely new perspective from which to tackle the question of Enlightenment interdiscursivity.

Melanie Walsh:
Right—because we are analyzing journal article titles, specifically, and because we are counting the connections between all words that appear in those titles (all words except stop words, numbers, and abbreviations), our semantic network reveals, in part, how titling conventions also helped shape, broker, and facilitate the print discourse networks of the Enlightenment. This approach makes visible the textual features of the discourse that are so ubiquitous as to seem almost mundane or invisible to human researchers, helping to provide

a sense of the scale and significance of such features as well. When we feed our computer programming script 19,794 scientific and literary journal article titles published between 1750 and 1815, for example, we discover that a simple word like "Nachricht" actually has one of the highest degrees in this semantic network, connecting almost 2500 other words and concepts.

Drawing attention to the potential significance of genre tags is certainly one of the contributions that we would like to make here. But it's by no means the only contribution or the end of the story. Though words that indicate genre, such as "Nachricht," connect many other words and concepts, the many words and concepts that they connect are often extremely diverse. This kind of constellation, precisely because it is so large and diverse, often seems to lack cohesion or intuitive meaning when considered as a cluster. More substantive nouns, however, such as "Bildung," "Geschmack," "Vernunft," or "Mensch," have fewer overall connections, but these few connections are often more immediately intuitive and thus more interesting to consider as a cluster. Finally, as we've said before, we are also very interested in words that act as brokers between other crucial words and concepts, not just the most dominant words with the largest number of connections.

Matt Erlin:
Investigating this brokering function with regard to the genre tags that Melanie mentions led to what I consider to be some of our most interesting results. If we look at the list of highly connected terms (i.e., those with the highest degree score), we find some revealing discrepancies. Some of these genre tags, such as "Übersetz(ung)(en)" (translations) and "Fragment(e)" (fragments) are far more likely to appear in titles from literary journals. By contrast, the term "Beschreib(ung)(en)" is demonstrably more prominent in titles from scientific journals, in this case by an adjusted ratio of 13 to 1. "Abhandl" is another example of a term that is heavily weighted toward scientific journals. In these cases, the discrepancies are less intuitive and I think they deserve further investigation. Moreover, a selection of these tags appears frequently in titles from both types of journals. Among these are such terms as "Beitrag" (contribution), "Bemerk" (remark), "Fortsetz(ung)(en)" (sequel), "Auszug" (excerpt), "Vergleich" (comparison), and "Beispiel" (example).

Taken together, these results invite a new perspective on the conceptual history of the period, pointing us toward practices of knowledge formation operating in a cognitive space that is less familiar to scholars of the period. By less familiar, I mean that neither are they "keywords" of the period in the sense of such terms as "Bildung," "Kritik," or "Mensch," nor do they really align with the current preoccupations of media studies approaches, at least not those with a more materialist bent. To my mind, they direct us toward an ideational infrastructure of the German Enlightenment, one reminiscent of Foucault's model of a discursive order that regulates the possible range of statements across disciplines.[26] In this regard, they can help to identify intersections between literary and natural scientific discourse as well as to find categories that serve to distinguish them. More concretely, although I think that the terms mentioned thus far can all be accurately described as genre tags, they in fact refer to certain kinds of operations that are at once genre-determining and cognitive. A term like "Auszug" points to specific procedures of knowledge reception and reframing, whereas "Bemerk" suggests a particular—provisional? informal?—relationship to knowledge. Presumably, not all knowledge at all times would be considered an appropriate focus for a brief comment. To the extent that these procedures are especially prominent in periodical literature, they provide additional source material for the thesis proposed by Gustav Frank, Madleen Podewski, and Stefan Scherer, namely, that nineteenth-century cultural journals serve as "small archives" ("kleine Archive") and can play a key role in revealing the "evolution of knowledge" ("Evolutionsprozesse des Wissens").[27] Some of these procedures appear to be relatively common in both scientific and literary knowledge formation—not only that of excerpting ("Auszug") or commenting but also argument by example ("Beispiel") and by comparison ("Vergleich"). The same equality does not seem to hold for description, however, as the skewed frequency in the case of "Beschreib" indicates. Both "Beobacht(ung)" and "Betracht(ung)" are terms with high connectivity, but the former appears more frequently in scientific journals by an adjusted ratio of roughly 24 to 1, whereas the latter is only about twice (2.38 times) as likely to appear in science titles. I would like to know why.

26. See Yvonne Wübben, "Forschungsskizze: Literatur und Wissen nach 1945," in *Literatur und Wissen*, ed. R. Borgards *et al.*, p.5–16 (10).
27. Frank, Podewski, and Scherer, "Kultur—Zeit—Schrift," p.31.

5. Crystal Hall and Birgit Tautz: Is network analysis a form of nonlinear reasoning? If so, is there a particular place for this method @1800?

Matt Erlin:
I am wary of asserting that network analysis *per se* is nonlinear, especially because its application in the fields of sociology and biology is intended to generate answers to specific research questions (e.g., understanding the cell cycle). But I would definitely say that our applications of network analysis to the journal metadata caused our original project to ramify in unforeseen ways. By their very nature, network visualizations invite multiple points of entry. Adopting the terminology of Deleuze and Guattari, we can describe them as rhizomatic rather than arborescent—although, technically speaking, a hierarchical tree-like network is still a network.

Melanie Walsh:
Absolutely—though I agree that network analysis does not inherently lead to nonlinear reasoning, these multiple points of entry definitely encourage the exploration of multiple perspectives and lines of inquiry at the same time. Ego networks are, to my mind, a great example here.

An ego network is oriented around a singular focal node, or "ego," where all other nodes in the network must have at least n connections to the ego. All nodes are egos, and any node can be the focal point of an ego network. Basically, it's a way of looking at a network from the "perspective" of any individual node. Because any of the 16,532 nodes in our 1750–1815 scientific-literary semantic network can be analyzed and visualized as an ego network, the network can be "entered" from, or viewed from the perspective of, any Enlightenment word or concept in the dataset.

Thus, we can look at our semantic network from its most macro, structural perspective (see Figure 36), or we can shift and enter the network through the perspective of "Beobacht" or "Betracht" or "Bildung," focusing only on the words and concepts that are most strongly connected to these selected ego nodes (see Figures 38a, 38b, and 38c).[28]

---

28. These ego networks have been filtered to include only nodes with an edge weight of at least 2 (in other words, only words and concepts with which the ego node has appeared in at least two article titles).

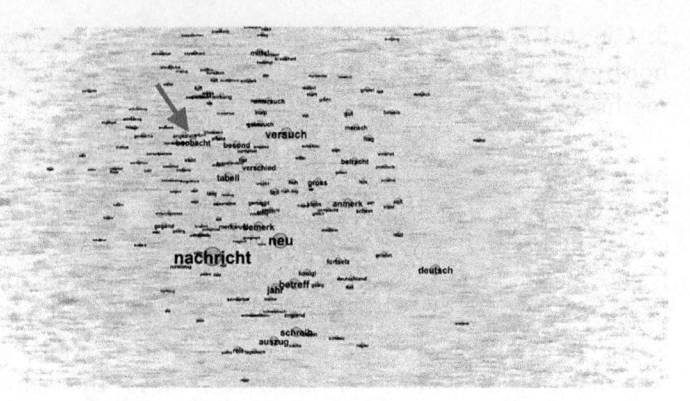

Figure 38a: Inset of Figure 36, network diagram of non-stop word terms used in article titles in the database Journals of the German Enlightenment, 1750–1815. Size indicates degree. Ego network of "Beobacht" highlighted. Visual created by Matt Erlin and Melanie Walsh.

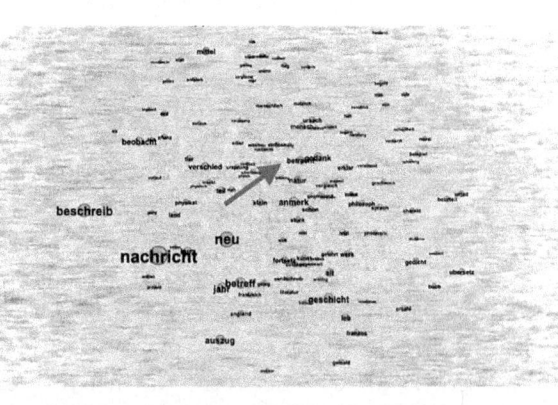

Figure 38b: Inset of Figure 36, network diagram of non-stop word terms used in article titles in the database Journals of the German Enlightenment, 1750–1815. Size indicates degree. Ego network of "Betracht" highlighted. Visual created by Matt Erlin and Melanie Walsh.

These are shifting pictures of the same network, shifting perspectives of Enlightenment print discourse—only a few among the hundreds possible. This simultaneity and multiplicity, when explored and acknowledged, expands our understanding of how scientific and literary concepts functioned during this time period.

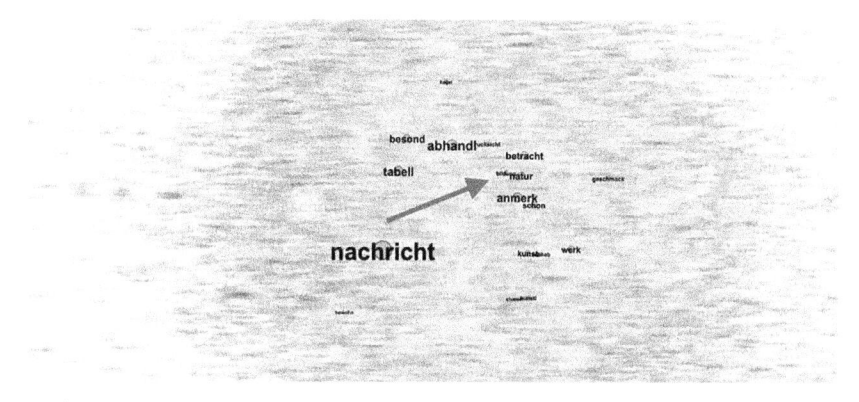

Figure 38c: Inset of Figure 36, network diagram of non-stop word terms used in article titles in the database Journals of the German Enlightenment, 1750–1815. Size indicates degree. Ego network of "Bildung" highlighted. Visual created by Matt Erlin and Melanie Walsh.

One final way in which network visualizations can encourage nonlinear reasoning is by allowing user interactivity. In a later stage of the project, I would love to create an interactive version of our Enlightenment semantic network and make it available to explore online. This interactivity would hopefully allow others to test their own arguments and make their own hypotheses by playing with, responding to, and learning from the dynamics of the network. It would also, of course, allow others to challenge and expand our arguments.

Matt Erlin:
As far as the question of a particular place is concerned, I would return to the beginning of our discussion. I hope that our project, even at this provisional stage, has demonstrated that network analysis can open up new perspectives on Enlightenment print culture and the Enlightenment more generally. But I don't think we have fully resolved the question of how to integrate this approach into the kind of thesis-driven journal article or book chapter with which humanities scholars are most familiar. Thus, one answer might be that yes, network analysis has a place in our toolkit, but one that is limited to initial exploration of a dataset, to generating research questions rather than answering them. Part of the problem stems from the aforementioned "rhizomatic" effect of the method. Every discrete analysis reveals possibilities for related or clarifying analyses,

many of which seem just as interesting as the original, and it can be difficult for scholars to winnow their results. Based on what I have seen from colleagues in literary studies and in other disciplines, however, I do think that network analysis has tremendous potential to provide answers as well as new questions, especially in light of the growing body of eighteenth-century scholars focusing on corpora (periodical literature, case studies, encyclopedias, correspondence) that lend themselves to quantitative approaches. It is just a matter of time. But now I'm wondering if I misinterpreted the question. Perhaps the issue is whether the period around 1800 constitutes an especially appropriate object for these techniques?

Melanie Walsh:
That's a great question, actually—and an especially interesting one for me to think about as a postwar/contemporary literature scholar. In fact, it's hard for me not to spin that question into another set of questions: Does the period around 1800 constitute a more or less especially appropriate object for network analysis than our contemporary moment, also heralded as highly networked? What is the relationship, if any, between the period around 1800 and the contemporary moment as objects of network analysis?

The former is mostly a provocation and clearly reductive: More than one period can be appropriate for network analysis, and different periods can be appropriate in different ways. But I think it's useful to compare these two different, highly networked periods, or at least to keep them both in mind, because it is the recent explosion of network analysis techniques and computational methods that has allowed us to see the networked nature of the Enlightenment in a new way, and it is the Enlightenment that has preceded and partly laid the groundwork for these recent developments. So, yes, I think there's a special place for network analysis techniques @1800, but that special place is partly contingent upon studying @1800 now.

I'll conclude by mentioning one way in which studying the Enlightenment now has struck me as being particularly well suited for network analysis, which is the way in which knowledge spread, ideas evolved, and intellectual communities formed through Enlightenment journal publication. Journal publication is really an ideal object for network analysis, as journal metadata lends itself easily to becoming elements in a network (authors, journals, or words can become nodes; co-publication or co-appearances can become edges). Because journal publication proliferated during the eighteenth century, and because journal publication was such an important vehicle for social and intellectual culture, applying network analysis techniques to journal publication can potentially reveal how major segments of Enlightenment culture developed in, through, and across print networks. That's what we're hoping to reveal, anyway. That's why we're dedicated to using network analysis @1800, despite all of its rhizomatic effects.

K/Cosmopolit* in Enlightenment journals: of networks and translation

BIRGIT TAUTZ

Bowdoin College

Cosmopolitanisms

Cosmopolitanism is in vogue. While it may strike us as fairly modern, cosmopolitanism is actually a storied idea that has become a conceptual swagger. But in both the broader scholarly context of European intellectual history and this volume, I consider the term to be a product of the eighteenth-century world. It is equally tied to the 1789 *Declaration of the rights of man*, which sought to establish— in the political context of the French Revolution—human rights as natural rights, and to Immanuel Kant's oeuvre, in which the essay on perpetual peace stands out for its proposed regulation of people's and national interests in a global context but which develops a more broadly and multifaceted understanding of cosmopolitanism as a philosophical category, expositing several semantic variations in the process.[1]

Cosmopolitanism's ancient roots faded into the background as Anglo-American practitioners labored to construe its Enlightenment roots, without accounting for what Mary Helen McMurran describes as "its discursive flexibility" which, "[i]n Britain and France, especially from the 1760s to the 1790s, [developed] the cosmopolite [... as] a creature of rhetoric rather than a robust theory."[2] In other words,

Thanks to Crystal Hall for assistance in asking the right questions and finding plausible readings and for pointing me to invaluable scholarship in the digital humanities. Quyen Ha and several colleagues at Bowdoin helped with accessing and visualizing the data.

1. Pauline Kleingeld, "Six varieties of cosmopolitanism in late eighteenth-century Germany," *Journal of the history of ideas* 60:3 (1999), p.505–24.
2. Mary Helen McMurran, "The new cosmopolitanism and the eighteenth century," *Eighteenth-century studies* 47:1 (2013), p.19–39, recaps the revival of

the *concept* of cosmopolitanism came to stand for a legal as well as intellectual framework or reach, while also encompassing the *subject's agency* or simply signifying a *metaphor* in language. It marked an intellectual territory that appears convoluted, meshing great names (Kant) and texts (*Declaration*) with expressive ambiguity unfolding linguistically between two words—"cosmopolite" and "citizen of the world"—and what McMurran labels "a conspicuous absence of straightforward identification with the cosmopolitan by the authors who use the term." Cosmopolitanism marked *a style, a rhetorical habitus* or *assertion*, whose *communal intention* encapsulated hierarchies as well as universal goals. All of these points of entry target (and circumscribe) a diffuse conceptual and linguistic network, to say the least. It is one that effortlessly traverses three different languages: English, French, and German, and that draws attention to the fragility and amorphousness of all networks, whether they comprise concepts, people, or objects.

Indeed, as this essay examines the keyword k/cosmopolit* in eighteenth-century German-language journals,[3] "cosmopolitan" is presumed to form a node in late-eighteenth-century networks. But networks of what? To begin with, of concepts and terms. Accordingly, my approach to the corpus, generated from the Zeitschriften der Aufklärung (Journals of the Enlightenment) collection resembles McMurran's "analysis of Eighteenth-Century Collections Online (ECCO) searches." At first glance, the architecture of search functions (keyword, author, subject, etc.) looks similar in both databases. While ECCO allows full-text access and the search of more than 180,000 titles (across all genres) published in Britain (and to a smaller extent elsewhere) during the eighteenth century, Journals of the Enlightenment contains digital images of 196 German-language journals from the long eighteenth century. Here, as Matthew Erlin and Melanie Walsh describe in their contribution to the current volume,

---

cosmopolitanism in the last twenty years—especially in the work of Martha Nussbaum and *Public culture*'s volume *Cosmopolitanism*—in order to work toward a "prehistory of Kant" (McMurran, "The new cosmopolitanism," p.22). This and the following quotes from McMurran are from p.21–22.

3. I am using the same database as Erlin and Walsh in their contribution to this volume, working with the University of Bielefeld's database Zeitschriften der Aufklärung (Journals of the German Enlightenment): http://ds.ub.uni-bielefeld. de/viewer/collections/zeitschriftenderaufklaerung/ (last accessed July 3, 2023). Subsequent references to the database appear in the main text as Journals, Journals of the Enlightenment, or Enlightenment Journals.

the search does not extend to full text, but only to "author," "title," and the somewhat nebulous property "identifier." The database was built according to the Index deutschsprachiger Zeitschriften 1750–1815 (Index of German-language journals 1750–1815) and the index's terms inform the capture of content and hits.[4] Using the general expressions k/cosmopolit* and weltbürger* in word searches, the algorithm returns results according to the index's pattern; the results mostly track the word stem in titles. Occasionally, though, the search digs deeper, locating the words used in the full text.

My resulting corpus is small, but the search identified articles that point to the generative patterns of a conceptual and linguistic network, in which k/cosmopolit* joins together, among other things, terms, persons, and styles, enabling us to explore cosmopolitanism's genealogy further, even beyond the confines of this volume. Since the late eighteenth century, we have perceived cosmopolitanism as an attitude, mindset, or style signaling, first and foremost, *openness*. The concept has often engendered its own criticism, not only because it implies juxtapositions and gestures of "othering" (almost always narrow viewpoints and provincialism), but also—and certainly since it has gained currency in modernity—because it is often used as an antidote to nationalism and patriotism in scholarly debates. Cosmopolitanism has become a catch-all phrase deployed in interdisciplinary contexts. With its often-imprecise meaning, it has morphed into the high-minded concept—indeed, the ethical imperative—that we wield today.[5]

Cosmopolitanism then serves as a stand-in, a vehicle that helps tell a story of historiographical and intellectual dominance, namely

---

4. A concise description of the database can be found at http://ds.ub.uni-bielefeld. de/viewer/collections/zeitschriftenderaufklaerung/. On the role and impact of the Index deutschsprachiger Zeitschriften, created by the Göttinger Akademie der Wissenschaften, see http://idrz18.adw-goettingen.gwdg.de/ (last accessed July 3, 2023). The application of the index is similar to the Library of Congress subject headings. While they are a post facto lens of interpretation that we use to access content, they also potentially exclude text that would have existed in relation to a term/semantic field in its historical moment but is no longer recognized as a connection. See Crystal Hall's contribution in the current volume.

5. Tapping into this rich conceptual history, Kwame Anthony Appiah has deployed cosmopolitanism's practical usage in the twenty-first century. Cosmopolitanism—along with worlding—seems to take the place of erstwhile universalism in order to avoid its ideological pitfalls, embrace an element of transcendence (of the global), and acknowledge the particular, difference, identity and equality, etc. See Kwame A. Appiah, *Cosmopolitanism* (New York, 2006).

how networks devolve (or evolve!) into neat narratives of tradition. Cosmopolitanism resembles "a boundary object" (i.e., its conceptual use in different disciplines converges without eliminating disciplinary differences). Boundary objects show how commonalities among disciplines were formed and pragmatically deployed, providing a common denominator or rhetorical device that mediates incongruities in information. Here, cosmopolitanism as a boundary object marks intersecting boundaries—of different social spaces, people, knowledge reservoirs, and styles, for example—and dispenses with the idea of immutable objects; it is flexible (to say the least).[6]

I am also interested in investigating whether ideas travel smoothly across languages, as McMurran insinuates. My examination therefore begins with and hinges on a term (or term cluster), k/cosmopolit*. In loose dialogue with some of the other essays in the volume, I aim to show how k/cosmopolit*—and, by extension, the discourse on cosmopolitanism unfolding in eighteenth-century journals—put pressure on concepts that emerged in the eighteenth century that are central to the various networks discussed in this volume: the nation and Europe, dominant genres and materially bound media, spaces organized and traveled in and through, acts of imitation undertaken, and cultural participation or exclusion. Collectively, these terms mark boundaries or realms of thought and directions in lines of thinking.

However, k/cosmopolit* is exemplary for two reasons: In the broader context of late-eighteenth-century language use, the term often conjures up another idea, namely translation, particularly when it appears in tandem with *Weltbürger(tum)*, the German-language expression for citizen(ry) of the world. Thus, this essay includes an examination of k/cosmopolit* vis-à-vis weltbürger* in the Journals of the Enlightenment, illustrating the limits of data-driven analysis and its visual representation. Furthermore, k/cosmopolit* reminds the literary scholar of a text by Christoph Martin Wieland, *Das Geheimnis des Kosmopolitenordens* (*The Secret of the order of cosmopolites*, 1788; hereafter referred to as *Cosmopolitan order*). The cultural legacy of text and author post-1800 suggests prominence—if we assume, as has been done in established literary historiography, a causal or foundational role for individual works. Can such a role be verified or disproved through its relation in networks? Does it generate its own

---

6. *Working with Leigh Starr: boundary objects and beyond*, ed. Geoffrey C. Bowker, Stefan Timmermans, Adele E. Clarke, and Ellen Balka (Cambridge, MA, 2016), p.35–36.

ego network, affirming Wieland's centrality, or does the text merely represent a passage point?

What we shall see is that Wieland's text foreshadows cosmopolitanism's career as a diffuse and diffusing concept. Although Wieland's use of the word *Kosmopolit* (cosmopolite) allegedly co-engineered its multifaceted presence in different disciplines, it failed to establish conceptual clarity; nevertheless, it centered an emerging debate. In other words, k/cosmopolit*—at once a designation of person and, with a *, a standardized expression of an attribution—comes with a twist, exemplifying and possibly complicating our understanding of *any* late-eighteenth-century cognitive figure. We know very little about *how* concepts work. Instead, we find ourselves entrapped in describing *what* they achieve.[7] Rather than understanding processes, we work with presumed end points or results only. Rather than seeing multifaceted networks, we fall back on the linear histories we deduce from them. At its obverse, then, k/cosmopolit* perhaps tells a story of extracting terms from the "great unread,"[8] but, by bringing cosmopolitanism's legacy in dialogue with its generic and networked (re)emergence at the advent of modernity, we can also make a plea for alternative histories that unfold in historical moments and confined places (rather than temporally driven narratives of history).

When choosing between calculating cosmopolitan's centrality index—by comparing the shortest and longest paths in a semantic network and thus also defining its eccentricity—within the journal and analyzing k/cosmopolit* in relation to Wieland's text and the broader "cosmopolitan discourse" playing out across the journals, I opted for the latter. Why? Aside from practical reasons (aka the missing data for the entirety of eighteenth-century German language materials and the nonexisting full-text readability across the Enlightenment Journals), I see digital humanities' role as ancillary. I am not interested in tackling "the great unread" for its own sake—that is, mining all digitally available texts in order to level neglected and by-now canonical texts. Rather, I seek to understand how and where concepts were formed by individual actors inventing and imposing them on a broader writerly public or, rather randomly, by simply emerging in "the great unread." Pursuing this limited text analysis will allow us to speculate on how

7. I loosely paraphrase from Maike Oergel, *Zeitgeist: how ideas travel* (Berlin, 2019), "Introduction," p.1–7.
8. Margaret Cohen, "Narratology in the archive of literature," *Representations* 108:1 (2009), p.51–70 (60).

canonical texts and authors acquired their privileged status in cultural history, since, by directing attention to the journals, we capture a larger literary and intellectual life, one that extends beyond individual authors and texts.

The study of a corpus addresses relations among a multitude of texts. Their connection is not necessarily apparent or even visible through conventional reading methods, but computational methods inform the reading of individual texts in the network. For example, to what extent was the legacy of Wieland's *Cosmopolitan order* enabled through a contemporaneous discourse that picked up on the term k/cosmopolit*? Were there other forces at work in elevating this text into the canon? Network analysis permits us to elucidate upon erstwhile postulated networks such as the one centered on Wieland's text by laying bare the invisible, contemporaneous forces at work in forming constellations whose story has yet to be told. As this essay unfolds, we will also see that the eighteenth-century journals invite further lines of questioning: Does cosmopolitanism operate as a node in our rethinking, à la Caroline Levine,[9] of networks and literary and social forms around 1800, or does it pervade as an edge—threatening to rip apart a worldview that came to establish the eighteenth century as modern, forward-directed, and indeed historical? Here, too, the "boundary object" proves useful: More than a ready-made term that can center scholarly communication as well as public presentation, it becomes conceptual currency that renders the intersection between "network" and "history" by marking the limits of both.

K/Cosmopolit* against its afterlife (or the erasure through translation)

In the German language, terms derived from k/cosmopolit* straddle the turn of the nineteenth century but have been felled by translation— in particular, through *Verteutschung* (Germanification). This linguistic act seeks to accomplish two things: finding a suitable expression in the target language, German, and simultaneously prompting a nation- alizing move by designating a germane origin. In other words, in this context, translation seeks to establish full equivalency or identity. Or so it seems when examining k/cosmopolit*'s (i.e., the term's) afterlife,

---

9.   Caroline Levine, *Forms: wholes, rhythms, hierarchies, networks* (Princeton, NJ, 2015), "Network," p.112–31.

which scholars have fused with the legacy of weltbürger*. In doing so, they have claimed an interchangeability of the terms.

Sigrid Thielking's *Weltbürgertum* (*World citizenry/citizenship*, 2000) and Andrea Albrecht's *Kosmopolitanismus* (*Cosmopolitanism*, 2005) participate in this trend: the emergence of a conceptual and linguistic network of k/cosmopolit* that hinges upon translation but, consistent with translation's increasing relegation to the discursive margins around 1800, tries to undo the translated in favor of originality, both by transplanting the term into the German language and by claiming the equivalency of weltbürger*. Both books treat *Weltbür-gertum* (world citizenship) and cosmopolitanism as synonyms, despite the terms' somewhat separate paths around 1800. But first things first. Both Thielking and Albrecht suggest that cosmopolit* and weltbürger* belong to a network, without elucidating upon the ways in which networks operate or what this stark observation means in the world of conventional, conceptual, and even broader cultural history. Whereas Albrecht recasts a conceptual history that associated cosmopolitanism with education and erudition and advocates for a pluralistic and discursive modeling of the term that will inevitably splice and multiply conceptual semantics,[10] Thielking emphasizes, by summarizing the distinguishing characteristics of *Weltbürger* around 1800, that the term not only appeared to complement patriotism and nationalism, but also worked as an instrument of compensation, countering the excess of patriotism and nationalism.[11] Throughout, she also directs our attention toward the philological dimension of weltbürger*, namely by surveying the various semantic meanings and fields conjured by the Grimms' *Deutsches Wörterbuch* (*Dictionary of the German language*, 1854–1961; hereafter referred to as the Grimms' *Dictionary*).

Therein, it seems, lies a moment of origin, a gesture that points to when the conceptual conflation of both terms, cosmopolitanism and *Weltbürger*, began. Thielking attributes meaning to the various compound words with *Weltbürger* that resemble the six kinds of cosmopolitanism that Kleingeld has discerned in German philosophy around 1800: moral, political, legal, cultural, and economic cosmopol-itanism, as well as a Romantic notion of unity that is tied up with

10. Andrea Albrecht, *Kosmopolitismus: Weltbürgerdiskurse in Literatur, Philosophie und Publizistik um 1800* (Berlin, 2005), p.29 and 56.
11. Sigrid Thielking, *Weltbürgertum: kosmopolitische Ideen in Literatur und politischer Publizistik seit dem 18. Jahrhundert* (Munich, 2000), p.9–15.

universal applicability.[12] I provide a contrast to this seamless substitution of one term with another, demonstrating instead that usage varied somewhat before the Grimms' *Dictionary* intervened with the self-styled authority of the titular namesakes. Furthermore, both Thielking and Albrecht refer exclusively to canonical authors who have defined the study of cosmopolitanism for nearly two centuries. Although Albrecht argues for the inclusion of noncanonical texts and texts of different genres, such texts serve, at best, to confirm and shore up the canonical status of well-worn materials. For both scholars, Enlightenment journals matter little, because they feature often-anonymous authors, pilfered and reprinted texts, poached translations and retranslations. These authors remain irrelevant and "unread" unless they became prominent as literary history was written.

The last observation takes us back to Wieland. He was an important public figure in the eighteenth century, who was dispatched to the Weimar court as an educator because of the fiction and treatises he wrote but has nevertheless been relegated to the realm of highly specialized literary scholarship. In fact, today his name is mostly associated with *Cosmopolitan order*. Credited with having established "Kosmopoliten" (cosmopolites) in modern German, the text avails itself of metaphors and forms that turn out to be a red herring with respect to cosmopolitanism's linguistic legacy. Indeed, the spirit that Wieland attributes to the cosmopolite and the working of the treatise within broader, networked cosmopolitanisms in the journals may shed new light on the persistence of the concept across time and beyond the canonical texts—without necessarily confirming Wieland's role as an inventor or first user.[13]

The data-driven environment of eighteenth-century journals casts k/cosmopolit*'s conceptual legacy in a diffuse light. While it accords a crucial role to Wieland's text—it reveals how the symbiosis of k/cosmopolit* and weltbürger* works in an individual text—the term's use in the Enlightenment Journals exposes the (partial) noncongruity of the German-language term *Weltbürger* and *Kosmopolit* (cosmopolite), a borrowed term from French. Semantic networks revolving around k/cosmopolit* and weltbürger* point to new directions in researching both the contemporaneous context and its aftermath. In the remainder of this essay, I suggest that the proliferation of small forms, networked

12. Kleingeld, "Six varieties of cosmopolitanism," p.505–24.
13. See also Ghanbari's essay on "first letters" in the current volume.

through the medium of the journal, may have established cosmopolitanism's reach and meaning over time. At once obscured and freely circulating, the term "brokered" among different networks, extracting meaning from one and infusing others with meaning, but always away from or at least in tension with canonicity and the long-presumed role of individual authors in centering and even directing discursive phenomena. This, we shall see, was a later invention.

***

Though considerably less numerous than those in ECCO, the materials housed in the Enlightenment Journals pose an obstacle to any conventional reading practice that would explore all journals in their entirety while seeking to identify themes, contents, and genres. What I am chronicling here is a reading approach combining the possibilities of *distant reading* with the necessity of *close reading*, as shaped by the conventions of literary interpretation. The promise to read comprehensively, albeit distantly, is predicated on so-called metadata, and uses selection criteria or descriptors applied by others (e.g., an old-fashioned index, evocative titles, comprehensive bibliographies) to construct their reading material as vast bodies of texts (or datasets) waiting to be *explored*. Using statistical methods to mine data, digital humanities imparts methods of "reading" and analyzing texts that seem unsurpassed in terms of the quantity of materials that can be managed, as well as the validity and comprehensiveness of results. Digital humanities asserts an aura of scientific evidence and indeed standardization, conjuring up a sense of objectivity. Using digital humanities methods comes with an altered approach to documenting results. At times, the descriptive passages in this essay and its online component outshine analysis and interpretation, pinpointing the usefulness of this fairly new approach, as well as its limitations, and charting next steps. Description is meant to direct the reader toward an integral online component of the argument, an accompanying supplement to the digital exhibit that is paired with a summary of the limitations of each essay.

While perusing the supplement, we take a step back to ask the question: What is topic modeling? And what is its relationship to standardized data and persuasive arguments, on the one hand, and to "pretty pictures" that simulate exactness but conceal deceptive promises on the other? The topic model captured by the digital supplement website offers one way of approaching networks around

1800; it illustrates semantic connectivity that shapes but does not constitute a neat network that can be described. However, as we shall see, the topic model allows us to predict which conceptual direction and context k/cosmopolit* takes. As Erlin and Walsh emphasize in their contribution to the current volume, the Journals of the Enlightenment database is somewhat deceptive: While the journals are *accessible in full text*, they are *not searchable in full text*. The application of any search term produces results generated through metadata and more nuanced (i.e., full-text) searches of entries' titles.

A search of k/cosmopolit* in the database reveals fifty-six occurrences in titles or subjects of journal contributions. This number accounts for spelling variations (k versus c; capitalization/noncapitalization) but not for all genre permutations. While I separated reviews from original texts for further analysis, I did not distinguish individual, one-piece texts from sequels that break one text into different installments. (For example, Wieland's *Cosmopolitan order* was published in two installments and thus shows up as two separate texts.) My grouping in genres combines close, traditional readings of full text (passages) with paratextual references labeling the text as "review," "translation," "speech," "treatise," and so on in a subheading of the text. More than half of the texts (thirty-three) are complete or partial reviews of "cosmopolitan texts": books, pamphlets, plays, and other types of writing that either reference k/cosmopolit* in their title and are therefore captured via a keyword search or, in the absence of these overt markers, have previously been indexed as "cosmopolitan." (In a next step of our research, especially if we decide to focus on genres, the corpus could be expanded by including all the works merely referenced, announced, or reviewed here.) Of the remaining, nonreview texts in journals, seven tackle philosophical-historical topics. Another six profess to offer general—we would call them popular—definitions of who a cosmopolite is, while another half dozen can be classified as social commentary. Formally, this thematic eclecticism avails itself of various genres: Treatises stand next to poems and anecdotes, plain definitions, announcements, speeches, and reports; we find scientific papers as well as fictional(ized) accounts.

In the examples from the accompanying website, the semantic interpretation via *keywords in context* dominates, displaying the most salient terms across the k/cosmopolit* corpus and allowing for a persuasive clustering into four fairly distinct topics that are modeled by using probability to reveal underlying patterns, or clusters, of words. These co-occur in similar patterns with one another in a large amount of text. Topic modeling is widely appreciated for its remarkable illustrative power because it reveals, with great persuasion and the object-like clarity of visual representation, "topics" within a body of texts. The "topics" appear intuitively and logically combined, and are assigned numbers by an algorithm; they can be grouped under umbrella terms or descriptors chosen by scholars and called "labels." The underlying principles and code are the same used by Crystal Hall in her contribution to the current volume; what differs is the visual representation. In the present essay's online accompaniment, the topics are represented by circles or bubbles of different sizes.

Frequency and relationships among the salient terms drive the clusters or topics, which, in turn, can be labeled accordingly to assist in the further reading and discussion of the results. For example, after applying the algorithms, we assigned the following labels in the three-topic model: "nation versus humankind" (topic 1), "France" (topic 2), and "global miscellanea" (topic 3; global is understood literally and figuratively in the sense of an all-encompassing range of references and semantics).[14] We then turned to the four-topic model for greater precision, but the overlapping circles indicate that the number of topics is too large; in this case, "nation" and "Europe" can be surmised as intersecting.[15] Since, in the four-topic figure, two topics overlap, we reverted to the three-topic model. A slightly different picture presents itself if we do not account for spelling variation (k/c) and examine only the kosmopolit* corpus.[16] As we repeat the gradual increase of topics, we achieve a well-differentiated four-topic model. Here, we observe a divergence, if not an opposition, between patriotism and a global framework, a distinction that subsequently defined cosmopolitanism's conceptual legacy. Accordingly, the derived topics (labels) are: "bourgeois nation and politics" (topic 1), "France" (topic 2), "global miscellanea" (topic 3), and "genealogy" (topic 4). The split between topic 4 and topic 1 suggests, however tacitly, how

14. See the interactive figure available in the digital collaboration hub for this volume and also at https://learn.bowdoin.edu/network-1800/k-cosmopolit/K-cosmopolitFullText3_Topic/TopicModel/index.html (last accessed July 3, 2023).
15. See the interactive figure available in the digital collaboration hub for this volume and also at https://learn.bowdoin.edu/network-1800/k-cosmopolit/K-cosmopolitFullText4_Topic/TopicModel/index.html (last accessed July 3, 2023).
16. See the interactive figure available in the digital collaboration hub for this volume and also at https://learn.bowdoin.edu/network-1800/k-cosmopolit/ (last accessed July 3, 2023).

conceptual *history* relies on the language of life sciences to tell its story in the nineteenth century, and also how it becomes imbued with national impetus, the effects of which I discuss in detail below.

In designing the approach, I faced the same vexing question that has preoccupied the still-evolving field of topic modeling: How does one define the perfect, or at least the ideal, number of topics? And, while the short answer is "by trial and error," the program provides embedded techniques to test any experimentation. We can observe this method by comparing the three-topic model with the four-topic model in both k/cosmopolit* and kosmopolit*.[17] This internal differentiation is generally considered an indicator to determine whether the direction of modeling (in this case an increase rather than a decrease in the number of topics) is correct. Conversely, the overlapping of circles would indicate that the number of topics is too large because clusters participate in other clusters, failing to delineate a discrete topic. In our case, moving to a four-topic model for k/cosmopolit* and a five-topic model for kosmopolit* produced overlaps, which is not surprising given our small corpus.[18] The topic model can be supplemented, if not corrected,[19] by a decade-based reading (see Figure 39).

Since our data sample is very small, we must counteract the deceptive story that the graphs may tell. Noticeable are the outliers: There are very few texts in the 1760s (1) and 1770s (5) or in the

17. See the interactive figure in the digital collaboration hub for this volume and also at https://learn.bowdoin.edu/network-1800/k-cosmopolit/ (last accessed July 3, 202).

18. See among others, Erik L. Peterson and Crystal Hall, "'What is dead may not die': locating marginalized concepts among ordinary biologists," *Journal of the history of biology* 55 (2022), p.219–51, https://doi.org/10.1007/s10739-020-09618-1 (last accessed July 3, 2023). An alternate application of the topic model disregards available metadata and "natural text boundaries" assigned by the respective journal and chunks all text into portions of equal size. This method is statistically more accurate and must be used in generating self-learned topics. See David Newman *et al.*, "Evaluating topic models for digital libraries," *Proceedings of the 10th annual joint conference on digital libraries* (June 2010), p.215–24. However, for our project, metadata as well as the hidden "distortions of data" (that is, the impact of an unusually large text) are important and the subject of a subsequent study.

19. Informal discussions among GitHub communities have cast doubt on the usefulness of topic modeling. Additional limitations include knowing the number of topics (K) ahead of time, the bag-of-words model that rejects sentence structure as meaningful, and the static assumption that does not capture change over time. See Rachel Sagner Buurma, "Fictionality of topic modeling," *Big data & society* 2:2 (July 2015), p.1–6.

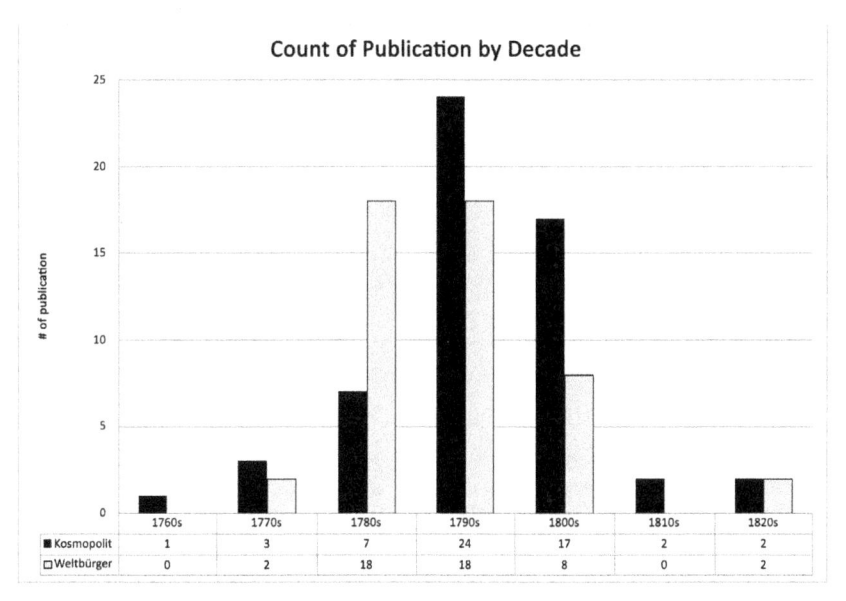

Figure 39: Bar chart of the publications that use Kosmopolit* (black) and Weltbürger (gray) in the Zeitschriften der Aufklärung (Journals of the Enlightenment) database 1760–1829, divided by decade. Visual created by Quyen Ha.

1810s (2) and 1820s (4). With the exception of the 1810s, these texts also deviate in their thematic focus and/or formal genre: Among the outliers, an obscure literary dialogue in which one of the characters is named "Cosmopolites" is joined by a dialogue of an unclear genre; there is also an anecdote, a reference to a piece of fiction (*literarische Notiz*), and a text about a Bible group that employs cosmopolitan terminology. The bulk of the k/cosmopolit* discourse is in the 1780s, 1790s, and 1800s, and grows after the publication of Wieland's *Cosmopolitan order*. In fact, three of the seven texts from the 1780s were written by Wieland in 1788 and 1789: Aside from the *Order*, he authored an address to the French National Assembly in 1789. The 1790s see an uptick in reviews, texts without titles, and treatises that attempt conceptual definitions of cosmopolitanism (albeit not in reference to Wieland's text). Toward the end of the 1790s, travel texts—so-called cosmopolitan journeys (*Wanderungen*)—proliferate, while the 1800s see a resurgence of letters and annals, a new historiographic genre. Only one text seems to tap into the subtext of Wieland's *Cosmopolitan order*, shaped by a thus-neglected word in its title ("secrets"): An 1808 treatise addressed to the cosmopolitan

Logen (Freemason lodges) connects with what the legacy of Wieland's text often conceals, namely[20] the language of secret societies and real or presumed indebtedness to Freemasonry. Despite the uptick in quantity after its publication, by delving deeper into the texts—that is, by reading in conventional ways—we cannot determine that any *qualitative* discursive shift was *caused* by Wieland's text: There was no proliferation in serializing, adapting, or reviewing *Cosmopolitan order*. Instead, the reviews revolve around popular genres, notably travel texts. Reviews keep the travelogues in the public discourse.

There is no evidence of any causal relationships between k/cosmopolit* in Wieland's text and k/cosmopolit* in the broader journal culture. What is noticeable, however, is the discursive establishment of the cosmopolite as a critical authority, as a self or persona. The cosmopolite appears as the writer of letters, the traveler, or the philosopher—in short, the sovereign subject of the texts—and is replicated, multiplied, and even serialized through the reviews. The cosmopolite claims the authority to speak and write. At the same time, the notion of cosmopolitanism absorbs semantic shades aligned with the various public spheres and actions that Kleingeld describes. In becoming all-encompassing, cosmopolitanism also becomes conceptually burdened; clearly identifiable meaning seems ever more elusive.

In contrast, prior to the publication of Wieland's text (and despite the scarcity of data), cosmopolitanism generally alluded to France and/or signified a concept that was imported through translation: A French journal is named as the source for one of the 1776 texts, and another (from the same year) is addressed to cosmopolitans who are always looking toward the other side of the Rhine River, if not traveling back and forth. Wieland himself embraces this origin and direction when addressing the French parliament in his other 1788 text. Cosmopolitanism thus *relates* to nation in various ways: While alignment with the French nation insinuates eventual opposition to the idea of a German nation, several texts center the relational terminology through paratexts that rope Germany into the discourse.

20. I am deliberately avoiding any discussion of Wieland and Freemasonry. Dan Wilson's scholarship is recommended reading here; it provides important insights into Wieland at the Weimar court and secret societies in classical Weimar. See W. Daniel Wilson, *Geheimräte gegen Geheimbünde: ein unbekanntes Kapitel der klassisch-romantischen Geschichte Weimars* (Stuttgart, 1991) and "Intellekt und Herrschaft: Wielands *Goldner Spiegel*, Joseph II. und das Ideal eines kritischen Mäzenats im aufgeklärten Absolutismus," *MLN* 99:3 (1984), p.479–502.

For example, several texts across the corpus indicate Germanness by including "Germania" next to or as the place of publication. Often, "the cosmopolitan speaker" alludes to patriotism or the nation, but not always as foils.

Whenever k/cosmopolit* appears in proximity to Christianity, it is imbued with secularism. This, in turn, suggests a conceptual closeness to the smaller corpus of *Weltbürger*, which is also more compressed: There are thirteen search returns between 1783 and 1792 in the Enlightenment Journals. Among them, three texts forge a strict delineation of the k/cosmopolit* from a religiously observant person; in the other texts, the citizen of the world presents as an enlightened person. The term weltbürger* expands the corpus to forty-eight returns, split formally into twenty reviews, twenty treatises, and eight other texts that can be loosely classified as fiction. The term's somewhat prolific usage predates 1788 (sixteen returns), and takes us into the 1790s (eighteen returns) and the 1800s (eight returns) (see Figure 39). The two small corpora thus lay bare a slight discrepancy in the usage of weltbürger* versus k/cosmopolitan*. Whereas the use of the former tilts somewhat toward the 1780s–1790s, the use of the latter picks up in the 1790s and 1800s. Similarly, weltbürger* appears in more and in a broader range of journals (nineteen, versus fifteen for k/cosmopolit*) but in 16 percent fewer entries overall; in addition, the k/cosmopolit* corpus features four texts of substantive length (forty-five to sixty-four pages), whereas weltbürger* includes only one text in the long-text rubric.[21] Therefore, based on the pure use of words (in titles), Wieland's *Cosmopolitan order* may well have had an impact, loosely suggesting the more frequent use of k/cosmopolit* across a variety of texts. However, these texts are otherwise unrelated to Wieland's text. Moreover, the genre descriptors suggest the opposite of any direct impact, connecting k/cosmopolit* not to philosophy but instead to travel. The presence of weltbürger* prior to Wieland pointedly suggests that importation of the French term was not necessary at all. Does Wieland's legacy consist in what was, by all means, a superfluous act?

Not so fast. The additional 1780s weltbürger* texts are the two parts of *Cosmopolitan order*. Despite not using the term in the title, Wieland's text appears in the corpus, along with two other 1797 texts, a poem ("Cosmopoliten" ["Cosmopolites"]), authored by M, and a treatise

---

21. Additional elements of quantitative analysis led me to conclude that the full-text topic model would skew results too much.

by F. R. Ricklefs ("Ueber Cosmopolitismus" ["About cosmopolitanism"]). Famous and forgotten authors appearing in both datasets
suggest that late-eighteenth-century prominence, which clearly distin-
guishes Wieland, played no role in the data-driven reading. Similarly,
both searches capture approximately the same number of works
(three) that do not reference k/cosmopolit* and weltbürger* in the title.
Both corpora contain few texts that overtly point to translation. Yet,
whereas k/cosmopolit*'s references to translation predate 1788, the
two weltbürger* references occur in 1793 and 1780.[22] These seemingly
errant observations allow us a glimpse into the pitfalls and (hidden)
depths of topic modeling while helping to contour a productive
relationship between *distant reading* and *close conventional reading*.

All of the available methods for topic modeling share a basic
problem: The data-driven visualizations make sense unless and
until one reads the texts conventionally. At first, topic models seem
circuitous because the researcher needs to pre-identify or suggest
the parameters for the model in a *quantitative* way by specifying
the number of topics the algorithm is asked to create, and often
by intuiting the qualitative descriptor or label when it comes to
settling on the eventual number of topics. (We detailed this process
for the three-topic model vis-à-vis the four-topic model above.) It
is in confirming or contradicting a hunch about a theme—in this
case, cosmopolitanism's conceptual tie to patriotism and universalism
established *in and as traditional intellectual history*—that I see the
promise of topic modeling when applied to a large dataset involving
eighteenth-century German-language texts. In planting the seed for
a "naturalized," growth-driven narrative through the symbiosis of
the topics "genealogy" and "nation," topic modeling illustrates how
the simplification and unification of a conceptual linear history may
have already happened at the beginning and over the course of the
nineteenth century.

Furthermore, the database's search algorithm uses what we might
call early-wave distant reading, as it relies on indexes constructed
according to good old-fashioned philological principles. They were
developed by an individual indexer, notecards by his side. One of the
indexes, devoted to reviews, emphasizes journals that published this

---

22. W. F. Graf von Schmettau, "Gedanken eines Weltbürgers bei Gelegenheit des
    jezigen Frankenkrieges," *Schleswiges Journal* 3 (1793), p.451–58; "Rezension
    Charron, P.; Möller [Übersetzer]: Die wahre Weisheit oder Sittenlehre des
    Weltbürgers," *Allgemeine deutsche Bibliothek* 42 (1780), p.107–108.

genre, while indexing, in general, is informed by and grounded in the scholarly habits of the nineteenth century that sought to inventory the archive of the nation. These early philological practices centered around literary writing and other corpora supporting and sustaining the imaginary path toward political unity. Considered against this historical moment, the searches' double grabbing of the three entries in the absence of weltbürger* in the title seems less random: One text by Wieland, *Cosmopolitan order*, was firmly lodged in the nineteenth-century memory as an indicator of a secular, universal Enlightenment and ensuing progress—which, as we shall see, early philologists labeled *Weltbürger*—while the two unknown authors' texts were published in prominent, aspirational venues: Both Schiller's literary magazine *Die Horen* and the journal *Deutsches Magazin* supported the idea of a *Kultur-nation*, an image grounded in language and thought. In foregrounding these aspects, topic modeling exposes the (dis)connections between great or canonical and forgotten or unread texts of varying genres in German. It brings attention to the *form*s of thought and expression, asking repeatedly: How do conventional reading models—all of which emphasize narrative progress toward a cosmopolitan mindset and habitus, that is, the pragmatic opportunities of the new cosmopolitanism—relate to the network-derived topics that emphasize political form, a link to France, and some predetermined, natural inclination, while expressing concomitant differences?[23]

Forging the national or making "the untranslatable" disappear

Despite its uptick in the 1790s and an overall steady prominence in the Enlightenment Journals, the French *Lehnwort* (borrowed word) k/cosmopolit* appears to become "unread"—or a restricted term only used by authors such as Wieland (or Immanuel Kant for that

---

23. Pethes has responded to this question in the context of historical modes of distant reading, an aspect that I have touched upon here. He believes that, in the early nineteenth century, periodicals' authors may have sensed their own position as manufacturers of nascent "distant readings." Accordingly, they were aware that they presented recycled material, unbalanced views, and filtered news and genres through a variety of metatexts. While certainly true, this model assumes that the author is the originator/center of discourse. Nicolas Pethes, "Serial individuality: eighteenth-century case study collections and nineteenth-century archival fiction," in *Distant readings: topologies of German culture in the long nineteenth century*, ed. Matt Erlin and Lynne Tatlock (New York, 2014), p.115–32.

matter)—when we consider its fate in the Grimms' *Dictionary*. This magnum opus of nineteenth-century philology, and the linguistic foundation of the German nation, claims to reveal the etymology as well as the contemporary usage of all its entries, in some cases going back centuries. The dictionary thus serves as an end point of lexical importation because it is only interested in the genealogy of the German language. For the Grimms, k/cosmopolit* deserves no stand-alone entry, although *Kosmopolit*—often with a parenthetical note pointing to its French origins—appears in other entries, first and foremost in "Weltbürger," "weltlich," and "weltling." But the dictionary's understanding of *Weltbürger* conveys not, as McMurran suggests for the English equivalent, a mere rendering of cosmopolitan in the vernacular. It is not simply a variation that alternates with k/cosmopolit*, depending on genre, appeal to readers, or author's intention. While weltbürger* appears, in the Journals of the Enlightenment, in limited but neutral use as an attribute of a (secular) enlightened person who acts with a worldly, not to say universal, intent or aspiration, the Grimms pivot to the nation. Although k/cosmopolit* maintains an overall more robust presence than weltbürger* in the Journals, the Grimms manage to expunge it from the *German* dictionary. Their turn to the vernacular means *recording* in order to *document* language use of *the past*, while also delineating language in service to a *future*, politically unified nation. They transform the concept (i.e., domesticate it), by "rendering unread" the multifaceted k/cosmopolit*.

In contrast, weltbürger* does not disappear from the dictionary (albeit, perhaps, from the journals), but returns with force. The Grimms treat the word as a "Schlagwort der Aufklärungszeit" (a key term of or short-cut to the Enlightenment), allegedly riding "on the wings of the French cosmopolite" (*beflügelt*).[24] Their word choice is telling, implying perhaps that cosmopolite predated or, in any case, brought into the open *Weltbürger*, which in turn absorbed all foreign connotations and offered an effective substitute. It fully encapsulated the spirit of the period. However, in order to establish weltbürger*'s nineteenth-century discursive dominance, the Brothers Grimm needed to assign it an origin. Though conceding the term's earlier existence in German, they attribute its discursive force to casting

---

24. *Deutsches Wörterbuch von Jacob und Wilhelm Grimm*, 32 vols. (Leipzig, 1854–1961), dwb.uni-trier.de/de/die-digitale-version/online-version (last accessed July 3, 2023), vol.28, col.1557. Hereafter referred to as *DWB*.

aside the French original. They disregard *Kosmopolit*'s coexistence as a stand-alone concept: As we have seen, it was an eighteenth-century word that showed up next to and indeed eclipsed, around 1800, the "original" German pseudo-synonym *Weltbürger*. The brothers relegated the term to the margins of the dictionary by declaring it essentially untranslatable: To them, it remained French. But, as *Kosmopolit* came to embody the limits of language and, ultimately, nation, *Weltbürger* took on slightly negative connotations in their dictionary: standing for restlessness, for individuals without residence who acted like nomads.[25] It thus equated, although no source is listed, the Journals' cosmopolitan travelers, whose wise sovereign actions had marked k/cosmopolit*'s usefulness as term and concept in small genres.

Ultimately, then, the Enlightenment Journals redirect our gaze toward this vexing relationship between translation and original on the one hand and the relative importance of journalistic, epistemic, and literary genres on the other. Both "discoveries" point to a messiness, a great unread that was forgotten or left behind when a national literary and cultural tradition was made and order imposed on what today presents as massive data. While the term k/cosmopolit* displays only once in cross-reference to "Übersetzung" (translation) in the Journals, it engenders a pairing with the other term, weltbürger*, and paves the way for simply considering them synonymous. Wieland's use of both words illustrates how both conflation and conceptual separation happened and how these discursive moves were tied to both the forms of network and linear cultural history.

Entering the (national) author or translation as a boundary object?

Somewhere between the predominance of k/cosmopolit* in the Journals, the feebler presence of weltbürger* in the same venue, and the Grimms' decisive philological intervention, shifts and ruptures happened, which allowed the Grimms to assert philological depth rather than mere politically motivated national intention. The term k/cosmopolit* takes on an *indexical quality*,[26] simultaneously harboring and expunging the rise of boundaries. The different words point to the

25. *DWB*, vol.28, col.1557.
26. In allusion to Brad Pasanek and Chad Wellmon, "The Enlightenment index," *The Eighteenth century: theory and interpretation* 56:3 (2015), p.359–82.

past and present, while inviting diverse participation in discourse. Thus k/cosmopolit* replicates cosmopolitanism's incipience and discursive rise while opening itself up to being co-opted for pragmatic purposes, whether to signal something as trivial as everyday worldliness or something as ambitious as universal political intention. The uneven coexistence between k/cosmopolit* and weltbürger* points to contested worldviews and mundane language use, but it also reveals efforts to impose an authoritative order on an increasingly messy perception of peoples' environs. The ordering impulse of the Grimms' *Dictionary* succeeded, by relegating each term to different discursive and medial realms[27] and expunging k/cosmopolit* from the German language in the process. Such arrangements focus network and linear histories in different, albeit intersecting ways—which brings us back to Wieland's *Cosmopolitan order.*

Wieland uses both words, *Kosmopolit and Weltbürger,* inviting what I believe to be a misreading of the two words as synonymous terms, while simultaneously laboring to keep them separate. When the rhetorical strategies of the essay are parsed, patterns of literal translation, disciplinary transposition, and hermeneutical interpretation become visible, suggesting new discursive and disciplinary uses of cosmopolitan concepts. Above all, Wieland institutes the role of the inventor or first user, reminding the reader of his writing fourteen years earlier in the same place, *Der teutsche Merkur (The German Mercury).* Identifying himself as the author of the *Abderiten*-novel, he recalls that he was the first to make the cosmopolites' existence public. Beyond this, he also documents the evidence in a footnote.[28]

In its opening passage, *Cosmopolitan order* thus plants what would become the trademark of German philology and its principled

27. See also Andrea Albrecht, "Kosmopolitische Ideale: das weltbürgerliche Engagement des Göttinger Literarhistorikers Friedrich Bouterwek," *Europa: alte und neue Welten* 3 (2004), p.80–85 (80): "Öffnet man zudem die nationalphilologisch verengte Perspektive, wird deutlich, dass sich an den Weltbürgerbegriff ein europaweit geführter »Kampf um Benennungen« [...] knüpfte." See also the still highly relevant essay by Kleingeld, "Six varieties of cosmopolitanism," and Andreas Klinger, "Was ist ein Weltbürger? Kosmopolitismus in Literatur, Philosophie und Publizistik um 1800 [review of *Kosmopolitismus. Weltbürgerdiskurse in Literatur, Philosophie und Publizistik um 1800* by Andrea Albrecht, 2005])," *IASLonline* (March 10, 2007), http://www.iaslonline.de/index.php?vorgang_id=1744 (last accessed July 3, 2023).

28. Christoph Martin Wieland, "Das Geheimnis des Kosmopolitenordens," *Der teutsche Merkur* 3 (1788), p.97–115 (97). The second part ("Zweytes Kapitel") was published in the same venue: *Der teutsche Merkur* 4 (1788), p.121–45.

approach to the textual past. (Like the Grimms' work, this too represents a crude form of archiving a distant reading pattern; it is fundamentally networked in its architecture.) Yet what drives the essay, its narrative telos, comes from a continued appeal to a secret waiting to be revealed in the future. Wieland goes on to perform an explication or revelation. Through this quirky rhetorical move, he exposes a rhetoric of translation that paves the way for cosmopolitan direction. In other words, the introduction encapsulates the seeds of the forms of a network and of narrative linear history that is marked by both repetitions and aspirations for wholeness.

Wieland claims that cosmopolitans (i.e., the cosmopolitan spirit) need to act in hiding because naming and proclaiming would make them cease to exist, but what he has in mind is their infinite and unlimited work (in the sense of *werken*), which he is afraid will be curtailed by identification. To name something means to limit it, and any progress will come in the form of a repeated, more successful, or complete attempt at naming (or understanding). Even the letter of a word confines its spirit, although, to be sure, the word "cosmopolitan" existed. It was unused, Wieland claims, and hence it was abused: "[C]ertain people believe […] to coopt a name that nobody claimed and treat it like a lost object."[29] Yet using the name seems like idle decorum ("mit dem Kosmopoliten: oder Weltbürger-Titel decorierten") that runs the risk of depleting the spirit or intent.[30] Indeed, Wieland seems to underscore the parallelism between the imported French and the genuinely German word, thus easing the reflexive replacement of one with the other. But the transition into the popular failed, compelling Wieland to reenter the debate on cosmopolitanism after fourteen years, ready to reveal a secret.

While Wieland refuses to say whether interchangeable use reflects self-illusion (i.e., the self's conflation of word and spirit), he concedes that the attempts at understanding and developing the concept of *Weltbürger* (citizen of the world) coincided with an impulse toward a general, universal Enlightenment (*Erleuchtung der Welt*); here, he seems to be in agreement with the trends we saw for *Weltbürger* in the journals. But he also insists that the belief in or trends toward universal Enlightenment led to confusion about cosmopolites'

29. "so glauben gewisse Leute […] wenn sie sich eines Nahmens, a welchen mehrere Jahre lang niemand Anspruch zu machen schien, als einer gleichsam verlassenen Sache bemächtigten"; Wieland, "Geheimnis," p.99.
30. Wieland, "Geheimnis," p.99.

influence on all things material (*Imperium orbis*). This influence does not mean, Wieland suggests, that cosmopolites universally and in unison work toward Enlightenment institutions or forms—theirs is not an immediate material impact. For *Cosmopolitan order* cannot be institutionalized and must move freely and unrestrained. (Of course, Wieland himself invites the conflation of terms by using *Orden*, which recalls monastic institutions, rather than *Geist* or *Ordnung*, which were synonymous with a communal spirit.) He concludes with the hope and plea that the time has come for German lands to lift the veil of secrecy, emphatically underscoring that cosmopolites will win in the eyes of reasonable and good human beings. He proclaims, albeit in different terms, the age of Enlightenment, only five years after a spirited debate in the *Berlinische Monatsschrift* that culminated in Kant's "What is Enlightenment?" essay. This is, of course, the rhetoric of all-pervasive, innate, and thus universal reason. It is also, according to Wieland's introduction, the *spirit* of language rather than its *form*.[31]

In separating spirit and form lies the messiness and elusiveness of translation: Form identifies, while spirit obscures, meanders, and travels. The form, or word, while critiqued by Wieland for its label stealing, led him nevertheless straight to a conflation of *Weltbürger/Kosmopolit* in his own text; he uses both to mean "citizen of the world," which in turn inspired the Grimms' definition "as a person thinking in global terms or terms of the entire world."[32] Subsequently, according to the Grimms, "Lessing, Göthe, Schiller [saw themselves] as citizens of the world."[33] Nevertheless, Wieland's resistance to naming both cosmopolites and their impact gives way to the more circumspect reading on the part of the Grimms, who attribute a potential threat to Wieland's elusive cosmopolite: "a freewheeler, without homeland and

31. The English translation of the title is helpful here. We find both *Order of the cosmopolites/cosmopolites' order* and *Cosmopolitan order*, indicating the move toward the spirit, away from persons. See Torsten Walter, *Staat und Recht im Werk Christoph Martin Wielands* (Wiesbaden, 1995). Several points in Walter's argument are relevant here: Walter reads *Geheimnis des Kosmopolitenordens*— correctly, I believe—as exposing the limits of political power, emphasizing the natural laws of community, and based on Leibniz's and Wolff's philosophy of "developing clarity," i.e., reason. He maintains (or resurrects) Koselleck's claim that there are two big intellectual trends in the eighteenth century, the Republic of Letters and Freemasonry.

32. "Mensch von weltweiter gesinnung." All quotes from Wieland in this paragraph are from *DWB*, vol.28, col.1557.

33. "Lessing, Göthe, Schiller [fühlten] sich als weltbürger."

without obligation as a citizen of a country."[34] In other words, where Wieland deliberately sought to evade the form of identification, the Grimms impose form through personification.

In *Cosmopolitan order*, we are left with the nongraspable and ultimately untranslatable spirit. Surely, Wieland endorses a revelation of the community's essence at this point in time in 1788. But by positing the structure of an allegory—that the introduction shares, by the way, with philosophical narratives such as Lessing's parable of the rings in *Nathan the wise* (1779) and his *Education of humankind* (1780)—Wieland edges closer to the untranslatable and toward the hermeneutics of allegories, which will always maintain a difference and rely on a medium—a linguistic stand-in that marks both this difference and that which cannot be translated—for expression.[35] We are left with a cognitive figure that always must remain in movement (and perhaps without finite form). What appears as a vague and nearly hollow term is actually marred by networks that seek to rearrange its reach and claim to universal, all-encompassing form. Cosmopolitanism's "brokered" effectiveness is constantly challenged and in flux. Whereas, in the digital reading of networks, nodes like nation, books, or genres nonetheless connote forms, often suggesting wholeness or closeness, cosmopolitanism seems elusive at best. Its claim proliferates by promising a free (read: formless) and meandering spirit. It engenders an idea that transcends limitations and pervades—true to its presumed reach—globally. It can only be expressed by entering the authority of a sovereign individual that controls it—in other words, by giving it form—in this case, through the repeated marshaling of cosmopolites (i.e., persons inhabiting the cosmopolitan spirit), as well as through Wieland, a first user who assures connection to the past and the literary historiography of the future. Translation formed but one boundary, aiding the morphing of cosmopolites into cosmopolitanism considerably.

Conclusion

I have mapped the intersection of narrative and network in only a small corpus around 1800, proposing how we may rethink (national) literary and cultural historiography in networked terms. Above all,

---

34. "ein freizügiger ohne festen heimatsitz und staatsbürgerliche bindungen an ein bestimmtes vaterland."
35. *Welt* appears as "untranslatable" in Barbara Cassin, *Dictionary of untranslatables*, translated by Emily Apter *et al.* (Princeton, NJ, 2014).

cosmopolitanism proves to be an element of stubborn resistance—indeed, a boundary object that, in today's network terms, binds the centering image of the node with the decentering, spectral effects of the edge. Cosmopolitanism intersects many nascent disciplinary discourses and rhetorical configurations whose multifaceted nature is eclipsed in the cultural turn toward more linear narratives of history. The ideas of multiple concepts of cosmopolitanism, on the one hand, and multidirectional acts of translation, on the other, complicate any neat (that is, linear) narratives of Enlightenment. But they also cast in a new light any history of genre, canon formation, or historiographies of national literature and identity, not least because they intersect anonymous networks (often revolving around a term) and canonical author intentions. We reconstructed these intersections and their inflections in narratives in order to make cosmopolitanism, yet again, a productive rather than hollow term. Whereas any exploration of k/cosmopolit* reminds us of the limits that existing studies of cosmopolitanism expose, examining the expression indicates the potential that comes with distant readings. It allows us to account for the phenomenon of translation around 1800 and to take seriously the interrelations among different texts—whether they belong to the canon or not.

Epilogue: new networks?

CRYSTAL HALL AND BIRGIT TAUTZ

If nothing else, reading the essays and working with the materials in the digital collaboration hub space accompanying this book underline an important insight: Networks are constantly *in flux*. Network analysis, recourse to knowledge architecture, and modes of documentation are constantly in flux. *Digital humanities* and what scholars and the public might understand by this are constantly in flux. So are more conventional literary historiography and theory, despite following a more predictable narrative pattern. *Conventional literary and historical-cultural scholarship* and *data-driven readings* are not in opposition to each other but form new, constantly shifting arrangements that are also mutually enhancing: Newly developed reading methods and ways of *visualizing* their findings have helped us understand networks that were formed by people, things, and texts more than 200 years ago, which have been legendary for their presumed cultural impact. But, rather than being stand-ins for groups of actors united in intention-driven projects, these networks have turned out to be unstable. They reveal that eighteenth-century publics did not magically dissolve into imaginary communities that shared common goals, purposes, and future ideals—or a telos of existence. We started our project by associatively linking such established, stable, and retroactively constructed narratives to what we called *linear readings* of cultural histories. Now we note that linearity as a descriptive term falls short of what we set out to critique—and is not completely absent from the alternate stories we tell. At the very least, modes of thinking inspired by digital humanities, and in some cases the application of digital and data-driven methods, have exposed the fragility of thinking in either–or oppositions. These methods have also allowed us to discover hitherto forgotten practices and redirect attention to multiple eighteenth-century pasts that co-existed.

Thus, as the lines of *relating* the important *key terms* in *social capital, material cultures,* and *reading* are in flux and constantly rearranging, the terms themselves are challenged as well. Uncovering these dynamic constellations thus takes the place of preserving or uncovering something that was stable or hidden. What strikes us as a perhaps banal observation comes to the fore in outgrowths, networks, afterthoughts, and notes created by several of the individual essays, which often had to be edited out of the final versions of these essays. In a similar fashion—while, in the language of visual representation of network analysis, flux can be articulated by edges between perceptively stable nodes—the things, people, and places behind them are dynamic as well. Visual representations of networks allow snapshot-like glimpses into the segments of the cultures we chose to highlight in the three sections—Sean Franzel's erstwhile conclusion of his essay, "Serial inventories," notes the recourse to a however tempting juxtaposition of dynamism and stability. And, while we frequently attribute "stable archiving" to digital projects, Franzel delineates the deceptiveness of promising a better archive with more stability. As editors of this volume, we not only concur but feel that such a conclusion far exceeds the scope of his essay, capturing instead the nature of the entire project. With Franzel's permission, we moved it here instead:

> The digitization of print holdings is commonly understood in terms of creating *stable archives* that are stocked and made accessible to various users. Digitization is then positioned as *a remedy to the decay and ephemerality* of materials such as nineteenth-century newspapers, as a kind of building, a shoring up of stable, permanent repositories. This has perhaps culminated in the utopian horizon of a project like the National Digital Public Library spearheaded by Robert Darnton.[1] But I would suggest that an overemphasis on tropes of *stability and permanence* can obscure the fact that we always already use and are reliant upon a *plurality of archives*, which are characterized by varying levels of incompleteness and incompatibility, by varying levels of usability and searchability, and by the decay of digital data

---

1. See Robert Darnton, "The National Digital Public Library is launched!," *New York review of books* (April 25, 2013), http://www.nybooks.com/articles/2013/04/25/ national-digital-public-library-launched/ (last accessed July 4, 2023). We thank Sean Franzel for permission to shorten his essay and move this important section here.

itself.[2] The plurality and partiality of resources and tools are features of scholarly life (and all medial storage) both before and after the shift to digital media, and the periodical, in particular, is well suited to model this kind of incompleteness—in contrast, perhaps, to the more self-enclosed, self-sufficient structure of the book.

That Franzel's astute reflection on the all-too-easily presumed advantages of the digital made it into this epilogue is a perfect testament to the way humanists work now and even more so in the future: recording preliminary results, engaging in published forum discussions, and writing for ongoing discussion rather than to conclude a debate, which has often resulted in asserting a scholarly truism and closing a proverbial archive on any given research inquiry. These iterative principles often but not always come with the scalable reading practices through which thinking informed by digital humanities folds into established processes and vice versa. They have also guided much of our collaboration here. Several other scholars gave talks at the Network@1800 symposium/Humboldt Kolleg (April 2017), which served as inspiration for the design of this book and its accompanying digital exhibit, even though they did not make it into this final, seemingly permanent documentation. Together, they make a plea for an ongoing debate, a mode of scholarship in which the present volume serves as a node rather than a completed, closed narrative. Exposing the false oppositions between stability and flux, between fixed entities (such as the archive, books, places) and relations, and between amorphous yet boundary-driven concepts and key terms that provide structure and order thus makes for an important accomplishment of this project. At the same time, we observe that any efforts to delineate conceptual clarity and uniformity—to impose order and comprehensiveness—are always already surpassed the moment their story is told or written. Incompleteness and incompatibility, as well as tension within and across cultures, describe the eighteenth century as well as our own conditions and frameworks for reconstructing bygone times. So where does this leave our project and, more broadly, our approaches to the intellectual, material, and social cultures of the eighteenth century, specifically Germany's, within an international context?

To some extent, expanding upon one of Franzel's key insights about the deceptively nostalgic stability that promises to encapsulate

---

2.   On this feature of the decomposition of digital data, see Wendy Hui Kyong Chun, "The enduring ephemeral, or the future is a memory," *Critical inquiry* 35:1 (2008), p.148–71.

the past, we note a curious similarity between the eighteenth century and our own efforts to approach the eighteenth century. As we argue for the above-described openness, fractures, and incongruities, we note that eighteenth-century writers described a similar landscape, albeit not as an inspirational goal. They perceived it as epistemological chaos, a surplus of methods and writing, and a universe that needed to be managed. And, amid today's open inquiries and advocacy for the plurality of method and documentation, a similar ordering impulse takes shape and begins to prevail. As we write this, several "keyword projects" are in the works or about to be completed, following on the tails of publications that sought to reorder and reapproach linear histories or thematic accounts of cultural histories. Keywords propose a manner of organizing an epistemological landscape that cannot manage its eternal contradictions: Its primary form may be that of a network and may betray a demonstrated interest in wanting to seem nonhierarchical and nonlinear—that is, altogether open—but it also projects completeness and indefinite reach. Keywords then evolve as the best approximation of wholeness and "secured knowledge," or, if you will, stability amid chaos.[3]

Inevitably then, this project ends up chronicling abandoned lines of inquiry and failed innovation, while repositioning—à la keywords project—important conceptual pairs in a new, refined understanding. For example, in designing the digital exhibit, we could not help note abandoned efforts (or those of the contributors) to mount resources that we thought could generate and be used to document an engagement with knowledge that would bridge the many divides that exist between scholarly and popular discourse, as well as creative and scholarly discourse, which could highlight prominent cultural activities such

3. We thank Daniel Purdy for conversations about keyword projects and the status of networks that seek to cross the popular/scholarly divide. Examples of keyword projects include *Keywords for today: a 21st century vocabulary*, ed. Colin MacCabe and Holly Yanacek (Oxford, 2018); *Information: keywords*, ed. Michele Kennerly, Samuel Frederick, and Jonathan E. Abel (New York, 2021); the large-scale, in all likelihood hybrid, format of the *Goethe-lexicon of philosophical concepts*, ed. Clark Muenzer and John Smith, https://goethe-lexicon.pitt.edu/ GL (last accessed July 4, 2023); and the curated colloquy on critical semantics developed for and housed at the digital platform Stanford Arcade: https:// arcade.stanford.edu/colloquies/critical-semantics-new-transnational-keywords (last accessed July 4, 2023). The latter project showcases many aspects of the state of collaborative, networked, and digitally born scholarship discussed in this epilogue.

as appropriation, borrowing, and cultural transfer. In the process of examining the distribution of Goethe's works across different continents and in multiple media markers of *Global Goethe today: relationships within the digital circulation of world literature*, Daniel Purdy and Burkhard Henke tried to create, consolidate, and mine a digital depository of allusions to and appropriations of individual characters, facets, and snippets of Goethe's works across different continents and multiple media in order to chart reconfigurations (and somewhat eccentric networks) of the production and distribution of Goethe's own work. In an age of globalized online platforms, it makes sense to chronicle Goethe's towering presence and the effects of *Weltliteratur* worldwide. But what the project revealed was that the architecture of one centralized website, while at first glance not directional in modeling new knowledge production and creating a space for marketing and collecting, is limited because the requirements for contributing, solidifying, evaluating, including, and maintaining resemble those of closed knowledge archives (similar to traditional libraries) and are read like a book. In other words, even the seemingly infinite possibility of accumulating and storing is faced with resistance to accumulation—even today, we encounter "management problems" yet again. Scholars are faced with the challenge of cataloguing and creating inventories or rules—not unlike the shopkeepers, librarians, collectors, and *salonnières* around 1800; the editors of splendid early editions of authors' works; and the publishers of travel books, print series, and declamatory prescripts. Their sheer open-ended resources are deceptive; in the end, they collapse under the accumulation of too much stuff and too many projects. They require a careful delineation of results, as illustrated by Conroy's seemingly modest claim about salons, their relevancy and make-up in pre- and postrevolutionary France, and their relatability to salons across Europe. Thus, for all their ambitious intentions, digital humanities also reminds us to remain unpretentious in the face of boldness. Digital projects, and, presumably, many traditionally conceived scholarly inquiries, remind us that scholarship is and should remain risk-taking. It not only pushes limits but always encounters limitation; projects in network analysis and, more broadly, digital humanities are not exempt from such limits.

The antiquated-looking website Goethezeitportal[4] is a prime example of these limits. Resembling a storage space for essays,

---

4. See http://www.goethezeitportal.de/home.html (last accessed July 4, 2023).

decidedly nonmultimedial, and thus not much more than an online journal (without the metadata aggregator), the website illustrates the shortcomings of a network documentation that itself adheres to non-network form. Not only does it simply defy expectations today (and involuntarily archive a past accomplishment), but such ambitious projects remind us that efforts to scale and to achieve large data-collecting projects are group projects that rely on constantly self-rearranging contributors and that still need to negotiate the intersection between conceptual work and collecting or mining work. They amplify the nascent stage in reflecting and defining this relationship; they also highlight the need to consider time frames and parameters for documenting research results.

Finally, work on this project has also underscored the effects of networks on coexistent terms that have generated productive and often unresolved, abridged, and abandoned debates in the study of European culture around 1800. A case in point is the effects on the conceptual pairing of local/global. While this is far from the only pair we could cite, it seems apt because of its frequent co-emergence with network. Here, networks often function as an attribute to illustrate personal, specific, and spatially concrete connections, frequently amplified by material exchanges. In combination with the local, networks serve to identify, while, combined with the global, networks accomplish the opposite and become all-encompassing. Together, these pairs allow for glimpses of the moment or the contemporaneous, in contradistinction to the long, often abstract and difficult to perceive duration of history that has privileged "nation" as a guiding concept. What shifting emphasis away from the local/global and toward the network illustrates is that networks neither identify precisely nor encompass everything. The larger the network, the more tenuous the unifying features that connect the nodes, with the nodes at the periphery likely marking the beginnings of a new network united by a stronger common descriptor. As such, networks disintegrate around the edges or overlap into obscurity—they certainly do so if we attempt to construct and resurrect any comprehensive qualities. Any efforts to eliminate eccentric elements or to offer complete and conclusive explanations—neat stories so to speak—prove to be counterintuitive because they undo any thinking in networked terms, instead working to bring back narrative causality and closure. What we hope to have shown is that networks' force consists in disruption and resistance; otherwise, they become meaningless. Networks encourage hitherto unasked questions. They spur alternate stories, uncover hidden parts of cultural histories, and envision novel architectures of representation. To analyze cultural networks comes not with the wholesale promise of new models for cultural historiography but with a more modest suggestion, which is to pay attention to nuance, incongruities, and the hidden potential of creative energies. Global Goethe quickly loses relevance without the nuance of the many uses of Goethe, his works, and his texts.

At the same time, to bring organizational concepts of the volume— social capital, material cultures, and reading—into today exposes the dual nature of cultural action and narrative. The project recalls the intricate and often fragile relations among places, people, and objects in Europe at a time when the national claim was both boldly resisted and supported. Uncovering these relations through the scholarly networks of the early twenty-first century is important for yet another reason: When first conceived, the European project revolved around a future-driven image of wholeness and community; now, however, it is increasingly challenged through local, regionalist, and nationalist rhetoric. Teleological and, more broadly, scholarly narratives are constantly on the verge of being undone through often local, disparate action and effects. Thus, even amid the plea for nonlinear narratives, we underscore the synergy that has characterized divergent manifestations of cultural modernity.

Ultimately then, while traditional cultural historiography has considered the effects of disruption and resistance an obstacle to be overcome, we conceive of networked thinking as a seed to generate new and alternative—in any case, nonhomogeneous—histories that invite being read, interrogated, and rearranged over and over again. By historically engendering binary opposites such as local/global and challenging them through form, networks, and even this book and its accompanying exhibit, networks chronicle their own limitations. They project a future that cannot be represented but merely invited, discussed, and depicted like a snapshot of part of an incomplete process. Thus, we both envision an architecture that can only be built by others and offer an invitation to take up the challenge of building it. This book is merely one chapter in a serial invention.

Contributors

Karin Baumgartner is Professor of German at the University of Utah, Salt Lake City, UT. Her research interests include German literature and culture in the eighteenth and nineteenth centuries, feminist and gender studies, travel literature, Swiss studies, and the digital humanities. She is the author of *Public voices: political discourse in the writings of Caroline de La Motte Fouqué* (2009) and the co-editor of *From multiculturalism to cultural hybridity: new approaches to teaching modern Switzerland* (2010) and *Anxious journeys: contemporary German travel literature* (2019). She has written numerous articles on German women writers during the Napoleonic Wars and their understanding of political discourse. She currently serves as the co-editor of *Die Unterrichtspraxis/Teaching German*.

Melanie Conroy is Associate Professor of French at the University of Memphis, TN. Her research explores literature and visual studies in modern French culture using digital mapping, as well as network and text analysis. She is the co-director of The Salons Project, a part of Mapping the Republic of Letters, as well as the director of Mapping Balzac. She is the author of *Literary geographies in Balzac and Proust* (2021). She is a current member of the centerNet Board and of the Board of H-France (where she is web editor), and the deputy treasurer of the Alliance of Digital Humanities Organizations.

Mary Helen Dupree is Associate Professor of German at Georgetown University in Washington, DC. She is the author of *The Mask and the quill: actress-writers in Germany from Enlightenment to Romanticism* (2011). Her research interests include late-eighteenth- and early-nineteenth-century German literature and culture, gender, performance studies, and theories of sound and the voice; she has published numerous chapters and articles on these subjects. She has been a member of the international research group Netzwerk Hör-Wissen im Wandel, which published *Wissensgeschichte des Hörens in der Moderne* (2017). With Sean Franzel, she co-edited *Performing knowledge, 1750–1850* (2015). Her current project is concentrated on the theory and practice of literary declamation in Germany from the mid-eighteenth to the early twentieth century.

Matt Erlin is Professor of German and Comparative Literature at Washington University in St. Louis, MO, where he also serves as a founding member of the Humanities Digital Workshop (HDW). He has published widely on eighteenth- through twentieth-century German, European, and North American literary and intellectual history. His most recent, co-authored publication, "Multi-retranslation and cultural variation: the case of Franz Kafka," appeared in *Target: international journal of translation studies* in 2022.

Sean Franzel is Associate Professor of German at the University of Missouri in Columbia, MO. He has published widely on media discourses in the eighteenth and nineteenth centuries. He is the author of *Writing time: studies in serial literature, 1780–1850* (2023) and *Connected by the ear: the media, pedagogy, and politics of the Romantic lecture* (2013), co-editor of *Performing knowledge: 1750–1850* (2015), and co-editor and co-translator of a 2018 volume of essays by the historian Reinhart Koselleck. He is a recipient of the Alexander von Humboldt fellowship for advanced researchers, and has served as the book review editor at the *Goethe yearbook*.

Nacim Ghanbari is Professor of German literature (Neuere Deutsche Literatur/Historische Semantik) at Universität Siegen, Germany. She is the co-editor of *Anna Louisa Karsch: Edition und Öffentlichkeit* (2022). Her research interests include the literary history of patronage in the eighteenth century, media history, and the theory of literary publics. She has published books and articles on German literature and culture in the eighteenth and nineteenth centuries, network theory, and practices of literary collaboration.

Crystal Hall is Associate Professor of Digital Humanities at Bowdoin College in Brunswick, ME. She is an affiliated faculty member in Italian studies and a founding member of digital and computational studies. Her research and teaching focus on the relationship between technology, textual expression, and the creation of knowledge. In addition to collaborating with colleagues across the liberal arts in their use of text analysis, her primary projects and publications relate to the reconstruction and study of Galileo Galilei's personal library.

Joachim Homann is the Maida and George Abrams Curator of Drawings at the Harvard Art Museums, where he oversees a comprehensive collection of European and American drawings spanning six centuries. His current projects include the first survey of Harvard's drawings of the landscape from 1780 to 1910. In 2023, he curated "American Watercolors, 1880–1990: Into the Light." Before returning to the Harvard Art Museums, where he had received his curatorial training, Homann held positions at the Bowdoin College Museum of Art in Brunswick, Maine, at Colgate University, and the University of Texas at El Paso. He studied in Göttingen, Munich, Karlsruhe, and Heidelberg and wrote a Ph.D. dissertation on art, politics, and the public sphere in Milan between 1770 and 1814, supported by the German Research Foundation.

Peter Höyng, Professor of German Studies at Emory University in Atlanta, GA, pursues an interdisciplinary approach to cultural productions within the German-speaking world, emphasizing Austrian cultural history. He recently edited and co-translated Hugo Bettauer's *The Blue stain: a novel of a racial outcast* (2017), and Arthur Rundt's *Marylin: a novel of passing* (2022). Another concentration of his has been theater, theater history, and performances of plays by contemporary authors such as George Tabori, Thomas Bernhard, and Elfriede Jelinek. As a third focal point, he is interested in the intersection of classical music and literature. To this extent, he has, for example, published several essays on Beethoven's keen interest in authors such as Schiller, Goethe, or Grillparzer.

Renata Schellenberg is Professor of German at Mount Allison University in Sackville, Canada. An eighteenth-century German scholar by training, she has published original work on authors such as Goethe, Herder, and Alexander von Humboldt, and maintains a keen interest in scientific literacy of this period. She has also written on print and material cultures in eighteenth-century Germanophone Europe. More recently, she has been exploring the subject of Goethe and warfare in the context of the French Revolution. Among recent nationally funded research projects is an SSHRC Insight Grant

(2022) focusing on the interplay of imperialism and ethnicity in the Hapsburg Empire in the early nineteenth century.

Birgit Tautz is Professor of German at Bowdoin College in Brunswick, ME. She is the author of *Translating the world: toward a new history of German literature around 1800* (2018) and *Reading and seeing ethnic differences in the Enlightenment: from China to Africa* (2007). Her research focuses on questions of German philosophy and literature in a global context during the long eighteenth century, material and book culture in the transatlantic world, and the limits and opportunities of digital methods in literary readings. A fellow of the Alexander von Humboldt Foundation, she has just finished a term as co-editor of the *Goethe yearbook*.

Melanie Walsh is Assistant Teaching Professor in the Information School at the University of Washington in Seattle, WA. Her research interests include digital humanities, data science, cultural analytics, and literature. She is the author of a free online programming textbook, *Introduction to cultural analytics & Python*, which is specifically geared toward humanities audiences. She is also co-editor of the Post45 Data Collective, a peer-reviewed, open-access repository for literary and cultural data.

Bibliography

Académie française, *Dictionnaire de l'Académie française*, 6th ed. (Paris, 1835).

Ackermann, Rudolph, *Repository of arts, literature, commerce, manufactures, fashions, and politics* (London, 1809–1829).

Adelung, Johann Christian, "Das Contor," in *Grammatisch-kritisches Wörterbuch der Hochdeutschen Mundart*, vol.1 (Leipzig, n.n., 1793), p.1348.

Albrecht, Andrea, "Kosmopolitische Ideale: das weltbürgerliche Engagement des Göttinger Literarhistorikers Friederich Bouterwek," *Europa: alte und neue Welten* 3 (2004), p.80–85.

–, *Kosmopolitismus: Weltbürgerdiskurse in Literatur, Philosophie und Publizistik um 1800* (Berlin, 2005).

Allgemeine Zeitung 178 (June 27, 1802).

Almon, John, *A Catalogue of books, with the prices: to be had at J. Almon's, bookseller and stationer, opposite Burlington-House, in Piccadilly* (London, J. Almon, 1774).

Apel, Friedmar, and Stefan Greif, "Über Kunst und Altertum," in *Goethe Handbuch*, ed. Bernd Witte *et al.*, vol.3 (Stuttgart, 1997), p.619–39.

Appiah, Kwame A., *Cosmopolitanism* (New York, 2006).

Apter, Emily, *The Translation zone: a new comparative literature* (Princeton, NJ, 2006).

Arndt, Ernst Moritz, *Der Rhein, Deutschlands Strom, aber nicht Deutschlands Grenze* (1813; Dresden, 1921).

Baetens, Jan, *A voix haute: poésie et lecture publique* (Brussels, 2016).

Baisch, Otto, *Johann Christian Reinhart und seine Kreise: ein Lebens- und Culturbild* (Leipzig, 1882).

Balzac, Honoré de, *The Gallery of antiquities*, in *The Works of Balzac*, translated by Katharine Prescott Wormeley, vol.15 (Boston, MA, 1896), p.1–184.

Baretti, Joseph, *A Grammar of the Italian language* (London, Hitch *et al.*, 1762).

Baudrillard, Jean, "Simulacra and simulations," in *Selected writings*, ed. Mark Poster (Stanford, CA, 1988), p.166–84.

Baumgartner, Karin, "Constructing Paris: flânerie, female spectatorship, and the discourses of fashion in *Französische Miscellen* (1803)," *Monatshefte* 100:3 (2008), p.351–68.

Beals, Kurt, "Redefining Dada: the avant-garde as network," talk delivered at the annual conference of the German Studies Association, San Diego, CA, September 2016.

Beethoven, Ludwig van, *Beethoven's conversation books*, ed. and translated by Theodore Albrecht, vol.1, no.1–8 (February 1818 to March 1820) (Woodbridge, 2018).

–, *Ludwig van Beethovens Konversationshefte*, ed. Karl-Heinz Köhler *et al.*, 11 vols. (Leipzig, 1972–2001).

Beethoven-Haus, Bonn, https://www.bthvn2020.de/ueber-uns/ueber-bthvn2020 (last accessed June 30, 2023).

Belgum, Kirsten, "Distant reception: bringing German books to America," in *Distant readings: topologies of German culture in the long nineteenth century*, ed. Matt Erlin and Lynne Tatlock (Cambridge, 2014), p.209–27.

Bender, John, "Novel knowledge: judgement, experience, experiment," in *This is Enlightenment*, ed. Clifford Siskin and William Warner (Chicago, IL, 2010). p.284–300.

Benjamin, Walter, *The Arcades project*, translated by Howard Eiland and Kevin McLaughlin (Cambridge, MA, 1999).

–, *Das Passagen-Werk*, in *Gesammelte Schriften*, ed. Rolf Tiedemann, vol.5 (Frankfurt am Main, 1982).

Benne, Christian, *Die Erfindung des Manuskripts: zur Theorie und Geschichte literarischer Gegenständlichkeit* (Berlin, 2015).

–, and Carlos Spoerhase, "Manuskript und Dichterhandschrift," in *Handbuch Literatur & materielle Kultur*, ed. Susanne Scholz and Ulrike Vedder (Berlin, 2018), p.135–43.

Berger, Bruno, and Heinz Rupp (ed.), *Deutsches Literatur-Lexikon: biographisch-bibliographisches Handbuch*, vol.2 (Bern, 1969).

Bertuch, Friedrich Justin, "Über die Wichtigkeit der Landes-Industrie-Institute für Teutschland," *Journal des Luxus und der Moden* (August 1793), p.407–17; (September 1793), p.458.

–, "Zusatz des Herausgebers," *London und Paris* 2:7 (1799), p.242–45.

–, and Karl August Böttiger (ed.), *London und Paris*, 30 vols. (1798–1815).

–, "Plan und Ankündigung," *London und Paris* 1:1 (1798), p.3–11.

Beutler, Ernst, "Goethes Jugendbriefe," in *Wiederholte Spiegelungen: drei Essays über Goethe* (Göttingen, 1957), p.5–30.

Birgfeld, Johannes, "Klopstock, the art of declamation and the reading revolution: an inquiry into one author's remarkable impact on the changes and counter-changes in reading habits between 1750 and 1800," *Journal for eighteenth-century studies* 31:1 (2008), p.101–17.

Bivens-Tatum, Wayne, *Libraries and the Enlightenment* (Sacramento, CA, 2012).

Black, Jeremy, *The British and the Grand Tour* (London, 1985).

Blair, Ann, *Too much to know: managing scholarly information before the modern age* (New Haven, CT, 2011).

Blanning, T. C. W., "The Grand Tour and the reception of neo-classicism in Great Britain in the eighteenth century," in *Grand Tour: Adeliges Reisen und europäische Kultur vom 14. bis zum 18. Jahrhundert*, ed. Rainer Babel and Werner Paravicini (Ostfildern, 2005), p.541–52.

Blei, David M., Andrew Ng, and Michael Jordan, "Latent Dirichlet allocation," *Journal of machine learning research* 3 (2003), p.993–1022.

Bödeker, Hans Erich, and Ernst Hinrichs (ed.), *Alphabetisierung und Literalisierung in Deutschland in der frühen Neuzeit* (Tübingen, 1999).

Bodenhamer, David J., "Narrating space and place," in *Deep maps and spatial narratives*, ed. John Corrigan, Trevor M. Harris, and David J. Bodenhamer (Bloomington, IN, 2015), p.7–27.

Bodmer-Gessner, Verena, "Heß, David," *Neue Deutsche Biographie* 9 (1972), p.1–2, https://www.deutsche-biographie.de/pnd116764570.html#ndbcontent (last accessed June 23, 2023).

Bolter, Jay David, and Richard Grusin, *Remediation: understanding new media* (Cambridge, MA, 1999).

Böning, Holger, "Das Intelligenzblatt—eine literarisch-publizistische Gattung des 18. Jahrhunderts," *Internationales Archiv für Sozialgeschichte der deutschen Literatur* 19:1 (2009), p.22–32.

Books of entertainment, &c. (London, n.n., 1773).

Böttiger, Karl August, "Der Leipziger MeßCatalog," *Neuste WeltKunde* 2:122 (May 2, 1798), p.485.

Bowker, Geoffrey C., Stefan Timmermans, Adele E. Clarke, and Ellen Balka (ed.), *Working with Leigh Starr: boundary objects and beyond* (Cambridge, MA, 2016).

Brandes, Helga, "The literary marketplace and the journal, medium of the Enlightenment," in *German literature of the eighteenth century: the Enlightenment and sensibility*, ed. Barbara Becker-Cantarino (Rochester, NY, 2005), p.79–102.

Brüggemann, Diethelm, "Gellert, der gute Geschmack und die üblen Briefsteller: zur Geschichte der Rhetorik in der Moderne," *Deutsche Vierteljahrsschrift für Literaturwissenschaft und Geistesgeschichte* 45:1 (1971), p.117–49.

Brüggemann, Heinz, "Luftbilder eines kleinstädtischen Jahrhunderts: Ekstase und imaginäre Topographie in Jean Paul: *Des Luftschiffers Giannozzo Seebuch*," in *Die Stadt in der deutschen Romantik*, ed. Gerhart von Graevenitz (Würzburg, 2000), p.127–82.

Buck-Morss, Susan, *The Dialectics of seeing: Walter Benjamin and the Arcades project* (Cambridge, MA, 1993).

Büttner, Frank, and Herbert W. Rott (ed.), *Kennst Du das Land: Italienbilder der Goethezeit* (Munich, 2005).

Buurma, Rachel Sagner, "Fictionality of topic modeling," *Big data & society* 2:2 (July 2015), p.1–6.

Buzard, James, *The Beaten track: European tourism, literature, and the ways to culture, 1800–1918* (New York, 1993).

"Cabinet, n.," in *OED online*, http://www.oed.com/view/Entry/25753?redirectedFrom=cabinet+edition& (accessed June 27, 2023).

Caldarelli, Guido, and Michele Catanzaro, *Networks: a very short introduction* (Oxford, 2012).

Calhoun, Charles C., *A Small college in Maine: two hundred years of Bowdoin* (Brunswick, ME, 1993).

Campe, Rüdiger, *Spiel der Wahrscheinlichkeit: Literatur und Berechnung zwischen Pascal und Kleist* (Göttingen, 2002).

Carpenter, Kenneth, "James Bowdoin III as library builder," in *The Legacy of James Bowdoin III* (Brunswick, ME, 1994), p.84–126.

Carpo, Mario, "Big data and the end of history," *International journal for digital art history* 3 (2018), p.21–35.

Carroll, Linda, *Thomas Jefferson's Italian and Italian-related books in the history of universal personal rights* (New York, 2019).

Cassin, Barbara, *Dictionary of untranslatables*, translated by Emily Apter *et al.* (Princeton, NJ, 2014).

Cassini, César-François, *Relation d'un voyage en Allemagne: qui comprend les opérations relatives à la figure de la terre & à la géographie particulière du Palatinat, du duché de Wurtemberg, du Cercle de Souabe, de la Bavière & de l'Autriche: fait par ordre du roi: suivie de la description des conquêtes de Louis XV, depuis 1745 jusqu'en 1748* (Paris, Imprimerie royale, 1775).

Chard, Chloe, *Pleasure and guilt on the Grand Tour: travel writing and imaginative topography 1680–1830* (Manchester, 1999).

Chesney, Duncan McColl, "The history of the history of the salon," *Nineteenth-century French studies* 36:1–2 (2007), p.94–108.

Chun, Wendy Hui Kyong, "The enduring ephemeral, or the future is a memory," *Critical inquiry* 35:1 (2008), p.148–71.

Cohen, Margaret, "Narratology in the archive of literature," *Representations* 108:1 (2009), p.51–70.

Comsa, Maria Teodora, *et al.*, "The French Enlightenment network," *The Journal of modern history* 88:3 (2016), p.495–534.

Conroy, Melanie, and Chloe Summers Edmondson, "The empire of letters: Enlightenment-era French salons," in *Networks of European Enlightenment*, ed. Chloe Edmondson and Dan Edelstein (Liverpool, Liverpool University Press / Voltaire Foundation, 2019), p.80–91.

Cousin, Victor, *De la société française au XVIIIe siècle, d'après le Grand Cyrus de Mlle Scudéry* (Paris, 1858).

Craveri, Benedetta, *The Age of conversation* (New York, 2006).

Czymmek, Götz, "Johann Christian Reinhart und Joseph Anton Koch als Landschafter," in *Heroismus und Idylle: Formen der Landschaft um 1800 bei Jacob Philipp Hackert, Joseph Anton Koch und Johann Christian Reinhart*, ed. Ekkehard Mai and Götz Czymmek (Cologne, 1984), p.19–29.

Dag- und Nachtstukken uit de Portefeuille van de gebroeders Spiritus Asper und Spiritus Lenis, vol.2 (Leeuwarden, 1833).

Darnton, Robert, "The National Digital Public Library is launched!," *New York review of books* (April 25, 2013), http://www.nybooks.com/articles/2013/04/25/national-digital-public-library-launched/ (last accessed July 4, 2023).

–, "What is the history of books?," *Daedalus* 111:3 (1982), p.65–83.

DeNora, Tia, *Beethoven and the construction of genius: musical politics in Vienna 1792–1803* (Berkeley, CA, 1995).

Deuling, Christian, "Aesthetics and politics in the journal *London und Paris* (1798–1815)," in *(Re-) writing the radical: Enlightenment, revolution and cultural transfer in 1790s Germany, Britain and France*,

ed. Maike Oergel (New York, 2012), p.102–18.

Deutsches Wörterbuch von Jacob und Wilhelm Grimm, 32 vols. (Leipzig, 1854–1961), dwb.uni-trier.de/de/die-digitale-version/online-version (last accessed July 3, 2023).

DiMaggio, Paul, "Cultural networks," in *The Sage handbook of social network analysis*, ed. John Scott and Peter J. Carrington (Los Angeles, CA, 2011), p.286–301.

Dodd, Charles, *An Autumn near the Rhine, or Sketches of courts, society, and scenery in Germany, with a tour in the Taunus Mountains in 1820* (London, 1821).

Dupree, Mary Helen, "Early Schiller memorials (1805–1809) and the performance of literary knowledge," In *Performing knowledge, 1750–1850*, ed. Mary Helen Dupree and Sean Franzel (Berlin, 2015), p.137–64.

–, "Elise in Weimar: 'actress-writers' and the resistance to classicism," in *The Enlightened eye: Goethe and visual culture*, ed. Evelyn Moore and Patricia Anne Simpson (Amsterdam, 2007), p.111–26.

–, "From 'dark singing' to a science of the voice: Gustav Anton von Seckendorff, the declamatory concert and the acoustic turn around 1800," *Deutsche Vierteljahrsschrift für Literaturwissenschaft und Geistesgeschichte* 86:3 (2012), p.365–96.

–, "Sophie Albrechts Deklamationen: Schnittstellen zwischen Musik, Theater, und Literatur," in *Verehrt. Verflucht. Vergessen: Leben und Werk von Sophie Albrecht und Johann Friedrich Ernst Albrecht*, ed. Rüdiger Schütt (Hannover, 2015), p.353–68.

–, and Sean Franzel (ed.), *Performing knowledge, 1750–1850* (Berlin, 2015).

Düwell, Susanne, and Nicolas Pethes (ed.), *Sprache und Literatur* 146 (2014), special issue: *Zeitschrift als Archiv.*

Edict of the grand duke of Tuscany, for the reform of criminal law in his dominions (London, n.n., 1789).

Electronic Enlightenment, http://www.e-enlightenment.com/ (last accessed June 23, 2023).

Emily Dickinson Archive, http://www.edickinson.org (last accessed June 30, 2023).

Emirbayer, Mustafa, and Jeff Goodwin, "Network analysis, culture, and the problem of agency," *The American journal of sociology* 99:6 (1994), p.1411–54.

Engelhardt, Christian Moritz (trans.), "Skizzen eines Engländers aus den deutschen Rheingegenden," *Morgenblatt für gebildete Stände* 274 (1818), p.1093–95.

Epistemes of Modern Acoustics, directed by Viktoria Tkaczyk, https://www.mpiwg-berlin.mpg.de/research/projects/RGTkaczyk (last accessed June 23, 2023).

Erlin, Matt, "Sammlung, Inventar, Archiv: Epistemologien der Liste im Roman des 19. Jahrhunderts," in *Archivfiktionen: Verfahren des Archivierens in Literatur und Kultur des langen 19. Jahrhunderts*, ed.

Daniela Gretz and Nicolas Pethes (Freiburg, 2016), p.363–84.

–, "Useless subject: reading and consumer culture in eighteenth-century Germany," *The German quarterly* 80:2 (2007), p.145–64.

–, and Lynne Tatlock (ed.), *Distant readings: topologies of German culture in the long nineteenth century* (New York, 2014).

Espagne, Geneviève, and Bénédicte Savoy (ed.), *Aubin-Louis Millin et l'Allemagne: le Magasin encyclopédique—les lettres à Karl August Böttiger* (Hildesheim, 2005).

Faulstich, Werner, *Die bürgerliche Mediengesellschaft (1700–1830)* (Göttingen, 2002).

"Ferdinand Ries," https://de.wikipedia.org/wiki/Ferdinand_Ries (last accessed June 30, 2023).

Feuchtmayr, Inge, *Johann Christian Reinhart, 1761–1847: Monographie und Werkverzeichnis* (Munich, 1975).

Ficacci, Luigi, *Giovanni Battista Piranesi: the complete etchings* (Cologne, 2011).

Fischer, Bernhard, "Poesie der Warenwelt: Karl August Böttigers Messberichte für Cottas *Allgemeine Zeitung*," in *Böttiger Lektüren: die Antike als Schlüssel zur Moderne*, ed. René Sternke (Stuttgart, 2012), p.55–74.

Fischer, Hannes, and Erika Thomalla, "Forschungsbericht: Literaturwissenschaftliche Netzwerkforschung zum 18. Jahrhundert," *Zeitschrift für Germanistik, Neue Folge* 26:1 (2016), p.110–17.

Folger Shakespeare Library, www. folger.edu/shakespeare (last accessed June 30, 2023).

Frank, Gustav, Madleen Podewski, and Stefan Scherer, "Kultur—Zeit—Schrift: Literatur- und Kulturzeitschriften als 'kleine Archive,'" *Internationales Archiv für Sozialgeschichte der deutschen Literatur* 34:2 (2009), p.1–45.

Franzel, Sean, "*Les Cris de Paris*: Lebendigkeit, Neuigkeit und Intermedialität in der urbanen Tableauliteratur um 1800," in *Belebungskünste: Praktiken lebendiger Darstellung in Literatur, Kunst und Wissenschaft um 1800*, ed. Nicola Gess, Agnes Hoffmann, and Annette Klappert (Paderborn, 2018), p.83–103.

—, "The Romantic lecture in an age of paper (money): Jean Paul's literary aesthetics across print and orality," *Romanticism and Victorianism on the net* 57–58 (2010), https://doi.org/10.7202/1006516ar (last accessed June 27, 2023).

Fredericksen, Burton, and Julia Armstrong, *Verzeichnis der verkauften Gemälde im deutsch-sprachigen Raum vor 1800*, 3 vols. (Munich, 2002).

Friedman, Sanford, *Conversations with Beethoven* (New York, 2014).

Fröhlich, Anke, *Landschaftsmalerei in Sachsen in der zweiten Hälfte des 18. Jahrhunderts: Landschaftsmaler, -zeichner und -radierer in Dresden, Leipzig, Meissen und Görlitz von 1720 bis 1800* (Weimar, 2002).

Fulton, Henry L., "An eighteenth-century best seller," *Papers of the Bibliographical Society of America* 66 (1972), p.428–33.

Des Galanten Frauenzimmers kluge Hofmeisterin aus dem Französischen ins Teutsche übersetzt (Leipzig, J. Thomas Fritsch, 1696).

Gay, Sophie, *Salons célèbres* (Paris, 1864).

Geertz, Clifford, "Thick description: toward an interpretive theory of culture," in *The Interpretation of cultures: selected essays* (New York, 1973), p.3–32.

Gellert, Christian Fürchtegott, *Gesammelte Schriften: Kritische, kommentierte Ausgabe*, ed. Bernd Witte, vol.4 (Berlin, 1989).

General index to twenty-seven volumes of the London magazine, viz. from 1732 to 1758 inclusive (London, n.n., 1760).

Ghanbari, Nacim, "Erste Briefe," in *Goethe medial: Aspekte einer vieldeutigen Beziehung*, ed. Margrit Wyder, Barbara Naumann, and Georges Felten (Berlin, 2021), p.9–25.

—, "Netzwerktheorie und Aufklärungsforschung," *Internationales Archiv für Sozialgeschichte der deutschen Literatur* 38:2 (2013), p.315–35.

Gilbert, Holly, "Folger Digital Texts," *Digital humanities at Geneseo* (2017), http://dh.suny-geneseoenglish.org/2017/09/20/folger-digital-texts/ (last accessed June 30, 2023).

Girardin, Delphine, *Œuvres complètes*, vol.4: *Lettres parisiennes* (Paris, 1860).

Giuffre, Katherine, "Mental maps: social networks and the language of critical reviews," *Sociological inquiry* 71:3 (2001), p.381–93.

Glinoer, Anthony, and Vincent Laisney, *L'Age des cénacles: confraternités littéraires et artistiques au XIXe siècle* (Paris, 2013).

Goethe, Johann Wolfgang von, *Berichte des freien Deutschen Hochstiftes zu Frankfurt am Main*, vol.11 (Frankfurt am Main, 1895).

–, *Briefe Anfang 1785–3. September 1786*, in *Historisch-kritische Ausgabe*, vol.6.1: *Texte*, ed. Volker Giel with assistance of Susanne Fenske and Yvonne Pietsch (Berlin, 2010).

–, *Goethes Briefe*, in *Goethes Werke*, vol.14 (Weimar, 1893).

–, *Italienische Reise*, in *Sämtliche Werke*, vol.15, ed. Karl Richter (Munich, 1992).

–, *Philipp Hackert: biographische Skizze, meist nach dessen eigenen Aufsätzen entworfen* (Tübingen, 1811).

–, *Sämtliche Werke: Briefe, Tagebücher und Gespräche*, 40 vols. (Frankfurt am Main, 1985–2013).

–, *Von 1823 bis zum Tode Carl Augusts 1828*, in *Sämtliche Werke, Briefe, Tagebücher und Gespräche*, vol.37, ed. Horst Fleig (Frankfurt am Main, 1993).

– (ed.), *Winkelmann und sein Jahrhundert: in Briefen und Aufsätzen* (Tübingen, 1805).

Goethezeitportal, http://www.goethezeitportal.de/home.html (last accessed July 4, 2023).

Goodman, Dena, *The Republic of Letters: a cultural history of the French Enlightenment* (Ithaca, NY, 1994).

Gosch, Josias Ludwig, *Fragmente über den Ideenumlauf* (Berlin, 2006).

Goßens, Peter, *Weltliteratur: Modelle transnationaler Literaturwahrnehmung im 19. Jahrhundert* (Stuttgart, 2011).

Gothaisches genealogisches Taschenbuch der freiherrlichen Häuser 58 (1908), p.717–20.

Göttert, Karl-Heinz, *Geschichte der Stimme* (Munich, 1998).

–, "Wider den toten Buchstaben: zur Problemgeschichte eines Topos," in *Zwischen Rauschen und Offenbarung: zur Kultur- und Mediengeschichte der Stimme*, ed. Friedrich Kittler, Thomas Macho, and Sigrid Weigel (Berlin, 2008), p.106–107.

Granovetter, Mark S., "The strength of weak ties," *American journal of sociology* 78:6 (1973), p.1360–80.

Greiling, Werner, "Kultur aus den 'zwei Hauptquellen' Europas: Friedrich Justin Bertuchs Journal *London und Paris*," in *Europa in Weimar: Visionen eines Kontinents* (Göttingen, 2008), p.138–58.

Griffiths, Anthony, *German printmaking in the age of Goethe* (London, 1994).

Guldi, Jo, "The common landscape of digital history: universal methods, global borderlands, longue-durée history, and critical thinking about approaches and institutions," in *Digital histories*, ed. Mats Fridlund and Mila Oiva (Helsinki, 2020), p.327–49.

Gunn, Simon, "The city of mirrors: the *Arcades project* and urban history," *Journal of Victorian culture* 7:2 (2002), p.263–75.

Habermas, Jürgen, *The Structural transformation of the public sphere: an inquiry into a category of bourgeois society*, translated by Thomas Burger (Cambridge, MA, 1978).

Hannan, Leonie, "Collaborative scholarship on the margins: an epistolary network," *Women's writing* 21:3 (2014), p.290–315.

Hansen, Jason D., *Mapping the Germans: statistical science, cartography, and the visualization of the German nation, 1848–1914* (Oxford, 2015).

Harvard University Library, *Catalogus librorum in Bibliotheca cantabrigiensi selectus, frequentiorem in usum Harvardinatum, qui gradu baccalaurei in artibus nondum sunt donati* (Cambridge, MA, Harvard University Press, 1773).

Hatch, Louis C., *The History of Bowdoin College* (Portland, ME, 1927).

Hearder, Harry, *Italy in the age of the Risorgimento, 1790–1870* (London, 1983).

Heinse, Wilhelm, "Über einige Gemählde der Düssendorfer Galerie," *Der teutsche Merkur* 4 (1776), p.3–14, 106–19; *Der teutsche Merkur* 3 (1777), p.117–35; *Der teutsche Merkur* 2 (1777), p.60–90.

Hess, David, *Die Badenfahrt* (Baden, 2017).

–, *Hollandia Regenerata* (London, n.n., 1797).

–, *Scherz und Ernst* (Zürich, 1816).

–, "Der wandernde Declamator," in *Enzyklopädie der deutschen Nationalliteratur oder biographisches-kritisches Lexikon der deutschen Dichter und Prosaisten seit den frühesten Zeiten; nebst Proben aus ihren Werken*, ed. O. L. B. Wolff, vol.4 (Leipzig, 1839), p.83–88.

Hirschi, Caspar, and Carlos Spoerhase (ed.), *Kodex: Jahrbuch der Internationalen Buchwissenschaftlichen Gesellschaft* 5 (2015), special issue: *Bleiwüste und Bilderflut: Geschichten über das geisteswissenschaftliche Buch*.

Holm, Christiane, "Goethes Papiersachen und andere Dinge des 'papierenen Zeitalters,'" *Zeitschrift für Germanistik* 21:1 (2012), p.17–40.

Homann, Joachim, "Giovanni Antolini's Foro Bonaparte: constitution of public space in Napoleonic Milan," in *The Political economy of art: making the nation of culture*, ed. Julie Codell (Madison, WI, 2008), p.111–23.

Horstmann, Jan, and Rabea Kleymann, "Alte Fragen, neue Methoden: philologische und digitale Verfahren im Dialog—ein Beitrag zum Forschungsdiskurs um Entsagung und Ironie bei Goethe," *Zeitschrift für digitale Geisteswissenschaften* (2019), DOI: 10.17175/2019_007.

Howard, Sara A., and Steven A. Knowlton, "The Library

of Congress Classification and subject headings for African American studies and LGBTQIA studies," *Library trends* 67:1 (2018), p.74–86.

Höyng, Peter, "'Shakespeare's Bruder': Beethovens Shakespeare-Rezeption und ihre unerhörten Folgen," in *Shakespeare im 18. Jahrundert*, ed. Roger Paulin (Göttingen, 2007), p.119–39.

Hughes, Linda K., *"Sideways!* Navigating the material(ity) of print culture," *Victorian periodicals review* 47:1 (2014), p.1–30.

Hüsgen, Heinrich Sebastian, *Nachrichten von Franckfurter Künstlern und Kunst-Sachen enthaltend das Leben und die Wercke, aller hiesigen Mahler, Bildhauer, Kupfer- und Pettschier Stecher, Edelstein-Schneider und Kunst-Gieser, nebst einem Anhang von allem was in öffentlichen und Privat-Gebäuden, merckwürdiges von Kunst-sachen zu sehen ist* (Frankfurt am Main, n.n., 1780).

Hüttner, C., "Beschauung des Gewölbes eines Londner Stationar. Cordovan. Verschiedene Arten und Benennung der Pappen, Karten, des Pergaments, des Zeichen-papiers," *London und Paris* 6:6 (1800), p.110–21.

–, "Beschluß der Beschreibung des Stationerladens. Quittungsbücher, Lineale, Huswifes und dergl.," *London und Paris* 7:1 (1801), p.26–27.

–, "Englischer Buchhandel. Vergleichung mit dem deutschen. Second-hand books. Lackington's Musentempel.

Completierhandel," *London und Paris* 2:7 (1799), p.237–45.

–, "Fortgesetzte Beschreibung des Stationers. Outsides, zum Vorsatzpapier der Buchbinder. Parchment-runners, um gleiche Linien zu zeichnen. Leserliche Handschriften der Engländer. Büchschen für Wachold-ergummi. Federspulen," *London und Paris* 6:7 (1800), p.195–222.

–, "Fortsetzung der Materialen welche ein Stationer verkauft. Verzierte Papiere, Rechnungszettel. Papierfiligran. Forell. Falzbeine. Dintenpulver," *London und Paris* 6:7 (1800), p.202–203.

Imbruglia, Girolamo, *The Jesuit missions in Paraguay and a cultural history of utopia (1568–1789)*, translated by Mark Weyr (Leiden, 2017).

"Inuentarium," in *Johann Heinrich Zedlers großes vollständiges Univer-sallexicon aller Wissenschaften und Künste (1731–1754)*, p.14 and 431, https://www.zedler-lexikon.de (accessed June 27, 2023).

"Inventory, n.," in *OED online*, http://www.oed.com/view/Entry/98981?p=e-mailA4LQTPDEZ./nE&d=98981 (accessed June 27, 2023).

Ittmann, John (ed.), *The Enchanted world of German Romantic prints, 1770–1850* (Philadelphia, PA, 2017).

Jameson, Fredric, "Marxism and postmodernism," *New Left review* 1:176 (1989), p.31–45.

Jannidis, Fotis, "TEI in der Praxis," *Jahrbuch für Computerphilologie*, http://computerphilologie.digital-humanities.de/praxis/teiprax.html (last accessed June 30, 2023).

Jaques, Susan, *The Caesar of Paris: Napoleon Bonaparte, Rome, and the artistic obsession that shaped an empire* (New York, 2018).

Jean Paul, *Titan (1802)* (Frankfurt am Main, 1983).

Jenaische Allgemeine Literaturzeitung 1 (1807).

Jockers, Matthew, *Macroanalysis: digital methods and literary history* (Champaign, IL, 2013).

Johnson, Samuel, "No. 2: the necessity and danger of looking into futurity," *The Rambler* (March 24, 1750), https://www.johnsonessays.com/the-rambler/no-2-the-necessity-and-danger-of-looking-into-futurity/ (last accessed June 28, 2023).

Jost, Erdmut, "Eintrittskarte ins Netzwerk: Prolog zu einer Erforschung des Empfehlungsbriefs," in *Briefwechsel: zur Netzwerkbildung in der Aufklärung*, ed. Erdmut Jost and Daniel Fulda (Halle an der Saale, 2012), p.103–43.

Kadushin, Charles, *Understanding social networks: theories, concepts, and findings* (Oxford, 2012).

Kaiser, Gerhard R., "Friedrich Justin Bertuch: Versuch eines Porträts," in *Friedrich Justin Bertuch (1747–1822): Verleger, Schriftsteller und Unternehmer im klassischen Weimar*, ed. Gerhard R. Kaiser and Siegfried Seifert (Tübingen, 2000), p.15–39.

Kale, Steven D., *French salons: high society and political sociability from the Old Regime to the Revolution of 1848* (Baltimore, MD, 2004).

–, "Women, the public sphere and the persistence of salons," *French historical studies* 25:1 (2002), p.115–48.

Keith, George, *A Catalogue of several libraries and parcels lately purchased, containing several thousand volumes of valuable and curious books in almost all languages, arts, and sciences* (London, n.n., 1759).

Kelly, Thomas Forrest, *First nights: five musical premiers* (New Haven, CT, 2001).

Kennerly, Michele, Samuel Frederick, and Jonathan E. Abel (ed.), *Information: keywords* (New York, 2021).

Kinderman, William, *Beethoven*, 2nd ed. (Oxford, 2009).

King, Geoff, *Mapping reality: an exploration of cultural cartographies* (New York, 1996).

Kirchner, Joachim, *Die Zeitschriften des deutschen Sprachgebiets von den Anfängen bis 1830* (Stuttgart, 1969).

Kirschenbaum, Matthew G., *Bitstreams: the future of digital literary heritage* (Philadelphia, PA, 2021).

Kittler, Friedrich, *Grammophone, film, typewriter* (Berlin, 1986).

Kleingeld, Pauline, "Six varieties of cosmopolitanism in late eighteenth-century Germany," *Journal of the history of ideas* 60:3 (1999), p.505–24.

Klingemann, August, *Schill oder das Declamatorium in Krähwinkel: eine Posse in drei Acten; Fortsetzung der deutschen Kleinstädter und das Carolus Magnus* (Helmstedt, 1812).

Klinger, Andreas, "Was ist ein Weltbürger? Kosmopolitismus in Literatur, Philosophie und Publizistik um 1800 [review of *Kosmopolitismus. Weltbürgerdiskurse in Literatur, Philosophie und Publizistik um 1800* by Andrea Albrecht, 2005])," *IASLonline* (March 10, 2007), http://www.iaslonline.de/index.php?vorgang_id=1744 (last accessed July 3, 2023).

Koch, Sabine, "Über die Düsseldorfer Gemäldegalerie," in *Tempel der Kunst: die Geburt des öffentlichen Museums in Deutschland 1701–1815*, ed. Bénédicte Savoy (Cologne, 2015), p.151–95.

Koschorke, Albrecht, *Körperströme und Schriftverkehr: Mediologie des 18. Jahrhunderts* (Munich, 1999).

Krajewski, Markus, *Paper machines: about cards and catalogues, 1548–1929*, translated by Peter Krapp (Cambridge, MA, 2011).

Krebel, Gottlob Friedrich (ed.), *Die vornehmsten Europäischen Reisen: wie solche durch Deutschland, die Schweiz, die Niederlande, England, Frankreich, Italien, Dännemark, Schweden, Hungarn, Polen, Preussen und Rußland, auf eine nützliche und bequeme Weise anzustellen sind; mit Anweisung der gewöhnlichsten Post- und Reise-Routen, der merkwürdigsten Oerter, deren Sehenswürdigkeiten, besten Logis, gangbarsten Münz-Sorten, Reisekosten etc., auch einer neuen Sammlung von Post- und Bothen-Charten, Post-Verordnungen, Post-Taxen etc.*, vol.1 (Hamburg, Herold, 1767).

Latour, Bruno, "Visualization and cognition: drawing things together," in *Knowledge and society: studies in the sociology of culture past and present*, ed. Henrika Kuklick (New York, 1986), p.7–13.

Léger-St-Jean, Marie, and Katie McGettigan, "Exploring transatlantic print culture through digital databases," *Amerikastudien / American studies* 63:2 (2018), p.159–81.

Levine, Caroline, *Forms: wholes, rhythms, hierarchies, networks* (Princeton, NJ, 2015).

Lilti, Antoine, *The World of the salons: sociability and worldliness in eighteenth-century Paris* (Oxford, 2015).

Long, Hoyt, "Fog and steel: mapping communities of literary translation in an information age," *The Journal of Japanese studies* 41:2 (2015), p.281–316.

–, "Toward a sociology of modernism: network analysis and avant-garde poetry in Japan," talk delivered at the annual conference of the American Association for Asian Studies, San Diego, March 1, 2013.

Löwe, Matthias, *Idealstaat und Anthropologie: Problemgeschichte der literarischen Utopie im späten 18. Jahrhundert* (Berlin, 2013).

Luther, Edith, *Johann Friedrich*

Frauenholz (1758–1822): Kunsthändler und Verleger in Nürnberg (Nuremberg, 1988).

MacCabe, Colin, and Holly Yanacek (ed.), *Keywords for today: a 21st century vocabulary* (Oxford, 2018).

Das malerische und romantische Deutschland, in zehn Sektionen (Leipzig, 1836–1842).

Mai, Ekkehard, and Götz Czymmek (ed.), *Heroismus und Idylle: Formen der Landschaft um 1800 bei Jacob Philipp Hackert, Joseph Anton Koch und Johann Christian Reinhart* (Cologne, 1984).

Mani, Venkat, *Recording world literature* (New York, 2017).

Mapping the Republic of Letters, http://republicofletters.stanford.edu (last accessed June 23, 2023).

Marshall, Joseph, *Travels through Holland, Flanders, Germany, Denmark, Sweden, Lapland, Russia, the Ukraine, and Poland: in the years 1768, 1769, and 1770: in which is particularly minuted, the present state of those countries, respecting their agriculture, population, manufactures, commerce, the arts, and useful undertakings*, 3 vols. (Dublin, printed for H. Saunders *et al.*, 1772).

Martin, Russell L., III, "North America and transatlantic book culture to 1800," in *A Companion to the history of the book*, ed. Simon Eliot and Jonathan Rose (Oxford, 2007), p.259–72.

Martin-Fugier, Anne, *La Vie élégante, ou la Formation de Tout-Paris, 1815–1848* (Paris, 1990).

Matthews-Schlinzig, Marie Isabel, and Caroline Socha (ed.), *Was ist ein Brief? Aufsätze zu epistolarer Theorie und Kultur / What is a letter? Essays on epistolary theory and culture* (Würzburg, 2018).

McMurran, Mary Helen, "The new cosmopolitanism and the eighteenth century," *Eighteenth-century studies* 47:1 (2013), p.19–39.

Merck, Johann Heinrich, "Über die letzte Gemälde Ausstellung in **," *Der teutsche Merkur* 4 (1781), p.167–78.

Meusel, Johann Georg, "Vorbericht," *Museum für Künstler und Kunstliebhaber* 1 (1787), p.1–4.

Meyer-Kalkus, Reinhart, *Geschichte der literarischen Vortragskunst* (Berlin, 2020).

–, *Stimme und Sprechkünste im 20. Jahrhundert* (Berlin, 2001).

Middell, Katharina, *"Die Bertuchs müssen doch in dieser Welt überall Glück haben": der Verleger Friedrich Justin Bertuch und sein Landes-Industrie-Comptoir um 1800* (Leipzig, 2002).

Mildenberger, Hermann, "'Deßhalb bitte ich Ihnen recht sehr, den schönen Vorsatz Italien zu sehn, doch ja nicht wie einen leichten Traum verwehen zu lassen': Johann Christian Reinhart und Friedrich Schiller," in *Johann Christian Reinhart: ein deutscher Landschaftsmaler in Rom*, ed. Andreas Stolzenburg and Herbert W. Rott (Munich, 2012), p.36–46.

Moore, John, *A View of society and manners in France, Switzerland, and Germany, with anecdotes relating to some eminent characters* (London, Strahan & Cadell, 1783).

Moretti, Franco, *Distant reading* (London, 2013).

–, *Graphs, maps, trees: abstract models for literary history* (New York, 2005).

Moses, Stéphane, "Goethes Entdeckung der französischen Landschaftsmalerei in Rom (1786–1788)," in *Rom–Europa: Treffpunkt der Kulturen: 1780–1820*, ed. Paolo Chiarini and Walter Hinderer (Würzburg, 2006), p.29–41.

Muenzer, Clark, and John Smith (ed.), *Goethe-lexicon of philosophical concepts*, https://goethe-lexicon. pitt.edu/GL (last accessed July 4, 2023).

Müller, Lothar, *White magic* (Malden, MA, 2014).

The Multigraph Collective, *Interacting with print: elements of reading in the era of print saturation* (Chicago, IL, 2018).

Muns, Lodewijk, "Gustav Anton Freiherr von Seckendorff, *alias* Patrik Peale: a biographical note," https://hcommons.org/ deposits/objects/hc:28472/ datastreams/CONTENT/content (last accessed June 23, 2023).

Muratori, Ludovico, *A Relation of the missions of Paraguay: wrote originally in Italian, by Mr. Muratori, and now done into English from the French translation* (London, J. Marmaduke, 1759).

Murray, John, *A Hand-book for travellers on the continent: being a guide through Holland, Belgium, Prussia, and northern Germany, and along the Rhine, from Holland to Switzerland* (London, 1836).

Netzwerk Hör-Wissen im Wandel (ed.), *Wissensgeschichte des Hörens in der Moderne* (Berlin, 2017).

"Neue Preisaufgabe an die Künstler Teutschlands," *Der neue teutsche Merkur* 1 (1800), p.33–44.

Newman, David, *et al.*, "Evaluating topic models for digital libraries," *Proceedings of the 10th annual joint conference on digital libraries* (June 2010), p.215–24.

Newman, M. E. J., *Networks: an introduction* (Oxford, 2010).

Nickisch, Reinhard M. G., *Die Stilprinzipien in den deutschen Briefstellern des 17. und 18. Jahrhunderts: mit einer Bibliographie zur Briefschreiblehre (1474–1800)* (Göttingen, 1969).

Nicolai, Christoph Friedrich, *Beschreibung einer Reise durch Deutschland und die Schweiz, im Jahre 1781, nebst Bemerkungen über Gelehrsamkeit, Industrie, Religion und Sitten*, 12 vols. (Berlin, Nicolai, 1783).

Nörtemann, Regina (ed.), *"Mein Bruder in Apoll": Briefwechsel zwischen Anna Louisa Karsch und Johann Wilhelm Ludwig Gleim*, vol.1 (Göttingen, 1996).

–, "Nachwort," in *"Mein Bruder in Apoll": Briefwechsel zwischen Anna Louisa Karsch und Johann Wilhelm Ludwig Gleim*, vol.2, ed. Ute Pott (Göttingen, 1996), p.523–55.

Nugent, Thomas, *The Grand Tour: containing an exact description of most of the cities, towns, and remarkable places of Europe: together with a distinct account of the post-roads and stages, with their respective distances* [...] *likewise directions relating to the manner and expence of travelling from one place and country to another, as also occasional remarks on* [...] *each respective country*, 4 vols. (London, Printed for S. Birt, D. Browne, A. Millar, and G. Hawkins, 1749).

Oergel, Maike, *Zeitgeist: how ideas travel* (Berlin, 2019).

Oesterle, Günter, and Thomas Falk, "Einleitung," in *Riskante Geselligkeit: Spielarten des Sozialen um 1800*, ed. Günter Oesterle and Thorsten Valk (Würzburg, 2015), p.9–24.

Owen, John, *Travels into different parts of Europe, in the years 1791 and 1792: with familiar remarks on places-men-and manners*, vol.2 (London, Printed for T. Cadell, jun. and W. Davis, 1796).

Pasanek, Brad, and Chad Wellmon, "The Enlightenment index," *The Eighteenth century: theory and interpretation* 56:3 (2015), p.359–82.

–, "Enlightenment, some assembly required," in *The Eighteenth centuries*, ed. David Gies and Cynthia Wall (Charlottesville, VA, 2018), p.14–39.

"Patrik Peale: aus einem Schreiben aus Schleswig," *Neue Schleswig-Holsteinische Provinzial-berichte* 20 (1811), p.234–36.

Pelham's Circulating Library, *Catalogue of Pelham's Circulating Library, no. 59, Cornhill: consisting of a chosen assortment of books in the various branches of literature* (Charlestown, MA, 1802).

Pelz, Annegret, *Reisen durch die eigene Fremde. Reiseliteratur von Frauen als autogeographische Schriften* (Cologne, 1993).

Pereira, H. B. B., I. S. Fadigas, V. Sennaa, and M. A. Moreta, "Semantic networks based on titles of scientific papers," *Physica A* 390 (2011), p.1192–97.

Peters, Ursula (ed.), *Künstlerleben in Rom: Bertel Thorvaldsen (1770–1844): der dänische Bildhauer und seine deutschen Freunde* (Nuremberg, 1992).

Peterson, Erik L., and Crystal Hall, "'What is dead may not die': locating marginalized concepts among ordinary biologists," *Journal of the history of biology* 55 (2022), p.219–51, https://doi.org/10.1007/s10739-020-09618-1 (last accessed July 3, 2023).

Pethes, Nicolas, "Serial individuality: eighteenth-century case study collections and nineteenth-century archival fiction," in *Distant readings: topologies of German culture in the long nineteenth century*, ed. Matt Erlin and Lynne Tatlock (New York, 2014), p.115–32.

–, "Verfahren und Formen," in *Literatur und Wissen: ein inter-*

disziplinäres Handbuch, ed. Roland Borgards *et al.* (Stuttgart, 2013), p.229–98.

Piles, Alphonse-Toussaint-Joseph-André-Marie-Marseille Fortia de, and Pierre-Marie-Louis de Boisgelin de Kerdu, *Voyage de deux Français en Allemagne, Danemark, Suède, Russie et Pologne, fait en 1790, 1792* (Paris, Desenne, 1796).

Piper, Andrew, *Enumerations: data and literary studies* (Chicago, IL, 2018).

Piranesi, Giovanni Battista, *Vedute di Roma: disegnate ed incise da Giambattista Piranesi*, vol.1 and 2 (Rome, n.n., 1769).

Porras, Stephanie, "Keeping our eyes open: visualizing networks and art history," *Artl@s bulletin* 6:3 (2017), p.41–49.

Pott, Ute, *Briefgespräche: über den Briefwechsel zwischen Anna Louisa Karsch und Johann Wilhelm Ludwig Gleim: mit einem Anhang bislang ungedruckter Briefe aus der Korrespondenz zwischen Gleim und Caroline Luise von Klencke* (Göttingen, 1998).

Proescholdt, Catherine W., "Johann Christian Hüttner (1766–1847): a link between Weimar and London," in *Goethe and the English-speaking world*, ed. Nicholas Boyle and John Guthrie (Rochester, NY, 2001), p.99–110.

Purdy, Daniel L., *The Tyranny of elegance: consumer cosmopolitanism in the era of Goethe* (Baltimore, MD, 1998).

Puschmann, Claudia, *Fahrende Frauenzimmer: zur Geschichte der Frauen an deutschen Wanderbühnen (1670–1760)* (Herbolzheim, 2000).

Radcliffe, Ann, *A Journey made in the summer of 1794, through Holland and the western frontier of Germany, with a return down the Rhine: to which are added, observations during a tour to the lakes of Lancashire, Westmoreland, and Cumberland* (London, printed for G. G. and J. Robinson, 1795).

Ray, Angela G., *The Lyceum and public culture in the nineteenth-century United States* (East Lansing, MI, 2005).

Ray, John, *Observations topographical, moral, & physiological made in a journey through part of the Low-Countries, Germany, Italy, and France: with a catalogue of plants not native of England, found spontaneously growing in those parts, and their virtues* (London, Printed for John Martyn, 1673).

Review of *A Descriptive journey through the interior parts of Germany and France including Paris: with interesting and amusing anecdotes by a young English peer of the highest rank, just returned from his travels* (1786), *Allgemeine Literatur-Zeitung* 273 (1786), p.313–16.

Review of Jacques-Antoine-Hippolyte Guibert and François E. Toulongeon, *Journal d'un voyage en Allemagne et en Prusse* (1803), *Allgemeine geographische Ephemeriden* 19 (1803), p.203–207.

"Rezension Charron, P.; Möller [Übersetzer]: Die wahre

Weisheit oder Sittenlehre des Weltbürgers," *Allgemeine deutsche Bibliothek* 42 (1780), p.107–108.

Richter, Dieter, *Von Hof nach Rom: Johann Christian Reinhart, ein deutscher Maler in Italien. Eine Biographie* (Berlin, 2010).

–, F. Carlo Schmid, Hans Schoenemann, and Michael Thumser, *Johann Christian Reinhart aus Hof: Aquarelle, Radierungen, Zeichnungen* (Berlin, 2011).

Riley, Thomas, "Goethe and Parker Cleaveland," *PMLA* 67:4 (1952), p.350–74.

Riou, Jeanne, Hartmut Böhme, and Jürgen Barkhoff, "Vorwort," in *Netzwerke: eine Kulturtechnik der Moderne*, ed. Jürgen Barkhoff, Hartmut Böhme, and Jeanne Riou (Cologne, 2004), p.7–16.

Robinson, G. G. J., *A Catalogue of books printed for and published by G. G. J. and J. Robinson* (London, Paternoster-Row, 1790).

Ruspini, Bartholomew, *Mr. Ruspini, earnestly recommends the following short observations to the perusal of the nobility, gentry, and others, but particularly to parents, and to those who have the care of young persons* (London, n.n., 1785).

Russel, John, *A Tour in Germany, and some of the southern provinces of the Austrian empire, in the years 1820, 1821, 1822*, 2 vols. (Edinburgh, 1824).

Rutland, Robert A., *"Well acquainted with books": the founding framers of 1787, with James Madison's list of books for Congress* (Washington, DC, 1987).

Sainte-Beuve, Charles-Augustin, *Portraits of celebrated women* (Boston, MA, 1868).

Saint-Fond, Barthélemy Faujas de, *Travels in England, Scotland and the Hebrides*, vol.1 (London, Ridgway, 1799).

The Salons Project, http://www.salonsproject.org (last accessed June 23, 2023).

Scheinfeldt, Tom, "Where's the beef? Does digital humanities have to answer questions?," in *Debates in the digital humanities*, ed. Matthew K. Gold (Minneapolis, MN, 2010), p.56–58.

Schiller, Friedrich, *Die Horen: eine Monatsschrift herausgegeben von Schiller* (1796; Darmstadt, 1959).

–, *On the aesthetic education of man in a series of letters*, ed. and translated by Elizabeth M. Wilkinson and L. A. Willoughby (Oxford, 1976).

–, *Schillers Werke: Nationalausgabe*, vol.20 (Weimar, 1962).

–, and Johann Wolfgang von Goethe, *Briefwechsel zwischen Schiller und Goethe in den Jahren 1794 bis 1805*, 6 vols. (Stuttgart, 1828–1829).

Schlaffer, Heinz, *Die kurze Geschichte der deutschen Literatur* (Munich, 2008).

Schlesische Provinzialblätter 50 (1809), p.54–60.

Schmettau, W. F. Graf von, "Gedanken eines Weltbürgers bei Gelegenheit des jezigen Frankenkrieges," *Schleswiges Journal* 3 (1793), p.451–58.

Schmid, F. Carlo, "'[...] da mein ganzes Vermögen meine

Hände und Kopf sind': Johann Christian Reinhart als Zeichner und Radierer,"in *Johann Christian Reinhart: ein deutscher Landschaftsmaler in Rom*, ed. Andreas Stolzenburg and Herbert W. Rott (Munich, 2012), p.8–25.

–, "'... Das Glueck, eine wahren Freund zu haben': Anmerkungen zu den Römischen Künstler-freunden Johann Christian Reinhart, Albert Christoph Dies, Joseph Anton Koch und Johann August Nahl dem Jüngeren," in *Ars et Amicitia: Beiträge zum Thema Freundschaft in Geschichte, Kunst und Literatur. Festschrift fuer Martin Bircher zum 60. Geburtstag am 3. Juni 1998*, ed. Ferdinand van Ingen und Christian Juranek (Amsterdam, 1998), p.623–43.

–, "Die Mahlerisch radirten Prospecte von Italien 1792–1798," in *Johann Christian Reinhart: ein deutscher Landschaftsmaler in Rom*, ed. Andreas Stolzenburg and Herbert W. Rott (Munich, 2012), p.227.

–, *Naturansichten und Idealland-schaften: die Landschaftsgraphik von Johann Christian Reinhart und seinem Umkreis* (Berlin, 1998).

Schmidt-Funke, Julia, *Karl August Böttiger (1760–1835): Weltmann und Gelehrter* (Heidelberg, 2006).

Schneider, Joh-Nikolaus, *Ins Ohr geschrieben: Lyrik als akustische Kunst zwischen 1750 und 1800* (Göttingen, 2004).

Scholz, Leander, and Hedwig Pompe, *Archivprozesse: die Kommunikation der Aufbewahrung* (Cologne, 2002).

Schöne, Albrecht, *Der Briefschreiber Goethe* (Munich, 2015). First published as "Soziale Kontrolle als Regulativ der Textverfassung: über Goethes ersten Brief an Ysenburg von Buri," in *Wissen aus Erfahrungen: Werkbegriff und Interpretation heute—Festschrift für Herman Meyer*, ed. Alexander von Bormann (Tübingen, 1976), p.217–41.

Schulz-Forberg, Hagen, "European travel and travel writing: cultural practice and the idea of Europe," in *Unravelling civilisation: European travel and travel writing*, ed. Hagen Schulz-Forberg (Brussels, 2005), p.13–42.

Shelley, Mary, "History of a six weeks' tour through a part of France, Switzerland, Germany, and Holland: with letters descriptive of a sail round the lake of Geneva, and of the glaciers of Chamouni [1817]," in *Women's travel writing: 1750–1850*, ed. Caroline Franklin, vol.2 (London, 2006), p.295–483.

Sickler, Friedrich, and Christian Reinhart (ed.), *Almanach aus Rom für Künstler und Freunde der Bildenden Kunst* (1810–1811), 2 vols. (Leipzig, 1984).

Siskin, Clifford, and William Warner (ed.), *This is Enlightenment* (Chicago, IL, 2010).

Skrandies, Timo, "Unterwegs in den Passagen-Konvoluten," in *Benjamin Handbuch: Leben, Werk, Wirkung*, ed. Burkhard Lindner (Stuttgart, 2006), p.274–84.

Smith, Henry A. (ed.), *Eutin–Heidelberg 1811: Briefwechsel des Studenten E. Hellwag mit seiner*

Familie in Eutin (Eutin, 2009).

Solbrig, Karl Friedrich, *Taschenbuch für die Freunde der Declamation*, 4 vols. (Leipzig, 1816–1818).

Solomon, Maynard, *Beethoven*, 2nd ed. (New York, 1998).

– (ed.), *Beethovens Tagebuch* (Mainz, 1990).

Sondermann, Ernst Friedrich, *Karl August Böttiger, literarischer Journalist der Goethezeit in Weimar* (Bonn, 1983).

Sowa, John, "Semantic networks," http://www.jfsowa.com/pubs/semnet.htm (last accessed July 3, 2023).

Spoerhase, Carlos, *Das Format der Literatur: Praktiken materieller Textualität zwischen 1740 und 1830* (Göttingen, 2018).

Staël, Mme de (Anne-Louise-Germaine), *Germany* (London, 1813).

Stanford Arcade, https://arcade.stanford.edu/colloquies/critical-semantics-new-transna-tional-keywords (last accessed July 4, 2023).

Starke, Mariana, *Letters from Italy: between the years 1792 and 1798, containing a view of the revolutions in that country, from the capture of Nice by the French republic to the expulsion of Pius VI. from the ecclesiastical state: likewise pointing out the matchless works of art which still embellish Pisa, Florence, Siena, Rome, Naples, Bologna, Venice, &c: with instructions for the use of invalids and families*, 2 vols. (London, 1800).

St. Clair, William, *The Reading nation in the Romantic period* (Cambridge, 2004).

Steiner, Uwe C., *Verhüllungs-geschichten: die Dichtung des Schleiers* (Munich, 2006).

Stendhal, *The Red and the black: a chronicle of the nineteenth century* (1830), translated by Catherine Slater (Oxford, 2009).

Sterne, Jonathan, *The Audible past: cultural origins of sound reproduction* (Durham, NC, 2003).

Stewart, Andrea, "'The limits of the imaginable': women writers' networks during the long nineteenth century," *Victorian review* 45:1 (2019), p.39–57.

Stockhausen, Johann Christoph, *Johann Christoph Stockhausens Grundsätze wohleingerichteter Briefe, nach den neuesten und bewährtesten Muster der Deutschen und Ausländer; nebst beygefügten Erläuterungen und Exempeln* (Helmstädt, Christian Friederich Weygand, 1751).

Stolzenburg, Andreas, "Biographie," in *Johann Christian Reinhart: ein deutscher Landschaftsmaler in Rom*, ed. Andreas Stolzenburg and Herbert W. Rott (Munich, 2012), p.101–103.

–, "'[…] der redlichste Mann in ganz Rom—fest und unverführbar': Johann Christian Reinhart und die Künstlerschaft in Rom 1790–1847," in *Johann Christian Reinhart: ein deutscher Landschaftsmaler in Rom*, ed. Andreas Stolzenburg and Herbert W. Rott (Munich, 2012), p.71–91.

–, and Herbert W. Rott (ed.), *Johann Christian Reinhart: ein deutscher Landschaftsmaler in Rom* (Munich, 2012).

Stone, Alva T., "The LCSH century: a brief history of the Library of Congress subject headings, and introduction to the centennial essays," *Cataloging & classification quarterly* 29:1–2 (2000), p.1–15.

Supplement au catalogue de livres françois, latins, etc. a Amsterdam, sur l'oude Turfmarkt & a Leipzig unter dem hohmannischen hausse auf der Peter-strasse (Amsterdam, Chez Arkstée et Merkus, 1767).

Swafford, Jan, *Beethoven: anguish and triumph* (Boston, MA, 2014).

Tatlock, Lynne (ed.), *Publishing culture and the "reading nation": German book history and the long nineteenth century* (Rochester, NY, 2010).

Tautz, Birgit, *Translating the world: toward a new history of German literature* (University Park, PA, 2018).

Te Heesen, Anke, "Der Ausstellungskatalog als Monographie: über Kataloge und ein neues Format des geisteswissenschaftlichen Publizierens," *Kodex: Jahrbuch der Internationalen Buchwissenschaftlichen Gesellschaft* 5 (2015), special issue: *Bleiwüste und Bilderflut: Geschichten über das geisteswissenschaftliche Buch*, ed. Caspar Hirschi and Carlos Spoerhase, p.231–48.

–, *The World in a box: the story of the eighteenth-century picture encyclopedia* (Chicago, IL, 2002).

<Text Encoding Initiative>, "Projects using the TEI," https://tei-c.org/Activities/Projects/ (last accessed June 30, 2023).

"Thé literaire beym Bürger Millin in der Nationalbibliothek," *London und Paris* 1:2 (1798), p.184–87.

Thielking, Sigrid, *Weltbürgertum: kosmopolitische Ideen in Literatur und politischer Publizistik seit dem 18. Jahrhundert* (Munich, 2000).

Thompson, C. W., *French Romantic travel writing: Chateaubriand to Nerval* (Oxford, 2012).

Towner, John, "Literature, tourism and the Grand Tour," in *Literature and tourism*, ed. Mike Robinson and Hans Christian Andersen (London, 2002), p.226–38.

Trilcke, Peer, "Social network analysis (SNA) als Methode einer textempirischen Literaturwissenschaft," in *Empirie in der Literaturwissenschaft*, ed. Philip Ajouri, Katja Mellmann, and Christoph Rauen (Münster, 2013), p.201–47.

Turner, Katherine, *British travel writers in Europe 1750–1800: authorship, gender and national identity* (Aldershot, 2001).

Tütken, Johannes, *Privatdozenten im Schatten der Georgia Augusta: zur älteren Privatdozentur (1734 bis 1831)*, vol.2 (Göttingen, 2005).

Tuttle, Richard, *The Thrill of the ideal: the Reinhart Project, with an* interview by Jarrett Earnest (New York, 2012).

"Unwissenheit und Stolz der Pariser Künstler: Millins Vorlesungen: das Cabinet der Antiken. Mionets Münzpasten," *London und Paris* 1:3 (1798), p.260–65.

Van Hoorn, Tanja, and Alexander Košenina (ed.), *Naturkunde in Wochentakt: Zeitschriftenwissen der Aufklärung* (Bern, 2014).

Van Vliet, Rietje, "Print and public in Europe 1600–1800," in *A Companion to the history of the book*, ed. Simon Eliot and Jonathan Rose (Oxford, 2007), p.247–58.

Vaughan, John Edmund, *The English guide book, c.1780–1870: an illustrated history* (Newton Abbot, 1974).

Vogl, Joseph, *Kalkül und Leidenschaft: Poetik des ökonomischen Menschen* (Zürich, 2002).

Von Breuning, Gerhard, *Memories of Beethoven: from the house of the black-robed Spaniards*, ed. Maynard Solomon (Cambridge, 1995).

Von Heinecken, Karl Heinrich, *Nachrichten von Künstlern und Kunst-Sachen* (Leipzig, Kraß, 1768).

–, *Nachrichten von Künstlern und Kunstsachen: zweiter Theil* (Leipzig, Kraß, 1769).

–, *Neue Nachrichten von Künstlern und Kunst-Sachen* (Leipzig, Breitkopf, 1786).

Von Knonau, Meyer, "Heß, David," *Allgemeine Deutsche Biographie* 12 (1880), p.273–77, https://www.deutsche-biographie. de/pnd116764570.html#adb-content (last accessed June 23, 2023).

Von Loesch, Heinz, and Claus Raab (ed.), *Das Beethoven-Lexikon* (Laaber, 2008).

Von Mechel, Christian, *Verzeichniß der Gemälde der Kaiserlich Königlichen Bilder Gallerie in Wien verfaßt von Christian von Mechel der Kaiserlich. Königlich Mitglied nach der von ihm Allerhöchsten Befehl im Jahre 1781 neuen gemachten Einrichtung* (Vienna, n.n., 1783).

Von Petersdorff, Dirk, *Mysterienrede: zum Selbstverständnis romantischer Intellektueller* (Berlin, 1996).

Von Seckendorff, Gustav Anton, "Aus Eutin," *Zeitung für die elegante Welt 161* (August 13, 1811), p.1287–88.

–, "Filadelfia: Literatur und Vergnügungen der Nordamerikaner," *Der neue teutsche Merkur* 2 (1791), p.168–72.

–, *Vorlesungen über Deklamation und Mimik*, 2 vols. (Braunschweig, 1816).

Wald, James, "Periodicals and periodicity," in *A Companion to the history of the book*, ed. Simon Eliot and Jonathan Rose (Oxford, 2007), p.421–33.

Walter, Torsten, *Staat und Recht im Werk Christoph Martin Wielands* (Wiesbaden, 1995).

Weingart, Scott, "Demystifying networks, part I & II," *Journal of digital humanities* 1:1 (2011), http://journalof-digitalhumanities.org/1-1/

demystifying-networks-by-scott-weingart/ (last accessed July 4, 2023).

–, *Exploring big historical data: the historian's macroscope* (London, 2015).

–, *The Network turn: changing perspectives in the humanities* (Cambridge, 2020).

Weise, Christian, *Christian Weisens Curiöse Gedancken von Deutschen Brieffen wie ein junger Mensch, sonderlich ein zukünfftiger Politicus, die galante Welt wohl vergnügen soll; in kurtzen und zulänglichen Regeln so dann in anständigen und practicablen Exempeln ausführlich vorgestellet; erster und andrer Theil* (Dresden, Johann Christoph Mieth, 1691).

Weithase, Irmgard, *Zur Geschichte der gesprochenen deutschen Sprache*, vol.1 (Tübingen, 1961).

Wellmon, Chad, *Organizing enlightenment: information overload and the invention of the modern research university* (Baltimore, MD, 2015).

White, James, *A Catalogue of books in various branches of literature* (London, n.n., 1797).

Wieland, Christoph Martin, "Das Geheimnis des Kosmopolitenordens," *Der teutsche Merkur* 3 (1788), p.97–115; 4 (1788), p.121–45.

–, "Vorrede des Herausgebers," *Der teutsche Merkur* 1 (1773), p.iii–xxii.

Wiethölter, Waltraud, and Anne Bohnenkamp (ed.), *Der Brief: Ereignis & Objekt* (Frankfurt am Main, 2010).

Wilford, John Noble, *The Mapmakers* (New York, 2000).

Wilkey, Edward, *Wanderings in Germany: with moonlight walks on the banks of the Elbe, the Danube, the Neckar, and the Rhine* (London, 1839).

Wilson, W. Daniel, *Geheimräte gegen Geheimbünde: ein unbekanntes Kapitel der klassisch-romantischen Geschichte Weimars* (Stuttgart, 1991).

–, *Das Goethe-Tabu: Protest und Menschenrechte im klassischen Weimar* (Munich, 1999).

–, "Intellekt und Herrschaft: Wielands *Goldner Spiegel*, Joseph II. und das Ideal eines kritischen Mäzenats im aufgeklärten Absolutismus," *MLN* 99:3 (1984), p.479–502.

Winckler, T. F., "Thé literaire beym Bürger Millin in der Nationalbibliothek," *London und Paris* 1:2 (1798), p.184–87.

Wohlfarth, Irving, "Die Passagenarbeit," in *Benjamin Handbuch: Leben, Werk, Wirkung*, ed. Burkhard Lindner (Stuttgart, 2006), p.251–74.

Wolff, Charlotta, "'Un admirateur des philosophes modernes': the networks of Swedish ambassador Gustav Philip Creutz in Paris, 1766–1783," in *Networks of European Enlightenment*, ed. Chloe Edmondson and Dan Edelstein (Liverpool, Liverpool University Press / Voltaire Foundation, 2019), p.173–200.

Wübben, Yvonne, "Forschungsskizze: Literatur und Wissen nach 1945," in *Literatur und Wissen: ein interdisziplinäres Handbuch*, ed. Roland Borgards *et al.* (Stuttgart, 2013), p.5–16.

Wurst, Karin, *Fabricating pleasure: fashion, entertainment, and cultural consumption in Germany, 1780–1830* (Detroit, MI, 2005).

Wyn Jones, David, *Music in Vienna 1700, 1800, 1900* (Woodbridge, 2016).

Young, Liam Cole, *List cultures: knowledge and poetics from Mesopotamia to BuzzFeed* (Amsterdam, 2017).

Zedler, Johann Heinrich, *Grosses vollständiges Universal-Lexikon*, vol.26 (1740; Graz, 1961).

Zeitschriften der Aufklärung, http://ds.ub.uni-bielefeld.de/viewer/collections/zeitschriftender-aufklaerung/ (last accessed July 4, 2023).

Zeitschrift für digitale Geisteswissenschaften, https://zfdg.de/ (last accessed July 4, 2023).

Index